GW01162014

Plants in Contemporary Poetry

Examining how poets engage with and mediate botanical life, *Plants in Contemporary Poetry* affords a glimpse into the ontologies, epistemologies, and semiospheres of flora and, by extension, the natural world. Highlighting the botanical obsessions of seminal poets writing in English today, the book calls attention to the role of language in deconstructing the cultural codes that limit an understanding of plants as intelligent beings. Ryan argues that, as poetic thought harmonizes with vegetality, writers gain direct knowledge of, and profound inspiration from, the botanical world. *Plants in Contemporary Poetry* provides a timely intervention in the prevailing tendency of ecocritical scholarship to date to examine animal, rather than plant, subjectivities and lifeworlds. A sensuous return to vegetal being is actualized in this study through a focus on the contemporary poetries of Australia, England, and the United States. The lively disquisition traverses a cross section of contemporary poetic genres from confessionalism and experimentalism to radical pastoralism and ecopoetry. Through readings of eight poets, including Louise Glück, Les Murray, Mary Oliver, and Alice Oswald, *Plants in Contemporary Poetry* centers on the idea of the botanical imagination and proposes a unique conceptual model the author calls *vegetal dialectics*. Drawing from developments in neuro-botany and contributing to the area of critical plant studies, the book also develops phytocriticism as a method for responding to the lack of attention to plants in ecocriticism, ecopoetics, and the environmental humanities. This ground-breaking study reminds readers that poetic imagination is as important as scientific rationality to appreciating the mysteries of plants on an increasingly imperiled planet. The book will appeal to a multidisciplinary readership in the fields of ecocriticism, ecopoetry, environmental humanities, and ecocultural studies, and will be of particular interest to students and researchers in critical plant studies.

John Charles Ryan is a poet and scholar who holds appointments as Postdoctoral Research Fellow in the School of Arts at the University of New England in Australia and Honorary Research Fellow in the School of Humanities at the University of Western Australia. From 2012 to

2015, he was Postdoctoral Research Fellow in the School of Communications and Arts at Edith Cowan University. His teaching and research cross between the environmental and digital humanities. He has contributed in particular to Australian and Southeast Asian ecocriticism and the emerging field of critical plant studies. He is the author, co-author, editor, or co-editor of 10 books, including the Bloomsbury title *Digital Arts: An Introduction to New Media* (2014, as co-author), *The Language of Plants: Science, Philosophy, Literature* (University of Minnesota Press, 2017, as co-editor and contributor), and *Southeast Asian Ecocriticism: Theories, Practices, Prospects* (Lexington Books, 2017, as editor and contributor).

Perspectives on the Non-Human in Literature and Culture

Birds and Other Creatures in Renaissance Literature
Shakespeare, Descartes, and Animal Studies
Rebecca Ann Bach

Race Matters, Animal Matters
Fugitive Humanism in African America, 1838–1934
Lindgren Johnson

Plants in Contemporary Poetry
Ecocriticism and the Botanical Imagination
John Charles Ryan

Plants in Contemporary Poetry
Ecocriticism and the Botanical Imagination

John Charles Ryan

Routledge
Taylor & Francis Group
NEW YORK AND LONDON

First published 2018
by Routledge
711 Third Avenue, New York, NY 10017

and by Routledge
2 Park Square, Milton Park, Abingdon, Oxon OX14 4RN

Routledge is an imprint of the Taylor & Francis Group, an informa business

© 2018 Taylor & Francis

The right of John Charles Ryan to be identified as author of this work has been asserted by him in accordance with sections 77 and 78 of the Copyright, Designs and Patents Act 1988.

All rights reserved. No part of this book may be reprinted or reproduced or utilised in any form or by any electronic, mechanical, or other means, now known or hereafter invented, including photocopying and recording, or in any information storage or retrieval system, without permission in writing from the publishers.

Trademark notice: Product or corporate names may be trademarks or registered trademarks, and are used only for identification and explanation without intent to infringe.

Library of Congress Cataloging in Publication Data
CIP data has been applied for.

ISBN: 978-1-138-18628-6 (hbk)
ISBN: 978-1-315-64395-3 (ebk)

Typeset in Sabon
by codeMantra

Printed and bound in Great Britain by
TJ International Ltd, Padstow, Cornwall

Contents

	Acknowledgments	ix
1	Introduction: The Botanical Imagination	1
2	Sacred Ecologies of Plants: The Vegetative Soul in Les Murray's Poetry	27
3	That Porous Line: Mary Oliver and the Intercorporeality of the Vegetal Body	53
4	It Healeth Inward Wounds: Bioempathic Emplacement and the Radical Vegetal Poetics of Elisabeth Bletsoe	81
5	From Stinking Goose-foot to Bastard Toadflax: Botanical Humor in Alice Oswald's *Weeds and Wild Flowers*	107
6	Consciousness Buried in Earth: Vegetal Memory in Louise Glück's *The Wild Iris*	135
7	That Seed Sets Time Ablaze: Judith Wright and the Temporality of Plants	163
8	On the Death of Plants: John Kinsella's Radical Pastoralism and the Weight of Botanical Melancholia	190
9	Every Leaf Imagined With Us: Vegetal Hope and the Love of Flora in Joy Harjo's Poetry	214
	Index	241

Acknowledgments

I wish to acknowledge the University of Western Australia in Perth, Australia, for an Honorary Research Fellowship in the Department of English and Cultural Studies, and the University of New England in Armidale, Australia, for a Postdoctoral Research Fellowship in the School of Arts. Both institutions provided invaluable assistance during the writing of this book. My appreciation goes to Karen Raber, the editor of the Routledge series Perspectives on the Non-Human in Literature and Culture, who was supportive of the project from its germinal stages. The editors and reviewers of the journals in which three chapters previously were published offered careful advice on style, structure, and content. Sincere thanks are due to Irene Sanz Alonso, Dianna Bell, Elaine Nogueira-Godsey, Flys Junquera Carmen Lydia, Bron Taylor, and Ted Toadvine.

A version of Chapter 2 was originally published as "Sacred Ecology of Plants: The Vegetative Soul in the Botanical Poetry of Les Murray." *Journal for the Study of Religion, Nature and Culture* 10.4 (2016): 459–484. My sincere thanks to Equinox Publishing for their kind permission to reprint the material.

A version of Chapter 7 was originally published as "That Seed Sets Time Ablaze: Vegetal Temporality in Judith Wright's Botanical Poetics." *Environmental Philosophy* (2016). doi:10.5840/envirophil2016121343.

A version of Chapter 8 was originally published as "On the Death of Plants: John Kinsella's Radical Pastoralism and the Weight of Botanical Melancholia." *Ecozon@: European Journal of Literature, Culture and Environment* 7.2 (2016): 113–133.

1 Introduction
The Botanical Imagination

> Imagination attempts to have a future.
> —Gaston Bachelard, *The Poetics of Reverie* (1971, 8)

Of the prevailing ideas about plants that inhabit the imagination, ballistics, I suggest, would not be at the top of the leaderboard. We tend to associate flora with aesthetics (beautiful flowers, delectable fruits, sublime forests) and poetics (poetry and poetic thoughts about flowers, fruits, and forests) rather than biomechanics, namely the rapid and occasionally targeted expulsion of projectiles. After all, for the most part, we think botanical life is sessile (unmoving), silent (lacking address), passive (acted upon by mobile life-forms), and, of course, pleasing (agreeable to the senses). Granted there are notable exceptions to the master narrative of the vegetal world as, indeed, vegetative in the pejorative sense of the descriptor as dull and unthinking. For instance, carnivorous orchids ensnare and consume insects, touch-me-nots recoil when contacted, and skunk cabbage emits a fetor that seduces pollinators but repulses people. On the whole, however, humankind envisages plants as mundane elements of the scenery (Pollan 2015); as the stuff we eat, process, and otherwise appropriate (Allen and Hatfield 2004); and as accoutrements to the less obscure—and more emotionally resonant and ethically valued—lives of animals and other non-plants (Taylor and Twine 2014). As a case in point from the history of philosophy, in *Creative Evolution* (1998, published originally in 1907), Henri Bergson reinscribed the age-old dualism demarcating between the zoological realm and its botanical counterpart. The thinker contended that "we should define the animal by sensibility and awakened consciousness, the vegetable by consciousness asleep and by insensibility" (Bergson 1998, 112). From his standpoint, the photosynthetic evolution of the plant—its uncanny ability to synthesize nutrients from water and carbon dioxide—"enables it to dispense with movement and so with feeling" (1998, 112).

Like many commentators both before and since him, Bergson framed animality in terms of the presumed deficiencies of vegetality. Despite his intimation that consciousness inheres within plants—albeit as a latent potential—he propounded a cerebrocentric (brain-centered) and, more precisely, neurocentric (nervous system-focused) model of intelligence that brought "two tendencies" into binary opposition (Bergson 1998, 113). These tendencies comprised, on one end of the spectrum, the "fixity and insensibility" of flora and, on the other, the "mobility and consciousness" of animals (1998, 113). To be sure, *Creative Evolution* at times is wholly fixated on fixity and engrossed with insensibility. Bergson negativized these so-called tendencies as the primary characteristics of botanical life. The mobility of animals renders their consciousness "more and more distinct, more and more ample" (1998, 112). Conversely, one doubts "whether nervous elements, however rudimentary, will ever be found in the plant" (1998, 112). Yet, how would Bergson—and his intellectual antecedents—have responded to the principle of vegetal ballistics in addition to recent findings in the field of plant neurobiology? Would they have been able to figure these illuminations of vegetal ontology into a negative calculus of flora? The ideas of cognition and ballistics in plants, indeed, trouble the characterization of photosynthetic life as dull, insensate, and spatially fixed. Of course, Bergson was unaware of the projectile mechanisms of plants such as white mulberry (*Morus alba*), a medium-sized tree native to China and historically central to the production of silk but also cultivated as an ornamental in Europe, including in the formal French gardens he would have encountered. Traveling at a rate in excess of half the speed of sound—more exactly, Mach 0.7 or 537 miles per hour—the pollen expulsion of white mulberry has been described as the fastest recorded biological motion (Taylor et al. 2006).

On close inspection, the mulberry is much more than a dullard, automaton, or passive substratum for the manipulations of birds, silkworms, and other more mobile creatures, including philosophers. Despite attributions of passivity to plants, the tree enacts behaviors of its own, notably those involving rapid ballistic movement wherein a projectile acquires all of its impetus prior to being launched (Vogel 2005, 167). Although anemophilous—or wind-pollinated—species are known to hurl pollen explosively through the air, the mulberry does so at a pace that approaches the hypothetical limit for botanical movement (Taylor et al. 2006, 19). Consequently, mulberry anthesis—the full process of flowering from style extension to pollen grain release—exceeds all known calculations of time motion, initial velocity, and power output in plants and rivals the speeds of the fastest terrestrial animals (Taylor et al. 2006, 23). As applied mathematician Jan Skotheim and evolutionary biologist Lakshminarayanan Mahadevan (2005) clarify, botanical life moves "all of the time, often too slowly to notice. Rapid movements, though rarer, are used by many plants in essential functions" (1308). Generalized as nastic movement, nonmuscular hydraulic propulsion in plants is moderated by internal water conveyance (Skotheim and Mahadevan 2005, 1308). Observations of nastic phenomena, nevertheless, are not confined to the province of contemporary botanical science. In the late eighteenth century, for instance, the English botanist James Edward Smith prodded the bud of a barberry (*Berberis communis*) specimen with a stick, after which one of the filaments—the stalk of the stamen—"instantly sprung from the petal with considerable force, striking its anthers against the stigma" (1788, 158). In this manner, Smith expedited the copulation of the male (stamen, filament, anther) and female (stigma, style, ovary) members of the barberry flower.

During provocations of other species in Chelsea Physic Garden, Smith further witnessed the rapidity of nastic movement. The stamen of pellitory (*Parietaria* spp.), are "very elastic [and] fly up, and throw their pollen about with great force" (1788, 162). Additionally, the pericarp, or *germen*, of yellow lucerne (*Medicago falcata*), "obtains its liberty by a sudden spring, in consequence of which the pollen is plentifully scattered about the stigma" (Smith 1788, 162). To be sure, the unsuspecting plants interrogated meticulously by the botanist exhibited a penchant for "explosive fracture," one of three categories of vegetal movement—along with swelling and shrinking, and snap-buckling—outlined by Skotheim and Mahadevan (2005, 1309). Notwithstanding the rationalization of plant motion in mechanical terms as the upshot of internal and external variables, a sense of wonderment is evident—indeed palpable—in scientific accounts of the principle. Of note is *The Power of Movement in Plants*, originally published in 1880, in which Charles and Francis Darwin employed the term *circumnutation* to describe the helical patterns of movement in the botanical world:

> [...] apparently every growing part of every plant is continually circumnutating, though often on a small scale. Even the stems of seedlings before they have broken through the ground, as well as their buried radicles, circumnutate, as far as the pressure of the surrounding earth permits. In this universally present movement we have the basis or groundwork for the acquirement, according to the requirements of the plant, of the most diversified movements.
> (Darwin and Darwin 2016, 2)

At the end of the disquisition, Charles and his son speculated famously that the tip of the radicle (the part of the embryo that becomes the primary root), with its "diverse kinds of sensitiveness," is analogous to the animal brain and mediates the processing of sensory information within the plant (Darwin and Darwin 2016, 419; also Chapter 6 of this volume).

It is not accidental that the Darwins reserved the contentious "rootbrain" hypothesis for the final lines of *The Power of Movement in Plants*. The proposal that plant mentation has an anatomical correlate instigated—and still instigates today—a radical leveling of botanical and zoological ontologies while retaining the essential difference between the two discrete domains of life. In contrast, the Aristotelian tradition elevated animals to the category of *anima sensitiva* (the sensitive soul) while confining plants to *anima nutritiva* (the nutritive soul), or the sphere of growth and reproduction (De Chadarevian 1996, 26; see Chapter 2 of this volume). Although providing the material foundation for higher-order soul-form teleologies, the plant itself remained fettered to the insensate realm. Highly responsive plants such as touch-me-not (*Mimosa pudica*) were considered anomalies indicating the tactile sensitivities of a few species. The idea of purposive growth movements in response to stimuli, however, threatened to unsettle the paradigm of irritability and the conception of botanical life (De Chadarevian 1996, 26). As a consequence, the renowned botanist Julius von Sachs rebuked the Darwins for careless and amateurish experiments that mistakenly embellished the plant as an agentic life-form (Baluška et al. 2009, 1121). Subsequent plant physiologists, nevertheless, emphasized that vegetal movement requires the kind of self-directedness indicating conscious being-in-the-world. In particular, Jagadis Chandra Bose opened the first volume of his treatise *Life Movements in Plants* (1995, published originally in 1918) by asserting that "the phenomenon of movement in plants under the action of external stimuli presents innumerable difficulties and complications" (1). For that reason, Bose (1919, 547–48) distinguished internally-induced autonomous movements from tropic responses prompted by unilateral external stimuli. As Dov Koller maintains in his evocatively titled *The Restless Plant* (2011, 5), nastic movements—such as mulberry bio-ballistics—should be regarded as autonomous because they are modulated by signals produced by the plant.

Vegetal Cognition and the Perils of Plant Neglect

It is indeed an exciting time for (re)considering vegetal being. The burgeoning area of plant neurobiology ever more apprises artistic, cultural, literary, and philosophical approaches to flora (for example, Gagliano, Ryan, and Vieira 2017; Irigaray and Marder 2016; Marder 2013, 2014). During the progression of *Plants in Contemporary Poetry*, I contextualize the botanical imaginings of eight poets from Australia, England, and the United States in relation to ideas emerging from this wide-ranging and dynamic field. My hope is that the present study will help to disclose the power of verse to anticipate and parallel scientific thought through a freedom of imagination unrestrained by—though conversant with—Aristotelian, Cartesian, Linnaean, and other prevailing discourses of botanical life. Reclaiming the wonderment underlying the experimental efforts of Bose, Darwin, Smith, and their scientific forebears, plant neurobiologists—by attending seriously to vegetal cognition—reconfigure the longstanding conception of plants as *anima nutritiva*, that is, as the inert substratum for the enactment of the life-worlds of organisms endowed with brains (Barlow 2008; Calvo 2016; Garzón 2007; Trewavas 2014, 2016; Van Loon 2016). Notwithstanding its critics (Alpi et al. 2007; Firn 2004; Struik, Yin, and Meinke 2008), plant neurobiology underscores the "downright erroneous" ascription of utter passivity to plants (Marder 2012, 2). In doing so, it provokes a paradigm shift from reductionist-mechanistic methodologies and principles toward "holistic, systems-based analysis of integrated and communicative" biological processes (Baluška and Mancuso 2007, 205).

From a holistic standpoint, plants are "much more complex than the sum of their constituents" and resist steadfastly the techno-industrial figurations that construct—and deconstruct—them as machines, motors, engines, clocks, instruments, and so on (Baluška and Mancuso 2007, 206). Rather than an automaton reacting to external stimuli in a generally predetermined fashion, the "intelligent plant" integrates aspects of communication, sensing, and emergence into its ontological bearing (Pollan 2013). But what are the implications of vegetal neglect—of conceptually reducing the plant to an insensate mechanical assemblage while discounting its subjectivity as a discerning participant in its world, and in ours? To be certain, the premise of the overlooked, or marginalized, plant is central to "critical plant studies"—the nascent area of inquiry into the vegetal world that incorporates diverse theoretical perspectives and methodological frames, including those of neuro-botany (Gagliano, Ryan, and Vieira 2017; Hall 2011; Marder 2013; Vieira, Gagliano, and Ryan 2016). Despite its relatively recent foregrounding—notably in terms of "plant blindness" (Nyberg and Sanders 2014; Wandersee and Schussler 1999; discussed later in this section), global botanical loss, and genetically manipulated species—the lamentation of vegetal neglect has cropped up consistently in different forms throughout botanical history. As an example from the post-Second World War era, botanist and former director of the New York Botanical Garden, William Robbins, began an address "The Importance of Plants" (1944) with the plain admission that "nothing I have to say here is new; all of it has been known for many years, some of it for a century or more. Yet I believe that the repetition from time to time of facts of fundamental import has its place [...] plants are the basis upon which all other life depends" (440).

Robbins' elucidation of the biospheric, scientific, economic, recreational, and cultural value of flora is as salient now as it was last century, particularly as the intensification of habitat degradation, invasive taxa, overharvesting, pollution, and climate change continues to fracture botanical communities globally (Dornelas et al. 2014). In a linguistic gesture conveying respect and admiration for flora, the botanist (1944) even personifies plants as "able chemists [...] there is no substitute for them" (441). Nonetheless, owing to the human inclination to background plants as landscapes, objects, or materials, one must be reminded regularly of the significance of vegetal life—or suffer the physical and existential consequences of complacency. In his view, the plant affords "an antidote for the artificiality and tension of city life" and fulfills a "deep-seated desire in all of us" for discourse with the other-than-human (Robbins 1944, 442). More specifically, gardening and other practices of cultivation facilitate healthful "traffic with the soil and the green things that grow from it" while engendering the virtues of "patience and philosophy" (Robbins 1944, 442). On this note, in Chapter 5, the theme of vegetal patience—the forbearance of plants in relation to their ontological and temporal comportment—is central to Alice Oswald's poetics of weeds and wildflowers. The idea, moreover, that vegetal life "pacifies and heals the body and the mind" (Robbins 1944, 442) resonates conspicuously in the work of Elisabeth Bletsoe in Chapter 4 and Joy Harjo in Chapter 9. As enacted by Bletsoe, Oswald, Harjo, and the other contemporary poets of this study, poetry makes available a lyrical means to counterbalance and redress the disregard implied by Robbins and, consequently, to bring emphasis to the multilayered capacities of plants beyond their unidimensional linkage to food, fiber, medicine, and the provision of resources.

In (re)turning human attention to botanical being, critical plant studies—one of the fields in which I position my green-streaked analysis of contemporary poetry—attempts to reverse the tendency denoted as *plant blindness*. Worried by the low priority given to threatened species and botanical communities within conservation discourse, biologists have put forward the notion of plant blindness to denote the tendency "among humans to neither notice nor value plants in the environment" (Balding and Williams 2016, 1192). As an inclination to overlook flora, to undervalue its global biocultural significance, or to render it appropriable matter in service to human desire, plant blindness highlights the physiological limits of visual processing in humans (Balas and Momsen 2014, 437). While we are able to register animals and other mobile organisms carrying out their lives within temporal frames comparable to our own, it is more of a perceptual challenge to apprehend the movements, patterns, needs, and potential dangers of plants and thus to come to appreciate their being-in-the-world. The limited popular esteem conferred to the botanical world relative to its utter indispensability could also reflect scientific, social, and educational prejudices prioritizing animals over plants (Manetas 2012, 8–9). Evoking the idea without naming the term, Randy Laist in his introduction to *Plants and Literature* (2013) maintains that "it is impossible to overstate the significance of plants to human life, and yet this simple fact is easily overlooked, taken for granted, or, perhaps, actively repressed in the semantic texture of urban, technological consciousness" (10). For Laist, common rhetoric tends to conceptualize botanical life as "a category of things that are alive like we are, but alive in a way that is utterly different, closed off from our capacity for empathy, omnipresent but unknown, seductive but unresponsive"

(2013, 14). While aural, visual, and textual productions throughout occidental history lay bare the symbolic prominence of botanical life—and of flowers especially; for instance, in relation to *le langage des fleurs* (Kranz 2017)—plants are of course much greater than the sum of their linguistic functions. To this end, the field of neuro-botany discloses at an ever-increasing rate, through laboratory- and field-based experimentation, that the plant enacts inherent modes of semiosis and meaning-making for the benefit of itself and other entities. How, then, might a neurobiological understanding of vegetal life—coupled to an awareness of the perils of plant neglect—influence ecocritical approaches to contemporary poetry?

On Imagining and Being Imagined by Literary Flora

The overarching concept of this study—the botanical imagination—respectfully invokes, builds on, and expands previous considerations of the imagination in some of the earliest and most formative scholarship in ecocriticism. For environmental critics on the whole, imagination signifies either the ability of the author to mediate the natural world in an evocative or persuasive manner, a quality emerging between text and referent during the process of mediation, or the capacity engendered within the reader, audience, or public to envision alternate scenarios to a future of unbridled techno-economic growth and rampant ecological devastation (Buell 1995; Heise 2008; Lynch, Glotfelty, and Armbruster 2012a). The preponderance of ecocritical approaches, however, remains ensnared in an anthropocentric and, at times, androcentric outlook on imagination. This is not to criticize ecocritical aspirations unnecessarily or unappreciatively, but instead to unveil prospects for the imagination through the concerted attention to the plant that, I suggest, has been a conspicuous lacuna in the "environmental turn in literary-critical studies" (Buell 2005, 1). To be certain, most ecologically-minded readers would sympathize with the assertion that the "environmental crisis involves a crisis of the imagination the amelioration of which depends on finding better ways of imaging nature and humanity's relation to it" (Buell 1995, 2). Lawrence Buell enunciates this position in *The Environmental Imagination* (1995), a seminal study of the American nature writing tradition. Buell further postulates that the resolution of intensifying environmental crises hinges on a collective envisaging of non-appropriative and non-hegemonic relations to the nonhuman realm.

Literary works facilitate this inspired (re)envisioning of nature. More specifically, environmental texts present a modality for galvanizing the progressive imagining—and re-imagining—of the natural world toward the actualization of ethically-based modes of exchange with other-than-human lives and milieux (Buell 1995, 7–8). In a sense analogous to Buell's early exposition, the more recent *The Bioregional*

Imagination (2012a, eds. Lynch, Glotfelty, and Armbruster) internalizes an idea of the imagination as a vital pathway for generating vibrant possibilities for living locally in bioregions and globally within the biosphere. The *human* imagination contributes to the generation of artistic works that integrate and promote place-based consciousness. Reciprocally, the imagination is molded by the power of these works to "ignite emotion, change minds, and inspire action" (Lynch, Glotfelty, and Armbruster 2012b, 12). Yet, what would be the implications of recognizing that forms of imagination inhere within nature itself and, more exactly, within the green things of everyday experience? Is it possible to approach imagination in ecocritical terms as a multispecies interplay of the emotions, minds, and actions of humans, plants, and others while, at the same time, avoiding the pitfalls of anthropocentrism? Jettisoning certain long-held presuppositions about botanical being—as unthinking, unfeeling, insensate, mute, immobile—how might we come to understand imagination as more than the exclusive province of either the intellective soul or of the ambulatory creature endowed with intelligence by virtue of its brainedness? In imagining plants, are we prepared for the impress of their imagining *us* in return, as all beings—vocal and less vocal, mobile and less mobile, patient and impatient, photosynthetic and less so—negotiate a collective future on an increasingly imperiled planet?

How do we imagine plants? How might plants imagine us? Although provoked by such questions—they are not designed to be rhetorical—I should clarify that *Plants in Contemporary Poetry* does not endeavor in any manner to "prove" or "refute" the existence of the imagination of the botanical kingdom through neurobiological evidence. The intent, moreover, is not to homogenize vegetal otherness through a form of personhood (see, for example, Hall 2011) emerging from the theorization of imagination as the interplay of agentic plants and non-plants. In this regard, my argument aligns with Michael Marder's (2012, 2013) critique of the metaphysical reckoning of subjectivity in terms of personhood or will. To be sure, the task of empirically demonstrating botanical phenomena is better left to the plant scientists of today and tomorrow who reveal more and more that vegetal sensitivity is not confined to a handful of anomalous species—such as the touch-me-not—but instead is an appropriate characterization of the whole floristic spectrum. Through intuition, attention, and sensoriality—in conjunction with ecologically-grounded witnessing over time and usually within the bounds of a place—contemporary poets versify a particular imaginative sphere. This is a dynamic sphere in which the lively plant activates and contributes to the process of poetization and, thereafter, remains as a corporeal trace within the poetic substratum. Rather than a reproduction or reconstitution of the vegetal form in the human mind, the poem conceived of as such embodies a dialectical back-and-forth between the lyrical exertions of the versifier and the autonomy of the vegetal presence inhabiting the poetic work.

This "opening of consciousness" (Bachelard 1971, 5) takes poetry beyond the unidimensional representation of plants in language and—turning to embrace botanical being—imbricates vegetal percipience within the substance of poetic imagination itself. In receiving diverse sensory impressions from the plant, the poeticizing mind enters a field of concourse—a plenum, a poetisphere—between vegetal nature, personal imagination, and collective cognizance of, and between, life-forms (Willey 1982, 860). As an upshot of the radical ascription of imagination outside of its normative bounds, poetry becomes the material exploration of potential in human and botanical subjects—and consequently highlights the instability of ontological delineations between both. In this context, the imaginative faculty serves as an intermediating zone at the threshold of rational thought, objective knowledge, and the specific corporealities of plants and others (Jones 1991, 95). My conception approximates Bachelard's notion of material imagination in which matter—in this instance, the vibrant matter of vegetal life—governs the form and expression of imagination (Jones 1991, 97). Contact with plant materiality provokes a carnal intensity of imagining through "the virile pleasure of *penetrating* substance, of *touching the inward parts* of substance, of coming to know what lies within the seed" (Bachelard 1991, 105, emphasis in original). In these terms, the botanical imagination can be regarded as "material becoming, a becoming which has a deep and inner source" (Bachelard 1991, 105)—a becoming with plants through poetry.

While this interpretation of imagination has the potential to expand critical approaches to contemporary environmental poetry—as the present study attempts to demonstrate—it is necessary to acknowledge previous studies of the nodes between vegetation and literary production. During the nineteenth century, for instance, a profusion of publications on Shakespeare's flora appeared, the most famous of which was Henry Ellacombe's *Plant-Lore and Garden-Craft of Shakespeare* (1896, first edition in 1878). Beginning alphabetically with aconitum and ending with yew before turning his attention to Shakespeare's gardens in the second part, Ellacombe (1896) commended the Bard's ability to "bring the plants and flowers before us in the freshest, and often in a most touching, way" (xii). Also in the late nineteenth century, the educator and botanist Leopold Hartley Grindon published *The Shakespeare Flora* (1883) with chapters on the woods, wildflowers, medicinal plants, garden settings, and wilderness environments of the poet's vegetal versifications. This genre of botanical criticism flourished through the twentieth century with studies such as Jessica Kerr's *Shakespeare's Flowers* (1968) and, later, into the twenty-first with the illustrated *Botanical Shakespeare* (Quealy and Collins 2017) and others. While elucidating the diverse meanings of plants in Shakespeare's botanical universe, these scholarly treatments as a whole underscore the symbolic potencies of flowers in his work. On the poetry of John Keats, furthermore, *The Consecrated Urn* (Blackstone 1959) developed a "botanico-physiologico-cosmogonical" (xii) methodology based on early twentieth-century theories of plant growth and form.

There are additional precedents in botanical criticism by contemporary scholars that should be mentioned. Charlotte Otten's *Environ'd With Eternity* (1985) examines the *terraculture*—a neologism comprising botany, agriculture, horticulture, gardening, and related natural science pursuits—of sixteenth- and seventeenth-century sources, featuring an extended discussion of "the ontology of vegetable smells" (97) in the poetic works of these periods. Molly Mahood's *The Poet as Botanist* (2008) investigates "the ways in which poets see plants" (1) through the verse of eighteenth-, nineteenth-, and twentieth-century male poets, namely Erasmus Darwin, Wordsworth, Crabbe, Clare, Ruskin, and Lawrence. More recently, *Plants and Literature* (2013, edited by Randy Laist) has added considerably to the burgeoning interdisciplinary area of critical plant studies. The volume does contain an analysis of the symbolism of fruit in Christina Rossetti's narrative poem "Goblin Market," published originally in 1862 (Yoshida 2013). As a whole, however, Laist's edited collection foregrounds the representation of vegetal life in novels, notably Jane Austen's *Mansfield Park* from 1814, Frank Norris' *The Pit* from 1903, and Virginia Woolf's *Jacob's Room* from 1922. The emphasis on the botanical aspects of novels is also apparent in *Bloom* (King 2003), a study of eighteenth- and nineteenth-century works of fiction. King centralizes the relationship between marriage and blossoming through the heuristic of the "bloom narrative" (4). Added to this mélange of botanical criticism is the sizeable ecocritical literature of forests, indicated by Jeffrey Theis' *Writing the Forest in Early Modern England* (2009), John Knott's *Imagining the Forest* (2012) on the arboreal narratives of Michigan and the Upper Midwest of the United States, and Albrecht Classen's *The Forest in Medieval German Literature* (2015). Notwithstanding this spectrum of botanical criticism, studies of plant life in contemporary poetry are curiously few and far between (Ryan 2017).

Phytocriticism and the Life-Worlds of Plants in Poetry

The foregoing discussion circumscribed *botanical criticism* as a plant-based form of criticism attentive to the representation of vegetal life—forests, trees, bushes, flowers, herbs, orchids, wildflowers, garden plants—in cultural artifacts, including, but not limited to, literary works. In its diffuse form to date, this green-minded ecocritical specialization has been wont to centralize the figurative potencies of flora as symbols, metaphors, tropes, linguistic devices, and narrative artifices. In a poignant instance of botanical aperçu, Buell reads William Faulkner's short story "The Bear" as a narrative in which "treeness matters but the identities and the material properties of the trees are inconsequential" (1995, 10). Buell's analysis, indeed, is germane to other literary depictions of, and approaches to, botanical subjects where vegetality—defined in terms of aesthetics, stasis, and standing-reserve—matters but the material life-worlds of the plants themselves remain peripheralized. To be sure, the premise that environmental crisis entails a crisis of the imagination has been determinative to ecocritical thought since the incarnation of the field in the 1990s as a cross-pollination of intellectual currents in British cultural studies, New Criticism, Post-Structuralism, Indigenous studies, and the American ecology movement (Buell 2005, 1–28). Nonetheless, I submit, the environmental predicament will be neither assuaged nor resolved as long as imagination remains the rarefied province of the cognitive hominids that collectively precipitated the catastrophe in the first place. Hence, to the formulation of botanico-criticism I superadd the botanical imagination as the dialectical interchange of the imaginative potentialities of plants and non-plants.

The particular mode of botanico-criticism enunciated and put into practice in this study—one that draws from neurobiological standpoints that confer greater agencies and capacities to plants—will be labelled *phytocriticism*. In acknowledging the plant as a cognitive entity that is able to behave, decide, feel, learn, and remember, phytocriticism assesses the extent to which vegetal dynamism figures into the shape of cultural productions, including environmental texts in which botanical life supplies an active presence. The methodological framework I am proposing recognizes that plant ontology integrates forms of bio-attention, notably directedness toward light, heat, chemicals (Chamovitz 2012), sound (Gagliano et al. 2017), and kin (Bais 2015) in addition to discernment between self and non-self (Depuydt 2014). Just as ecocritical practice has opened dialogue with the biological sciences in order to assess the fidelity of literary representations and discourses against ecological realities (Love 2003), so too does phytocriticism engage emergent ideas in botanical science and, more precisely, in plant neurobiology as part of its analytical slant. Whereas the plant has been cast as the zero-point of behavior against which to contrast the animal, neuro-botany counterpoises the zoo- and anthropocentric ascription of cognition and instead looks toward "behavior at the *plant-coupled-with-its-environment* level" (Garzón 2007, 211, emphasis in original). Bearing in mind the field of phytosemiotics as the exploration of vegetal sign systems (Kull 2000) stemming from the theoretical work of Jakob von Uexküll (2010) in the early twentieth century, critics can speak of the vegetal *Umwelt*—life-world or being-in-the-world—as the plant enacts certain behaviors in relation to the botanical system to which it is integral.

Enfolding perspectives from neuro-botany, phytocriticism broadens the unidimensionality of "floral symbolism in poetry" (evident, for example, in Lang 1961 and elsewhere). As a consequence, the methodology responds to Buell's call for alternatives to reductive critical models according to which a plant "seems to be nothing more than a textual function and one comes to doubt that the author could have fancied otherwise" (1995, 5). In contrast to a limited focus on the utilities vegetal subjects provide to texts, the approach orients toward the prospect of plant-thinking and thus confers "a new prominence to vegetal life" (Marder 2013, 3), specifically in the milieu of ecopoetics. Reconfiguring the understanding of plants as passive objects, phytophenomenology marks the "fruitful interdisciplinary combination of phenomenology, botany and population ecology" (Marder 2012, 7). Building firmly on Marder's phytophenomenological intervention, the approach leveraged in *Plants in Contemporary Poetry* situates botanical life at the fulcrum of literary criticism and recognizes the plant within "the elemental terrain it inhabits without laying claim to or appropriating it" (Marder 2013, 8). A phenomenological mode of botanical criticism, moreover, prompts the questions, "How does the world appear (or not appear) to a plant? What is its relation to its world? What does it strive to, direct itself toward, or intend?" (Marder 2013, 9). Able to function independently of Cartesian limitations, poetry makes available a means for responding to—and being guided by—questions of vegetal being-in-the-world. While preserving the alterity of vegetal nature, phytocriticism also embraces the commonalities between beings, particularly in relation to the material fundaments on which all plant and non-plant lives depend. The crucial acknowledgement of difference-within-sameness stands in contrast to literary analysis that either homogenizes the plant as a narrative backdrop or obscures its alterity through unbridled sentimentalization or metaphorization. As a botanically-oriented mode of ecocriticism, phytocriticism "lets plants maintain their otherness, respecting the uniqueness of their existence" (Marder 2013, 8).

Even though the methodology derives from present-day plant neurobiology, phytocriticism finds a surprising precedent in *The Consecrated Urn* (Blackstone 1959). In developing a morphological approach to the poetry of Keats, Blackstone (1959) makes an obscure allusion to the term, curiously by way of announcing the direction he did *not* intend to take in his study: "Still less do I pretend to erect a phyto-criticism" (xii). The inspiration for Blackstone's unusual slant on Keats arrived fortuitously through his reading of mathematician D'Arcy Wentworth Thompson's *On Growth and Form* and plant morphologist Agnes Robertson Arber's *The Natural Philosophy of Plant Form*, both published in the first half of the twentieth century (Blackstone 1959, xii). Reading these scientific works enabled Blackstone to recall that Keats received a medical training early in life and that the young poet had

Introduction 13

sketched plants in the margins of his lecture notebooks. According to Blackstone, the botanical drawings of Keats uncannily resembled those featured in Erasmus Darwin's *The Botanic Garden* (Darwin 1798; for a discussion of the text, see Chapter 5). Although abjuring all pretenses of "phyto-criticism," he contends that "Keats's poetry *is* a poetry of growth and form" (Blackstone 1959, xii, emphasis in original). These brief references from *The Consecrated Urn* resonate strikingly with the approach I have outlined in this section. Rather than plant morphology, it is plant neurobiology—including aspects of behavior, cognition, learning, and memory in the vegetal world—that inspires the study. Like Blackstone, I foreground the influence of the poets' formal or informal training as botanists (to a limited extent, Les Murray and John Kinsella in Chapters 2 and 8, respectively), horticulturalists (Elisabeth Bletsoe, Alice Oswald, Louise Glück, and Joy Harjo in Chapters 4, 5, 6, and 9, respectively), and conservationists (Judith Wright in Chapter 7, in particular). In lieu of the works of Thompson and Arber, however, the principal texts apprising my disquisition include *What a Plant Knows* (Chamovitz 2012), *Plant Behavior and Intelligence* (Trewavas 2014), *Plant Sensing and Communication* (Karban 2015), the popular account of vegetal intelligence, *Brilliant Green* (Mancuso and Viola 2015), and a trove of scientific papers on different dimensions of plant neurobiology.

Like ecocriticism more broadly, phytocriticism energizes the process of reformulating human assumptions about "the nature of representation, reference, metaphor, characterization, personae, and canonicity" (Buell 1995, 2). The phytocritical impulse of this study is to disclose the rootedness of botanical poetry in the vibrant materiality of nature and to embrace a conception of the plant as more than a textual artifice or insensate phenomenon. It has become clear that ontological distinctions between life-forms necessitate differing ecocritical methodologies. Confronted with the need to propel a transformation of language, the phytocritic intercedes in the totalization of botanical nature as environment, ecology, landscape, species, and, indeed, as plant. The green-inclined critic, moreover, approaches the environmental text as one in which the vegetal world is not simply a framing device but a presence and in which human responsibility to plants imprints upon the ethical fabric of the work (Buell 1995, 7). On this note, phytocritical practice and theory could combine effectively with developments in plant ethics (Hall 2014; Heyd 2012; Pouteau 2014; Swiss Confederation 2008; see also Chapter 8). Another compatible conceptual reference point for *Plants in Contemporary Poetry* is material ecocriticism, reflecting the premise that "the world's material phenomena are knots in a vast network of agencies" and which attends to the omnipresent "stories of matter" (Iovino and Oppermann 2014, 1). While society at large exploits botanical material for food, fiber, and medicine at an increasingly reckless pace, neuro-botany and related fields signal that the agencies of vegetal matter emerge as a function of the immense network of the *"plant-coupled-with-its-environment"* (Garzón 2007, 211).

Drawing connections between phytocriticism and the environmental humanities—of which Indigenous studies is an ever more essential part—proves to be a fertile direction, as Chapters 2 and 9 of the volume suggest. The conjunction with the environmental humanities brings posthumanist studies, animal studies, and multispecies theory (Haraway 2008, Kirksey and Helmreich 2010) into productive dialogue with phytocriticism. To be certain, emergent eco-humanities concepts and premises—such as "the entanglements of agential beings" (Rose et al. 2012, 3)—acquire particular resonances in the vegetal context when, for instance, we consider the knack of certain plants for entwining or, as Charles Darwin put it, circumnutating. While other specializations within ecocriticism have appeared in recent years, namely zoocriticism and geocriticism, a comparable approach to plants—those life-forms that constitute 99% of the biomass of the Earth (Trewavas 2002)—has not previously been available to environmental critics. Zoocriticism is defined as a practice of literary studies "concerned not just with animal *representation* but also with animal *rights*" (Huggan and Tiffin 2010, 18, emphasis in original). Emerging at the intersection of animal studies, ecocriticism, and postcolonialism, zoocriticism turns attention to issues of representation, protection, and conservation. Even so, Graham Huggan and Helen Tiffin (2010, 19) note the "uneven development" of zoocriticism relative to ecocriticism. Alongside zoocriticism, there has been noteworthy progress in geocritical practices that attend to topographical phenomena and the co-constitution of different forms of space (Finch-Race and Weber 2015, 161). In their introduction to *Ecocriticism and Geocriticism* (2016), Robert Tally and Christine Battista underscore the geocritical emphasis on space, place, and mapping in interpreting cultural materials, including texts. Given these companionable trajectories, the time is ripe to initiate phytocriticism as a plant-attentive practice inspired by the perspectives of vegetal neurobiology and allied areas of behavior, cognition, and sensing.

Vegetal Dialectics and Poetry as the Plant Itself

A phytocritical outlook emphasizes the agencies of botanical beings in poetic texts and considers how plants are rendered, evoked, mediated, or brought to life in and through language. Cognizant of the longstanding asymmetries between life-forms—codified, for instance, by the Aristotelian *scala naturae*, or great chain of being—phytocritical attention discloses, and redresses where possible, the marginalization of flora in cultural narratives. One of the tasks of the phytocritic is to identify the potentially negative construal of the vegetal world through the human proclivities for aestheticization (plants as pretty objects and picturesque

Introduction 15

scenery), appropriation (as expendable materials or throwaway matter), and figuration (as symbols, tropes, and linguistic artifices rather than presences, bodies, and sensory entanglements). At the same time, the plant-inflected genre of ecocriticism I have sketched evaluates the ethical orientation of texts and the degree to which narratives prompt "the moral consideration of plants for their own sake" (Swiss Confederation 2008, 8). The potency of phytocriticism derives not exclusively from its highlighting of anti-ecological treatments of plants but also in its foregrounding of the heterogeneous ways vegetal life has been integral to literary invention. This critical practice, moreover, reveals how green-minded writers cherish and respect plants immensely, as exemplified by the versifiers featured in this study. Phytocriticism accordingly furnishes the methodological tack of *Plants in Contemporary Poetry* and potentizes the examination of the formative role of botanical being in the work of American, Australian, and British poets of the contemporary period. Within my development of the phytocritical model, however, there is an additional component to be noted here. I shall characterize the theoretical optic underlying the mode of interpreting the botanical poetry selected in this study as a *vegetal dialectics*.

What is a vegetal dialectics and how can it enhance understanding of contemporary botanical poetry? The origin of the dialectics concept, of course, lies in the classical philosophies of Socrates and Plato, subsequently reformulated by Hegel, Marx, Engels, Adorno, and many other theorists (Bhaskar 1993, Gadamer 1976, Norman and Sayers 1980). Although interpreted in numerous and often incompatible ways—a broad survey of which is outside the scope of this discussion—dialectics generally signifies the modulation of the oppositions inherent to conventional discourse. The concept points to a capacity to encompass ordinarily dichotomized positions—particularly those pertaining to, and gestated by, language—within an integrated frame of reference. Roy Bhaskar (1993) defines a dialectic as "anything from any relation between differential elements" (396). Inhering within dialectics, for Bhaskar, is potential freedom from de-agentification according to which processes of dualistic disembodiment and reductionistic reification trigger the enervation of groups or agents (1993, 396). Put differently, dialectics prioritizes "the rejection of rigid antitheses" (Norman and Sayers 1980, Preface) and foregrounds the generative tension of contradictoriness. Theodor Adorno develops a comparable position in *Negative Dialectics* (2004, published originally in 1966), arguing that "the dialectical primary of the principle of contradiction makes the *thought of unity the measure of heterogeneity*. As the heterogeneous collides with its limit it exceeds itself" (5, emphasis added). For the German philosopher, dialectics heralds "the qualitative variety of experience" and "unfolds the difference between the particular and the universal" (Adorno 2004, 6). In the context of ecocriticism and the nonhuman, Timothy Morton (2007,

185) accentuates the potential of dialectical interplay between states of subjectivity and objectivity, resulting in a subject-object duality (fluid complementarity) rather than a dualism (rigid opposition). For Morton (2007), a dialectical mode of literary criticism "bends back upon itself" and therein counters a Hegelian dialectics privileging the "reconciliation of the self to the other, who turns out to be the self in disguise" (13, 196). In other words, dialectics preserves alterity.

In the light of these theorizations, a vegetal dialectics is marked by the oscillation of states of difference and sameness between plants and non-plants. In preserving the irreducible otherness of flora, a dialectics provides a conceptual space for comprehending that "the absolute familiarity of plants coincides with their sheer strangeness" (Marder 2013, 4). What is more, a dialectics modulates the binarizing discourses surrounding plant nature—notably, as lacking thought, feeling, sensation, and response—and enables the subjectivities and agencies of vegetal being to come forth. This non-dualistic mode, furthermore, destabilizes the relegation of the plant to the zero-point of behavior, experience, and intelligence against which the capabilities of the animal are tuned to in sharp relief. As a consequence, a dialectics intersects with phytophenomenological exploration of "the intentionality inherent in plant life" (Marder 2012, 3). As humans engage with the distinct subjectivities of the botanical realm from a non-oppositional standpoint—as contradictoriness transforms into complementariness—the plant is no longer "an object readily available for the subject's manipulation" (Marder 2013, 7). A dialectics accordingly makes it possible for critics to think of plants in terms of *lives* (their complex phenomenological experiences as individuals and communities) rather than unidimensionally as *life* (a scientific totalization levied, in this context, as *botanical life*). The lively plant is one that *lives*, one in possession of a life, one that expresses and enacts its subjectivity within a life-world; it is not merely the plant homogenizable as the blunt biological denomination *plant life*, negativized in the image of animal life and human life. Within criticism itself, a plant-inflected dialectics provokes consciousness of the intrinsic faculties of vegetal life *and* lives to affect bodies and to be embodied (Chapter 3); to empathize and to be empathized with (Chapter 4); to remember and to be remembered (Chapter 6); and to hope and to be hoped for (Chapter 9).

As such, botanical poetry becomes the material semiosis of vegetal being and vitalizes the reformulation of engrained ideas about the botanical world. In this regard, Donna Haraway (2008) observes the "heterogeneous material-semiotic entanglements" between species and the transactions of "corporeal semiosis" whereby meaning inheres within embodied being-in-the-world and somatic being-between-worlds (236, 243). Not a representation of a botanical thing, the poem in a corporeal-semiotic sense is "the thing itself" (Marder 2012, 5). As stated above, my conceptualization of plant-focused poetry aligns with the idea of the poem as an ecosystem. This bold characterization collapses the traditional distinction between text and referent (Buell 1995, 10). I follow ecopoetic theory in arguing that the form of a poem can approximate the integrated systems of the natural world (Finch-Race and Weber 2015, 163). Environmental rhythms can become the metrics of the poem (for a case in point, see, in particular, Chapter 4 of this volume on the work of Bletsoe). Poetic structures can fluctuate with the circumstances of the versifier and the life-worlds of ecological subjects (Finch-Race and Weber 2015, 163). To be certain, the premise that "nature and poetry are mutually determinative" reverses the traditional ascription of meaning to botanical nature through poetic and other artistic representation (Finch-Race and Weber 2015, 164). While entanglement between vegetal and human subjects takes shape in poetry—as the chapters of this study reveal on a poet-by-poet basis—the audience remains affected by "what is nonidentical with us" (Morton 2007, 185). Through poetry, the dialectics of strangeness and familiarity entices us deeper into the lives of plants where we are confronted both by their radical otherness and profound sameness.

Book Structure and Thematic Overview

As detailed previously in this chapter, *Plants in Contemporary Poetry* responds to the prevailing tendency within ecocritical scholarship to examine animal, rather than plant, subjectivities and life-worlds. The sensuous return to vegetal being is actualized here through a focus on contemporary Anglophone poetry written during the last 70 years; that is, since the end of the Second World War (Makaryk 1993, vii). Along the way, my disquisition traverses a cross section of contemporary poetic genres, including confessionalism, postconfessionalism, experimentalism, radical pastoralism, radical landscape poetry, and, of course, ecopoetics. The oldest texts discussed within the ambit of contemporary poetry are *The Ilex Tree* (1965) by Les Murray and Geoffrey Lehmann (Chapter 2), *No Voyage and Other Poems* (1965) by Mary Oliver (Chapter 3), and *The Moving Image* (1946) by Judith Wright (Chapter 7). Most of the work, however, was originally published within the last 30 years. At the time of my writing, seven of the eight poets are living; Judith Wright passed away in 2000. Concerning its structure, the book adopts a thematically-based and author-focused approach that eschews either overall chronological sequencing according to the release dates of the works or political organization according to the poets' countries of origin. Instead, each chapter explores in detail a salient theme emerging within the botanical oeuvre of a poet—soul, body, empathy, humor, memory, time, death, and hope (love), in that order—and aligns the thematic analysis with historical thinking and current developments in the science of plant cognition. Extracts from published interviews with, and prose writings by, the poets contextualize their literary practices by disclosing their botanical affinities.

18 Introduction

The study accordingly opens with the vegetative soul in Australian poet Les Murray's work, progresses through a number of intervening themes, including botanical humor (Chapter 5) and plant death (Chapter 8), then concludes on a poignant note with American writer Joy Harjo's botanically-attuned versifications through the optics of vegetal hope and the love of flora (Chapter 9). A prominent technique deployed by contemporary poets to see the world from the perspectives of sessile lives is personification, entailing the attribution of personae to abstract things and other-than-human entities (see, in particular, Chapters 2, 4, 5, 6, and 9). Communicating in the first (botanical) person, vegetal speakers come to life through a material imagination shared by poet and plant. Rather than ventriloquizing vegetal being—and constructing plants in the human image—personification helps to elicit the intrinsic capacities of flora for sensibility and sensation. The position I take counterbalances the persistently negative view of the technique—both in literary theory and popular discourse—as a form of quaint sentimentalization or human-centered reverie. While advocating its benefits, the eighteenth-century natural philosopher Joseph Priestley (1833) argued that personification "converts every thing we treat of into thinking and acting beings. We see *life*, *sense*, and *intelligence*, every where" (434, emphasis in original). For Priestley, "if the resemblance be sufficiently strong, and other circumstances favour the figure, the impropriety of the personification gives not the least offence" (1833, 434). Rather than "an empty archaism," personification signifies the instability of ontological categories and—significantly for this study—confers "sensibility, voluntary motion, life, action, affection, sympathy, perception, intelligence" (Keenleyside 2009, 447, 449). The fearless personifications of Oswald and Glück especially threaten to upend "the sacred distinction between Thing and Person [upon which] all Law human and divine is grounded" (Coleridge 1829, 197; see Chapters 5 and 6).

Notwithstanding the topical specificity of each chapter, certain themes cut across the preponderance of poetic works discussed. A conspicuous one pertains to the use of plant nomenclature. While some poetry incorporates common names, frequently in titles—for instance, Glück's "Snowdrops" (1992)—other verse makes extensive use of scientific monikers. Bletsoe's *Pharmacopœia* (2010) is noteworthy for employing both; hence the sequence contains poems like "Monkey-flower (*Mimulus guttatus*)" and "Foxglove (*Digitalis purpurea*)" (105–6). Naming, of course, is implicated in the reduction of plant lives (a heterogeneity) to plant life (a homogeneity). As Londa Schiebinger (2004) contends, Linnaean binomialism attempted to expunge the "medicinal usages, biogeographical distribution, and cultural valence" (197) from botanical appellations and, moreover, from plant histories. Rendered in terms of genus and species, the individual plant became nothing more than a signifier of its hierarchization. By intertwining different nomenclatural forms with first-hand observations of plants, botanical poets approximate a

Rousseauian "poetico-scientific language" that follows the contours of vegetal nature (Willey 1982, 859). The precise use of naming reflects the poet's exposure to different botanical epistemologies, including Indigenous, scientific, ecological, folkloric, and medicinal discourses. As a case in point, Murray's spiritual-poetic ecology of flora hybridizes Aboriginal Australian, Christian, ecological, and experiential perspectives on the plants of coastal New South Wales (Chapter 2). What is more, an inclination characterizing many poets—Murray, Oliver, Bletsoe, Oswald, Glück, Wright, and Kinsella included—is to render one plant per poem. This model of versification might reflect a consciousness of the species as one of the defining memes of modernity. In its attention to the complex transactions between animate beings and inanimate things, however, Harjo's poetry presents an exception to this pattern (Chapter 9).

A pronounced biogeographical distribution—from Western Australia to South West England, from desert environments to woodland habitats—is a distinguishing feature of *Plants in Contemporary Poetry*. Nonetheless, there are distinct commonalities of literary praxis, especially in terms of the importance of gardening and walking to poets and poetry. For the botanical versifiers of this study, these two body techniques constitute a mode of interrelation and inscription as significant as the act of writing itself. Horticultural and ambulatory methods underlie a phytophenomenological return to "the things themselves" according to which poetry comes to embrace the aspects specific to each experience of botanical being (Marder 2013, 7). Gardening is particularly foundational to the work of Oswald, Glück, and Wright. Accordingly, these poets join an esteemed lineage of others like Wordsworth for whom "composing poetry and gardening were intertwined" (Buchanan and Buchanan 2001, 25). After reading classics at Oxford, Oswald studied at the Royal Horticultural Society then worked as a gardener at Chelsea Physic Garden, Dartington Hall Estate, and elsewhere. Facilitating immersion in plant life-worlds, such experiences inform the distinctive humor found throughout *Weeds and Wild Flowers* (Chapter 5). Although not professionally trained in horticulture, Glück raised a flower garden in Vermont from which the Pulitzer Prize-winning *The Wild Iris* emerged. Glück's poetization of memory in plants derives in part from this sustained encounter with vegetal life through tending flowers (Chapter 6). Still, the cultivation of flora in contexts other than gardening has been influential to the apprehension of vegetal ontology by the poets I discuss. Kinsella writes about his experiences replanting degraded habitats in the poem "Harsh Hakea (or Elements of the Subject's Will)" (2011). Heightened by the practice of helping to restore environments, an embodied sense of "botanical nativism" (Kerr 2012, 195) is vital to Kinsella's radical pastoralism and addresses the grief of witnessing profound plant loss over time (Chapter 8). Central to Harjo's poetics of hope is the plant and, more specifically, the annual *boskita*, or Green Corn Ceremony, celebrating the ripening of a new crop of maize and marking the beginning of a new year. Harjo resists what she calls the "dehumanization of plants" not by anthropomorphizing them but by embracing them as kin (Chapter 9).

In addition to practices of cultivation, walking offers the poet a means to interact viscerally with plants (see Chapters 3, 4, 5, 6, and 7 in particular). When performed over time and through the seasons, perambulation becomes a textual act revealing the plant as a being in process rather than a static thing (Buell 1995, 8). The connection between walking and poetry, however, is not the province of the last 30 years—the contemporary period in focus in this book. During the first half of the twentieth century and in the spirit of Thoreau, for instance, the Swiss writer Robert Walser felt compelled to walk in order "to invigorate myself and to maintain contact with the living world, without perceiving which I could not write the half of one more single word, nor produce the tiniest poem in verse or prose" (Walser 1957, 77). As for botanically-concerned poets, non-mechanized self-propelled movement spurred Walser (1957) "on to further creation" and "is always filled with significant phenomena, which are valuable to see and to feel" (78). One must perambulate with "open and unclouded eyes" so as to "sink into the deepest and smallest everyday thing" (Walser 1957, 78, 79). On this note, Oliver's poetic insights into vegetal being and, more precisely, the plant-human intercorporeality of her work take shape through the combination of walking, sensing, reflecting, and writing (Chapter 3). The lived space of vegetal poetry, therefore, emerges as a function of the bodily orientation of plant and non-plant subjects, including the writer-walker. Moreover, walking is foundational to Bletsoe's development of a sense of bioempathic emplacement through medicinal flora (Chapter 4). To be sure, Bletsoe is not only a botanizer but a herborizer: one who sets off on foot to observe, consider, or wildcraft healing plants. Wright's work, furthermore, alludes to instances of walking among botanical communities. As a result of her extended sensory exposure, plant temporalities become distinguishable from human chronos (Chapter 7). Walking thus potently dispels "the illusion of plant immobility" by elucidating "the difference in the time scales of human and plant lives" (Marder 2012, 3).

Conclusion: The Poetisphere of Our Time

In examining the ways poets engage with and mediate botanical lives, *Plants in Contemporary Poetry* affords a glimpse into the ontologies, epistemologies, and semiospheres of flora and, by extension, the natural world. Highlighting the florally-focused inclinations and obsessions of some of the leading versifiers in English today, this book calls attention to the capacity of language to deconstruct the cultural codes that limit understanding plants as percipient beings with their own teleological pulsations. As poetics entrains with vegetal being, poets gain direct knowledge of—and are inspired by—the comportments, capacities, negotiations, and interrelations of the life-worlds of plants with which they interact and in which they too are embedded. Uniquely bringing plant neurobiology to bear on ecocritical practice, this study underscores poetry's "(necessarily imperfect and incomplete) approximation to the locus of vegetal being" (Marder 2013, 63) through the work of poets who, despite their stylistic and biogeographical differences, share an enduring affinity for plants of all shapes, sizes, and habits. In *The Poetics of Reverie* (1971, 25), Bachelard asks, "How can we enter the poetisphere of our time?" In closing this introduction, I suggest that the question is an ecocritical one and, more precisely, a phytocritical one. Entering the poetisphere of our time at the threshold of plants and language necessitates learning about, from, and with our photosynthetic fellow-beings. In disrupting the normative conception of subjectivity (Cvrčková, Žárský, and Markoš 2016, 3) and violating the criteria defining individuality in the natural world (Clarke 2012, 321), the lively plant insinuates its body, soul, wisdom, and imaginings into everyday milieux. From a dialectical standpoint, to imagine the plant is always-already to imagine *with* the plant. Such a realization shifts not only our approach to poetry but to the world(s) all beings share.

Bibliography

Adorno, Theodor W. 2004. *Negative Dialectics*. Translated by E.B. Ashton. London: Taylor and Francis. Original edition, 1966.

Allen, David, and Gabrielle Hatfield. 2004. *Medicinal Plants in Folk Tradition: An Ethnobotany of Britain and Ireland*. Portland, OR: Timber Press.

Alpi, Amedeo, Nikolaus Amrhein, Adam Bertl, Michael Blatt, Eduardo Blumwald, Felice Cervone, Jack Dainty, Maria Ida De Michelis, Emanuel Epstein, Arthur Galston, Mary Helen Goldsmith, Chris Hawes, Rudiger Hell, Alistair Hetherington, Herman Hofte, Gerd Juergens, Chris Leaver, Anna Moroni, Angus Murphy, Karl Oparka, Pierdomenico Perata, Hartmut Quader, Thomas Rausch, Christophe Ritzenthaler, Alberto Rivetta, David Robinson, Dale Sanders, Ben Scheres, Karin Schumacher, Herve Sentenac, Clifford Slayman, Carlo Soave, Chris Somerville, Lincoln Taiz, Gerhard Thiel, and Richard Wagner. 2007. "Plant Neurobiology: No Brain, No Gain?" *Trends in Plant Science* 12 (4): 135–36. doi:10.1016/j.tplants.2007.03.002

Bachelard, Gaston. 1971. *The Poetics of Reverie: Childhood, Language, and the Cosmos*. Translated by Daniel Russell. Boston, MA: Beacon Press. Original edition, 1960.

———. 1991. "The Hand Dreams: On Material Imagination." In *Gaston Bachelard, Subversive Humanist: Texts and Readings*, edited by Mary McAllester Jones, 102–6. Madison: University of Wisconsin Press.

Bais, Harsh. 2015. "Shedding Light on Kin Recognition Response in Plants." *New Phytologist* 205 (1): 4–6. doi:10.1111/nph.13155

Balas, Benjamin, and Jennifer Momsen. 2014. "Attention 'Blinks' Differently for Plants and Animals." *CBE: Life Sciences Education* 13 (3): 437–43. doi:10.1187/cbe.14-05-0080

Balding, Mung, and Kathryn Williams. 2016. "Plant Blindness and the Implications for Plant Conservation." *Conservation Biology* 30 (6): 1192–99. doi:10.1111/cobi.12738
Baluška, František, and Stefano Mancuso. 2007. "Plant Neurobiology as a Paradigm Shift Not Only in the Plant Sciences." *Plant Signaling and Behavior* 2 (4): 205–7.
Baluška, František, Stefano Mancuso, Dieter Volkmann, and Peter Barlow. 2009. "The 'Root-Brain' Hypothesis of Charles and Francis Darwin: Revival After More Than 125 Years." *Plant Signaling and Behavior* 4 (12): 1121–27.
Barlow, Peter. 2008. "Reflections on 'Plant Neurobiology'." *Biosystems* 92 (2): 132–47.
Bergson, Henri. 1998. *Creative Evolution*. Mineola, NY: Dover Publications.
Bhaskar, Roy. 1993. *Dialectic: The Pulse of Freedom*. London: Verso.
Blackstone, Bernard. 1959. *The Consecrated Urn: An Interpretation of Keats in Terms of Growth and Form*. London: Longmans, Green and Company.
Bletsoe, Elisabeth. 2010. *Pharmacopœia and Early Selected Works*. Exeter: Shearsman Books.
Bose, Jagadis Chandra. 1919. *Life Movements in Plants*. Vol. 2. Calcutta: Bengal Government Press.
———. 1995. *Life Movements in Plants*. Vol. 1. Delhi: D.K. Publishers. Original edition, 1918.
Buchanan, Carol, and Richard Buchanan. 2001. *Wordsworth's Gardens*. Lubbock: Texas Tech University Press.
Buell, Lawrence. 1995. *The Environmental Imagination: Thoreau, Nature Writing, and the Formation of American Culture*. Cambridge, MA: Belknap Press of Harvard University Press.
———. 2005. *The Future of Environmental Criticism: Environmental Crisis and Literary Imagination*. Malden, MA: Blackwell Publishing.
Calvo, Paco. 2016. "The Philosophy of Plant Neurobiology: A Manifesto." *Synthese* 193 (5): 1323–43. doi:10.1007/s11229-016-1040-1
Chamovitz, Daniel. 2012. *What a Plant Knows: A Field Guide to the Senses*. Brunswick, Australia: Scribe Publications.
Clarke, Ellen. 2012. "Plant Individuality: A Solution to the Demographer's Dilemma." *Biology and Philosophy* 27 (3): 321–61. doi:10.1007/s10539-012-9309-3
Classen, Albrecht. 2015. *The Forest in Medieval German Literature: Ecocritical Readings from a Historical Perspective*. Lanham, MD: Lexington Books.
Coleridge, Samuel Taylor. 1829. *Aids to Reflection in the Formation of a Manly Character, on the Several Grounds of Prudence, Morality, and Religion*. Burlington, VT: Chauncey Goodrich.
Cvrčková, Fatima, Viktor Žárský, and Anton Markoš. 2016. "Plant Studies May Lead Us to Rethink the Concept of Behavior." *Frontiers in Psychology* 7 (622): 1–4. doi:10.3389/fpsyg.2016.00622
Darwin, Charles, and Francis Darwin. 2016. *The Works of Charles Darwin: The Power of Movement in Plants*. Edited by Paul Barrett and R.B. Freeman. London: Routledge.
Darwin, Erasmus. 1798. *The Botanic Garden: A Poem, in Two Parts*. 5th ed. New York: T. and J. Swords.

De Chadarevian, Soraya. 1996. "Laboratory Science Versus Country-House Experiments: The Controversy Between Julius Sachs and Charles Darwin." *The British Journal for the History of Science* 29 (1): 17–41.

Depuydt, Stephen. 2014. "Arguments For and Against Self and Non-Self Root Recognition in Plants." *Frontiers in Plant Science* 5 (614). doi:10.3389/fpls.2014.00614

Dornelas, Maria, Nicholas Gotelli, Brian Mcgill, Hideyasu Shimadzu, Faye Moyes, Caya Sievers, and Anne Magurran. 2014. "Biodiversity Change but Not Systematic Loss." *Science* 344: 296–99. doi:10.1126/science.1248484

Ellacombe, Henry. 1896. *The Plant-Lore and Garden-Craft of Shakespeare*. London: Edward Arnold. Original edition, 1878.

Finch-Race, Daniel, and Julien Weber. 2015. "The Ecocritical Stakes of French Poetry from the Industrial Era." *Dix-Neuf* 19 (3): 159–66. doi:10.1179/1478731815Z.00000000084

Firn, Richard. 2004. "Plant Intelligence: An Alternative Point of View." *Annals of Botany* 93 (4): 345–51. doi:10.1093/aob/mch058

Gadamer, Hans-Georg. 1976. *Hegel's Dialectic: Five Hermeneutical Studies*. Translated by P. Christopher Smith. New Haven, CT: Yale University Press.

Gagliano, Monica, Mavra Grimonprez, Martial Depczynski, and Michael Renton. 2017. "Tuned In: Plant Roots Use Sound to Locate Water." *Oecologia* 184 (1): 151–60. doi:10.1007/s00442-017-3862-z

Gagliano, Monica, John Ryan, and Patrícia Vieira, eds. 2017. *The Language of Plants: Science, Philosophy, Literature*. Minneapolis: University of Minnesota Press.

Garzón, Francisco Calvo. 2007. "The Quest for Cognition in Plant Neurobiology." *Plant Signaling and Behavior* 2 (4): 208–11.

Glück, Louise. 1992. *The Wild Iris*. New York: HarperCollins Publishers.

Grindon, Leo. 1883. *The Shakespeare Flora: A Guide to All the Principal Passages in Which Mention Is Made of Trees, Plants, Flowers, and Vegetable Productions*. Manchester, UK: Palmer and Howe.

Hall, Matthew. 2011. *Plants as Persons: A Philosophical Botany*. Albany, NY: State University of New York Press.

———. 2014. "Talk Among the Trees: Animist Plant Ontologies and Ethics." In *The Handbook of Contemporary Animism*, edited by Graham Harvey, 385–94. New York: Routledge.

Haraway, Donna. 2008. *When Species Meet*. Minneapolis: University of Minnesota Press.

Heise, Ursula. 2008. *Sense of Place and Sense of Planet: The Environmental Imagination of the Global*. New York: Oxford University Press.

Heyd, Thomas. 2012. "Plant Ethics and Botanic Gardens." *PAN: Philosophy Activism Nature* 9: 37–47.

Huggan, Graham, and Helen Tiffin. 2010. *Postcolonial Ecocriticism: Literature, Animals, Environment*. New York: Routledge.

Iovino, Serenella, and Serpil Oppermann. 2014. "Introduction: Stories Come to Matter." In *Material Ecocriticism*, edited by Serenella Iovino and Serpil Oppermann, 1–17. Bloomington: Indiana University Press.

Irigaray, Luce, and Michael Marder. 2016. *Through Vegetal Being: Two Philosophical Perspectives*. New York: Columbia University Press.

Jones, Mary McAllester. 1991. *Gaston Bachelard, Subversive Humanist: Texts and Readings*. Madison: University of Wisconsin Press.
Karban, Richard. 2015. *Plant Sensing and Communication*. Chicago: University of Chicago Press.
Keenleyside, Heather. 2009. "Personification for the People: On James Thomson's 'The Seasons'." *ELH* 76 (2): 447–72. doi:10.1353/elh.0.0044
Kerr, Heather. 2012. "Melancholy Botany: Charlotte Smith's Bioregional Poetic Imaginary." In *The Bioregional Imagination: Literature, Ecology, and Place*, edited by Tom Lynch, Cheryll Glotfelty and Karla Armbruster, 181–99. Athens: The University of Georgia Press.
Kerr, Jessica. 1968. *Shakespeare's Flowers*. Chicago: Johnson Books.
King, Amy. 2003. *Bloom: The Botanical Vernacular in the English Novel*. Oxford: Oxford University Press.
Kinsella, John. 2011. "Harsh Hakea (or Elements of the Subject's Will)." *Literary Review* no. 54 (3): 132–55.
Kirksey, S. Eben, and Stefan Helmreich. 2010. "The Emergence of Multispecies Ethnography." *Cultural Anthropology* 25 (4): 545–76.
Knott, John. 2012. *Imagining the Forest: Narratives of Michigan and the Upper Midwest*. Ann Arbor: University of Michigan Press.
Koller, Dov. 2011. *The Restless Plant*. Edited by Elizabeth Van Volkenburg. Cambridge, MA: Harvard University Press.
Kranz, Isabel. 2017. "The Language of Flowers in Popular Culture and Botany." In *The Language of Plants: Science, Philosophy, Literature*, edited by Monica Gagliano, John Ryan and Patrícia Vieira, 193–214. Minneapolis: University of Minnesota Press.
Kull, Kalevi. 2000. "An Introduction to Phytosemiotics: Semiotic Botany and Vegetative Sign Systems." *Sign Systems Studies* 28: 326–50.
Laist, Randy. 2013. "Introduction." In *Plants and Literature: Essays in Critical Plant Studies*, edited by Randy Laist, 9–17. Amsterdam: Rodopi.
Lang, Nancy Helene. 1961. *Flower Symbolism in the Poetry of T.S. Eliot*. Oxford, OH: Miami University Press.
Love, Glen. 2003. *Practical Ecocriticism: Literature, Biology, and the Environment*. Charlottesville: University of Virginia Press.
Lynch, Tom, Cheryll Glotfelty, and Karla Armbruster, eds. 2012a. *The Bioregional Imagination: Literature, Ecology, and Place*. Athens: University of Georgia Press.
Lynch, Tom, Cheryll Glotfelty, and Karla Armbruster. 2012b. "Introduction." In *The Bioregional Imagination: Literature, Ecology, and Place*, edited by Tom Lynch, Cheryll Glotfelty and Karla Armbruster, 1–29. Athens: University of Georgia Press.
Mahood, Molly. 2008. *The Poet as Botanist*. Cambridge, UK: Cambridge University Press.
Makaryk, Irene Rima. 1993. *Encyclopedia of Contemporary Literary Theory: Approaches, Scholars, Terms*. Toronto: University of Toronto Press.
Mancuso, Stefano, and Alessandra Viola. 2015. *Brilliant Green: The Surprising History and Science of Plant Intelligence*. Translated by Joan Benham. Washington, DC: Island Press.
Manetas, Yiannis. 2012. *Alice in the Land of Plants: Biology of Plants and their Importance for Planet Earth*. Berlin: Springer.

Marder, Michael. 2012. "Plant Intentionality and the Phenomenological Framework of Plant Intelligence." *Plant Signalling and Behavior* 7 (11): 1–8. doi:10.4161/psb.21954

———. 2013. *Plant-Thinking: A Philosophy of Vegetal Life*. New York: Columbia University Press.

———. 2014. *The Philosopher's Plant: An Intellectual Herbarium*. New York: Columbia University Press.

Morton, Timothy. 2007. *Ecology Without Nature: Rethinking Environmental Aesthetics*. Cambridge, MA: Harvard University Press.

Murray, Les, and Geoffrey Lehmann. 1965. *The Ilex Tree*. Canberra: Australian National University.

Norman, Richard, and Sean Sayers. 1980. *Hegel, Marx and Dialectic: A Debate*. Brighton, UK: The Harvester Press.

Nyberg, Eva, and Dawn Sanders. 2014. "Drawing Attention to the 'Green Side of Life'." *Journal of Biological Education* 48 (3): 142–53. doi: 10.1080/00219266.2013.849282.

Oliver, Mary. 1965. *No Voyage and Other Poems*. Boston: Houghton Mifflin.

Otten, Charlotte. 1985. *Environ'd with Eternity: God, Poems, and Plants in Sixteenth and Seventeenth Century England*. Lawrence, KS: Coronado Press.

Pollan, Michael. 2013. "The Intelligent Plant: Scientists Debate a New Way of Understanding Flora." *The New Yorker* December 23 and 30: 92–105.

———. 2015. "Foreword." In *Brilliant Green: The Surprising History and Science of Plant Intelligence*, edited by Stefano Mancuso and Alessandra Viola, xi–xiii. Washington DC: Island Press.

Pouteau, Sylvie. 2014. "Beyond 'Second Animals': Making Sense of Plant Ethics." *Journal of Agricultural and Environmental Ethics* 27 (1): 1–25.

Priestley, Joseph. 1833. *English Grammar: Lectures on the Theory of Language and Universal Grammar*. London: Rowland Hunter.

Quealy, Gerit, and Sumie Hasegawa Collins. 2017. *Botanical Shakespeare: An Illustrated Compendium of all the Flowers, Fruits, Herbs, Trees, Seeds, and Grasses Cited by the World's Greatest Playwright*. New York: HarperCollins.

Robbins, William. 1944. "The Importance of Plants." *Science* 100 (2603): 440–43.

Rose, Deborah Bird, Thom van Dooren, Matthew Chrulew, Stuart Cooke, Matthew Kearnes, and Emily O'Gorman. 2012. "Thinking Through the Environment, Unsettling the Humanities." *Environmental Humanities* 1 (1): 1–5.

Ryan, John. 2017. "In the Key of Green? The Silent Voices of Plants in Poetry." In *The Language of Plants: Science, Philosophy, Literature*, edited by Monica Gagliano, John Ryan and Patrícia Vieira, 273–96. Minneapolis: University of Minnesota Press.

Schiebinger, Londa. 2004. *Plants and Empire: Colonial Bioprospecting in the Atlantic World*. Cambridge, MA: Harvard University Press.

Skotheim, Jan, and Lakshminarayanan Mahadevan. 2005. "Physical Limits and Design Principles for Plant and Fungal Movements." *Science* 308 (5726): 1308–10.

Smith, James Edward. 1788. "Some Observations on the Irritability of Vegetables." *Philosophical Transactions of the Royal Society of London* 78: 158–65.

Struik, Paul, Xinyou Yin, and Holger Meinke. 2008. "Perspective: Plant Neurobiology and Green Plant Intelligence: Science, Metaphors and Nonsense."

Journal of the Science of Food and Agriculture 88 (3): 363–70. doi:10.1002/jsfa.3131

Swiss Confederation. 2008. *The Dignity of Living Beings with Regard to Plants: Moral Consideration of Plants for Their Own Sake*. Translated by Jackie Leach Scully. Bern: Federal Ethics on Non-Human Biotechnology ECNH.

Tally, Robert, and Christine Battista. 2016. "Introduction: Ecocritical Geographies, Geocritical Ecologies, and the Spaces of Modernity." In *Ecocriticism and Geocriticism: Overlapping Territories in Environmental and Spatial Literary Studies*, edited by Robert Tally and Christine Battista, 1–15. Houndsmills, UK: Palgrave Macmillan.

Taylor, Nik, and Richard Twine. 2014. "Introduction: Locating the 'Critical' in Critical Animal Studies." In *The Rise of Critical Animal Studies: From the Margins to the Centre*, edited by Nik Taylor and Richard Twine, 1–15. New York: Routledge.

Taylor, Philip, Gwyneth Card, James House, Michael Dickinson, and Richard Flagan. 2006. "High-Speed Pollen Release in the White Mulberry Tree, *Morus alba* L." *Sexual Plant Reproduction* 19 (1): 19–24. doi:10.1007/s00497-005-0018-9

Theis, Jeffrey. 2009. *Writing the Forest in Early Modern England: A Sylvan Pastoral Nation*. Pittsburgh, PA: Duquesne University Press.

Trewavas, Anthony. 2002. "Plant Intelligence: Mindless Mastery." *Nature* 415 (6874): 841. doi:10.1038/415841a

———. 2014. *Plant Behaviour and Intelligence*. Oxford: Oxford University Press.

———. 2016. "Intelligence, Cognition, and Language of Green Plants." *Frontiers in Psychology* 7: 1–9. doi:10.3389/fpsyg.2016.00588

Uexküll, Jakob von. 2010. *A Foray into the Worlds of Animals and Humans: With a Theory of Meaning*. 1 ed. Minneapolis: University of Minnesota Press. Original edition, 1934.

Van Loon, Leendert. 2016. "The Intelligent Behavior of Plants." *Trends in Plant Science* 21 (4): 286–94. doi:10.1016/j.tplants.2015.11.009

Vieira, Patrícia, Monica Gagliano, and John Ryan. 2016. "Introduction." In *The Green Thread: Dialogues with the Vegetal World*, edited by Patrícia Vieira, Monica Gagliano and John Ryan, ix–xxvii. Lanham, MD: Lexington Books.

Vogel, Steven. 2005. "Living in a Physical World II: The Bio-ballistics of Small Projectiles." *Journal of Biosciences* 30 (2): 167–75.

Walser, Robert. 1957. *The Walk and Other Stories*. Translated by Christopher Middleton. London: Calder. Original edition, 1917.

Wandersee, James, and Elisabeth Schussler. 1999. "Preventing Plant Blindness." *The American Biology Teacher* 61 (2): 82–86.

Willey, Susan. 1982. "The Poetic Imagination: Of Myopia, Botany, and Electromagnetism." *MLN* 97 (4): 849–61.

Wright, Judith. 1946. *The Moving Image: Poems*. Melbourne: The Meanjin Press.

Yoshida, Akemi. 2013. "Temptation of Fruit: The Symbolism of Fruit in Christina Rossetti's 'Goblin Market' and in the Works of D. G. Rossetti and J. E. Millais." In *Plants and Literature: Essays in Critical Plant Studies*, edited by Randy Laist, 75–84. Amsterdam: Rodopi.

2 Sacred Ecologies of Plants
The Vegetative Soul in Les Murray's Poetry

> I am lived. I am died.
> I was two-leafed three times, and grazed,
> but then I was stemmed and multiplied,
> sharp-thorned and caned, nested and raised,
> earth-salt by sun-sugar. I am innerly sung
> by thrushes who need fear no eyed skin thing.
> —from "Cockspur Bush," *Translations from the Natural World*
> (Murray 2012, 35, ll. 1–6)

As Chapter 1 explained, scientific research in plant neurobiology increasingly reveals the percipience of vegetal life (for example, Trewavas 2016). As a case in point, the pilpil (*Boquila trifoliolata*), a climbing vine found in the temperate rainforests of Chile and Argentina, mimics the leaf size, shape, color, and position of at least eight different tree hosts (Gianoli and Carrasco-Urra 2014). Long associated with mammals, birds, and insects, complex forms of mimicry have been recognized in plants as mechanisms for enhancing fitness, survival, and wellbeing (Burns 2010). In another study, botanists suggest that the Venus flytrap (*Dionaea muscipula*) can count to five. The carnivorous plant tallies the number of times its trigger hairs have been touched before releasing its trap and secreting an enzyme cocktail, ensuring that insects—rather than raindrops or non-organic debris—are encaged and eventually digested (Böhm 2016). What is more, experiments in plant communication indicate that Douglas firs (*Pseudotsuga menziesii*) and other species use a system of underground "tree talk" mediated by mycorrhizal networks to increase the long-term resilience of forest communities (Gorzelak et al. 2015). As anthropologist Jeremy Narby observes in his book *Intelligence in Nature* (2006), nonhuman life displays an uncanny capacity for self-directed decision-making and percipient behavior.

If plants are intelligent, do they also have souls? To be sure, the possibility of vegetal ensoulment stirs the human imagination with glimpses of talking trees, floral sprites, garden muses, sylvan dryads, and other mythological plant-people hybrids (Giesecke 2014). Yet, the simple but provocative question—one a whimsical child, overly-imaginative adolescent, or quixotic adult inclined toward mystical reverie might ask—has in surprising ways influenced the course of occidental thought. For Aristotle, the answer was affirmative but weak and contingent on a hierarchy. In his schema, anything—or, more precisely, any*body*—that is alive necessarily has a soul. He characterized the elusive life principle as "an actuality or formulable essence of something that possesses a potentiality of being ensouled" (Aristotle 2000, book II.2). In the writings of the ancient philosopher, vegetal life possesses a base variant of soul known as vegetative or nutritive. As a result of Aristotelian thinking, the concept of the vegetative soul according to Saint Thomas Aquinas and subsequent Western commentators embeds hierarchical typologies delineating between the ensoulment of plants, animals, and humans. This philosophical lineage coupled the vegetative soul to gross materiality and deprived plants of the intellective faculties of higher-order soul-forms. As the upshot of their philosophical marginalization, plants are lesser ensouled, stripped of intelligence, and rendered inferior to the zoological domain (see Chapter 1). Tracing the idea of the plant soul from Aristotle to Aboriginal Australian cosmologies, this chapter examines the enlivened reclamation of vegetal being in the work of contemporary Australian poet, novelist, and critic Les Murray (b. 1938). Despite the hierarchies propounded by Western discourse, the vegetative soul figures prominently in the work of Murray, a writer who critics regard as "the leading Australian poet of his generation" (Coetzee 2011, sect. 7) and whose 50-year corpus of work consistently engages environmental themes with steadfast attention to the nonhuman life of rural New South Wales, Australia (Clark 2002, 2003, 2007; Dunkerley 2001).

How might poetry become a vehicle for expressing the percipient attributes of flora? Murray's work provides a response to this question by countering the premise that plants lack intelligence and bear only a rudimentary soul. Through lyrical engagement with the intentionalities of flora, the poet approaches the botanical domain as a sentient locus of spiritual realization and multispecies exchange. Murray's sacred ecology of plants bridges Christian and Indigenous Australian concepts of nature while paralleling recent scientific evidence for plant intelligence. Murray integrates cosmological aspects from Indigenous societies across Australia that consider plants spiritually meaningful participants in creation or Dreaming narratives (Clarke 2011, 23–33). The traditional stories of the Myall Lakes area of mid-coastal New South Wales—near the town of Bunyah where Murray writes and resides—foreground the dialogical relationships between intelligent vegetal protagonists, the natural order, and the human domain. After the sky deity Gulambarra is speared to death, his mother's tears give rise to a specimen of mangrove tree, still in existence today, called the crying tree (Paulson 2016). Murray speaks a little of the Worimi language Gadjang (Alexander 2000, 315), and is familiar with other Dreaming narratives of the region, such as those gathered in *Gumbaynggirr Yuludarla Jandaygam* (*Gumbaynggirr Dreaming Story Collection*) (Morelli 2010).

The sacred ecology of plants at work in Murray's poetry points to two dimensions of the vegetal soul. On the one hand, there is the intrinsic plant soul, existing regardless of human ascriptions of ensoulment to the botanical world. On the other, there is the ability of plants to catalyze the sacred experiences of humans—to nourish our souls and to provide living portals to divine experience in everyday consciousness. The botanical verse of Murray brings plants to life through this dialectic as ensouled beings with capacities proper to their modes of existence, which remain sensorially accessible yet metaphysically elusive to human subjects. By conferring ensoulment to vegetal life, Murray counters the "valorization of reason at the expense of dream and the body" (Clark 2002, 21). Murray's vegetal ensoulment, hence, forms part of his broader critique of Cartesian rationalism and European Enlightenment values that underlie the prioritization of the intellect over the body and the relegation of the other-than-human world to insentient matter (Clark 2002). Moreover, in its hybridization of diverse ontologies, Murray's botanical poetry concretizes his theory of convergence (see Murray 1977) between Indigenous and Anglo-Australian, and ecological and agrarian views of plants. His theory is certainly relevant to addressing the urgencies of the Anthropocene today. In an era of profound loss of botanical diversity—where one in five species globally is threatened with extinction (Royal Botanic Gardens, Kew 2016)—Murray's post-Aristotelian, post-Enlightenment vision of vegetal life invites us to consider the percipience of flora as well as the ethics of human-plant relations. Imagining the botanical world around us in this way is the first step toward valuing plants and devising sustainable means of living with—rather than displacing and eradicating—these non-animal beings.

Murray's Botanical Imagination: Conceptions of the Sacred Plant

Murray's botanically-inclined poetry interweaves the traditional knowledge of the Worimi and other Aboriginal groups of the mid-coastal areas of New South Wales with the Christian beliefs of Anglo-Australian settler culture. His sacred ecology of plants centers on some of the most ancient and drought-tolerant plant species known. Operating within this Australian context, a sacred ecology—which I define as a state of plant-animal-human souls in dynamic exchange with the material landscape—embodies the qualities of antipodean plant life: unique, endemic, ancient, adaptive, xeriphilic, and sensorial. Australia's extremely arid, fire-prone landscape with generally low-fertility soils consists of flora that is sclerophyllous (bearing hard leaves and best adapted to Mediterranean-type climates) and xeromorphic (shaped by adaptation to prolonged drought conditions) (Crisp and Cook 2013, 303). In total, Australia counts over 17,000 species of flowering plants, an unparalleled 16 endemic plant families found nowhere else on the planet, and more than half of the mangrove species of the world (Steffen et al. 2009, 10). Eucalypts and acacia trees dominate the botanical makeup of the landmass; and most plant species come principally from the Myrtaceae (myrtle), Proteaceae (protea), and Fabaceae (legume) families. In the late Cretaceous period (roughly between 145.5 and 65.5 million years ago), Australia formed part of the ancient supercontinent Gondwana. Around 45 million years ago in the late Eocene epoch, the Australian landmass separated from Antarctica, effectively isolating species for millions of years and resulting in the pronounced biological diversification (Steffen et al. 2009, 9). As a result, a staggering 91% of Australian flowering plants are endemic (Steffen et al. 2009, 8).

Considering Australia's high biodiversity, the prominent role of plants in the imagination of one of the country's seminal poets is expected. As Gary Clark (2007) observes, a dominant theme in Murray's work is the appreciation of "the very distinctive biogeographical and climatic patterns of the Australian continent" (438). Murray's textualization of this distinctiveness extends to ancient events, such as the transition of Gondwana rainforests into fire adapted eucalypt habitats, as well as the more recent impacts of settlement-era land clearing and plant eradication campaigns (Clark 2007). Despite tendencies toward botanical nativism, Murray is not obsessively—or ideologically—only concerned with endemic Australian plants, those species extant within the environment at the time of British colonization. Murray's view of vegetative ensoulment, instead, applies to both original and introduced plant taxa. I suggest that the poet's sensory contact with the flora of the rural coastal and inland regions of New South Wales, in conjunction with his knowledge of natural history and a positive outlook on the potentialities of vegetative ensoulment, forms a triad giving rise to a sacred ecology of plants. Moreover, Murray propounds the broader ideal of cultural convergence, which provides the conceptual grounding for vegetal ensoulment in his poetry with respect to Worimi and other Indigenous Australian values.

It is not a coincidence that the title of Murray's first published collection, *The Ilex Tree* (1965), co-authored with Australian poet Geoffrey Lehmann, evokes an ancient plant with the ability to speak and express itself otherwise. The work appeals to the Western pastoral tradition both in its title and through an epigraph from Eclogue VII of Virgil's *Eclogues* (circa. 37 BCE). Eclogue VII relates:

> It happened Daphnis sat beneath a singing ilex.
> Thyrsis and Corydon had drawn up both their flocks—
> Thyrsis his ewes and Corydon his goats, all udder-
> Swollen. Arcadians both, the boys were in their bloom.
> (Virgil 2010: 51, ll. 1–5)

Rather than "singing," in the translation quoted by Murray and Lehmann in the epigraph, the ilex is a "whispering" plant being (Matthews 2001, 39). Along with the vines, trees, bees, and insects of other long poems, including the *Georgics* (ca. 29 BCE), the whispering ilex—a common holly but also an expressive subject with its own voice—exemplifies the animistic conception of plants as sacred beings in Virgil (Thomas 1988, 263) and also conveys Murray's identification with a metaphysics of flora not constrained by Enlightenment-based ratiocination. To be sure, Murray's poetry hybridizes different cultural understandings of flora and leads to a syncretic interpretation of vegetative ensoulment that draws from Ancient Greek, Indigenous Australian, and Christian traditions.

Murray's fellow feeling for the natural world and the eminence of animals, plants, and landscapes in his poetry reflect the poet's country upbringing on a dairy farm in the town of Bunyah between Forster and Gloucester—and between the Aboriginal districts of Coolongolook and Bucca Wauka—in the Manning River delta system of NSW (Alexander 2000; Murray 2005). It is at least partly because of a childhood in the countryside that all manner of plants—both domesticated and wild, introduced and native, ground-hugging and skyward-reaching—factor into Murray's botanical imagination, providing the vehicles for his poetic expression of animism. His father Cecil Allan accrued substantial knowledge of the plant life—especially the woodlands—he cleared on his property. Murray recalls his father assessing the suitability of a living tree for timber by listening closely for "pipes" (or hollow inner sections) on tapping the trunk with his fingers (Alexander 2000, 15). In 1986, Murray returned to his family farm and "spirit country" in Bunyah to take up residence and pursue a living as a writer after numerous years residing in urban areas. During this period of transition to rural life, Murray's interest in local plant ecologies intensified, as evident in his poetry and prose.

The title of his prose non-fiction work, *The Paperbark Tree* (1992), invokes the *Melaleuca* genus of nearly 300 species, most of which occur in Australia. The collection celebrates the vegetative landscape in a manner evocative—in tone and content—of other seminal works of Australian natural history, namely Vincent Serventy's *Dryandra* (1970), George Seddon's *Sense of Place* (1972), and Eric Rolls' *A Million Wild Acres* (1981). For instance, an excerpt from *The Paperbark Tree* reveals Murray's technical knowledge of eucalypt growth in the context of the rural landscape of New South Wales:

> Eucalypts are by and large extremely fussy about their requirements for drainage and soil chemistry, and really the best way to 'plant' them is to fence grazing animals out and see what comes up. Heads of trees are left on the ground after felling, to shed their masses of seed and replenish the forest with their species.
>
> (Murray 1992, 386)

Even the metaphorical characterization of eucalypts as "fussy" suggests the trees' responsiveness and capacity for affect. Rather than a hollow trope or a hackneyed mode of personification, the choice of the adjective "fussy" represents the material-semiois of plants in Murray's poetry. The qualifier connects the ecology of eucalypts to an idea of plant ensoulment.

On the whole, Murray's botanical imagination is inclusive and integrative. It is not restricted to technical appreciation of flora—for instance, "drainage and soil chemistry"—nor to the practical interventions of a conservationist-cultivator "planting" the land. His sacred ecology is grounded in the discourses of natural history and science, but also engenders dialogue with non-Western epistemologies, particularly those of Indigenous Australian cultures, including the Worimi of Murray's spirit country. In other words, the poet's consciousness of vegetal life hybridizes his own observations of farming country; acute awareness of the exchanges between domesticated and non-cultivated species; and appreciation of different cultural knowledges. In his poetry, empirical understanding acquired through both scientific awareness and personal experience melds with an understanding of plants as ensouled beings who manifest the sacred in and through their everyday ontologies. For Murray, traditional Indigenous environmental practices and narratives (such as the crying tree Gulambarra and the place-specific knowledge the story contains) are vital to this integrative impulse because of their attunement to the cycles of primordial flora (Clark 2003, 41–42). His ongoing critique of the impacts of European modernity—including the colonial appropriation of the Australian landmass and the dispossession of Indigenous societies throughout the country—involves poeticizing alternative modes of subjectivity (Clark 2003, 42), including the voices of plants, animals, rocks, water, and other elements of the landscape.

Rather than commenting on or describing plants objectively, Murray thus strives to enable percipient plant subjects to speak through poetry. A notion of ensoulment is forwarded most persuasively in *Translations from the Natural World*—a collection of poems that represents an "attempt to speak *for* nature, the majority being short dramatic monologues by various beings, animate and inanimate" (Dunkerley 2001, 80, italics in original). The collection demonstrates the role of polyvocality in Murray's notion of cultural convergence, defined as his "hoped-for integration or fusion of what he considers Australia's three main cultures, the Aboriginal, the urban, and the rural" (Kane 1996, 194). In order to facilitate such integration, Murray aligns his work with Indigenous beliefs, thus allowing plants and other beings to speak—both through the poet and the medium of their own language (Clark 2003, 43). It would, however, be infelicitous to claim that the form of plant ensoulment found in Murray's work is strictly a fusion of Woremi or other

Indigenous cultures and ancient Greek allusions gleaned from canonical sources such as the *Eclogues*. A fuller appreciation of vegetative ensoulment as plants speaking through Murray's poetry also requires deliberation on his long-standing Christian faith and his investment in poetry itself as a means for manifesting God as the divine. Consider the strongly religious overtones of "The Broad Bean Sermon:"

> beans upright like lecturing, outstretched like blessing fingers
> in the incident light, and more still, oblique to your notice
> that the noon glare or cloud-light or afternoon slants will uncover
> [...]
> like edible meanings, each sealed around with a string
> and affixed to its moment, an unceasing colloquial assembly,
> the portly, the stiff, and those lolling in pointed green slippers....
>   (Murray 2007, 13, ll. 16–18, 22–24)

For Murray, poetry summons the sacred. Since the mid-1960s, he has consistently dedicated his work "to the glory of God." Raised a Presbyterian, Murray converted to Catholicism around the time of the publication of *The Ilex Tree*. As he comments in *The Paperbark Tree*, poetry is "the prime channel through which I ever achieve (or am given) any apprehension of ultimate and divine things" (Murray 1992, 252). Murray's perspective that poetry is a hierophany or a manifestation through which the sacred presents itself to us echoes historian of religion Mircea Eliade. The principle of hierophany signifies the presentation of the sacred to our awareness or *"that something sacred shows itself to us"* (Eliade 1957, 11, emphasis in original). In their spiritual timbres, hierophanies range from the ordinary phenomenal domain of objects, stones, or plants to unseen noumenal manifestations. With respect to the Australian context many of his poems, such as "The Buladelah-Taree Holiday Song Cycle" (2007, 20–30), convey a belief that the sacred is communicated to mortal beings through the interplay of Indigenous and Christian traditions. In other words, cultural convergence also entails religious and spiritual convergence. The poet is in dialogue with the sacred of different knowledge systems, including traces of plant ensoulment from the ancient Greek tradition, plant-based Indigenous spiritualities suggested by the Worimi Dreaming, and the ideas drawn from the Western literatures, symbologies, and faiths imported to Australia from elsewhere.

The process of translation between the sacred and the everyday, between the nonhuman and the human, takes place within—rather than outside of—poetic language (Davidson 2013). This outlook is evident in his poem "Poetry and Religion" in which he asserts:

> Religions are poems. They concert
> our daylight and dreaming mind, our
> emotions, instinct, breath and native gesture
>
> into the only whole thinking: poetry.
> Nothing's said till it's dreamed out in words
> and nothing's true that figures in words only.
>
> (Murray 2007, 94, ll. 1–6)

On this note, critic Lyn McCreddon (2005, 166) argues that Murray's hybridic conception of the sacred through poetry involves three enactments: (a) the ordinary world as a locus of the sacred; (b) the cultural convergence of Indigenous country, rural life, and the city; and (c) propheticism in which the poet is a messenger of the divine and poetry his device. The tendency in Murray's poetry to bring forth that which is normally regarded as beyond representation includes the plant soul. I suggest that Murray pursues an ideal of poetry as a conversation with the divine in relation to—rather than on the margins of—the community of beings ontology of Australia's Indigenous cultures (with specific awareness of the Worimi and other local groups) and the discourses of his Catholic faith.

On the (Plant) Soul: From Aristotle to Aquinas

In order to contextualize Murray's reclamation of the plant soul, it is vital to consider the dominant Western discourses of ensoulment. In the treatise *De Anima* (or, *On the Soul*), written in approximately 350 BCE, Aristotle recognized that plants have souls, albeit in proportion to a hierarchical matter-mind continuum. In the Aristotelian *scientia de anima*, the vegetative (or nutritive) soul is the primitive essence out of which emerge the higher order sensitive soul of animals and the intellective (or imaginative) soul of human beings (Boer 2013, 216–17). As the apotheosis of ensoulment, humans bear the gift of intellection and, thus, possess all three soul-forms, whereas animals are limited to two and plants to one. In comparison to the souls of mobile, expressive, and cogitating animals—including us—the soul of a plant cannot exceed the limits of its mute carnal constitution. Consequently, the nutritive soul is its "only psychic power" (Aristotle 2000, book II.2). In Aristotle's entelechy, the potentiality of plant ensoulment is marked by self-nourishment, seeding, flowering, upward and downward growth, movement, decay, and other modes specific to vegetal lives, but excludes percipience, cognition, and intelligence—which belong to the (hum)animal. In other words, plants "live, and yet are not endowed with locomotion or perception" (Aristotle 2000, book I.5).

My intent here is neither to revise Aristotle's claims in any significant way nor to venture a structured rejoinder to the age-old question of plant soul. Without a doubt, the task is better left to metaphysicians to decide if contemporary poetry has anything to do with the venerable idea of soul. Instead, before returning to Les Murray's botanical inclinations, I shall put forth that the idea of vegetative soul has been influenced by the presuppositions underlying dominant Western views of plants as largely unmoving, insensitive, and unintelligent materials—as existing indeterminately somewhere between a rock and an animal. The most cursory reading of *De Anima* reveals the Aristotelian privileging of the zoological at the expense of the vegetal. Even in light of its origins before the proto-botanical writings of Aristotle's student Theophrastus (see, for instance, *Enquiry into Plants*, 1916) and the much later development of scientific botany, *De Anima* promulgates an early bias toward plants as lesser beings mired in sessility. At the same time, the treatise stigmatizes plant materiality, the so-called nutritive—which, as we increasingly realize, ensures that the planet's vital systems flourish (Trewavas 2014) (see Chapter 3).

Along the same lines, Saint Thomas Aquinas' *Commentary on De Anima* (*In Libros De Anima Expositio*), written ca. 1268 CE, reinscribed the Aristotelian schema in his tripartite division between the nutritive, sensitive, and rational soul. He delineated the vegetative (or nutritive) principle as "that part of soul in which even [merely] nutritive things—i.e., plants—participate" (Aquinas 1999, 139, interpolation in original). For Aquinas, as for Aristotle, the soul was a fundamental life principle that cannot be denied to living things—even the basest and least sentient. As a originary manifestation along the chain, the plant soul constituted the "first soul, which is called the nutritive soul, and which in plants *is* their soul, while in animals it is *part* of their soul" (Aquinas 1999, 183, italics in original). The nutritive (plant) soul is a foundational essence; the sensitive (animal) and rational (human) souls cannot exist independent of it. For this reason, unlike its counterparts, the primitive vegetative soul can manifest "without the sensitive and intellective principles, but these cannot exist without the nutritive" (Aquinas 1999, 114).

According to these thinkers, the vegetative soul embodied the means of multidirectional growth and self-nourishment unique to plants. The phototropic movement of leaves and flowers upward in dynamic relation to the downward extension of roots—coupled to nutritional mechanisms autonomous of animals, much later described in terms of photosynthesis—rendered the vegetal world the baseline of ensoulment. According to this framework, if it were completely deficient in formulable essence, the plant would be relegated to the category of inanimate objects alongside rocks. Animal essence must emerge from somewhere (or something) living; the vegetative soul becomes its default source and imperfect medium: "less complete beings with souls exist for more complete beings with souls" (Aquinas 1999, 169). It is important to acknowledge, however, that Aristotle as author of, and Aquinas as commentator on, *De Anima* did confer ensoulment to the botanical kingdom in the first place. These philosophers moreover contemplated the divisibility of vegetative soul—i.e., whether the modularity of plants (their ability to be split yet remain alive) yields multiple souls—"as in the case of plants which when divided are observed to continue to live [...] showing that in their case the soul of each individual plant before division was actually one, potentially many" (Aristotle 2000, book II.2).

Regardless of these allowances from the history of philosophy and religion, plant potentiality—a key principle in Aristotelian entelechy—is subordinate, yet oddly intrinsic, to animal and human ensoulment. Eschewing plant-animal-human oppositions, Elaine Miller in her book *The Vegetative Soul* (2002) links the plant soul to the eighteenth and nineteenth century concept of creative genius as plantlike subjectivity. According to Miller (2002), "the vegetative soul is radically opposed to the figure of organism as autonomous and oppositional; its stance toward the world is characterized by the promise of life and growth" (5). In her view and in contradistinction to sharply individuated animals and humans, plants undergo processes of metamorphosis that constantly transfigure their subjectivities. Nonetheless, for Miller, invoking critic M. H. Abrams' notion of "vegetable genius" (1953) in the history of Romantic criticism, the vegetative soul is at best a trope for the relationship between nature and unconscious, spontaneous creativity. In reference to the connection between nature, genius, and literary analysis, Abrams (1953) pointed out a "recourse to vegetable life as a model for the coming-into-being of a work of art [that] had, in fact, engendered the fateful concept that artistic creation is primarily an unwilled and unconscious process of mind" (173). Here, rather than a material essence that is possessed by botanical life—as nascent, for better or worse, in the writings of Aristotle and Aquinas—the plant soul is figured as a metaphor in service to humanity's intellectual and artistic trajectories. Hence, Miller, Abrams, and the Romantic critics under scrutiny in Abrams' *The Mirror and the Lamp* appear to diverge from plant life's "actuality [...] of being ensouled" (Aristotle 2000, book II.2).

Australia and Other Contexts: Murray's Sacred Ecology of Plants

Murray's work demonstrates lyrical engagement with the possibility of plants as sentient, intelligent beings with souls rather than as passive automatons, aesthetic backdrops, or the mute foils of animality. Some poems allow ensouled plants to speak for themselves. Contemplate, as an example, the "self-espaliered" plant in his poem "Creeper Habit" whose "branches twine and utter/coated leaves" (Murray 2007, 16, ll. 4, 14–15). Although it has "little choice" (l. 17) and "spreads where it can" (l. 19), the creeper is an autonomous, adaptive, and aware being who can decide for itself. In order to outline Murray's sacred ecology of plants further, I want to remain a while longer with the idea of plant soul and its relationship to the sacred in the Australian context. Considering Murray's tendency to lyricize New South Wales flora—as well as his sustained interest in Worimi and other Indigenous environmental knowledge, alongside what he calls cultural convergence—the Australian dimensions of his poetry require further consideration.

As explained in Chapter 1, a prevailing theme of *Plants in Contemporary Poetry* is the principle of the vegetal dialectic: that plants affect and are affected; experience and are experienced; feel and are felt; sense and are sensed; remember and are remembered; imagine and are imagined; and so forth. The science of plant neurobiology increasingly affirms that vegetal life exhibits a disposition toward intelligent behavior that enhances its evolutionary survival. This body of scientific research also marks a deepening of our understanding of our diverse physical and cultural transactions with flora (Trewavas 2014). Such an appreciation of vegetal potentiality expands the ambit of human-plant interactions beyond a narrow utilitarian paradigm of flora as foods, fibers, dyes, medicines, ornaments, or otherwise consumable things; and beyond a principally metaphorical approach to plants and their organs as texts or tropes. Take, for instance, the prevalence of root, rhizome, flower, and leaf as symbolic mechanisms in literary history and criticism (see Olney 1980). In light of this and with respect to the plant soul, there is another productive dialectic that should be considered. On the one hand, the plant is ensouled (i.e., inherently bears a soul or spirit by virtue of its nature) and, on the other, the plant is an object, home, conduit, or stimulus of the spiritual experience, insight, or awakening of human beings.

Appreciating the difference I highlighted above requires discerning between the terms *soul*, *spirit*, and *sacred*. In its etymological roots, the Greek word *psychê*, for soul, similar to the Latin *anima*, originally signified "breath, breeze, or wind" (Frede and Reis 2009, 1). According to ancient cosmologies, the body was considered ensouled with its first breath at birth. In contrast, mortality was the cessation of breath and, thus, soul. The Modern English word *soul* stems from Old English *sáwol*, the Old Saxon *sêola*, and several cognate terms denoting "sea" and semantically inscribing the belief that human souls originated in and returned to sacred lakes following the passing of their physical forms. Correspondingly, *spirit* stems from the Latin *spiritus* for "breath." With their related etymologies in *breath*, the terms *soul* and *spirit* are used interchangeably in my discussion of the plant soul in Murray's poetry. Unaware of the function of plants in the global carbon cycle, Aristotle regarded the vegetative soul as unable to breathe and, consequently, base and incomplete (Marder 2013, 31). Other philosophers, such as Hegel, denied ensoulment to plants not for their lack of breath but for their deficiency of the inward-turned qualities (emotion, reflection, consideration) attributed to the psyche (Marder 2011, 87). The German idealist Johann Gottlieb Fichte, however, preferred to conceptualize the vegetative soul as primary movement in nature. The first breath of anima and psychê constituted the first movement of nature, which first provoked vegetal potentiality and then provided the substance for animalistic soul-forms: "the soul of the plant is not only the principle of a determined organization, (is not only the interpenetration and union of different chemical forces,) but is, moreover, the first principle of a *motion* in nature; it is the moving principle" (Fichte 1869, 503, italics in original). In brief, as the derivation of the term *soul* implies, the plant soul is linked to breath—a condition rendered more momentous and all-encompassing when we consider the ongoing gaseous exchanges with vegetal life that make animal existence possible in the first place.

The Aristotelian vegetative soul is primitive and foundational—supplying the substrate for the sensitive and intellective souls of animals and humans, respectively. However, as evident in traditional Indigenous Australian cosmologies, such as the Worimi Dreaming, the boundaries between plant-animal-human ensoulment are not so bluntly drawn. For a myriad of past and present cultures, a sacred plant is an actual vegetable being with a formulable essence and the potentiality for ensoulment (for example, Cusack 2011). In distinction to powerful mythological flora, such as the ash of Norse cosmology or Yggdrasil, real species in the landscape unveil their percipient capacities and their sacred qualities recognized by generations of people. Among the Kamilaroi, Eora, Darkinjung, and Wiradjuri people of eastern and central NSW, for instance, the woody outgrowths on the lower trunks of many trees are understood as the seats of the arboreal Dreaming ancestor Daramulun (Clarke 2011, 24). Sacred plants, including Dreaming trees, can also be sources of physical sustenance, providing edible leaves and sap—and thus bridging the gap between sacred and commonplace plants.

The case of Daramulun, however, highlights the distinction between the vegetative soul—as internal to the plant—and the living plant as a sacred vessel, or home, for creation beings and dispossessed human souls. The outgrowths offer a medium—a seat—for a Dreaming spirit, but what of the souls of the trees themselves? What is the relationship between a sacred ecology of plants and the vegetative soul; the spiritual projections of humankind; and the interpenetrations of vegetal and human ensoulment? Part of the answer to this question might lay in religious historian of Mircea Eliade's concept of the sacred. Following the work of French sociologist Émile Durkheim, Eliade (1957) positioned the sacred as "the opposite of the profane" (10). From his perspective, the principle of hierophany denoted the presentation of the sacred to our awareness or *"that something sacred shows itself to us"* (Eliade 1957, 11, italics in original). In their spiritual tones, hierophanies range from the ordinary phenomenal domain of objects, stones, or plants to unseen noumenal manifestations such as God through Jesus in the Christian tradition. For Eliade, the sacred opposed and, indeed, transcended the material domain perceptible to the senses. With plants and stones in mind, he explained that "the sacred tree, the sacred stone are not adored as stone or tree; they are worshipped precisely because they are *hierophanies*, because they show something that is no longer stone or tree but the *sacred*, the *ganz andere* [wholly other]" (Eliade 1957, 12, italics in original). Eliade posited a gulf between the profane and the sacred, demarcating the sacred from ordinary locales, everyday matters, and commonplace beings, including plants.

As a hierophany, the tree manifests the sacred, but its material basis—its nutritive constitution—remains profane. In contrast to Eliade's dichotomy, a non-typological approach would shun the theorization of the profane as the foil for the sacred. An idea of the sacred inhering within the profane—or the phenomenon within the noumenon—would conceive of a sacred plant as a body and spirit, and as a wellspring of sustenance, insight, and ensoulment. The sacred that I have in mind is nascent in anthropologist Jack Goody's (1961) critique of the sacred-profane dichotomy and his rejection of "Durkheim's assumption [the basis for Eliade's model] that the sacred-profane dichotomy is a universal feature of people's views of the human situation" (155). From Goody's (1961, 154) perspective, the sacred-profane opposition is the residue of nineteenth-century intellectualists who propounded logico-experimental paradigms at the expense of traditional societies.

A sacred ecology of plants—particularly in Murray's collection *Translations from the Natural World* (2012)—is grounded in an appreciation of Dreaming stories, as well as direct experience of NSW flora. While visually evocative of Australian plant life, Murray's poetry also draws from a heightened sense of embodiment through haptic, olfactory, and gustatory feedback. Clark (2002) characterizes the body as "one of the fulcrums of Murray's thought" representing a movement away from Cartesian rationalism and toward the "reinstatement of the body as a substratum of language, rationality, meaning and metaphor" (21). The resulting immediacy of his sensory transactions with plants (e.g., gum trees, melaleuca shrubs, and herbaceous wildflowers) converges with an awareness of ecological exchanges and a spiritual consciousness of landscape that hybridizes a range of belief systems. In Murray's botanical imagination, the souls of plants are immanent in the ecological phenomena that can be verified through perception; multisensorial human-plant encounter is a pathway to the noumenal. To appreciate Murray's sacred ecology of plants, is to recognize its basis in sensory experience and Indigenous Australian worldviews—a critical position not taken by commentators on the spiritual and environmental aspects of his work (for example, Kane 1996; McCredden 2005).

As a living entity requiring reciprocal obligations, country is a place of belonging, where Dreaming—or creation—narratives focus on the actions of ancestral entities in the form of plants, animals, winds, fire, stars, and celestial bodies (Turpin 2007, 95). Acknowledging its life generating qualities, anthropologist Deborah Bird Rose (1996) describes country aptly as "nourishing terrain"—as a sentient and conscious topography that "gives and receives life" and thus commands respect and ethical regard (7). Kombu-merri philosopher Mary Graham asserts that the perception of land as sacred shapes social interactions, cohesion, and identities. From Graham's perspective, land comprises plants, animals, interspecies relations, and the activities of Dreaming ancestors—not merely visual landscape features or physiographic regions. She argues that "the land, and how we treat it, is what determines our human-ness. Because land is sacred and must be looked after, the relation between people and land becomes the template for society and social relations. Therefore all meaning comes from land" (Graham 2008).

Ethnobotanist Philip Clarke identifies interplay between the sacred and profane in the ontologies of Australian Aboriginal cultures. Rather than the foil of the profane, the sacred is ubiquitous in the landscape and its flora. He observes that "the Aboriginal landscape is considered full with sacred plant manifestations. Even when plants do not represent the actual Ancestors, they may be seen as having been involved with Dreaming activities in the Creation" (Clarke 2011, 23–24). The spiritual qualities of plants infuse everyday awareness. This in turn prompts a sympathetic human outlook on the environment as suffused with sacredness: "Aboriginal people see plants as sacred signatures in their country that, along with topographic features such as hills, creeks and waterholes, came into existence through the actions of Dreaming Ancestors" (Clarke 2011, 24). A sacred ecology ascribes percipience, intelligence, and subjectivity to vegetal life in relation to the mundane world and the spiritual domain of Dreaming ancestors. Clarke (2011, 26) also refers to the idea of "plants as spirit homes" in which spirits occupy particular botanical formations, which are then recognized by people as dangerous or forbidden. "Spirit home" expresses the notion of extrinsic plant soul: a vegetation community (thicket, hollow, forest) or individual plant is territorialized by displaced human souls.

The sacred ecology at the center of my approach to Murray's poetry builds on anthropologist Fikret Berkes' research on traditional environmental knowledge. Seeking a post-positivist framework of human-environment relations—one which resists the mechanistic reduction of ecological systems to their structural components—Berkes observes that the ecological practices of many Indigenous peoples inculcate nature with sacredness (Berkes 2012, 11–12). For Berkes, an expansive, non-reductionistic conception of ecology—beyond a narrow scientific paradigm—rejects the materialist tradition of plants as mute matter (that is, as mere chemicals, cellulose, anatomical parts) and embraces the sacred as "unity" in nature. The premise of a sacred ecology involves distributed subjectivity and an inclusive community of beings ontology (Berkes 2012, 286). His book *Sacred Ecology*, however, makes no mention of soul. In fact, most allusions to flora in the text reflect the ethnobotanical tradition of plants as usable objects: medicines, foods, fibers, and so on. Berkes moreover makes no distinction between intrinsic (soul in nature) and extrinsic (human soul manifested in or projected on nature) senses of the soul. In contrast, his model posits the natural world as a theater for human dramatization of the sacred rather than as a living substratum for the ensoulment of animate and inanimate things.

Loci of Soul: Eucalypt Trees, Gum Forests, and Lightning Strikes

As sacred entities, plants are neither merely mechanistic vessels for displaced human souls nor screens for the spiritual projections of humans. The vegetative soul is a complete manifestation of plantness, rather than an imperfect medium for the development of higher animalistic entelechies. In Murray's verse, a sacred ecology of plants materializes independently of the hierarchical schemas of Aristotle and Aquinas in which the vegetative is the basest soul-form, and the sensitive and intellective is the highest. The poietic potentialities of plants—their capacities for ensoulment as expressed in ecological expressions of growth, decay, transformation, and movement upward, downward, and rhizomatically—figure significantly in "Flowering Eucalypt in Autumn" (2007, 65–66). The poem reflects an immersive sense of interspecies transformation during the autumn months of March, April, and May when the tree becomes a self-governing community of beings. The eucalypt's copious flowering and associated production of nectar provoke exchanges within an ensemble of living things. This results in a state of pronounced activity transliterated by Murray from ecological to poetic language:

> That slim creek out of the sky
> the dried-blood western gum tree
> is all stir in its high reaches:
>
> its strung haze-blue foliage is dancing
> points down in breezy mobs, swapping
> pace and place in an all-over sway.
> (Murray 2007, 65–66, ll. 1–6)

Even the "high reaches" of the tree—those arboreal zones typically outside of everyday human grasp—reverberate with the bustle of flowers, birds, insects, and other organisms. A metaphor extending to both

42 Sacred Ecologies of Plants

natural science and Indigenous knowledge, "dried-blood" denotes the astringent kino gum produced by Australian eucalypts and used by many Aboriginal cultures as a medicine (Clarke 2011).

Murray brings botanical transformation to life, spurning the preconception of plants as insensate things through the twists and turns of lyrical language. Instead, the eucalypt is "a spray in its own turned vase" (Murray 2007, 66, l. 19)—a metaphor inverting an aesthetics that positions flora as pleasing, though static, objects deferential to and acted upon monologically by animal life. The poem's internal vitality and movement are linked to the animate qualities of the eucalypt within its ecosystem. The co-becoming of poetic meaning and vegetal ensoulment is concretized in the nodes between plant, insect, animal, and human lives. To reiterate Miller's idea, the vegetative soul speaks to "the promise of life and growth" (2002, 5). In "Flowering Eucalypt in Autumn," Murray reveals that the vegetative soul is imbued with the promise of the "tough delicate/raucous life" of the other soul-forms of the autumnal eucalypt system (2007, 65, ll. 17–18). This does not exclude the intellective soul of Murray himself as participant-observer-poet in the scene. The active participles of foliage dancing, mobs swapping, and fragrance crisping synergistically function with the poiesis of phrases such as night-creaking and fig-squirting bats, food bristling, and petals drizzling. The rendering of the quintessentially Australian botanical landscape is neither static, delimited strictly by visual data, nor confined to plants alone.

The poem's sensuous specifics are mimetic of the eucalypt, the autumn season, and the mounting ecological activity, therein expressing what Paul Carter (1996: 331) defines as middle voice: the folding of time "in the sense that it dissolves the subject-object relation, grounding each in the other, continuously redefining both in terms of each other, so that the two sides exist echoically or simultaneously" (1996, 331). In the same poem, Murray's memory of the shedding of the petals of a Japanese plum tree causes him to ask:

> what kind of exquisitely precious
> artistic bloom might be gendered
> in a pure ethereal compost
>
> of petals potted as they fell.
> From unpetalled gum-debris
> we know what is grown continually.
>
> (Murray 2007, 66, ll. 25–30)

In contrast to the cosmopolitan plum flowers with their universally embraced beauty, ancient provenance, and associations with Europe, Asia, and America, the "swish tatters" of the eucalypt flowers underlie the evolution to the Australian landmass itself, evoked in the image of "a crusted/riverbed with up-country show towns" (Murray 2007, 66, ll. 32–33). Unlike the plum, the vegetative soul of the eucalypt is chthonic. Its sacred ecology is specific and adapted to the rural locale that Murray lyricizes. In other poems, Murray enunciates the idea of being spiritually at home and bio-regionally emplaced within the eucalypt forests of the inland NSW environment. "The Gum Forest" opens with the following unequivocal couplets:

> After the last gapped wire on a post,
> homecoming for me, to enter the gum forest.
>
> This old slow battlefield: parings of armour,
> cracked collars, elbows, scattered on the ground.
>
> New trees step out of old: lemon and ochre
> splitting out of grey everywhere, in the gum forest.
>
> (Murray 2007, 31, ll. 1–6)

The regenerative processes of the forest unfold before the speaker's senses. The emergence of vegetal being is rhythmic and processual, yet stupefying and all-enveloping. As new trees spring from the old and the colors of the natural world transform from dull to vibrant, one might be reminded of Aristotle and Aquinas' speculation over the divisibility of the vegetative soul.

Notwithstanding the speaker's immersion in the eucalypt scene, one "can never reach the heart of the gum forest" (Murray 2007, 31, l. 10). In other words, a glimpse and grasp of the plant soul is both limitlessly accessible to ordinary perception while ultimately ineffable. The instance the poet begins to synthesize the sensory information acquired through rapture in the forest, the plant soul—which is one and many, a condition of "being singular plural" (Nancy 2000) or, in other words, a community of ecologically threaded souls—evades and exceeds him. Such are the "mysteries of the gum forest" (Murray 2007, 31, l. 22). The structure of "The Gum Forest" mirrors the oscillation between entrée and elusion—the tension between being allowed into and being barred from the sacred plant. Murray's concrete observations of ecology are in line with his recognition of the forest's elusiveness and the limits of language in communicating the vegetal sacred. As in "Flowering Eucalypt in Autumn," the lyricizing of ecological interdependencies is the one method available to the poet-observer grappling with the vegetative soul as a community of beings, as a sacred ecology before him:

> Flooded-gums on creek ground, each tall because of each.
> Now a blackbutt in bloom is showering with bees
> but warm blood sleeps in the middle of the day.

> The witching hour is noon in the gum forest.
> Foliage builds like a layering splash: ground water
> drily upheld in edge-on, wax-rolled, gall-puckered
> leaves upon leaves. The shoal life of parrots up there.
>
> (Murray 2007, 31, ll. 14–20)

Flooded-gum is *Eucalyptus grandis*, a species occurring throughout coastal areas of NSW on loamy alluvial soils. Additionally, blackbutt is *Eucalyptus pilularis*, also common to the region. For Murray, the vegetative soul of the gum community and its individual trees diverges sharply from the "autonomous and oppositional" figures of (animal) organisms and their expressions of percipience (Miller 2002, 5). The ecological principle of "each tall because of each," as observed by the speaker, brings about the transformation of vegetal subjectivities—from old to young, from short to tall, from plant to insect and animal species. A sacred ecology is a "communion of subjects, not a collection of objects" (Berry 1999, 82), each and the whole bearing a soul.

In Murray's botanical imagination, the forest is a locus of plant ensoulment, on the one hand, and human spiritual experience, on the other. Rather than a substratum for human gestures toward the divine—objectified, reduced, and split off from the intellective soul—the gum forest is the sacred immanent in its material presence, sensory expression, and ecological relation. Not a threatening domain to be subjugated or dominated by zoological energies, the forest is an epicenter of reverie, reverence, rejuvenation, and enlightenment: "Delight to me, though, at the water-smuggling creeks,/health to me, too, under banksia candles and combs" (Murray 2007, 31, ll. 24–25). The allusion to *Banksia*—another quintessentially Australian genus of around 170 species—contextualizes the poem further in the plant life of Murray's home-place (see Collins, Collins, and George 2008 on banksias). The sensoriality of the eucalypt forest initiates catharsis and a heightened contemplative state: "singed oils clear my mind, and the pouring sound high up" (Murray 2007, 32, l. 29).

The poem concludes with a powerful final image that entwines the forest with the preternatural, earth with sky, nutritive with sensitive and intellective: "Why have I denied the passions of my time? To see/lightning strike upward out of the gum forest" (2007, 32, ll. 30–31). What echoes—on initial inspection—as an inwardly-looking and brooding question can subsequently be read as a transcendental device of rhetoric in line with Murray's theory of cultural convergence and my extension of Berkes' idea of sacred ecology. For diverse Indigenous cultures, lightning expresses the activities of spirit beings. It directly articulates—rather than superficially symbolizes—the world of Dreaming ancestors. Lightning strikes are spirits manifested on earth, and can confer powers of healing and clairvoyance to the living (Johnson 2014, 28). As an example, speakers of the language Kunwinjku in western Arnhem Land in the Northern Territory of Australia recognize Namarrgon, the Dreamtime ancestor who heralds the arrival of the Wet Season and is responsible for the violent lightning storms that occur during that time of year (Ploum 2012, 93). Axes attached to his body allow him to split dark clouds and produce lightning. The activities of Namarrgon also indicate the optimal time to harvest bush foods like Kakadu plum (*Terminalia ferdinandiana*). In the Christian tradition, numerous passages also allude to lightning as an encounter with God and divine inspiration so potent as to disperse enemies; for example, in Book 2 of Samuel, "out of the brightness of his presence bolts of lightning blazed forth" (qtd. in Elwell 1991, 191).

The Sacred as Plant Presence: Figs, Sunflowers, and Stone Fruits Speak

The poems "Flowering Eucalypt in Autumn" and "The Gum Forest" link the potentialities of plant ensoulment to the transformations of eucalypt trees and their habitats. The sensitive and intellective souls of bees, birds, mammals, and humans coexist in an even, non-binary field of ecological relation to the vegetative soul. Contrary to Aristotle's assertion that plants "live, and yet are not endowed with locomotion or perception" (2000, book I.5), research in botanical science demonstrates that the vegetal world abounds with movement at various scales, such as the transit of complex signals via volatile compounds (Baluška and Ninkovic 2010), as well as evolutionarily-structured forms of sensory perception (Mescher and De Moraes 2015). It goes without saying that Aristotle and Aquinas lacked the access that modern plant-thinkers have to scientific studies in botanical signaling and behavior, or neurobotany. The long-standing hierarchical construction of the vegetative soul, nevertheless, has been formative to modern views of plants. Such reconsideration—indeed, an aim of *Plants in Contemporary Poetry*—situates the intuitions, insights, and experiences of poets such as Murray in relation to emerging scientific trends. Whereas the previous section focused on readings of two botanical poems narrated from a human speaker's perspective, the final section of this chapter examines representative examples from *Translations from the Natural World*. The poems of Part II, entitled "Presence," involve vegetal life addressing the reader in the first (plant) person.

In *Translations*, presence is vegetative ensoulment—"an actuality or formulable essence of something that possesses a potentiality of being ensouled" (Aristotle 2000, book II.2). Of all Murray's works, *Translations* grapples most consistently with the vegetative soul by adopting the perspectives of vocal plants within a sacred ecology of interacting beings. The inherent difficulty of speaking for nature has been a central concern for ecocritics and rhetoricians (for example, Manes 1996; McDowell 1996; Watts 2001). After all, these poems are ineluctably Murray's subjective interpretation at work on behalf of figs, sunflowers, and stone fruits. The word choices, metaphors, and enjambments—though prompted and shaped by flora—remain his. Nonetheless, the tenor of the mediation and the poetic impulse to approximate, and bring to life, the plant soul in his poetry is striking. For instance, the poem "Strangler Fig" opens with the propinquity of a plant's address and alludes, in the second line, to the Worimi nomenclature of the common *Ficus* species:

> I glory centennially slow-
>
> ly in being Guugumbakh the
>
> strangler fig bird-born to overgrow
>
> the depths of this wasp-leafed stinging-tree
>
> through muscling in molten stillness down
>
> its spongy barrel crosslacing in overflow
>
> even of myself as in time my luscious fat
>
> leaves top out to adore the sun forest high
> (Murray 2012, 31, ll. 1–8, line spacing in original)

The reverse-nominalization of glory (noun) as glory (verb) presents an intriguing intertextual reference to the normal dedication of his books, "to the glory of God" (Murray 2012, 4). The self-professed glory of the fig intersects with the glory of God. Accordingly, the "bird-born" overgrowing of the tree by the strangler fig is both a divine and ecological—sacred and everyday—manifestation. The plant is of the spirit and within its body. As conveyed through the active participles muscling and cross-lacing, in conjunction with somatic descriptors, such as "luscious fat leaves," the ensouled fig gestures in a language without words, or at least those recognized as such by linguists.

For Murray, the idea of the vegetative soul requires abandoning the Aquinian pronouncement that "less complete beings with souls exist for more complete beings with souls" (Aquinas 1999, 169). The poietic growth and decay of plants are akin to the transubstantiation of water to wine, wine to blood, bread to flesh, spirit to lightning:

> and my shade-coldest needs touch a level that
>
> discovered as long yearned for transmutes
>
> my wood into the crystal mode of roots

and I *complete* myself and mighty on

buttresses far up in combat embraces no

rotted traces to the fruiting rain surface I one.
(Murray 2012, 31–32, ll. 10–12, emphasis added, line spacing in original)

Significantly, through this process of transformation, the vegetative soul becomes complete unto itself. The notion of plant soul extant as a whole within an ecologically-based "communion of subjects" (Berry 1999, 82) is metaphysically intensified in "Sunflowers," in which the ubiquitous field plant declares, with a forceful pitch:

I am ever fresh cells who keep on knowing my name
but I converse in my myriads with the great blast Cell
who holds the centre of reality, carries it behind the cold
and on out, for converse with a continuum of adorers:

The more presence, the more apart. And the more lives circling you.
(Murray 2012, 65, ll. 1–5)

The sunflower is a temporally spacious being in dialogue with God and synchronized with the origins of the universe; its lack of human language embodies a conversation with an all-encompassing sacred— which is corporeal presence. Yet, the vegetative soul in its ecological milieu cannot always entrain to the elusiveness of the sacred. There is a dynamic tension between expulsion and inclusion, banishment and salvation, transcendence and obscuration, body and spirit. As the poem concedes, "the more presence, the more apart. And the more lives circling you" (Murray 2012, 65, l. 5). This presence—this vegetative soul that embodies the universal sacred—is the upshot of the sunflower's locomotion and perception: "*Falling, I gathered such presence that I fused to Star, beyond all fission*" (Murray 2012, 65, l. 6, emphasis in original). Through these examples, we see in plain sight the elements of Murray's sacred ecology: soul, sense, poiesis, materiality, and relation.

The collectivity of a sacred ecology of plants—as a communion of ensouled subjects—is a theme further developed in "Stone Fruit." The poem, again rendered in the first (plant) person, eschews the preconception that the vegetal world cannot register interiority; including emotion, reflection, and other qualities attributed to the psyche. Instead, the stone fruit as a presence materializes from "the inner world, singular and many" (Murray 2012, 75, l. 1). Rather than propounding the hierarchy of vegetative, sensitive, and intellective—plants, animal, and human—souls, the poem troubles the order by advancing a concept of animal within plant, as the fruit announces:

> I appear from the inner world, singular and many, I am
> the animals of my tree, appointed to travel and be eaten
> since animals are plants' genital extensions, I'm clothed in luscious
> dung but designed to elicit yet richer, I am modelled on the sun
> (Murray 2012, 75, ll. 1–4)

The fruit's ensoulment involves sensuous embodiment within a sacred ecology and in relation to the other subjects with whom it exchanges: "perfumed, flavoured by the mouthless, by insect-conductors who kill/ and summon by turns" (ll. 10–11). As in other examples of Murray's botanical imagination, the inner world—the plant soul within its sacred ecology—paradoxically remains (in)accessible, as the enigmatic final lines of the poems signify:

> [...] I'm to tell you there is a future and there are
> consequences, and they are not the same, I emerge continually
> from the inner world, which you can't mate with nor eat.
> (Murray 2012: 75–76, ll. 11–13)

Conclusion: The Lives of Ensouled Plants

As evident in Murray's poetry, the ensoulment of plants—as active, percipient, and responsive beings—is related to the materiality of their habitats and the exigencies of their lives through phases of growth, decay, flowering, seeding, spatial movement, and physical gesture. The botanical imagination forwarded by Murray reclaims the ancient idea of the vegetative soul in radically new terms that integrate spiritual traditions as part of an ideal of cultural convergence. The vegetative soul, in Murray's conception, is etched in the transactions between plants, insects, animals, soil, rocks, and humans. The wild and domestic plant species of the inland areas of New South Wales constituting Murray's spirit country are simultaneously ensouled and earthed. Not the mute, immobile, and insensate things connoted pejoratively by the term "vegetative", Murray's poeticized plants are active, self-directed, percipient, and responsive beings involved in the spiritual and material lives of humans.

Through plant ensoulment, Murray attempts to counteract the denial of voice to nature by Enlightenment rationalism and hierarchies of soul originating with Aristotle. Rather than a device deployed solely for literary ends, Murray's vegetal ensoulment has implications for our current time of great biodiversity loss. In Australia, 40% of forests have been cleared, with the highest rates of removal since 1970 occurring in Queensland and NSW (Bradshaw 2012). Yet, despite widespread environmental degradation, botanists estimate that Australia retains 7% of all known plant species on the planet (Australian National Herbarium 2009). Re-imagining plants—as their self-directed ensoulment in Murray's poetry enables us to do—is foundational to protecting the world's botanical heritage that remains and restoring that which has been fragmented or lost. If plants are intelligent and have souls, then there should be a moral imperative to consider the vegetal world as more than an aesthetic backdrop for human perception, an impediment to colonial or modern process, or a source of food, fiber, and medicine valuable only in utilitarian terms. As forester Peter Wohlleben writes in his book *The Hidden Life of Trees*, trees—and, I argue, plants more broadly—"should be allowed to fulfill their social needs, to grow in a true forest environment on undisturbed ground, and to pass their knowledge on to the next generation" (2016, 138). The passing on of knowledge—between plants, animals, insects, humans, and others—will only be preserved through a transformation of societal values. By recognizing the vegetal soul within the vegetal body, Murray's ensoulment of plants offers a catalyst for this urgent transformation. Building on the idea of a sacred ecology of plants, the next chapter will explore Mary Oliver's poetization of the vegetal body.

Bibliography

Abrams, Meyer Howard. 1953. *The Mirror and the Lamp: Romantic Theory and the Critical Tradition.* London: Oxford University Press.
Alexander, Peter. 2000. *Les Murray: A Life in Progress.* Oxford, UK: Oxford University Press.
Aquinas, Thomas. 1999. *A Commentary on Aristotle's De Anima.* Translated by Robert Pasnau. New Haven, CT: Yale University Press. Original edition, circa. 1270 ACE.
Aristotle. 2000. *On the Soul.* Accessed 23 May 2017. http://classics.mit.edu//Aristotle/soul.html
Australian National Herbarium. 2009. "Australian Flora Statistics." *Information about Australia's Flora.* Accessed 23 May 2017. www.anbg.gov.au/aust-veg/australian-flora-statistics.html
Baluška, František, and Velemir Ninkovic, eds. 2010. *Plant Communication from an Ecological Perspective.* Dordrecht: Springer.
Berkes, Fikret. 2012. *Sacred Ecology.* 3rd ed. New York: Routledge.
Berry, Thomas. 1999. *The Great Work: Our Way into the Future.* New York: Random House.
Boer, Sander Wopke de. 2013. *The Science of the Soul: The Commentary Tradition on Aristotle's* De Anima, *c. 1260-c. 1360.* Leuven: Leuven University Press.
Böhm, Jennifer. 2016. "The Venus Flytrap *Dionaea muscipula* Counts Prey-Induced Action Potentials to Induce Sodium Uptake." *Current Biology* 26 (3): 286–95.

Bradshaw, Corey. 2012. "Little Left to Lose: Deforestation and Forest Degradation in Australia Since European Colonization." *Journal of Plant Ecology* 5 (1): 109–20.

Burns, Kevin. 2010. "Is Crypsis a Common Defensive Strategy in Plants? Speculation on Signal Deception in the New Zealand Flora." *Plant Signaling and Behavior* 5 (1): 9–13.

Carter, Paul. 1996. *The Lie of the Land*. London: Faber & Faber.

Clark, Gary. 2002. "Transmuting the Black Dog: The Mob and the Body in the Poetry of Les Murray." *Antipodes* 16 (1): 19–24.

———. 2003. "History and Ecology: The Poetry of Les Murray and Gary Snyder." *Interdisciplinary Studies in Literature and Environment* 10 (1): 27–54.

———. 2007. "Environmental Themes in Australian Literature." In *A Companion to Australian Literature Since 1900*, edited by Nicholas Birns and Rebecca McNeer, 429–44. Rochester, NY: Camden House.

Clarke, Philip. 2011. *Aboriginal People and Their Plants*. Dural Delivery Centre, NSW: Rosenberg.

Coetzee, J. M. 2011. "The Angry Genius of Les Murray." *The New York Review of Books* 29 September. Accessed 23 May 2017. www.nybooks.com/articles/2011/09/29/angry-genius-les-murray/

Collins, Kevin, Kathy Collins, and Alex George. 2008. *Banksias*. Melbourne: Blooming Books.

Crisp, Michael, and Lyn Cook. 2013. "How was the Australian Flora Assembled Over the Last 65 Million Years? A Molecular Phylogenetic Perspective." *Annual Review of Ecology, Evolution and Systematics* 44: 303–24. doi:10.1146/annurev-ecolsys-110512-135910

Cusack, Carole. 2011. *The Sacred Tree: Ancient and Medieval Manifestations*. Newcastle upon Tyne: Cambridge Scholars Publishing.

Davidson, Toby. 2013. *Christian Mysticism and Australian Poetry*. Amherst, NY: Cambria Press.

Dunkerley, Hugh. 2001. "Unnatural Relations? Language and Nature in the Poetry of Mark Doty and Les Murray." *Interdisciplinary Studies in Literature and Environment* 8 (1): 73–82.

Eliade, Mircea. 1957. *The Sacred and the Profane: The Nature of Religion*. Translated by Willard Trask. Orlando, FL: Harcourt Books.

Elwell, Walter. 1991. *Topical Analysis of the Bible: A Survey of Essential Christian Doctrines*. Peabody, MA: Hendrickson Publishers.

Fichte, J.G. 1869. *The Science of Rights*. Translated by A. E. Kroeger. Philadelphia, PA: J. B. Lippincott.

Frede, Dorothea, and Burkhard Reis. 2009. "Introduction." In *Body and Soul in Ancient Philosophy*, edited by Dorothea Frede and Burkhard Reis, 1–20. Berlin: Walter de Gruyter.

Gianoli, Ernesto and Fernando Carrasco-Urra. 2014. "Leaf Mimicry in a Climbing Plant Protects Against Herbivory." *Current Biology* 24 (9): 984–87.

Giesecke, Annette. 2014. *The Mythology of Plants: Botanical Lore from Ancient Greece and Rome*. Los Angeles: J. Paul Getty Museum.

Goody, Jack. 1961. "Religion and Ritual: The Definitional Problem." *The British Journal of Sociology* 12 (2): 142–64.

Gorzelak, Monika, Amanda Asay, Brian Pickles, and Suzanne Simard. 2015. "Inter-plant Communication through Mycorrhizal Networks Mediates Complex Adaptive Behaviour in Plant Communities." *AoB Plants* 7: plv050. doi:10.1093/aobpla/plv050

Graham, Mary. 2008. "Some Thoughts about the Philosophical Underpinnings of Aboriginal Worldviews." *Australian Humanities Review* 45. Accessed 23 May 2017. www.australianhumanitiesreview.org/archive/Issue-November-2008/graham.html

Johnson, Dianne. 2014. *Night Skies of Aboriginal Australia: A Noctuary.* Sydney: Sydney University Press.

Kane, Paul. 1996. *Australian Poetry: Romanticism and Negativity.* Cambridge, UK: Cambridge University Press.

Manes, Christopher. 1996. "Nature and Silence." In *The Ecocriticism Reader: Landmarks in Literary Ecology*, edited by Cheryll Glotfelty and Harold Fromm, 15–29. Athens: The University of Georgia Press.

Marder, Michael. 2011. "Plant-Soul: The Elusive Meanings of Vegetal Life." *Environmental Philosophy* 8 (1): 83–99.

———. 2013. *Plant-Thinking: A Philosophy of Vegetal Life.* New York: Columbia University Press.

Matthews, Steven. 2001. *Les Murray.* Manchester: Manchester University Press.

McCredden, Lyn. 2005. "The Impossible Infinite: Les Murray, Poetry, and the Sacred." *Antipodes* 19 (2): 166–71.

McDowell, Michael. 1996. "The Bakhtinian Road to Ecological Insight." In *The Ecocriticism Reader: Landmarks in Literary Ecology*, edited by Cheryll Glotfelty and Harold Fromm, 371–91. Athens: The University of Georgia Press.

Mescher, Mark and Consuelo De Moraes. 2015. "Role of Plant Sensory Perception in Plant-Animal Interactions." *Journal of Experimental Botany* 66 (2): 425–33.

Miller, Elaine. 2002. *The Vegetative Soul: From Philosophy of Nature to Subjectivity in the Feminine.* Albany: State University of New York Press.

Morelli, Steve, ed. 2010. *Gumbaynggirr Yuludarla Jandaygam: Gumbaynggirr Dreaming Story Collection.* Nambucca Heads, NSW: Muurrbay Language and Culture Cooperative Limited.

Murray, Les. 1977. "The Human Hair Thread." *Meanjin* 36 (4): 550–71.

———. 1992. *The Paperbark Tree: Selected Prose.* Manchester, UK: Carcanet.

———. 2005. "Les Murray, The Art of Poetry No. 89." Interview by Dennis O'Driscoll. *The Paris Review.* Accessed 23 May 2017. www.theparisreview.org/interviews/5508/les-murray-the-art-of-poetry-no-89-les-murray

———. 2007. *Selected Poems.* Melbourne: Black Inc.

———. 2012. *Translations from the Natural World.* Manchester, UK: Carcanet.

Murray, Les, and Geoffrey Lehmann. 1965. *The Ilex Tree.* Canberra: Australian National University.

Nancy, Jean-Luc. 2000. *Being Singular Plural.* Stanford, CA: Stanford University Press.

Narby, Jeremy. 2006. *Intelligence in Nature: An Inquiry into Knowledge.* New York: TarcherPerigee.

Olney, James. 1980. *The Rhizome and the Flower: The Perennial Philosophy-Yeats and Jung*. Berkeley: University of California Press.

Paulson, Toni. 2016. "Gulambarra and the Crying Tree." *Saltwater, Freshwater Aboriginal Stories*. Accessed 23 May 2017. http://pacificcoast.com.au/itineraries-and-trails/aboriginal-stories/forster-worimi/

Ploum, Albrecht. 2012. "Iconography, Science and Lightning Figures." *Australian Aboriginal Studies* 2: 87–95.

Rolls, Eric. 1981. *A Million Wild Acres: 200 Years of Man and an Australian Forest*. Melbourne: Nelson.

Rose, Deborah Bird. 1996. *Nourishing Terrains: Australian Aboriginal Views of Landscape and Wilderness*. Canberra: Australian Heritage Commission.

Royal Botanic Gardens, Kew. 2016. *The State of the World's Plants Report*. Kew: Royal Botanic Gardens.

Seddon, George. 1972. *Sense of Place: A Response to an Environment, the Swan Coastal Plain, Western Australia*. Nedlands: University of Western Australia Press.

Serventy, Vincent. 1970. *Dryandra: The Story of an Australian Forest*. Sydney: A. H. and A. W. Reed.

Steffen, Will, Andrew Burbridge, Lesley Hughes, Roger Kitching, David Lindenmayer, Warren Musgrave, Mark Stafford Smith, and Patricia Werner. 2009. *Australia's Biodiversity and Climate Change*. Melbourne: CSIRO Publishing.

Theophrastus. 1916. *Enquiry into Plants and Minor Works on Odours and Weather Signs*. Translated by Arthur Hort. London: William Heinemann.

Thomas, Richard. 1988. "Tree Violation and Ambivalence in Virgil." *Transactions of the American Philological Association* 118: 261–73.

Trewavas, Anthony. 2014. *Plant Behaviour and Intelligence*. Oxford: Oxford University Press.

———. 2016. "Plant Intelligence: An Overview." *BioScience* 66 (7): 542–51.

Turpin, Myfany. 2007. "Artfully Hidden: Text and Rhythm in a Central Australian Aboriginal Song Series." *Musicology Australia* 29 (1): 93–108.

Virgil. 2010. *Eclogues*. Translated by Len Krisak. Philadelphia: University of Pennsylvania Press.

Watts, Eric King. 2001. "'Voice' and 'Voicelessness' in Rhetorical Studies." *Quarterly Journal of Speech* 87: 179–96.

Wohlleben, Peter. 2016. *The Hidden Life of Trees: What They Feel, How They Communicate—Discoveries from a Secret World*. Carlton, VIC: Black Inc.

3 That Porous Line
Mary Oliver and the Intercorporeality of the Vegetal Body

> Never in my life
> had I felt myself so near
> that porous line
> where my own body was done with
> and the roots and the stems and the flowers
> began.
> —from "White Flowers," *New and Selected Poems*
> (Oliver 1992, 59, ll. 31–36)

Research at the microscopic level increasingly reveals remarkable congruencies between human, mammalian, and botanical bodies. Plant cells and animal neurons share more structural features in common than scientists previously recognized (Baluška 2010; Barlow 2008). Root hairs, pollen tubes, and other actively dividing anatomical zones in plants resemble the threadlike axons that conduct electrical impulses between neurons in animals. Moreover, the hormones mediating plant-to-plant communication are essential for regulating processes within animals and bear an uncanny similarity to neurohormones (Baluška and Mancuso 2009, 291). Endocannabinoids shown to govern all dimensions of human and animal physiology—including brain and nerve tissue generation in adults—are nearly identical in structure to psychoactive compounds found in hemp (*Cannabis sativa*) (Prenderville, Kelly, and Downer 2015). As biologists explain, co-evolution has brought about a wealth of organic compounds known as secondary metabolites with pronounced influence on human bodies and minds, which only have marginal effects on the plants that synthesize them (Speed et al. 2015). What is more, vegetal beings manufacture a broad spectrum of other neurologically active compounds such as ethylene, a gas produced in response to plant injuries which has also been employed as an anesthetic in Western medicine since the 1920s (Barlow 2008, 142; Dillard 1930).

Within the field of signaling and behavior, the corporeal kindredness between plants, animals, and humans coalesces further with the revival of the root-brain hypothesis that was initially postulated by Charles Darwin (with laboratory assistance from his son Francis) in the late nineteenth century (Baluška et al. 2009). In locating neuronal activity in the root apex, the Darwins eschewed the classical paradigm of vegetal life as devoid of the capacity for self-directed movement involving sensory perception and coordinated by a brain-like nexus. The Darwinian root-brain theory radically reconfigured the plant body as an analogue animal or human with its anterior root-brain in the soil and posterior reproductive organs (flowers) and waste disposal mechanisms (leaf and stem stomata) suspended in a matrix of air (Baluška and Mancuso 2009, 288). Published in 1880, *The Power of Movement in Plants* ends on an expansive note, suggesting that "[...] it is impossible not to be struck with the resemblance between the foregoing movements of plants and many of the actions performed unconsciously by the lower animals" (2016, 418; see also Chapter 1). This assertion presages the modern biological principle of "inclusivity" (Barlow 2008, 136–37) integrating plant and animal evolution through a shared "logic" (Meyerowitz 2002, 1485). In particular, the Darwins exalted the tip of the radicle (the segment of a plant embryo that turns into the primary root) as the nervous epicenter of vegetal life and as the most "wonderful" structure of the plant body, capable of distinguishing between subtle differences in pressure, moisture, temperature, and object densities (2016, 418). The famous final sentence of the treatise contends that the radicle "acts like the brain of one of the lower animals; the brain being seated within the anterior end of the body, receiving impressions from the sense-organs, and directing the several movements" (Darwin and Darwin 2016, 419). Research continues to explain that the tip of the root apex—theorized over 130 years ago by the Darwins—mediates sensory perception and corresponds physiologically to the neuronal processes of animals and humans (Baluška and Mancuso 2009, 289).

As this chapter will suggest, the science of vegetal, zoological, and human bodily affinities has provocative resonances in the work of Mary Oliver (b. 1935) who is widely regarded as one of the foremost ecopoets in contemporary American literature (Bryson 2005, 75–98; Christensen 2002; Davis and Womack 2006, 37–49; Elder 1996, 217–28; McNew 1989). Sensuously evoking nonhuman nature, especially the landscape of Cape Cod, Massachusetts where she resides, Oliver's ecopoetry has been faithfully examined through the optics of human embodiment (Bonds 1992; Graham 1994), spiritual transcendence (Burton-Christie 1996; Davis 2009; Mann 2004; Ullyatt 2011), and posthumanist subjectivity (Christensen 2002). Despite the conspicuous vegetal themes and subjects of her more than 50 year oeuvre, foregrounded in collections such as *White Pine* (1994) and *Blue Iris* (2006), commentators have not specifically drawn attention to Oliver's engagement with botanical life and sensorial rendering of human-plant transactions. In contrast to such an emphasis, critical studies of Oliver tend to prioritize the birds, mammals, insects, reptiles, and other mobile creaturely subjects of her verse within its broader ecological concerns (for instance, Bryson 2005, 75–98; Malamud 2003, 32–34). Regardless of the critical lacuna, through its cross-species and relational basis, Oliver's vegetal poetics lyrically recasts the stigma of plant sentience as merely parapsychological or pseudoscientific—depreciatory associations, in part, embedded in public consciousness since Peter Tompkins and Christopher Bird's *The Secret Life of Plants* (1973) (for a critique of this text, see Baluška and Mancuso 2009, 286). In their percipience and embodiment—mediated by the language of poetry—Oliver's embodied vegetal subjects present a counterforce to the Aristotelian-Linnaean impulse to reduce plant life hierarchically and mechanistically to components, compounds, nutritive souls, and taxonomic nomenclature.

Echoing the physiological human-botanical congruence of the root-brain hypothesis (Darwin and Darwin 2016) and the more recent assertions of plant signaling and behavior (Baluška 2010; Baluška et al. 2009; Barlow 2008), Oliver confers embodiment to vegetal life while educing the intricate nodes of contact between beings through a form of "intercorporeality" (Csordas 2008). Oliver's botanical poetry emphasizes the "multiple corporeal exchanges that continually take place in our everyday lives" (Weiss 1999, 5) with plants and other beings. I propose that the sensing body of Oliver as poet exists in dialogical exchange with the multitudinous bodies of nature, including those of lilies, trilliums, peonies, grapes, roses, and other everyday vegetal forms that co-inhabit her coastal terrain. As one of the fulcrums of the poet's thought, the body is permeable, heterogeneous, indeterminate, and resistive of firmly individuated subjectivity. Put differently, the intercorporeal body mediated in Oliver's poetics is distinctly posthuman (Haraway 2008; Hayles 2008), shaped by language via the intimacies of olfaction, gustation, and touch in conjunction with visual and auditory aesthetics. Following this argument, the ensuing discussion further advances the premise of vegetal dialectics that is central to *Plants in Contemporary Poetry*. While they facilitate the corporeal experiences and bodily emplacement of human subjects, plants are always already self-directed beings with discriminating internal sensory faculties (Chamovitz 2012; Karban 2015) and the potential for carnal presence in the world. Oliver engages the somatic registers of vegetal life as part of her ecopoetics not merely by figuring plants as human analogues; for instance, as having brains, lungs, skin, blood, and bones (although she regularly deploys an anatomical rhetoric of plants). More compellingly and boldly, the poet resists a botanical imagination of disembodied, transcendent reverie by attending to the sensorial immediacies of plants in the actual spaces of intercorporeal encounter.

Oliver's Vegetal Poetics: Transcendence and the Bodies of Nature

Born in 1935 outside Cleveland in Maple Heights, Ohio, Oliver published her first book of poetry *No Voyage and Other Poems* in 1965. Noteworthy among her more than 30 published collections to date are *American Primitive* (1983), recipient of the Pulitzer Prize for Poetry, and *New and Selected Poems*, winner of the National Book Award for Poetry in 1992 (Harde 2002). The broad public appeal of her "epiphanic nature poems," beyond literary or academic circles, ensures that Oliver is "far and away [America's] best-selling poet" whose books consistently dominate national listings of poetry in popularity and sales (Garner 2007). Understanding the plant-human intercorporeality of Oliver's verse calls for awareness of the pastoral dimensions of her early life in the Midwest and her more than 50 year residency in coastal Provincetown located at the tip of the hook-shaped Cape Cod peninsula in Massachusetts, within earshot of the Atlantic Ocean. Oliver is a largely reclusive writer who rarely grants media interviews or goes beyond brief allusions about her childhood (indeed, she is skeptical of the confessional tradition popularized by Anne Sexton, Sylvia Plath, and other female and male poet-predecessors) (Oliver 2011). Her work, however, discloses instances from a rather introverted and bucolic upbringing during which memories of trees and other nonhuman beings took shape. Within their ecological bearing, some of Oliver's poems express acute and haunting familial recollections. Her early collection *The River Styx, Ohio, and Other Poems* (1972) invokes the unincorporated community in rural north-eastern Ohio as well as the river of Greek mythology after which it was named. The work exemplifies her reclamation of an Ohioan heritage through lyrical remembrance and mythologization, prominent in poems such as "Spring in the Classroom," "Learning About the Indians," and "Night Flight."

"The Black Walnut Tree" from *New and Selected Poems* narrates the intimate overlays between botanical life and Oliver's ancestry. The poem traces the course of a "debate" between the poet-daughter and her elderly mother over an old black walnut tree (*Juglans nigra*) rendered disruptive and cumbersome with age, its "roots in the cellar drains" and leaves "[...] getting heavier/every year, and the fruit/harder to gather away" (Oliver 1992, ll. 11, 13–15). Defying the obvious utilitarian recourse of selling "the black walnut tree/to the lumberman" (ll. 3–4) in order to pay down an overbearing mortgage, daughter and mother resolve to allow the tree to live out its days, thus observing an ethics of vegetal nature within a sense of filial piety:

> [...] That night I dream
> of my fathers out of Bohemia

filling the blue fields
of fresh and generous Ohio
with leaves and vines and orchards.
What my mother and I both know
is that we'd crawl with shame
in the emptiness we'd made
in our own and our fathers' backyard.
(Oliver 1992, 201, ll. 21–29)

As immigrants from Eastern Europe who became winemakers and orchardists in the New World landscape of Ohio, Oliver's forefathers physically cultivated relations to the plants that sustained their diasporic communities. For the poet, to do away callously with the venerable black walnut would have been to purge the deep-seated corporeal articulations between vegetal and family life. During her solitary childhood, Oliver's empathic disposition toward plants matured through the combination of walking, observing, reflecting, and composing: "I spent a great deal of time in my younger years just writing and reading, walking around the woods of Ohio, where I grew up" (Oliver 2011). This bodily, creative habit carried over to her long tenure in Provincetown where, in the raw exposure to the elements, she felt "able to see the earth not as our reckless ambitions have rearranged it, but as it was created by those infinitely more mysterious forces: wind, storm, time" (Oliver 1991, 33). Sharing an inwardness with plants and aligning with non-Western ontologies (Rumi is one of her favorite poets), Oliver transgresses the Aristotelian-Linnaean paradigm that either mechanistically denies or hierarchically debases vegetal ensoulment: "To me, it's all right if you look at a tree, as the Hindus do, and say the tree has a spirit. It's a mystery, and mysteries don't compromise themselves" (Oliver 2011) (see Chapter 2 for a companionable attitude toward the vegetative soul in the poetry of Les Murray).

Rather than re-inscribing the Cartesian opposition between spirit and matter in her botanical writing, Oliver's transcendence is rooted in the heterogeneous bodies of vegetal nature and the ineluctable materiality of the earth. Ecocritic J. Scott Bryson (2005, 78) characterizes the prevailing intercorporeality of her poetics as "the body's fundamental relatedness to the rest of nature," while Laird Christensen (2002) examines Oliver's desire for embodied contact with the nonhuman other as a reconfiguration of the *cogito ergo sum* conception of self. Correspondingly, in her analysis of Pulitzer-winning *American Primitive*, Vicki Graham understands Oliver's embodiment as an inherently plural, porous, and immersive mode of contact between the poet-observer and nonhuman subjects, blurring a sharply delineated conception of human identity: "To merge with the nonhuman is to acknowledge the self's mutability and multiplicity, not to lose subjectivity" (1994, 353). Graham's feminist reading of Oliver's poetics reflects a theory of thinking *through* the body found in some schools of cognitive science. Such a position maintains that cognitive processes are distributed throughout the totality of an organism rather than narrowly confined to the central nervous system (brain and spinal cord) (see, for instance, Adams 2010). Graham observes that Oliver's verse mediates the interplay between sensation (feeling through the senses) and sense (thinking through the mind-body): "[...] evoking and then becoming another depends on direct, sensuous contact with the other, on using the body *rather than the mind* to apprehend it [emphasis added]" (1994, 355). Avoiding the binarism implicit in Graham's assertion and following the principle of embodied cognition, this lyrical becoming-other could more fruitfully be posited as a condition of *mind within body*, leading to non-dualistic modes of identification between Oliver and the commonplace, corporeal, and sentient vegetal beings populating her verse. Along similar lines, Douglas Burton-Christie (1996, 79) argues that the transcendent noumenal inheres within the everyday phenomenal—and vice versa—as Oliver "articulates an utterly particular and concrete sense of spiritual transformation that emerges in and through the ordinary, transfigured by poetic imagination."

Highlighting the interstices between ecological materiality, modes of embodiment, and spiritual transformation in Oliver's work, critics including Bonds (1992) and Bryson (2005) allude to "Landscape" from *Dream Work* (1986) for its articulation of nature as language and nature as perfection, respectively. More specifically, Bryson (2005, 80) construes the agentic potential of plants—their appearance of largely motionless poise in time and space—in negative terms as emblematic of the "the lack of ambition exhibited by nonhuman natural entities." I propose, however, that "Landscape" is illustrative of plant-human intercorporeality with its first two stanzas rendered as rhetorical questions ("Isn't it plain [...] Isn't it clear?") drawing attention to the omnipresence of vegetal bodies, from prostrate moss to ascendant black oaks:

> Isn't it plain the sheets of moss, except that
> they have no tongues, could lecture
> all day if they wanted about
>
> spiritual patience? Isn't it clear
> the black oaks along the path are standing
> as though they were the most fragile of flowers?
> (Oliver 2005, 1103, ll. 1–6)

The corporeal presence of moss is figured as a sheet protecting and, indeed, nurturing the earth on which the poet walks in a state of sensuous receptivity. Yet, the generic, nondescript title "Landscape" signals the potential perils of relegating botanical and other nonhuman communities to the backdrop of everyday consciousness as part of the scenery or as, what Michael Pollan terms, "the mute, immobile furniture of our world—useful enough, and generally attractive, but obviously second-class citizens in the republic of life on Earth" (Pollan 2015, xi). In "Landscape," poetry becomes a mechanism for fostering embodied perception of flora (here, moss and trees) that might otherwise become marginalized in consciousness— banished to the sides of the path. In Oliver's material-semiosis of plants, the obvious lack of a tongue and other zoological organs of vocalization does not preclude moss—a community of beings; a plural "they" rather than singular and inanimate "it"—from the fields of language, communication, knowledge, and spirituality. As Robin Wall elaborates persuasively in her book *Gathering Moss* (2003), irrespective of their diminutive form, mosses provide essential habitats for microorganisms, invertebrates, and other creatures. Beyond their ecocultural significance and despite their relatively stationary form, Oliver's sheets of moss are moreover ensouled, self-directed, and decision-making subjects who "[...] could lecture/all day *if they wanted* [emphasis added]." In Oliver's poetics, human spiritual yearning is misdirected when not guided by the wisdom of the body and nature (McNew 1989, 68).

In "Landscape," the ensoulment of moss—its "spiritual patience"— corresponds to, rather than transcends, its bodily habitus (and, in this instance, a bryophytic one): growing densely in mats, preferring cool shaded habitats, and anchored in the earth and to one another via filamentous rhizoids (see also Chapter 5 for the idea of plant patience). Moreover, the black oaks of the second stanza are not standing figuratively *like* fragile flowers. In contrast, they "are standing/as though they were the most fragile of flowers," implying qualities of coy self-awareness and cross-species recognition internal to—not linguistically projected upon—the oaks. Indeed, science is increasingly confirming Oliver's poetic insights into vegetal life garnered from her practices of walking, sensing, and writing. Trees and other members of the botanical kingdom communicate between each other and to companion species via electrical and chemical signals (Karban 2015). When a predator begins to graze the leaves of oaks, beeches, and spruces, electrical impulses register pain and set in motion a cascade of self-protective measures (Wohlleben 2016, 17–20). Through her sensitive and imaginative rendering of vegetal nature grounded in bodily exigencies of plants and nonplants, Oliver suggests that even the stateliest and most obdurate of flora is vulnerable to the caprices of a hyper-mobile humankind. Additionally, Oliver's subjectivity in "Landscape" is neither contingent on severance from the vegetal world nor on transcending the materiality of nature; instead she confers subjecthood to moss and black oaks by embracing their capacity for language and expression.

In their identification with nature and traces of intersubjective corporeal transformation, poems such as "Landscape" and others from her 50 year oeuvre beckon the question of Oliver's relationship to the Romantic imagination of Wordsworth and other precursors of the male-dominated landscape poetry tradition (see also Chapter 8). In an early study, Janet McNew (1989) argued that Oliver's spiritual realizations in nature are the opposite of Romantic transcendence, which in her view positions the terrene body and earthly desires as inferior to the rarified ideals of spirit and mind. McNew asserts that "Oliver's unpatrolled ego boundaries, her conviction that nature is also an articulate and conscious subject" differentiates her poetry from the Romantic construction of nonhuman beings as voiceless others (McNew 1989, 67). In McNew's assessment, Oliver's lyricism refrains from positioning the materiality of nature as a foil for Romantic longings. For instance, "Sleeping in the Forest" from *Twelve Moons* (1979) narrates the dissolution of individuated consciousness through contact with a feminized landscape. An embodied rhetoric of vegetal life in the poem traces the Earth's "dark skirts, her pockets/full of lichens and seeds" (cited and analyzed in McNew 1989, 61–62). Accordingly, critics align Oliver with contemporary feminist writers such as Mary Daly and Susan Griffin rather than her Romantic predecessors per se (Bonds 1992, 1; McNew 1989). Foregrounding the prominence of the proximal senses of touch, taste, and smell, Diane Bonds (1992, 7) propounds that Oliver's metaphysical searching is "always firmly located in the materiality of nature" and the bodies of the world. In comparable terms, McNew (1989, 69) observes that "physicality thus becomes the most visionary spirituality" in Oliver's writing. For McNew (1989, 72), the human soul in Oliver's verse does not transcend the body but rather synchronizes with it through natural cycles of change.

Oliver's spiritual vision of nature positioned with respect to the "vibrant matter" (Bennett 2010) of the world exhibits affinities with the work of iconic nineteenth-century nature writer Henry David Thoreau, particularly the multisensorial botanical vignettes of *Walden* (1882) and the posthumous *Faith in a Seed* (1993) and *Wild Fruits* (2000). Thoreau was unreservedly apprehensive of Cartesian reductionism as well as Carl Linnaeus' binomial system of plant classification (though he was appreciably sympathetic toward the morphological ideas of Johann Wolfgang von Goethe, the biogeographical approach of Alexander von Humboldt, and the sixteenth-century vitalism of John Gerard). In a journal entry from March 1859, Thoreau (2009, 546) warns that "the physiologist must not presume to explain [the growth of plants] according to mechanical laws, or as he might explain some machinery of his own making." In the same entry, Thoreau briefly puts forward a theory of effluence, eroding the categorical distinction between sense (mind) and sensation (body) by invoking the near-homophonous terms *essence* and *effluence*:

> The ultimate expression or fruit of any created thing is a fine effluence which only the most ingenuous worshipper perceives at a reverent distance from its surface even. Only that intellect makes any progress toward conceiving of the essence which at the same time perceives the effluence.
>
> (Thoreau 2009, 546)

In Thoreau's counter-Romantic vegetal philosophy, the aspirations of mind and spirit are contingent on bodily sensation. The breaking down of rigidly individuated subjectivity is epitomized by effluence as the flowing forth of something material (pheromones, compounds, exudates) into something else (subjects, bodies, intellects). As "one of the most direct heirs of Transcendentalism" (Morris 2010, 676), Oliver summons her Thoreauvian extraction, albeit with reticence, in "Going to Walden" from *The River Styx, Ohio and Other Poems* (1972), characterizing a pilgrimage to the fabled pond as "[...] not so easy a thing/As a green visit. It is the slow and difficult/Trick of living, and finding it where you are" (Oliver 1992, 239, ll. 10–12). Moreover, as John Elder notes, the middle of the title poem from *White Pine* (1994) almost duplicates the short narrative of Thoreau's second-hand anecdote of African elands exuding the fresh fragrance of the savanna when killed (Elder 1996, 217). Indeed, as is the case also in Oliver's poem, Thoreau (1990, 130) seemed to revel in the intercorporeality of the story recounted by an African hunter:

> [...] the skin of the eland, as well as that of most other antelopes just killed, emits the most delicious perfume of trees and grasses. I would have every man so much like a wild antelope, so much a part and parcel of nature.
>
> (Thoreau 1990, 130)

In pivoting toward bodily experience as a means of becoming "part and parcel of nature" and away from scientific concepts of flora, Oliver's botanical poetry glosses over genus-species nomenclature in favor of common or folk monikers (moccasin flowers, morning glories, skunk cabbage), unlike Kinsella, Wright, Glück, Bletsoe, and other poets featured in *Plants in Contemporary Poetry* who freely invoke technical names to varying degrees (Chapter 1 goes into further detail about the role of naming in botanical poetry). For Oliver, the Enlightenment-inspired pursuit of knowledge outside of oneself disrupts the intimacy of everyday embodied exchange with the non-human world:

> [...] there is nothing better than to be taken into the woods with people who can identify flashes of color and songs and behaviors.

But after a while I grew tired, not of the new knowledge itself, but of the constant seeking for it.

(Oliver 1991, 34)

The Vegetal Body: From the Doctrine of Signatures to the *Bauplan*

The previous section set the foundation for an approach to Oliver's vegetal poetics from an intercorporeal perspective that resists the transcendence of vegetal materiality. In narrativizing human-flora entanglements and affinities, Oliver eschews the hierarchical rendering of plants as disembodied automatons devoid of soul in comparison to their animal and human counterparts. In contrast, the preponderance of Oliver's botanical poems presents the agentic plant body as an animate, self-governing yet permeable subject enmeshed within the ecological community of which it is "part and parcel" (to echo her philosophical forebear Thoreau again). Moreover—and most distinctively—Oliver is cognizant of the Romantic implications of appropriating vegetal corporeality as a symbol, metaphor, or expedient rhetorical device. An example to the contrary is "Rage" from *Dream Work* (1986) in which she likens a young woman sexually abused by her businessman father to "a tree/that will never come to leaf" (ll. 27–28). On the whole, however, her poetry uses plant tropes judiciously. The vegetal corpus she poeticizes tends to be a sentient presence rather than a linguistic signifier of, for instance, the desecration of the female body and spirit mediated in "Rage." As a consequence, Oliver's textualization of the particular modes of plant embodiment approaches poet Francis Ponge's principle of *adéquation*. In literary scholar Sherman Paul's view, *adéquation*

> repudiates correspondence [symbolism] for equivalence: language is not to be used symbolically but only to define and describe [...] For symbolism displaces the things it uses where *adéquation* place them before us so freshly they claim our attention.
>
> (Paul 1992, 124–25)

I suggest that Oliver endeavors toward a "verbal representation [...] so close to the [vegetal] thing itself that it partakes of it" (Ponge qtd. in Paul 1992, 125). The interlinked human and plant bodies of Oliver's botanical imagination partake in cycles of co-becoming within the fabric of lyrical representation. The plant nature of Oliver's poetry, therefore, literally embodies the concept of intercorporeality as the material and sensory "interweaving of lived bodies both human and nonhuman" (Cataldi and Hamrick 2007, 13). In this way, I link her work to a Thoreauvian-Goethean tradition of plants that intersects with contemporary ideas concerning plant perception.

In linking Oliver's poetics to Thoreau and other transdisciplinarians, such as Goethe, who engaged in forms of dialogue with plants as agentic beings, it is illuminating to consider her verse within the context of historical, cultural, and scientific figurations of the vegetal corpus. Of particular note are the human-plant bodily affinities of the doctrine of signatures, developed in the medical systems of the ancient Greeks and Chinese but also extant in some practices of folk herbalism, as a means to recall the efficacy of botanical medicines in treating certain ailments (Pearce 2008). The doctrine is both a medical theory and mneumonic system in which "form recapitulates function—physical characteristics of plants reveal their therapeutic value" (Bennett 2007, 246). For instance, the sori (clusters of sporangia, which produce and hold spores) on the fronds of the common fern (*Asplenium scolopendrium*) resemble a spleen, which led ancient physicians to use the species to treat splenic dysfunction (Pearce 2008, 51). As another example, boneset (or feverwort, *Eupatorium perfoliatum*)—characterized by the unusual perforation of its leaves by its stems—evokes the image of a splint and, thus, was prescribed by doctors as a poultice for healing broken or fractured bones (Pearce 2008, 51). Although principally dismissed by modern medical practitioners and ethnopharmaceutical researchers as fanciful, subjective, and prescientific, the doctrine is effective for transmitting knowledge of the therapeutic value of plants between generations, particularly in preliterate societies with strong oral traditions (Bennett 2007, 250–53). Emphasizing the physical forms of herbs, critics tend to narrowly correlate the doctrine to the visual ability of humans (see, for example, Simpson and Conner-Ogorzaly 2001). To more fully understand the tradition, however, it is essential to recognize the olfactory, gustatory, and haptic indicators that empirically signify—even within the overwhelming technological context of today's allopathic medicine—the presence of bioactive compounds. Phytochemicals, such as poisonous alkaloids, possess bitter, astringent, and pungent qualities that register in the human body and through the proximal senses as strikingly as—and perhaps more acutely than—the corporeal forms taken in through one's eyes.

Centering on morphological congruences, the doctrine of signatures of ancient Roman and Greek provenance construed plant bodies as analogues of animals and humans. The naturalist Pliny the Elder (23–79 CE) is credited with introducing the doctrine to the West in his 37-book compendium *Naturalis Historia* (*Natural History*). For instance, Pliny regarded the spotted leaves of *consiligo* or lungwort (*Pulmonaria officinalis*) as visually suggestive of ulcerated lungs and thus useful "for those attacked by pulmonary tuberculosis [...] It is a sovereign remedy indeed for lung trouble in pigs and in all cattle, even though it is merely placed across the ear-lap [the external ear]" (Pliny 1949, Book 26, Chapter 21). Furthermore, in his extensive five-book *De Materia Medica* (*On Medical Material*), the physician and botanist

Pedanius Dioscorides of Anazarbos (40–90 CE) made some of the earliest elaborations of the doctrine, notably in his analysis of scorpion bites and the sedation of venomous arachnids. Aconite or monk's hood (*Aconitum* spp.) has "a root similar to the tail of a scorpion, glittering like alabaster. They say that the root of this applied to a scorpion makes him insensible" (Dioscorides 2000, 628). Similarly, heliotrope or turn-sole (*Heliotropium europaeum*) bears "white flowers inclining to purple, winding around like the tail of a scorpion [...] A decoction (taken as a drink with wine and also smeared on) is good for those touched by scorpions" (739).

As evident in the commentaries of botanists and herbalists from the sixteenth century onward, the doctrine of signatures came to reflect the belief that the Christian God imbues plants and other living things with signs. Accordingly, the divine semiotics of the vegetal world could be unraveled by astute observation and, therein, dismantled and reconfigured for human benefit through boiling, distilling, tincturing, powdering, and other medicine-making procedures. Such a perspective, however, decoupled agency from the plant body and—in its vacuum—positioned God's hand as the animating force imparting value to vegetal life. The Swiss-German philosopher and botanist Paracelsus von Hohenheim (1493–1541) expanded the doctrine of signatures through the concept of *similia similibus curantur* ("like cures like") with the insistence that "the soul does not perceive the external or internal physical construction of herbs and roots, but it intuitively perceives their powers and virtues, and recognizes at once their Signatum" (quoted in Bennett 2007, 248). The Paracelsian theory that God infuses plant bodies with signs of their healing applications influenced the Christian theologian Jakob Böhme (1575–1624). In his magnum opus *Signatura Rerum* (*The Signature of All Things*), Böhme claimed that "the whole outward visible world with all its being is a signature, or figure of the inward spiritual world" (Böhme 1651, 77). Sharing a belief in the divine Signatum with Paracelsus and Böhme, the botanist and herbalist William Coles (1626–1662) in *The Art of Simpling* contended that

> the mercy of God, which is over all his works, makes grass grow up on the mountains, and herbs for the use of men, and hath not only stamped upon them (as upon every man) a distinct form, but also given them particular signatures, whereby a man may read, even in legible characters, the use of them.
>
> (Coles 1657, 88)

The doctrine also factored into Nicholas Culpeper's contemporaneous *Complete Herbal* (1653) and persisted in medical textbooks of the 1800s as well as modern homeopathic and complementary medicine (Pearce 2008, 52) (see Chapter 4).

With the advance of the technoscientific paradigm of medicine in conjunction with the growth of the fields of plant physiology and morphology in the nineteenth and twentieth centuries, the doctrine of signatures began to fall into disrepute as unproven folkloric speculation. For instance, in *The Transit of Civilization from England to America in the Seventeenth Century*, American historian and novelist Edward Eggleston critiqued the philosophy of correspondences disparagingly as the tainted residue of the New World's British inheritance. Eggleston (1900, 55–56) contended that the doctrine presents an "obscure theory of sympathy and antipathy [belonging] to the overshadowing supernaturalism of the time, and to the geocentric and homocentric notions of the universe that gave value to things only in their relation to man." Despite Eggleston's critique, the doctrine from Pliny to Culpeper centralizes the congruences between plant, animal, and human bodies, as well as the primacy of direct, unaided, and sympathetic perception of plant materiality (leaves, stems, roots, flowers, exudates, fragrances, sensations). In the system of correspondences, though, vegetal bodies are reduced to—and valued in—exclusively human or animal terms and, to be more precise, homocentrically "only in their relation to man." Rather than a self-determined whole with agency of internal provenance, the plant is divinely signified in its parts and rendered consequential not in its full material presence but as a symbolic manifestation of God's will and mercy. The decline of the doctrine of signatures and related vitalistic beliefs paralleled the rise of reductionistic plant sciences focused on the isolation of anatomical parts, phytoactive compounds, and metabolic processes. During the 1800s, the advent of plant physiology in the experimental work of Swiss chemist Nicolas-Théodore De Saussure (one of the founders of photosynthesis) and German botanist Julius von Sachs (a caustic critic of Darwin and notably antagonistic to the root-brain hypothesis) began to erode the standing of vitalism. In preceding eras, the belief in an animating force independent of the chemical and physical components of organisms was foundational to understandings of nature, plants, herbs, and human-vegetal relations (Egerton 2012).

In particular, Sachs is considered the "father of plant physiology" for his research on seed germination, nutrient transport, and plant organ genesis (Harvey 1929). As a counterforce to the correspondence theory at the heart of the doctrine of signatures, his monumental *Lectures on the Physiology of Plants* (1887) contains exacting detail on plant organography (the description of organ structure and function), molecular form, nutrition, growth, "irritability" (including geotropism and heliotropism), and reproduction. The first lecture (out of a total of 47) posits a theory of the plant body as constituting "simply organised forms, in which all the processes necessary for the maintenance and reproduction of the individual are carried on in the limited space of microscopically small cells, in a scarcely ponderable mass of vegetable substance" (Sachs

1887, 1). From Sachs' point of view, the animating principle of vegetality depends on microscopic processes unfolding out of sight within the cell. His suggestion of a "scarcely ponderable mass" connotes, on the one hand, the plant body as a whole—inexplicable and irreducible and, hence, resistive of a physiological logos—and, on the other, the ubiquity of the vegetal corpus representing, as modern ecology tells us, 99% of the Earth's biomass (Trewavas 2002). Moreover, in Sachs' model, the completeness of the vegetal body hinges on the integration and efficiency of its cellular processes; hence, "with this division of physiological labour, the perfection of organisation of a living being increases" (Sachs 1887, 1). Contemptuous of Charles Darwin's investigations of the plant radicle, Sachs warned fellow botanists that experiments on roots necessitate "extensive knowledge of vegetable physiology." Ultimately Sachs would brand the Darwinian idea that "the growing point of the root, like the brain of an animal, dominates the various movements in the root" as sensational and founded on subpar experimental practices (Sachs qtd. in De Chadarevian 1996, 17–18).

Along with the physiological itemization of the internal vegetal body, the field of plant morphology (or phytomorphology) as the analysis of the external forms of plants, commenced in the late eighteenth century with the scientific work of Johann Wolfgang von Goethe (Kaplan 2001; Campbell 1911). Goethe initiated the tradition of pre-Darwinian comparative plant morphology, emphasizing the varieties of organization exhibited at the level of the whole plant and its organs (Kaplan 2001, 1712). In Goethe's conception, notwithstanding pronounced morphological diversity among flowering taxa, a *Bauplan* (body or ground plan) provides a core organizational assemblage—a biological blueprint—encoding the physical characteristics, such as symmetry, segmentation, and orientation, shared between plants (Kaplan 2001, 1717). On the basis of the inherent modularity of vegetal life, Goethe argued that flowers and fruits are repetitions of the foliage (Cabej 2013, 42). Published in 1790 (prefaced by a Goethe poem of the same title) introduces the

> laws of metamorphosis by which nature produces one part through another, creating a great variety of forms through the modification of a single organ [...] The process by which one and the same organ appears in a variety of forms has been called *the metamorphosis of plants*.
> (Goethe 2009, 5–6 [italics in original])

Holistic in focus and "ideal" in its conceptual generalization, the plant morphology of Goethe "sees things not by themselves but in an organismic relation to one another" (Bloch 1952, 313) yet without negating the aesthetic value of nature. Following Goethe, in the nineteenth and twentieth centuries Wilhelm Hofmeister achieved acclaim for his investigation of plant embryology while Karl Ritter von Goebel developed organography to underscore the importance of a causal approach to plant morphology (Kaplan 2001).

A more inclusive historical overview of the vegetal body than possible in this section would comprise the development of phytography, or descriptive botany, from Linnaeus onward (Moll 1934), the advent of scientific ecology as plant-environment relationality (Tansley 1947), and recent studies of bioperception that assign higher sensitivity to vegetal life (Karban 2015). Nevertheless, the philosophical transformations from the doctrine of signatures to the emergence of plant morphology elicit some considerations of relevance to a close reading of Mary Oliver's intercorporeality. The doctrine of signatures provokes the botanical imagination through its internalization of a sympathetic outlook on vegetal being emphasizing the correspondences between plant, animal, and human bodies. Although superficially appearing to foster empathic identification with the vegetal world, the doctrine is invariably constrained by its figuring of the plant corpus one-dimensionally through mammalian (human), utilitarian (medical), and nonsecular (Christian) ideologies. In place of engaging with the self-directed plant body, the doctrine renders plants as mammalian forms while relegating their agency to *signatum*—to God's divine impression on matter. In contrast, with its rationalistic Cartesian and Linnaean foundation, plant physiology comprehends the vegetal body as the efficient assemblage of interlocked cellular constituents. Along with the adoption of binomial nomenclature originating in Linnaeus, the formalization of the field in the early 1800s hastened the decline of the everyday knowledge of plants founded in sensory feedback and enshrined in correspondence theory. Whereas physiology turned attention to the plant's inner mechanics, morphology—and, in particular, the German lineage beginning with Goethe (Kaplan 2001)—emphasized external patterns and visible processes (metamorphosis) and, thus, developed a more holistic view of the vegetal corpus as *Bauplan* (the term *plan* itself connoting the internal self-governance of the plant body).

The Senses of Plants: Lyric Attention and Vegetal Percipience

The basic philosophical challenge for a writer such as Oliver with an empathic disposition toward plants is countering—through lyrical assertion—the conception of vegetal life as insentient matter, as part of the panorama and furniture, as a mechanism or code to be deciphered, and as a "scarcely ponderable mass of vegetable substance" (Sachs 1887, 1) to be denied agency and therein exploited recklessly. The

Goethean principle of *Bauplan*—attributing internal directedness to the plant and foregrounding the morphological interconnections within the vegetal body and between botanical taxa—figures prominently into current bioperception theory (Chamovitz 2012; Karban 2015; Mescher and De Moraes 2015; Trewavas 2014). Most of the characteristics once considered exclusive to brain and spinal cord cells—comprising the so-called "neuron doctrine" of perception—have also been identified in their non-mammalian equivalents (Guillery 2005). With the plant radicle regarded as the primary organ of sensory perception, once tenuous correspondences between zoological and botanical life manifest in laboratory conditions, particularly regarding the reception of light and magnetism (Baluška and Mancuso 2009, 295). Rather than propounding "an argument that plants are just like us" (Chamovitz 2012, 8), research into vegetal perception helps to redefine long-standing presumptions about the very nature of intelligence and sense. As František Baluška and Stefano Mancuso propose, "the discovery of convergent neuronal processes in animals and plants allows us to unite these two kingdoms" in a manner deviating from the segregation of *Animalia* from *Plantae* in the worldviews of Aristotle and Linneaus.

The premise that sensing plants are more genetically, ecologically, and physiologically kindred to animals than scientists previously believed contributes to eroding the rigid delineations between animals and plants in terms of their respective materialities: flesh in hierarchical comparison to cellulose, brains to roots, veins to phloem, and blood to sap. The harmonization of bodies also problematizes the Aristotelian *scala naturae* demarcating between organisms according to "powers of soul" in which vegetative ensoulment represented the basest and the intellective the highest (Lovejoy 2010, 58) (see Chapter 2 on Les Murray's poetry). At the same time, the understanding of plants as embodied agents negotiating their environments actively through complex sensorialities could counteract pernicious "zoocentrism" as the enfranchisement of animals—including humans—above all else (Callicott 1998, 462–63). Through their material registers, vegetal beings engage in somatic exchange with the conspicuously mobile bodies of insects, birds, mammals, and humans. Rather than one-directionally acting on the vegetal corpus, these bodies act with plants in co-constituted interrelation, enmeshed within shared lifeworlds. Extending the previous historical and scientific discussion, I argue that Oliver's poetry intersects with a Goethean-Thoreauvian appreciation of the plant as a whole being while intuitively invoking—through her direct experience—post-Darwinian ideas of vegetal sensing, behavior, and intelligence. The plant *Bauplan* of Oliver's poetry is neither overlooked as passive background nor consumed as dispensable matter but, instead, engaged with as material presence. More specifically, the principle of intercorporeality—as a catalyst of empathic interrelation with plants—is crucial to Oliver's rendering of olfaction, gustation, and tactile perception. While conduits for human embodiment—we smell, taste, and touch them—plants also have intrinsic forms of bodily apprehension and make use of sensory cues for shaping their environments and thus improving their long-term fitness.

Although antithetical to the intoxicating perfume of Thoreauvian effluence, the putrescent reek of skunk cabbage in Oliver's poem of the same name nevertheless galvanizes the writer into receiving the swamp plant internally like a "worshipper [...] at a reverent distance" (Thoreau 2009, 546). Emitting a rotten meat odor as a means to attract pollinators and prey, skunk cabbage (*Symplocarpus foetidus*) is also distinctive for thermogenesis, defined as the production of heat up to 20°C greater than the ambient temperature. This evolutionary mechanism enhances the volatilization of aromatic compounds over distances while melting the early spring snow surrounding the plant in its natural setting (Seymour and Blaylock 1999; Vereecken and McNeil 2010). Oliver narrates the vibrant material presence of *S. foetidus* in the poem's seamless alternation between human, vegetal, and insect bodies. The fetor of the wetland plant becomes the engrossing substance through which ecological reciprocity between human and nonhuman beings takes shape:

> You kneel beside it. The smell
> is lurid and flows out in the most
> unabashed way, attracting
> into itself a continual spattering
> of protein. Appalling its rough
> green caves, and the thought
> of the thick root nested below, stubborn
> and powerful as instinct!
>
> (Oliver 1992, 160, ll. 9–16)

Neither ethereal nor insubstantial, the "lurid" skunk cabbage signature is presented as a molten material that flows in accordance with the intention of the plant, gathering both human and insect bodies centripetally "into itself" in order to enable the self-actualization of the plant during the vernal season. In this excerpt, Oliver poeticizes olfaction as a primordial sense as "stubborn/and powerful as instinct" (although the structure of the two lines following the comma renders the grammatical subject ambivalently as either the root, the smell, or both). From a scientific perspective, neurobiological research demonstrates that smell is related intimately to memory and emotion. For instance, personally-significant odor-evoked memories correspond to heightened activity in the amygdala and hippocampus regions of the limbic system (Herz et al. 2004).

Regarded as the "paleomammalian complex" (a term now considered outmoded by comparative neuroscientists) the limbic system developed during the evolution of mammals, at least according to the much-disputed triune theory of the brain (MacLean 1990).

Instinctive, bold, and tactile in character, the pungent aroma "appalls"—sets up a dynamic sensory tension with—the visual architecture of the leaves and the terrene nature of the "thick root nested" in the ground. In her evocation of the vegetal *Bauplan*, Oliver parallels Charles Darwin's radicle-brain hypothesis in lyrical terms that position the cognitive nexus of the plant below the surface of the earth. For Oliver in the concluding declarative—and in contrast to the more "elegant and easeful" blossoms emerging later in spring—"what blazes the trail is not necessarily pretty" (1992, 160, ll. 25, 27). "Skunk Cabbage" recognizes vegetal intelligence in the primordial meshing of plants and other forms of life, as mediated by the palpability of smell and its material correlates (molecules, compounds, protein, and organs). Correspondingly, biologist Daniel Chamovitz in *What a Plant Knows* (2012, 20) observes that plants release odors—such as the "lurid" scent of *S. foetidus*—appealing to animals and humans while making certain ecological functions possible. He argues that plants also have a "highly sensitive" inherent form of olfaction, sensing their own odors (for instance, when their fruit ripens) and registering those of their neighbors threatened by grazing animals or voracious insects (Chamovitz 2012, 20). Other beings receive the volatile compounds emitted by plants, but vegetal life also has an intrinsic capacity for olfaction. Hence, plants are acted upon by humans, animals, and insects while, at the same time, they negotiate their environments for the benefit of themselves and the ecosystems of which they are part. Regarding the sophisticated olfactory communication of plants, Chamovitz (2012, 24) cites the phenomenon of "leaves-dropping" in which attacked trees transmit airborne hormonal signals to healthy neighboring trees to warn of impending danger. In the nineteenth century, Erasmus Darwin (1800, 125) (grandfather of Charles) comparably speculated about the presence of a sense organ directing "vegetable amourettes [lovers] to find each other; one probably analogous to our sense of smell which in the animal world directs the new-born infant to its source of nourishment." Despite these ideas, from Erasmus Darwin's amorous vegetables to Chamovitz's cognizant plants—many of which were supported experimentally yet dismissed at first by mainstream botany—vegetal beings have been denied olfactory agency due to the absence of a nervous system, or at least one reflecting an animalistic design.

Oliver implies vegetal olfaction in the drawing of organic bodies into the corpus of the skunk cabbage. This chapter has aimed to bring her poetry into discourse with historical and scientific notions of bioperception in order to elucidate the intercorporeal elements of her work. Extending intercorporeality to plants through an open-ended interpretation to the concept, Gail Weiss (1999, 5) asserts in her book *Body Images* that "to describe embodiment as intercorporeality is to emphasize that the experience of being embodied is never a private affair, but is always-already mediated by our continual interactions with other human and nonhuman bodies." Following Weiss' characterization, I maintain that Oliver's poetic intercorporeality recognizes vegetal embodiment as provoking sensory experience (the poet and insects perceive the skunk cabbage fetor) while possessing internal sensory ability (the skunk cabbage receives the materialities of other bodies through its senses). Never a private affair, even for plants, intercorporeality is furthermore apparent in the poem "Peonies" with its immediate use of anatomical correspondence to create empathic identification between poet, flower, and environment: "This morning the green fists of the peonies are getting ready/ to break my heart" (Oliver 1992, 21, ll. 1–2). Associated with the sharp somatic registers of fists and the heart, the peony blossoms—as evoked textually—impact the poet (and her audience) on emotional and visceral levels. Attracting other bodies into themselves—in a tactile manner redolent of the skunk cabbage previously discussed—the peonies magnetize ants "craving the sweet sap/taking it away/to their dark, underground cities" (Oliver 1992, 21, ll. 11–13). In this instance, the flowers' olfactory articulations express the "mindless mastery" (Trewavas 2002) of vegetal nature negotiating its ecological milieu volitionally, even in the absence of the neurological apparatus of animals:

> the flowers bend their bright bodies,
>   and tip their fragrance to the air,
>   and rise,
>   their red stems holding
>
> all that dampness and recklessness
>   gladly and lightly,
>   and there it is again—
>   beauty the brave, the exemplary,
>
> blazing open.
>   (Oliver 1992, 21–22, ll. 17–25)

Active verbs—bend, tip—combine with present participles—holding, blazing—to inculcate the textualized peony bodies with agency. Formulated as three short rhetorical questions (ll. 26–28) and a single long concluding question (ll. 29–36), the poem's latter stanzas bring into focus the "mingled bodies" (Serres 2008) of people in dynamic relation to flora. With its reference to filling "your arms with the white and pink flowers,/with their honeyed heaviness, their lush trembling,/their eagerness" (Oliver 1992, 22, ll. 32–34), the final question is unequivocal in its suggestion of peony agency. Oliver renders the visual beauty of the flowers in relation to the taste of sap, the sensation of vegetal movements, and the potent metaphysical implications of the speaker's realization of the permeability of plants to other bodies. The spirit of giving and receiving—of intercorporeal transaction based in smell and taste—is correspondingly palpable in "Roses, Late Summer" in which "the last roses have opened their factories of sweetness/and are giving it back to the world" (Oliver 1992, 95–96, ll. 24–25).

"Goldenrod" further thematizes human-plant intercorporeality—as a condition of somatic exchange—through poetic attention to a species common to northeastern North America. The vegetal subject is presumably the Canadian goldenrod (*Solidago canadensis*) native to the coastal region where Oliver lived prior to her relocation to southern Florida following the death of her partner Molly Malone Cook in 2005. As the dual sense of the speaker's embodiment in relation to the plant being observed, intercorporeality typifies the poem's progression. The "rumpy bunches" of goldenrods are "sneeze-bringers and seed-bearers" who exert a pull on the myriad bodies of nature. An assemblage of "bees and yellow beads and perfect flowerlets/and orange butterflies" coalesces (Oliver 1992, 17, ll. 3, 7, 8–9). Rather than an ocular spectacle taken from a detached position—and free of sneezing and other hazards of contact—the goldenrod collapses the perceptual distance by engaging the speaker bodily: its "glittering pandemonium/leaned on me" (Oliver 1992, 17, ll. 20–21). In eliding the distinction between the visual and tactile dimensions of the flower, Oliver disturbs the hierarchy of the senses through the goldenrod's glitter that leans. The synaesthesiac metaphor also counters the Western elevation of the distal senses (sight and hearing) over the proximal (smell, taste, and sensation)—a schema pursued since antiquity and enshrined in Aristotle's valorization of sight (Jütte 2005, 61–71). In the final stanzas, Oliver reverses this long-standing order by investing her faith more fully in the sensuous presence of vegetal being:

And what has consciousness come to anyway, so far,

that is better than these light-filled bodies?
  All day
    on their airy backbones
      they toss in the wind,

> they bend as though it was natural and godly to bend,
> they rise in a stiff sweetness,
> in the pure peace of giving
> one's gold away.
>
> (Oliver 1992, 18, ll. 28–36)

The speaker revels in plant materiality but not by privileging the body. In her analysis of *American Primitive*, Vicki Graham (1994, 357) observes that Oliver consistently reverses the traditional opposition between mind (sense) and body (senses). With the body as the foundation for abstract expression, the poet risks subordinating the non-physical to the physical (Graham 1994). In contrast, I maintain that the intercorporeality of Oliver's poetics recognizes spiritual insight as an emergent property of human and nonhuman bodies interacting.

Although the foregoing examples have centered on the human-vegetal encounter, Oliver's work also extends intercorporeality to the transactions between plants and animals. "Tasting the Wild Grapes" (Oliver 1982) centralizes gustation as the tasting, drinking, and eating of plants but with respect to the habitus of a fox. As "a muscled sleeve the color/of all October!" (ll. 11–12), the creature's movements harmonize with the temporospatial rhythms of the landscape. Elation mounts as the speaker awaits the unscripted appearance of the elusive animal:

> Walk
> quietly under these tangled vines
> and pay attention, and one morning
> something will explode underfoot
> like a branch of fire.
>
> (Oliver 1982, ll. 5–9)

Despite obvious differences in the respective mobilities of the subjects, the perambulation of the human synchronizes with the slow tangling of the vines and rapid movements of the fox. Similarly, for biologists Stefano Mancuso and Alessandra Viola (2015, 71), twining behavior enables vines to identify the objects most supportive of their growth, and demonstrates that vegetal life is endowed with the sense of touch. Far from static or passive, plants move their tendrils, leaves, roots, flowers, and other organs freely and with intention according to timescales often imperceptible to human consciousness (for a more extensive analysis, see Chapter 7 on time-plexity in Judith Wright's work). In Oliver's lyrical account, the wild taste of grapes mixes with the glimpse of the fox. Vegetal and zoological ephemeralities intersect and, in doing so, foreground the physical connections between the co-constituted beings of a place. The fox is "small-boned, thin-faced, in a hurry,/lively as the dark thorns of the wild grapes/on the unsuspecting tongue!" (Oliver 1982, ll. 16–18).

In its sharpness, the taking of plant food—thorns and all—into the body affirms the incontrovertibility of human and animal reliance on the vegetal corpus. Like Thoreau, who preferred the scent of grapes over their wild taste, Oliver relishes her immersion in the vine and the prospect of a small, piquant harvest of fruits. As these extracts from Oliver's extensive work reveal, her speakers smell and ingest plants as a means of immersive involvement with nonhumans. In other instances, however, Oliver implies a vegetal sense of taste by aligning plants with the anatomical features necessary for animal gustation. For example, trout lilies (*Erythronium* spp.) are distinguished for "[…] their spotted bodies/and their six-antlered bright faces,/and their many red tongues" (Oliver 2003, 87, ll. 19–21). As argued previously in this chapter, such a rendering of vegetal embodiment attempts to go beyond the symbolic deployment of anatomical tropes and, instead, moves toward the principle of *adéquation* as "verbal representation […] so close to the [vegetal] thing itself that it partakes of it" (Ponge qtd. in Paul 1992, 125). If we decide that her poetic exertions in this regard are viable, then Oliver's readers might look at the vegetal domain anew and become open to regarding plants as having tongues and faces as science has suggested that they really do possess sensory faculties. Literary critics also might feel liberated from the intellectual specters of pathetic fallacy and Romantic idealization that constrain analytical approaches to vegetal nature and its poetization by banishing the imagination from discourse. As creatures miraculously breathing with plants at all moments of existence, human beings might therefore come to see moccasin orchids and other species not as part of the background, but through the glitter of their somatic relations, as:

> the pink lungs of their bodies
>   enter the fire of the world
>   and stand there shining
>   and willing—the one
>
> thing they can do before
>   they shuffle forward
>   into the floor of darkness, they
>   become the trees.
>
> (Oliver 1992, 67, ll. 29–36)

Conclusion: Toward Intercorporeal Relations with Plants

Through the botanical verse of renowned American poet Mary Oliver read in the context of historical and scientific interpretations of the

That Porous Line 75

vegetal body, this chapter has asserted that plants mediate human experience of the world, and also that they are capable of corporeal perception. Oliver lyricizes vegetal embodiment as necessarily intercorporeal; plant presence emerges through contact and spirited exchange with humans, animals, insects, and other plants. Neither the anatomized body of the physiological tradition nor the metaphorized body of the doctrine of correspondences, the vegetal body she presents is that of the agentic plant. Considering the implications of Oliver's poetics, though, how might heightened consciousness of vegetal embodiment intersect with the future wellbeing of botanical life on an increasingly globalized, industrialized, and climatically-disturbed planet? By way of a conclusion to this discussion, I submit that in fostering corporeal affinities with plants, poetry helps to counter the deep-rooted view of the vegetal domain as dispensable material, mechanical assemblage, statistical abstraction, subservient biological class, or the silent backdrop to more imperative human affairs. Intercorporeality brings to the fore the potent awareness that human and nonhuman bodies are subjected to the same circumstances and partake in a common fate. The call to communion of Oliver's botanical poetics urges us to receive the embodied wisdom of plants, as in "The Sunflowers" with its entreaty: "[...] let us talk with those modest faces,/the simple garments of leaves,/the coarse roots in the earth/so uprightly burning" (Oliver 1992, 139, ll. 33–36).

Oliver's work propels its audience toward emotional recognition of plants—based in the particular bodily needs of both—as an essential step toward valuing botanical nature and cherishing the vegetated biosphere that graciously sustains all life, despite humanity's perilous disregard. The power of intercorporeality thus lies in its relationship to empathy, which can provoke and sustain the love of plants by dissolving the conceptual barriers that place us above them (see Chapter 4). And the wellbeing of that which is loved tends to be considered and protected. In his seminal essay "In Defense of the Land Ethic," the environmental philosopher J. Baird Callicott (1989, 154) makes a case for bio-empathy as the most significant moral position for establishing and defending the intrinsic value of nonhumans. Correspondingly, consider the positive values of empathy and love evident in "Black Oaks" in which the speaker confesses desirous "longing/for their thick bodies ruckled with lichen" (Oliver 1997, 5, ll. 7–10). Sharing in vegetal bodies through these kinds of intimacies, Oliver's poetry inflects empathic identification verging, at times, on botanical affection. For, as Oliver suggests, "[...] we must want to save our world. And in order to want to save the world, we must learn to love it—and in order to love it we must become familiar with it again" (1991, 34). Chapter 4 will further explore these themes through the notion of bioempathic emplacement in the work of British poet Elisabeth Bletsoe.

Bibliography

Adams, Fred. 2010. "Embodied Cognition." *Phenomenology and the Cognitive Sciences* 9 (4): 619–28.
Baluška, František. 2010. "Recent Surprising Similarities Between Plant Cells and Neurons." *Plant Signaling and Behavior* 2 (3): 87–89.
Baluška, František, and Stefano Mancuso. 2009. "Plants and Animals: Convergent Evolution in Action?" In *Plant-Environment Interactions: From Sensory Plant Biology to Active Plant Behavior*, edited by František Baluška, 285–301. Berlin: Springer-Verlag.
Baluška, František, Stefano Mancuso, Dieter Volkmann, and Peter Barlow. 2009. "The 'Root-Brain' Hypothesis of Charles and Francis Darwin: Revival After More Than 125 Years." *Plant Signaling and Behavior* 4 (12): 1121–27.
Barlow, Peter. 2008. "Reflections on 'Plant Neurobiology'." *Biosystems* 92 (2): 132–47.
Bennett, Bradley. 2007. "Doctrine of Signatures: An Explanation of Medicinal Plant Discovery or Dissemination of Knowledge." *Economic Botany* 61 (3): 246–55.
Bennett, Jane. 2010. *Vibrant Matter: A Political Ecology of Things*. Durham, NC: Duke University Press.
Bloch, Robert. 1952. "Goethe, Idealistic Morphology, and Science." *American Scientist* 40 (2): 313–22.
Böhme, Jakob. 1651. *Signatura Rerum: Or the Signature of All Things*. London: John Macock and Gyles Calvert.
Bonds, Diane. 1992. "The Language of Nature in the Poetry of Mary Oliver." *Women's Studies* 21 (1): 1–15.
Bryson, J. Scott. 2005. *The West Side of Any Mountain: Place, Space, and Ecopoetry*. Iowa City: University of Iowa Press.
Burton-Christie, Douglas. 1996. "Nature, Spirit, and Imagination in the Poetry of Mary Oliver." *Cross Currents* 46 (1): 77–87.
Cabej, Nelson. 2013. *Building the Most Complex Structure on Earth: An Epigenetic Narrative of Development and Evolution of Animals*. London: Elsevier.
Callicott, J. Baird. 1989. *In Defense of the Land Ethic: Essays in Environmental Philosophy*. Albany: State University of New York Press.
———. 1998. "'Back Together Again' Again." *Environmental Values* 7 (4): 461–75.
Campbell, Douglas Houghton. 1911. "A Sketch of the History of Plant Morphology in America." *The Plant World* 14 (5): 105–10.
Cataldi, Suzanne, and William Hamrick. 2007. "Introduction." In *Merleau-Ponty and Environmental Philosophy: Dwelling on the Landscapes of Thought*, edited by Suzanne Cataldi and William Hamrick, 1–15. Albany: State University of New York Press.
Chamovitz, Daniel. 2012. *What a Plant Knows: A Field Guide to the Senses*. Brunswick, Australia: Scribe Publications.
Christensen, Laird. 2002. "The Pragmatic Mysticism of Mary Oliver." In *Ecopoetry: A Critical Introduction*, edited by J. Scott Bryson, 135–52. Salt Lake City: University of Utah Press.

Coles, William. 1657. *The Art of Simpling: An Introduction to the Knowledge and Gathering of Plants*. London: J.G. for Nath.
Csordas, Thomas. 2008. "Intersubjectivity and Intercorporeality." *Subjectivity* 22 (1): 110–21.
Darwin, Charles, and Francis Darwin. 2016. *The Works of Charles Darwin: The Power of Movement in Plants*. Edited by Paul Barrett and R.B. Freeman. London: Routledge.
Darwin, Erasmus. 1800. *Phytologia: Or the Philosophy of Agriculture and Gardening*. Dublin: P. Byrne.
Davis, Todd. 2009. "The Earth as God's Body: Incarnation as Communion in the Poetry of Mary Oliver." *Christianity and Literature* 58 (4): 605–24.
Davis, Todd, and Kenneth Womack. 2006. *Postmodern Humanism in Contemporary Literature and Culture: Reconciling the Void*. Houndmills, UK: Palgrave Macmillan.
De Chadarevian, Soraya. 1996. "Laboratory Science Versus Country-House Experiments: The Controversy Between Julius Sachs and Charles Darwin." *The British Journal for the History of Science* 29 (1): 17–41.
Dillard, M.M. 1930. "Ethylene: The New General Anesthetic." *Journal of the National Medical Association* 22 (1): 10–11.
Dioscorides. 2000. *De Materia Medica*. Translated by Tess Anne Osbaldeston. Johannesburg: Ibidis Press.
Egerton, Frank. 2012. "History of Ecological Sciences, Part 43: Plant Physiology, 1800s." *The Bulletin of the Ecological Society of America* 93 (3): 197–219.
Eggleston, Edward. 1900. *The Transit of Civilization from England to America in the Seventeenth Century*. Boston, MA: Beacon Press.
Elder, John. 1996. *Imagining the Earth: Poetry and the Vision of Nature*. Athens: University of Georgia Press.
Garner, Dwight. 2007. "Sunday Book Review: Inside the List." *The New York Times*. Accessed 22 May 2017. www.nytimes.com/2007/02/18/books/review/18tbr.html?ref=paul_auster&_r=0
Goethe, Johann Wolfgang von. 2009. *The Metamorphosis of Plants*. Cambridge, MA: The MIT Press.
Graham, Vicki. 1994. "'Into the Body of Another': Mary Oliver and the Poetics of Becoming Other." *Papers on Language and Literature* 30 (4): 352–72.
Haraway, Donna. 2008. *When Species Meet*. Minneapolis: University of Minnesota Press.
Harde, Roxanne. 2002. "Mary Oliver (1935–)." In *Contemporary American Women Poets: An A-to-Z Guide*, edited by Catherine Cucinella, 263–67. Westport, CT: Greenwood Press.
Harvey, R.B. 1929. "Julius von Sachs." *Plant Physiology* 4 (1): 154–57.
Hayles, N. Katherine. 2008. *How We Became Posthuman: Virtual Bodies in Cybernetics, Literature, and Informatics*. Chicago: University of Chicago Press.
Herz, Rachel, James Eliassen, Sophia Beland, and Timothy Souza. 2004. "Neuroimaging Evidence for the Emotional Potency of Odor-Evoked Memory." *Neuropsychologia* 42 (3): 371–78. doi:10.1016/j.neuropsychologia.2003.08.009
Jütte, Robert. 2005. *A History of the Senses: From Antiquity to Cyberspace*. Translated by James Lynn. Cambridge, UK: Polity Press.

Kaplan, Donald. 2001. "The Science of Plant Morphology: Definition, History, and Role in Modern Biology." *The American Journal of Botany* 88 (10): 1711–41.

Karban, Richard. 2015. *Plant Sensing and Communication*. Chicago: University of Chicago Press.

Kimmerer, Robin Wall. 2003. *Gathering Moss: A Natural and Cultural History of Mosses*. Corvallis: Oregon State University Press.

Lovejoy, Arthur. 2010. *The Great Chain of Being: A Study of the History of an Idea*. New Brusnwick, NJ: Transaction Publishers.

MacLean, Paul. 1990. *The Triune Brain in Evolution: Role in Paleocerebral Functions*. New York: Plenum Press.

Malamud, Randy. 2003. *Poetic Animals and Animal Souls*. New York: Palgrave Macmillan.

Mancuso, Stefano, and Alessandra Viola. 2015. *Brilliant Green: The Surprising History and Science of Plant Intelligence*. Translated by Joan Benham. Washington, DC: Island Press.

Mann, Thomas. 2004. *God of Dirt: Mary Oliver and the Other Book of God*. Lanham, MD: Cowley Publications.

McNew, Janet. 1989. "Mary Oliver and the Tradition of Romantic Nature Poetry." *Contemporary Literature* 30 (1): 59–77.

Mescher, Mark, and Consuelo De Moraes. 2015. "Role of Plant Sensory Perception in Plant-Animal Interactions." *Journal of Experimental Botany* 66 (2): 425–33.

Meyerowitz, Elliot. 2002. "Plants Compared to Animals: The Broadest Comparative Study of Development." *Science* 295 (555): 1482–85.

Moll, J.W. 1934. *Phytography as a Fine Art*. Leiden: Brill.

Morris, Saundra. 2010. "Twentieth-Century American Poetry." In *The Oxford Handbook of Transcendentalism*, edited by Joel Myerson, Sandra Harbert Petrulionis and Laura Dassow Walls, 671–81. New York: Oxford University Press.

Oliver, Mary. 1965. *No Voyage and Other Poems*. Boston, MA: Houghton Mifflin.

———. 1972. *The River Styx, Ohio, and Other Poems*. New York: Harcourt Brace Jovanovich.

———. 1979. *Twelve Moons*. New York: Little, Brown and Company.

———. 1982. "Tasting the Wild Grapes." *Western Humanities Review* 36 (3): 263.

———. 1983. *American Primitive*. New York: Little, Brown and Company.

———. 1986. *Dream Work*. New York: Atlantic Monthly Press.

———. 1991. "Among Wind and Time." *Sierra* 76 (6): 33–34.

———. 1992. *New and Selected Poems*. Boston, MA: Beacon Press.

———. 1994. *White Pine: Poems and Prose Poems*. San Diego, CA: Harcourt Brace.

———. 1997. *West Wind: Poems and Prose Poems*. Boston, MA: Houghton Mifflin Company.

———. 2003. "Trout Lilies." *Southern Review* 39 (1): 87–88.

———. 2005. "Landscape." *Emerging Infectious Diseases* 11 (7): 1103.

———. 2006. *Blue Iris: Poems and Essays*. Boston, MA: Beacon Press.

———. 2011. "Maria Shriver Interviews the Famously Private Poet Mary Oliver." Accessed 22 May 2017. www.oprah.com/entertainment/maria-shriver-interviews-poet-mary-oliver
Paul, Sherman. 1992. *For Love of the World: Essays on Nature Writers*. Iowa City: University of Iowa Press.
Pearce, J.M.S. 2008. "The Doctrine of Signatures." *European Neurology* 60 (1): 51–52.
Pliny. 1949. *Natural History*. Translated by H. Rackham, W.H.S. Jones and D.E. Eichholz. Cambridge, MA: Harvard University Press.
Pollan, Michael. 2015. "Foreword." In *Brilliant Green: The Surprising History and Science of Plant Intelligence*, edited by Stefano Mancuso and Alessandra Viola, xi–xiii. Washington DC: Island Press.
Prenderville, Jack, Áine Kelly, and Eric Downer. 2015. "The Role of Cannabinoids in Adult Neurogenesis." *British Journal of Pharmacology* 172 (16): 3950–63. doi:10.1111/bph.13186
Sachs, Julius Von. 1887. *Lectures on the Physiology of Plants*. Translated by H. Marshall Ward. Oxford: Oxford University Press.
Serres, Michel. 2008. *The Five Senses: A Philosophy of Mingled Bodies*. London: Continuum.
Seymour, Roger, and Amy Blaylock. 1999. "Switching Off the Heater: Influence of Ambient Temperature on Thermoregulation by Eastern Skunk Cabbage *Symplocarpus foetidus*." *Journal of Experimental Botany* 50 (338): 1525–32.
Simpson, Beryl Brintnall, and Molly Conner-Ogorzaly, eds. 2001. *Economic Botany: Plants in Our World*. 3rd ed. Boston, MA: McGraw-Hill.
Speed, Michael, Andy Fenton, Meriel Jones, Graeme Ruxton, and Michael Brockhurst. 2015. "Coevolution Can Explain Defensive Secondary Metabolite Diversity in Plants." *New Phytologist* 208: 1251–63. doi:10.1111/nph.13560
Tansley, A.G. 1947. "The Early History of Modern Plant Ecology in Britain." *Journal of Ecology* 35 (1/2): 130–37.
Thoreau, Henry David. 1882. *Walden*. Vol. 1. Boston, MA: Houghton, Mifflin and Company.
———. 1990. *The Essays of Henry David Thoreau*. Edited by Richard Dillman. Albany, NY: NCUP.
———. 1993. *Faith in a Seed: The Dispersion of Seeds and Other Late Natural History Writings*. Washington, DC: Island Press.
———. 2000. *Wild Fruits: Thoreau's Rediscovered Last Manuscript*. Edited by Bradley P. Dean. New York: W.W. Norton.
———. 2009. *The Journal of Henry David Thoreau, 1837–1861*. New York: New York Review of Books.
Tompkins, Peter, and Christopher Bird. 1973. *The Secret Life of Plants: A Fascinating Account of the Physical, Emotional, and Spiritual Relations Between Plants and Man*. New York: Harper and Row.
Trewavas, Anthony. 2002. "Plant Intelligence: Mindless Mastery." *Nature* 415 (6874): 841. doi:10.1038/415841a
———. 2014. *Plant Behaviour and Intelligence*. Oxford: Oxford University Press.

Ullyatt, Gisela. 2011. "'The Only Chance to Love This World': Buddhist Mindfulness in Mary Oliver's Poetry." *Journal of Literary Studies* 27 (2): 115–31.

Vereecken, N.J., and J.N. McNeil. 2010. "Cheaters and Liars: Chemical Mimicry at Its Finest." *Canadian Journal of Zoology* 88 (7): 725–52.

Weiss, Gail. 1999. *Body Images: Embodiment as Intercorporeality.* New York: Routledge.

Wohlleben, Peter. 2016. *The Hidden Life of Trees: What They Feel, How They Communicate—Discoveries from a Secret World.* Carlton, VIC: Black Inc.

4 It Healeth Inward Wounds

Bioempathic Emplacement and the Radical Vegetal Poetics of Elisabeth Bletsoe

> pin-drop pollenfall &
> dazzling cryptographs
> of ultra-violet
>
>   explode
>
> the pyriform
> leaving that trace
>   of digitoxin
>
> palebuff
>
>   micro-
>   crystalline
>
> —from "Foxglove (*Digitalis purpurea*), Beech Hanger, Longstone Hill," *Pharmacopœia* (Bletsoe 2010a, 106, ll. 11–20)

While selflessly supplying us with food, fiber, material, oxygen, and other essentials on a constant basis, plants also provide medicinal substances vital to human wellbeing. The diverse herbal traditions of the world—often theorized in terms of ethnobiology, ethnobotany, and ethnopharmacology—enunciate a common understanding of vegetal life as an inimitable source of psychological rejuvenation and physical healing (see, for example, Pardo-de-Santayana, Pieroni, and Puri 2010). Many readers already are aware, for instance, that the ubiquitous bathroom vanity drug, aspirin—known pharmaceutically as acetylsalicylic acid, or ASA—derives from the willow, a tree medicinally employed by the Assyrians as early as 4000 BCE for treating musculoskeletal pain and by the Sumerians approximately 500 years later as an antipyretic, or fever-reducing, agent (Mahdi 2010, 318). In the eighteenth century, Reverend Edward Stone traced the effects of willow on pain, fever, and inflammation to the compound salicylic acid and conducted the first clinical trial of willow bark, specifically to treat ague, or malarial fever (Hatfield 2004, 370; Mahdi 2010, 318). As a further example from the history of European herbalism, in 1868 the French pharmacist Claude-Adolphe Nativelle isolated the cardiac glycoside, digitalin, from the seeds of the poisonous foxglove plant (*Digitalis purpurea*) (Kidambi and Massad 2014, 165). A controversial medicine with variable efficacy in treating heart failure and other ailments, digitalin—also mentioned in the above epigraph from Elisabeth Bletsoe—is known for severe side effects, including oculotoxicity. Vincent van Gogh depicted foxglove in his later painting *The Portrait of Dr. Gachet*, dated 1890, leading some to hypothesize that the artist was treated for epilepsy with digitalin, causing xanthopsia—a color distortion favoring yellowish hues—and pronounced halos around points of light (Kidambi and Massad 2014, 165).

Despite the taxonomization of plants and the pervasive bioprospecting of natural medicines around the globe, species with curative potential continue to be identified, even beyond the rainforests of the Amazon and the biodiverse river basins of the Himalaya. Rather than involving the discovery of a new species, however, sometimes this process entails the reevaluation of plants in everyday life, leading to therapeutic possibilities emerging from new perspectives on familiar flora. As a case in point, the benefits of dog-rose (*Rosa canina*) as a medicine and food have typically been associated with its fruits—also known as hips, heps, or haws—whereas the leaves have been discarded as waste. Yet recently researchers have confirmed the antimicrobial potential of the leaf extract, notably in countering biofilm, or bacterial aggregates (Živković et al. 2015). What is more, the examination of historical texts has garnered interest as a method for identifying plant metabolites with pharmacological potential. The formulations recorded in three major herbals of the Anglo-Saxon period (499–1066 ACE)—the *Old English Herbarium* (circa. 950), *Bald's Leechbook* (or *Medicinale Anglicum*, c. 950–1000), and the *Lacnunga* (or *Remedies*, c. 1000 ACE)—could provide insights into the use of plant-derived compounds in responding to significant health conditions impacting societies today (Watkins et al. 2011). These three texts document botanical remedies for lung diseases, skin maladies, eye disorders, headaches, fevers, and other prevalent ailments of the time and of equal relevance today. Applied as household medicines and by community healers throughout history, ordinary garden plants, including yarrow (*Achillea millefolium*), horehound (*Marrubium vulgare*), and St. John's wort (*Hypericum perforatum*), have been shown in laboratory trials to contain a suite of anti-inflammatory, antiviral, antitumoral, hypotensive, purgative, and vermifugal constituents of high interest to modern pharmacognosists (Watkins et al. 2011, 1071–73).

As intimated by these examples, the extraction of compounds from diverse species of flora fulfills the ideal of herbal plants as reducible principally to their chemistries. As a hallmark of post-Renaissance medical evolution, reductive rationalism shifted scientific emphasis away from whole living specimens and toward the invisible (to the naked eye) yet isolatable phytochemicals enclosed within them (Hechtman 2012, 105).

Such a perspective on the vegetal world is inscribed in the discourse of the active ingredient—exemplified by digitalin but also figured in terms of secondary metabolites—as the appropriable quintessence of the medicinal plant (Harborne 1984). A consequence of phytochemical thinking, nevertheless, is the chemicalization of flora and the ensuing relegation of the vibrant energetic and bodily dimensions of plants to outmoded folklore or unquantifiable ideation. In terms of yielding viable medicines, the value of an extractive approach to secondary metabolites and other primary constituents is indisputable, as the histories of willow, St. John's wort, and other herbs demonstrate. What phytochemical rhetoric risks through its assertions is the peripheralization of the non- or pre-scientific histories of reciprocal exchange between people and plants in Europe, North America, Oceania, and elsewhere. The phytochemical bias expels alternate expressions of herbal knowledge to the hinterlands of the mainstream medical paradigm. An example of this marginalization is the doctrine of signatures, degraded as quaint herbal superstition (Bennett 2007; Pearce 2008) but, nevertheless, foregrounding the correspondences and connectivities between human bodies and medicinal flora (see Chapter 3 for a related discussion of the intercorporeality of Mary Oliver's botanical poetry).

The objectification of plants I am describing—which invariably leads to their construal as lesser-endowed with lives, rights, and privileges—also extends to the medical paradigms of today that, at the same time, utterly depend on denatured vegetal substances. Despite its predominance, the anatomization of botanical life into its chemical components is a comparatively recent development within Western herbalism and a distinctly scientific approach to acquiring plant-based knowledge. In comparison, in the floristically-rich Hippocratic and Galenic traditions of the second century CE, the principle of *holon* denoted the integration of the cosmos, human bodies, natural elements, and nonhuman beings (Pitman 2014, 28). Hippocratic philosophy linked the behavior of air—in the environment and the body—to cosmic air and, as a result, associated diseases with prevailing environmental, seasonal, and celestial conditions (Pitman 2014, 28). An empathic conception of the vegetal—which, I propose, is one characteristic of pre-Linnaean botanical knowledge systems—disrupts the presumption that humans merely act upon—taxonomize, pick, harvest, process, consume, transport, and trade—immobile and insentient plant matter. Through principles of reciprocation, co-enervation, and bioempathy, a dialogical ethos of vegetal life eschews the totalizing diminution of the botanical agent to its molecular constituents. This is indeed the broad historical and philosophical background to contemporary British writer Elisabeth Bletsoe's *Pharmacopœia*, a sequence of eleven poems originally published in 1999 as a chapbook by Odyssey Poets Press and reissued by Shearsman Books as the final section of *Pharmacopœia and Early Selected Works* (2010a). Bletsoe invokes the language of prescientific European herbal traditions rooted in bioempathic connections between human and vegetal beings. By poeticizing the legacies of herbal plants vis-à-vis their ecological, biogeographical, and cultural specificities, Bletsoe's poetry overcomes phytochemical reductionism and enables us to reimagine the therapeutic agency and healing potential of commonplace vegetal life—or what some call cosmopolitan plants or noxious weeds. Building on Harriet Tarlo's (2000, 2007, 2011, 2013) articulation of radical landscape poetry, I characterize Bletsoe's radical vegetal poetics in terms of resistance to the perilous scientific reduction and cultural backgrounding of the plant world.

The Radical Plant: Bletsoe's Experimental Vegetal Poetics

Even a cursory inspection of medical herbalism discloses the phytochemical rhetoric of plant compounds identified, extracted, processed, and administered through a suite of techniques. Representative of this specialized knowledge, which has become the prevailing view of medicinal plants, a recent issue of the *Journal of Herbal Medicine* contains discussion of boswellic acid (a molecule derived from the resin of the genus *Boswellia*), phenolic compounds of Davidson's plum (*Davidsonia pruriens*), and flavenoid extracts of *Dorema aucheri*, a species found in the mountains of Iran (Pendry 2016). Considering the reductive impulse of such an approach to the herbal realm, it would seem that the human ability to envision and engage healing plants—in their vibrant wholeness—has been largely overtaken by technical terminologies and narrowed by the logic of chemicalization. Elizabeth Bletsoe's poetics counterbalances phytochemical discourse not by rejecting or circumventing it, but by incorporating scientific and other technical language of medicinal flora into palimpsestic open-form verse referent to the curative traditions of vegetal life and the specific locales where herbal plants live. However, in lieu of the epistemology of reductionism Bletsoe's writing internalizes bioempathy as an integrative perspective on the agency of the medicinal plant in relation to human corporeality, health, and healing. Theorized in more detail in the next section of this chapter, bioempathy is not a distant yearning for identification with nonhuman lives, but, in contrast, denotes the deep-seated corporeal resonances that already exist between emplaced beings. From this point of view, human-plant entanglement is a persistent material negotiation enacted in the present rather than an inaccessible Romantic ideal attained at an undeterminable future juncture. Hence, bioempathy supplies a pivot point for considering the immediacy of vegetality in *Pharmacopœia* and, more specifically, for illuminating the poet's conception of the cosmopolitan medicinal plants (foxglove, stinging nettle, lady's bedstraw, and others) narrated in the sequence.

Born in 1960 and raised in Dorset in South West England, Elisabeth Bletsoe has trained as a homeopath and currently works as a curator at Sherborne Museum (Noel-Tod 2013). In its palpable eclecticism, her poetry flouts the categorizations of contemporary British literature, particularly those related to nature writing, ecopoetics, ecofeminism, L=A=N=G=U=A=G=E poetry, experimentalism, and the avant-garde. Nonetheless, according to Jeremy Noel-Tod (2013), Bletsoe's poetization of ancestral knowledge of nature through the splitting and compounding of words links her at least partly to "a tradition of radically eccentric British modernism" (56). Steve Spence (2010, para. 1) suggests that her writing stands astride New Age sensibilities and the urban, language-based experimentation associated with London and Cambridge. Harriet Tarlo (2011), moreover, characterizes her as a radical landscape poet whose innovations with form, diction, voice, and sound aim to give rise to intimate non-Romantic congruences between language, text, and environment. Still, other commentators further connect her verse to the revival of the shamanic figure in British poetry (Mortuza 2013, 27). Titled after a portmanteau denoting a protective spirit, her chapbook *The Regardians: A Book of Angels* (Bletsoe 1993) blends images of shamanic rituals and entities with wide-ranging historical allusions. An example from the collection is "The 'Oary Man," which summons the presence of a medieval shaman in lines of direct address: "I find your traces/over the park gates/in a frosted scrollwork of ivy" (Bletsoe 2010a, 69, ll. 17–19). Despite her reticence toward literary labeling, Bletsoe is nevertheless a mesmerizing performer of her own work and is known also for her collaborations with visual artists, as apparent in the origami microbook *Missal Birds* (Bletsoe and Hatch 2013) (see also Chapter 5 for a discussion of performance and cross-genre collaboration in Alice Oswald's work). An example of her enactment of the oral tradition, a reading of "Votives to St. Wite" makes use of dramatic pauses corresponding to the spatial breaks, gaps, deletions, interruptions, and insertions of the text itself. The spoken presentation of the poem thus renders the difficult and archaic terminology of the poem melodic through alliteration, elocution, modulation of reading speed, and other aural techniques.

In addition to *Pharmacopœia* and *The Regardians*, Bletsoe has published the collection *Landscape from a Dream* (2008), featuring the "Birds of the Sherborne Missal" sequence (47–58), as well as the earlier chapbook *Portraits of the Artist's Sister* (1994), loosely based on the female subjects of Edvard Munch's paintings, lithographs, letters, and journals. On the whole, Bletsoe's work has variously been described as an "anomaly," "healthily independent," and "one of the rare gems in modern British poetry" (Tim Allen qtd. in Bletsoe 2010a, back cover). To be sure, Bletsoe stands out among botanical poets for in-depth engagement with herbal traditions, contexts, ideas, and historical sources. Heterogeneous influences—from botany, ecology, geography, and history to homeopathy, psychology, folklore, and mythology—underlie a poetic praxis that sinuously tracks between pastoral and urban vegetal subjects and settings (Spence 2010, para. 1). Juxtaposing colloquial and specialized lexicons while hybridizing disparate materials, Bletsoe's method has been termed "incantatory organisation" (Spence 2010, para. 2)—a characterization that, fittingly or otherwise, positions her poetry in proximity to New Age spiritualities and shamanic traditions. Like Bletsoe, other writers in *Plants in Contemporary Poetry* bring the interstices between plants and place to the fore. Kinsella prominently does so in "Resurrection Plants at Nookaminnie Rock" (Chapter 8). Leveraging dimensions of science for lyrical effect, Murray (Chapter 2), Glück (Chapter 6), and Wright (Chapter 7) also disclose awareness of place and reveal conversance with ecological tenets. Unlike most vegetally-attentive writers, Bletsoe's botanical consciousness foregrounds the topographical specificities of plants and the long-standing European cultural traditions—especially those involving medicine, nutriment, and spirituality—of which they are a part.

In most examples of criticism, a standard description of Bletsoe is as a poet of place (for example, Alexander and Cooper 2013; Hooker 2011). It is true that much of her poetry is place-referent, demonstrated, for instance, by the exclusive focus on the South West sedimentary landscapes of Dorset in *Landscape from a Dream*. The eponymous lead poem of the collection is suffixed with "Purbeck coast from Swanage to Kimmeridge" (Bletsoe 2008, 16). Michael Peverett (2010) describes Bletsoe's consistent declarations of geographical situatedness as "topographic notes" (para. 1). In his review of the essay and poetry anthology by leading British nature writers, *Towards Re-Enchantment*, Jeremy Hooker (2011) makes a reference to the temporality of place that is central to "Votives to St. Wite" (Bletsoe 2010b). According to Hooker (2011), the long poem is a "verbal palimpsest" that is modernist in form and enacts "temporal duality" (para. 9). The poem materializes the phenomenon of place in the present tense of lyrical encounter but also through Bletsoe's invocation of the past people, practices, events, and objects that have shaped the *genius locus* of the present. Both the anthology and the poem lay emphasis on topographical re-enchantment—seeing place anew and learning to appreciate its multi-dimensionality—as a process invariably contingent on language. For Bletsoe, at least in her contribution to the anthology, re-enchantment centers on St. Wite, the saint of Whitchurch Canonicorum, and the south-west Dorset environs where the village is located. The result is "poetic embodiment, in which St. Wite's is 'wedded' to the place, an incarnate spirit present in the total ecology, natural and geological, and in language—words of her own time, and words of now" (Hooker 2011, para. 10). Neal Alexander and David Cooper allude to Bletsoe's enigmatic, boundary-eliding work in their study of space and place in post-war British poetry since

1945. In voicing environmental concerns, contemporary writers such as Bletsoe, Michael Longley (b. 1939), Kathleen Jamie (b. 1962), and others make explicit the implicit correlation between local and global conditions (Alexander and Cooper 2013, 7). While strongly attentive to place, Bletsoe is not provincial in her environmental imagination but, to the contrary, puts into textual practice what Ursula Heise (2008) terms "eco-cosmopolitanism," or "environmental world citizenship" (10).

Bletsoe responds to place as a wellspring of identity, stability, and attachment but also as a pattern of temporally-enacted relations through which nature and culture come into dialogue (Alexander and Cooper 2013, 7). Although literary critics underscore the essential function of place in Bletsoe's poetry, the relationship between plants, topos, and language remains principally unaddressed in their analyses. This lacuna comes as a surprise considering that each title of the eleven poems of *Pharmacopœia* conspicuously arranges the colloquial and taxonomic names of the plant subject side by side, immediately followed by the location of encounter with the species (Bletsoe 2010a, 101–11). Accordingly, the sequence begins with "Stinking Iris (*Iris foetidissima*) Kilve" (Bletsoe 2010a, 101), denoting in both appellations the distinctive plant fetor and its topos—the village in West Somerset, England, located within the Quantock Hills Area of Outstanding Natural Beauty. In the same way, *Pharmacopœia* concludes with "Tormentil (*Potentilla erecta*) Dartmoor" (Bletsoe 2010a, 111) in reference to the moorland region of southern Devon—one of the many locales where the poem's cosmopolitan vegetal protagonist profusely grows. Not only a poet of place, as most observers agree, Bletsoe is hence a poet of flora whose receptivity to botanical being courses through even her less obviously plant-occupied poems. Topographically located, after both the fictitious Egdon Heath of Thomas Hardy's *The Return of the Native* and the real-life Puddletown Forest recreation area of Dorchester, "Rainbarrows" from *Landscape from a Dream* enfolds allusions to the heathland ecosystems of the area but without the sustained botanical fixation of *Pharmacopœia*. For instance, in reference to the steep cliff walls and extensive marshlands of the Isle of Purbeck (located about 20 miles to the east of Puddletown) we learn, through haptic and sonic diction, of "the lazarus-rattle of dried heather/as the wind slitters off from the Purbecks" (Bletsoe 2007, unpaginated, ll. 6–7). Further along, the poet incorporates the obscure term "vell" (for a salted calf's stomach), configuring place in respect of the corporeal immediacy of encounter with landscape and the intensification of long-standing historical interconnections between nature and culture. Bletsoe thus points to "[…] the vell of heath where/splinters of history continually discharge/at the surface of the present" (2007, unpaginated, ll. 32–34).

Yet, to appreciate Bletsoe's vegetal poetics more completely, we should turn to Harriet Tarlo's characterization of her work as "radical landscape poetry" while, simultaneously, considering the function of the plant within the contemporary poetic orientation outlined by Tarlo. So far this chapter has suggested that *Pharmacopœia* and Bletsoe's other green-spirited poetry eschew the chemicalization of plants for a holistic view of botanical life suffused with ancestral connotations and actualized through "incantatory" synthesis of, among other things, interspecies (and inter-being) polyvocality, diverse historical insinuations, and specific geographical referents. Put another way, as Spence (2010, para. 4) fleetingly notes, Bletsoe narrativizes plants in *Pharmacopœia*, intertwining their natural and social histories through references to diverse herbal and nutritional values. Following Tarlo, what does it mean to consider Bletsoe a "radical botanical poet" (i.e., as one who spurns aestheticization and objectification for an agentic view of plants)? And precisely how does her poetry liberate vegetal life from narrative peripheralization and therein provide a lyrical counterweight to the abstract reduction of flora into chemical constituents, taxonomic signifiers, and overly generalized classifications, such as genus and species? In formulating the concept of radical landscape poetry, Tarlo (2011) observes that urban environments were regarded once as more apposite subject matter for experimental praxis. For Tarlo (2011, 8), however, "radical" refers not to an ecopolitical stance propagated by poets but to the exploration of, and experimentation with, formal poetic techniques—particularly regarding the spatial layout of the text, or the *mise-en-page*—addressing landscape, ecology, environmental subjects, and nonhuman beings. Tarlo (2011, 10–11) makes a crucial distinction between more polemically-driven ecopoetry, or ecopoetics, and radical landscape poetry in which only some work engages explicit environmental concerns. She (2011, 11) asserts that "ecopoet" and "landscape poet" are not transposable designations because the former traverses broader political spheres beyond local landscapes.

Thus associated with avant-garde, experimental, and Linguistically Innovative Poetry (LIP)—rather than ecopoetics per se—radical landscape poetry explores the imbrications between poet, environment, form, and diction (Tarlo 2000, 149). Whereas the pastoral tends to sentimentalize the countryside and its inhabitants, the radical mode seeks a more realistic—though not necessarily literal—representation of landscape, agriculture, rural economies, and the social and cultural issues of past and present (Tarlo 2011, 11). The genre, as articulated by Tarlo, further acknowledges that, rather than a phenomenon with firm boundaries in time and space, nature *is* perpetual change. The poet writing in the radical mode encounters—and might embrace—an indeterminedness marked by persistent ambiguities, doubts, and paradoxes that upend any unified conception of environment, land, or landscape (Tarlo 2011, 12). Such a recognition of the natural world as an exceedingly mutable category prompts "a radical questioning of the idea that land can be translated into words, and of the idea that we can fully perceive or understand the 'nature' we find around us" (Tarlo 2000, 151). It is specifically Bletsoe's use of open-form—in which the page becomes a de-Romanticized, phenomenal space—that distinguishes her writing as radical landscape/botanical poetry (Tarlo 2011, 8; Widger 2016, 365). Open-form interrogates, and also experiments with, the congruences between poetic structures and environmental subjects (Tarlo 2013, 113). As the form of the poem (or recitation), space of the page (or reading), and dimensions of the rendered place (or plant) interdigitate, the materiality of the text (or performance) is vitalized. To this effect, Bletsoe juxtaposes prose blocks, irregular poetic stanzas, and disparate found texts, with each of these components occupying a discrete space on the page (Tarlo 2011, 9). Typographical variance, notably italicization and the liberal use of quotation marks, further enables heterogeneous materials and voices to reach a kind of dialogue across space and time.

In its "self-conscious attention to text" (Tarlo 1999, 104) and linguistic experimentation with herbal subjects, *Pharmacopœia* exemplifies the capacity of radical botanical writing to intervene in the rigid conceptualization of plants as mute, immobile, and insensate things. Bletsoe's writing tacitly brings into focus the cultural codes governing human-plant interactions, specifically those which render the vegetal as appropriable matter to be dispatched without the slightest afterthought. Although *Pharmacopœia* summons and celebrates the European history of herbal medicine-making, it does not do so uncritically. Instead of construing a prelapsarian botanical idyll centered on healing flora, the sequence underscores the limits of predominantly functional, utilitarian, or aesthetic relationships to vegetal life. Depicting the plant agent of each poem as a plurality in itself—as an accretion of its biological, topographical, nomenclatural, cultural, and mythological impetuses—Bletsoe broadens our view of plantness and problematizes the supposition that the telos of medicinal flora is to satisfy human ends (Tarlo 2011, 14). The palimpsesting of historical texts—ancient herbals, medieval illuminated manuscripts, and nineteenth-century fiction—is one method through which Bletsoe generates diverse imaginative access points into the worlds of cosmopolitan plants seamlessly living alongside and within human communities (Tarlo 2011, 14–15). The recycling of texts, images, and motifs, moreover, contributes an "ecological element" to Bletsoe's radical landscape/botanical praxis while problematizing the notion of poetic originality and the myth of poet-as-individual-genius (Tarlo 2011, 15). As with other comparably syncretic and transgressive writing about vegetal nature, *Pharmacopœia* appropriates the discourse of the dominant paradigm—in this case, botany and medicine—with sometimes unanticipated results for readers and listeners. In an interview with poet, editor, and publisher Tim Allen, Bletsoe elaborates on the transformation of staid scientific language into surprisingly arresting erotic diction:

I read *Pharmacopœia* to one group and a very straight, shy Irish woman was smiling behind her hand until the end when she burst out laughing and said 'Oh, that's really filthy!'—apparently starchy botanical terminology can be subverted into something quite erotic.
(qtd. in Spence 2010, para. 4)

Neither a disembodied nor cerebral work, despite its intellectual aims and occasionally obscure references, *Pharmacopœia* resonates with an eroticism—a magnetic attraction between bodies, a bioempathic intertwining of beings, things, and ideas—that parallels many human relationships to land, and especially to plants and flowers. In its ostensible concern with herbal flora, the sequence thus capitalizes on the traditional association of flowers with love. Consequently *Pharmacopœia* can be further understood as a work of *vegetal eros* (love as the essence of vegetal being and the foundation of ecological exchanges between plants and others) (Tarlo 2011, 15) and *phytophilia* (the human love of plants that inspires creative practices) (Marder and Vieira 2013).

Bioempathic Emplacement: Theorizing Cosmopolitan Herbs

Up to now, this chapter has distinguished *Pharmacopœia* as an intensely heterogeneous text with numerous possible interpretations; for instance, as a narrative of vegetal eros and phytophilia, as a work of radical vegetal poetics, as a palimpsest of diverse historical sources, as a register of nonhuman and other marginalized voices, as a lyrical response to reductive phytochemicalization, as a counterpoint to the logic of the active ingredient, and, more simply, as a poetry of place. Radical landscape/botanical poetry—indeed, one of many descriptions of Bletsoe's work—inflects an intimate sense of locality and concretizes the idea of place vis-à-vis actual living flora, plant science terminology, botanical appellations, naming practices, and the histories of humans using plants (Tarlo 2007, para. 15). Opposing the romanticization and sentimentalization of plants, and especially their sexual anatomies, this experimental poetic mode remains steadfastly critical of the "hierarchies, systems and epistemologies" that dictate botanical understandings (Tarlo 2007, para. 17). Rather than a narrative backdrop, aesthetic accessory, or sexualized object, vegetal nature, as a result, becomes more of a participant in the poetic process and, at best, a cherished, valued, and, even, loved agent in knowledge-formation. This section goes one step further by highlighting *bioempathy* as the essential principle underpinning the representation of cosmopolitan herbs in *Pharmacopœia* and elsewhere in Bletsoe's body of work. Theorizing medicinal flora through the interlinked optics of place and bioempathy (or what I will refer to as *bioempathic emplacement*), as Bletsoe does, provides a revitalizing alternative to the extractive chemical model of herbal therapeutics in widespread currency in both specialist science and popular culture. As an outlook on Bletsoe's vegetal praxis, bioempathic emplacement discloses herbal nature as a function of where plants grow and with whom—or with what—they relate. *Pharmacopœia* not only represents medicinal plants holistically and innovatively on the page but also signifies poetry's potential to preserve and, indeed, rejuvenate the ancient herbal traditions often banished to the periphery of modern phytochemical discourse.

In understanding bioempathic emplacement and its relevance to the medicinal flora of *Pharmacopœia*, a practical starting point is the emergence of empathy as a concept in nineteenth century German psychology of aesthetics. The word *empathy* derives from the Ancient Greek term *empatheia* for affection, passion, feeling, and emotion (Selles 2011, 9). Logician Hermann Lotze (1817–1881) and aesthetician Robert Vischer (1847–1933) were among the principal early formulators of the term *Einfühlung* for "in-feeling" (Selles 2011, 9). Lotze contributed to the foundations of *Einfühlung* through his three volume work, *Microcosmus*, published between 1856 and 1864. Although privileging human sentience, sensation, and aesthetic sensibility, Lotze nevertheless believed that nonhuman beings and inanimate objects can be the subjects of empathic feeling:

> Not is it only into the peculiar vital feelings of that which in Nature is near to us that we enter—into the joyous flight of the singing bird or the graceful fleetness of the gazelle [...] we not only expand into the slender proportions of the tree whose twigs are animated by the pleasure of graceful bending and waving; nay, even to the inanimate do we transfer these interpretative feelings, transforming through them the dead weights and supports of buildings into so many limbs of a living body whose inner tensions pass over into ourselves.
> (Lotze 1885, 585–86)

In 1873, Vischer expanded the existing concept *Mitfühlung* (sympathy) by introducing *Einfühlung*—in addition to *Anfühlung* (attentive feeling), *Nachfühlung* (responsive feeling), and *Zufühlung* (immediate feeling)—in his doctoral thesis, *On the Optical Sense of Form* (Debes 2015, 296). Building on Lotze's idea of empathic identification, Vischer characterized *Einfühlung* as the spontaneous and unconscious projection of the body "and with this also the soul—into the form of the object" (Vischer 1994, 92). Phenomenologist Theodor Lipps (1851–1914)—whose work influenced Freud—subsequently drew from Vischer's thought and further elucidated *Einfühlung* in his disquisition *Empathy and Aesthetic Pleasure* appearing in 1906. Lipps claimed that the perceiving subject imbues the perceived object with affection and, as a consequence, lays bare the emotional state of that which is apprehended (Nowak 2011,

305–6). The British psychologist Edward Titchener translated Lipps' conception of *Einfühlung* as "empathy" for "feeling into" and in contradistinction to "sympathy" for "feeling with." Through this interpretative process from Lotze to Titchener, the word *empathy* entered parlance beyond psychology and aesthetics.

This short sketch of the nineteenth-century history of empathy suggests that "feeling into" the natural world involves somatic identification necessarily based in human experience. One could argue that empathy is always bioempathic in that the former is mediated by the resonances, proximities, and entanglements between bodies of diverse kinds. It comes as no shock, then, that contemporary environmental philosophers have turned to empathy in postulating an ecologically equitable and stable future. For instance, eco-aesthetician Arnold Berleant (1993, 16), following Lipps, sees empathy as harmonizing human appreciation and the perceived nonhuman through physical attunement, bodily correspondence, and co-constructed consciousness. He further explains that "when empathy with a physical movement takes place, there is a consciousness that is wholly identical with the movement" (Berleant 1993, 16). Absent of either subject-object absorption or identity-eroding merger between beings, empathy offers a practicable ecological value based on "feeling oneself into the aesthetic object, an activity that engages not just our attention but also kinaesthetic sensations" (Berleant 1993, 17). In other words, empathy dissolves aesthetic distance and constrains objectification—indeed, two important implications for the vegetal world. The subject-object co-constitution at the heart of Berleant's idea of empathy is also evident in Thomas Nagel's landmark article "What Is It Like To Be a Bat?" (1974)—although it should be noted that neither Berleant nor Nagel invokes the term *bioempathy* per se. As a means to develop a critique of reductionism, Nagel takes on the problem of extrapolating from our lives to the interior worlds of others. Contending that such an extrapolation is defensible, Nagel concludes that a phenomenology of nonhuman experience is invariably and intrinsically grounded in human affective states. Feeling into what is apprehended reveals the insufficiencies of logos-driven demarcations and brings us face-to-face with the irreducible: "Reflection on what it is like to be a bat seems to lead us [...] to the conclusion that there are facts that do not consist in the truth of propositions expressible in a human language" (Nagel 1974, 441).

Contemporary environmental ethicists enlist the term *bioempathy* to specify the moral implications of empathy for nonhuman beings, particularly in relation to intrinsic value theory. In this regard, German theologian Albert Schweitzer (1875–1965) developed an early life-centered will-to-live model bridging reason and empathy, which has since been critiqued as anthropocentric (Martin 2007, 34). One of its principal critics, J. Baird Callicott, in his essay "In Defense of the Land Ethic"

(1989, 154), nevertheless, considers bioempathy to be an important moral resource for arguing for the intrinsic value of nonhumans. Callicott asserts that altruistic behavior and empathic identification are evolutionary mechanisms safeguarding interspecies cooperation. For Marder (2012), however, in acute contrast to Callicott and Nagel, plant life discloses the limits of empathy as a form of "totalizing vitalism" (260). The danger of empathy lies in its engrained and inexorable human-centeredness that risks eliding the alterity—the difference—of vegetal being: "When humans empathize with plants, they, thus, ultimately empathize with themselves, turning the object of empathy into a blank screen, onto which essentially human emotions are projected" (Marder 2012, 263). In his view, empathy assumes commonality and thus threatens to homogenize the ontological difference of vegetal life in "the substantial sameness of the empathizer and the empathized with, united by the fact that both are living beings" (Marder 2012, 260). Rather than a source of constructive ecological affect, vegetal empathy based in human self-recognition and projection—in *Einfühlung* as "feeling into"—presupposes that integration between plant "world-hood" and human being-in-the-world is viable in the first place (Marder 2012, 264). Empathy as "feeling into" potentizes narcissistic identification with plants, invariably leading back the egoistic self while elevating "exclusively human subjects, who rely on it to construct their ideal selves or to retrieve alienated features of their own existence" (Marder 2012, 271). Despite its commitment to non-anthropocentric vegetal ethics, Marder's critique frames empathy prevailingly through the plant-cathexis of the human who becomes conscious of vegetal suffering. His position, moreover, excludes the possibility of what could be called "feeling together" or "feeling into in response" in which the sensing plant projects, extends, identifies, and imbues in return. If plants are supremely sensitive lifeforms, as research indicates (Karban 2015; Trewavas 2014, 2016; Trewavas and Baluška 2011), then the possibility that they can reciprocate empathic gestures should at least remain a subject of debate.

Vegetal empathy is thus bioempathic feeling *into* and *with* plants that conversely entails openness to being affected by plant gestures in response. Rather than one-sided recognition of vegetal suffering or solipsistic identification with botanical communities in decline, a bioempathy of plants, I suggest, encompasses the persistent exchanges (somatic, sensory, energetic, emotional, conscious, unconscious, etc.) that confer benefits and losses to the plant and non-plant agents involved. To be sure, as the next section of this chapter elaborates, Bletsoe's *Pharmacopœia* and the ancient herbal systems summoned in the sequence disclose a bioempathy of plants that materializes *in* and *through* place. Given her work's distinctive constellation of various elements, *bioempathic emplacement*—or the enactment of bioempathy in close connection to topos—is essential to elucidating Bletsoe's radical vegetal poetics in the light of its prominent topographical and botanical anchorings. Most conspicuously, alongside the distinctive incorporation of nomenclature and locales in the poem titles, *Pharmacopœia* begins with the pronouncement, "we cannot emotionally separate a flower from the place or conditions we find it in" (Bletsoe 2010a, 99). Authored by British poet, critic, and naturalist Geoffrey Grigson (1905–1985), the epigraph vigorously resonates with Bletsoe's radical landscape/botanical mode and sets the tenor for the collection. Like Bletsoe, Grigson assayed disparate botanical sources in publications such as *A Herbal of All Sorts* (1959). His disquisitions on the natural history of the British countryside, for instance in *The Shell Country Alphabet* (2009, originally appearing in 1966), touch upon the magical, supernatural, folkloric, and medicinal features of local flora, including details gleaned from John Gerard's exhaustive classic of the early modern period, *Herball, or Generall Historie of Plantes*. Gerard delineated "the place," "the time," "the names," and other attributes of herbal species. His description of "the place" of wild parsley (*Apium* spp.), for instance, notes that the species "is found by pond sides in moist and dankish places, in ditches also having in them standing water, and oftentimes by old flocks of Alder trees" (Gerard 1597, 867). Writing during this period, Paracelsus (1493–1541) additionally believed that every place enfolds its own specific diseases and remedies: "There is no disease but hath his own proper and peculiar medicine and remedy: and every place furnisheth you with simples enough for its cure" (qtd. in Tobyn 2014, 92). In the classical era, preceding Gerard and Paracelsus, on the medicinal virtues of wild carrot (*Daucus carota*), the Roman historian and naturalist Pliny the Elder in *Historia Naturalis* remarked—in a correspondingly place-focused manner—that "the cultivated form has the same as the wild kind, though the latter is more powerful, especially when grown in stony places" (qtd. in Grieve 1971, 161).

In contrast to the commoditized medicinal substances in worldwide circulation—historically and contemporarily—via economic networks disassociated from place, herbal paradigms of the classical and early modern periods engaged the sites of cultivation, soil virtues, weather conditions, hydrological patterns, regional exigencies, energetic ebbs and flows, and other place-specific factors that potentize plant medicines (Pitman 2014). The medicos and healers of these periods understood the origin of diseases and the efficacy of herbal agents as upshots of the particularities of place. Rather than extractive reductionism founded on chemical makeup—an epistemology that became available on the heels of Baconian empiricism in the late sixteenth and early seventeenth centuries and the advent of the scientific revolution—such theories reveal the relevance of bioempathic emplacement to pre- and nonscientific plant-thinking. While my aim here is absolutely not to propound a revision of Western herbal medicine history and thus diminish its complex ecosocial, corporeal, energetic, and temporal dimensions, I do wish to posit bioempathic emplacement as a viable framework for approaching this history and, by extension, Bletsoe's *Pharmacopœia*. Indeed, place cultures the plant while the plant cultures place—dialogically and reciprocally (Gagliano 2017). For vegetal, human, and other life, emplacement is a function of embodied self-recognition in space but is also a mode accentuating the interstices between things, events, scales, and scapes. To be emplaced bioempathically is to project *into*, resonate *with*, and vibrate *in response to* other beings. Bioempathy therefore reveals that human manipulation of herbal plants is not reducible to asymmetrical acts of ascendancy over vegetal nature. While we affect the medicinal plant, so the plant impacts us in return. As we reach toward the herb, so it gestures back, even in its processed or so-called devitalized state. In projecting cognition and sensation outward from ourselves to exploit the plant, its intelligence perfuses us. It might be possible, then, to counter-conceptualize botanical substances in terms of vegetal gesture into the world. In this regard, secondary metabolites—substances generated by specific botanical groups but contributing directly neither to plant growth nor development (Pichersky and Gang 2000)—can be theorized as bioempathic traces through which vegetal and non-vegetal bodies engender contact, relation, and provocation.

Although a more satisfying fleshing out of these assertions is not achievable within the structure of the present discussion, my goal is nevertheless to re-emphasize the convergence of Bletsoe's work with topographically-centered, whole-plant, pre- and nonscientific herbal knowledge systems. Bioempathically emplaced medicinal personae lie in proximity to the poet-herbalist-folklorist herself gesturing to the plant—dissolving aesthetic detachment and upsetting the primacy of reductionism—as part of a contrapuntal interspecies praxis. Accordingly, *Pharmacopœia* reveals that place and plant also culture poet, while the converse is true. With its weight on the vegetal, my conception of emplacement extends—but also tests—the notion of botanical cosmopolitanism as "the emergence of new [plant-based] forms of culture that are no longer anchored in place" yet, hopefully, without abnegating or diminishing—as I fear Heise does—ancestral ties to place for "[plant-based] territories and systems that are understood to encompass the planet as a whole" (2008, 10). The vegetal beings of *Pharmacopœia* emblematize cosmopolitan flora as intimately tethered to place but concurrently able to flourish in diverse habitats distributed across vast geographical scales—and, in some cases, ubiquitously across the globe. Notwithstanding their medicinal and nutritive affordances, cosmopolitan botanical taxa can be denigrated as weeds—as unloved plants out of place yet paradoxically emplaced almost everywhere beside us (Mabey 2012). The "weed" as a cultural and biological category of plantness will be considered in Chapter 5 in relation to the poetry of Alice Oswald. For Bletsoe, however, the topographical orientation of *Pharmacopœia* is always inherently global; its plants are place-rooted cosmopolitans.

More Grateful and Aromatic: *Pharmacopœia* and Plant Being

The previous section proposed *bioempathic emplacement* as an optic for illuminating the gravitation of herbal nature toward human and other bodies—and vice versa—and for understanding the balance between the scales of exchange that take place among and between lifeforms. My position counters the narrow association of empathy with "feeling into" vegetal suffering—that is, as a cathexis of the plant subjugated by local, regional, and global impetuses, not limited to climate change, deforestation, biodiversity loss, illicit trade of endangered species, weed eradication campaigns, plant blindness, the fracturing of ethnobotanical heritage, and so forth. To the contrary, bioempathy points to the topographical intersubjectivities, intimacies, impulses, intentionalities, and exchanges, which beings enact—consciously and otherwise—between themselves on an ongoing basis. Rather than a rarified emotional projection, empathy as such is part and parcel of the vibrant fabric and foundation of inter-being. The idea of an eco-cosmopolitanism of plants also helps to disclose the bioempathic emplacement developed in Bletsoe's work vis-à-vis the multiscale resonances of medicinal flora. Syncretic and genre-blurring poetry, such as *Pharmacopœia*, is especially well-poised to embrace the dimensions of vegetal ontology peripheralized in other discourses, notably phytochemicalization. Despite his reserve concerning empathy as an ethical value, Marder (2012) nevertheless concedes that poetry is an amenable medium for empathizing with plants. Poetry enables the detection of certain aspects of vegetal life in ourselves, in lieu of the egoistic recognition of aspects of ourselves in vegetal life. As a consequence of "reversing the trajectory of narcissistic identification" (Marder 2012, 265), poetry can generate empathy—in its most ethical incarnation—and facilitate understanding of the vegetal registers *within us*.

Turning toward the radically empathic *Pharmacopœia*, we discover in the first poem, "Stinking Iris (*Iris foetidissima*) Kilve," the principal elements of the sequence. Bletsoe's approach integrates topographical references, common plant names, and taxonomic technicalities, along with tacit references to nineteenth-century literature, citations to texts from the history of botany, invocations of figures from Greek mythology, and insinuations of her own field praxis (Tarlo 2013, 116). Disparate allusions and sources—such as these and others still—render each poem a prism through which to apprehend a cosmopolitan vegetal subject. Native to the open woodlands of Western Europe and Northern Africa, the affectionately-dubbed stinking iris grows just as well in shaded, semi-shaded, and unshaded locations and tolerates relatively inhospitable environments, such as calcareous sea cliffs (Plants for a Future 2012). However, *A Global Compendium of Weeds* categorizes the stinking iris as a naturalized weed, "casual alien" and "garden thug" both outside and inside its original range (Randall 2012, 546). The plant is also known by the alternate colloquial appellations, fetid iris, stinking gladwin, and roast beef plant—all of which connote its putrid smell—but also by the mellifluous, though archaic, name *flower-de-luce*, an Anglicization of the French *fleur de lis* for "flower of the lily." Although "lis" means "lily," *fleur de lis* also has colloquially been used in referring to irises as well. At the same time, Bletsoe's usage of *flower-de-luce* in the fifth line implicates her work with the wider literary history of this floristic idiom propagated, for instance, in Henry Wadsworth Longfellow's pastoral poem "Flower-de-Luce" (1867) and its lyrical exaltation of an apparently less-malodorous but unspecified counterpart to *Iris foetidissima*: "Beautiful lily, dwelling by still rivers,/Or solitary mere,/Or where the sluggish meadow-brook delivers/Its waters to the weir!" (7, ll. 1–4).

The first stanza of "Stinking Iris" evokes—in a manner diffusely reminiscent of Longfellow's poetization of the lily—a cosmopolitan vegetal presence adapted to the threshold area between land and water. To this effect, Bletsoe (2010a) foregrounds the ecotonal dwelling place of the stinking gladwin in the opening lines, "sea-cliffs &/a green confluence of/ waters" (101, ll. 1–3). In particular, the ampersands here and elsewhere are redolent of notetaking in the field. Extending Tarlo's (2011) analysis, I suggest that one of the cornerstones of radical landscape/botanical poetry is unmediated contact with plants in their milieu of dwelling, frequently noted by the botanical poet working in the field and then transposed to the page as a poem emerges and evolves. Traces of the field praxis textually persist as ampersands and other shorthand notations, but also in allusions to the "fossil triturate" and "charred letters" of the calcareous Kilve environment (Bletsoe 2010a, 101, ll. 8–10). Diverting sharply from Longfellow's quixotic adulation, "Stinking Iris" disrupts the pastoral idyll of the Kilve coast through the occasionally painful sensation of encounter: "daggered leaves/of flower-de-luce/cut your smile/in slices of salt light" (Bletsoe 2010a, 101, ll. 4–7). Following the commentary of Hooker (2011), there is a two-fold rendering of place in "Stinking Iris." The poem's initial and middle sections depict place in terms of the immediacy of poetic encounter—"a country where you are"—as well as corporeal responsiveness to its botanical denizens evident in phrases, for instance, describing iris anatomy as "a delicate/recurve of tepals" (Bletsoe 2010a, 101, ll. 16–18). Place is additionally the coalescence of its historical elements and forces, as contrastingly emphasized in the poem's final three short stanzas. The summoning of the Neolithic Carnac stones of Brittany, the Elysian Fields of Greek mythology, and Iris as the messenger of Zeus and female counterpart to Hermes makes it possible for the poem to transcend its own temporal and topographical demarcations.

The cosmopolitan personae of *Pharmacopœia* are broadly distributed, not only geographically and across space, but also historically and across cultures. Further along, the radical poetics of "Stinking Iris" unfold in the poem's final, inter-textual reference: "'growing more grateful & aromatic/as it dries'" (Bletsoe 2010a, 101, ll. 24–25). The source of the quoted material is *Botanicum Officinale* (1722) written by the Scottish gardener and apothecarist Joseph Miller who served as Demonstrator of Botany and Horti Praefectus (Director) of Chelsea Physic Garden between 1740 and 1748. Miller, in turn, drew from Samuel Dale's *Pharmacologia* (1693), according to physician-botanist Richard Pulteney who observed later in the eighteenth century that "the Summary of the Virtues [of *Botanicum Officinale*] is, in most instances, a translation from the *Pharmacologia* of Dale" (1790, 103). To be sure, the subtitular descriptions "a compendious herbal" and "an account of all such plants as are now used in the practice of physick, with their descriptions and virtues" distinguish Miller's *Botanicum Officinale* as a pre-Linnaean apothecarists' reference providing succinct profiles of herbs, including growing conditions and medicinal attributes. Surprisingly for the botanically-curious reader, however, the phrase extracted by Bletsoe refers not to an iris—foul-smelling or otherwise—but to sweet flag, or calamus (*Acorus* spp.). Although resembling an iris in habit, calamus bears leaves that "are much longer and narrower than the *Iris*, or Flower de luce" (Miller 1722, 12). But like the iris, sweet flag "has a strong Smell, not so pleasant, while green" and also occupies "watery Places in *England* [italics in original]" (Miller 1722, 13).

My tracing of medicinal plant knowledge dispersal from seventeenth-century herbals to contemporary botanical poetry is not intended as a means to expose technical fault lines within Bletsoe's palimpsesting. Rather, the distinction between iris and calamus in the source text *Botanicum Officinale* and Bletsoe's subsequent appropriation of an *Acorus* species descriptor for a poem expressly about *Iris foetidissima* affirm both the pre-Linnaean paradigms of flora and the experimental poetic modes within which she works. Referring to calamus, which, as Miller observed, is sweet-scented when dry and, hence, known alternately as sweet flag, the English *flag* appeared in the late fourteenth century—most likely from the Germanic *flæg* for "yellow iris"—at which time the term referred to flora inhabiting moist places, or generally any reedy or rush-like plant, including irises (Harper 2017). For that reason, the Reverend James Stormonth's *Etymological and Pronouncing Dictionary* (1876) describes iris as "the fleur-de-lis or *flag* flower [emphasis added]" (297). In the far-reaching European history of vernacular naming prior to the genus-species convention, fewer delineations were drawn between certain plants, or the distinctions that existed were based on criteria varying from place to place, culture to culture, and language to language (Allen and Hatfield 2004, 36). As Foucault argued in *The Order of Things* (2005), plant naming before binomialism made use of the resemblances, virtues, legends, stories, heraldry, medicaments, foodstuffs, ancient beliefs, and travelers' observations linked to a plant as part of "the whole semantic network that connected it to the world" (140). Viewing the situation as pandemonium, Linnaeus sought to standardize biological naming in *Systema Naturae*, first published in 1735, through a Latinate nomenclature that could be applied globally (Jarvis 2007). In relation to this historical context, it should appear tenable that some folk botanical taxonomies categorize iris and calamus together as *flags*.

Through the placement of the *Botanicum Officinale* extract in the poem's final lines, Bletsoe challenges the formal distinction between stinking iris (*Iris foetidissima*) and sweet flag (*Calamus* spp.), tacitly emphasizing their analogous habits, habitats, effusions, and phenomenological shifts (in this case, from fetid to aromatic). She accordingly calls attention to the diverse systems of folk taxonomy that, in their biocultural anchorings, countered—and still counter—binomial totalization in favor of folk distinctions. In keeping with the radical landscape mode, Bletsoe's vegetal poetry also moves sinuously between nearness and distance—between concreteness and abstraction—granting entrée to vegetal nature while, at other times, barring the reader's access to it (Tarlo 2011, 14). To be sure, the movement between revealing and concealing is a principal feature of "Stinking Iris." The title notably appeals to olfaction (a corporeal sense involving propinquity between subjects), but the poem itself oscillates between multiscalar perspectives—from the sea cliffs to the fossils underfoot, from the Kilve countryside to the Elysian Fields—before returning full circle to smell in the final found-text from Miller. As an experimental genre, radical landscape poetry exhibits "self-conscious attention to text," foregrounding silence and space while exploiting the gaps, excisions, and asymmetries of the page (Tarlo 1999, 104). Changes in diction, form, and typography enable "Stinking Iris" to approximate the actual experience of *Iris foetidissima* in its coastal milieu. The poem structures language in proportion to topos and flora while tracking iris poiesis across temporal changes in its olfactory (e.g., roots stinking), tactile (leaves cutting), visual (waters converging), and affective (stones desiring) dimensions.

Upending taxonomic determinism, Bletsoe's citation of *Botanicum Officinale* also signifies the transformation of the olfactory register of the iris/calamus as it dries or decomposes over time. Rather than static in their perceived immobility and situatedness, plants are exceedingly mutable and cosmopolitan lifeforms (Vieira, Gagliano, and Ryan 2016). As Bletsoe shows us through the radical plant poetics of *Pharmacopœia*, human sensorality also transforms in response to place and flora. Bioempathic emplacement is thus capacious enough to account for the diverse exchanges between human presence, vegetal nature, and phenomenal place. We come into relation through feeling *into* and *with* other beings—including through our noses and on our skin—while opening ourselves, in return, to the effects of those who are affected by us. This chapter has suggested that one form of bioempathic emplacement is the synergism between human beings and medicinal flora that *take place*. More broadly, Bletsoe's poem helps reclaim the marginalized tradition of *Iris foetidissima*—and, for that matter, other plants depicted in the sequence—as a medicinal agent once common in European herbal practice. Widely used during the Anglo-Saxon period, the rhizomes of stinking iris were ingested as purgatives—or cathartic—substances until the early nineteenth century (Allen and Hatfield 2004, 332). Gerard (1597) recorded stinking iris, or spurgewort, preparations as "effectual against the cough; they easily digest and consume the gross humors [...]; they purge colour and tough phlegm; they procure sleep, and help gripings within the belly" (60). He also noted the prevalent usage of stinking iris among the residents of Somerset, located about 16 miles inland from Kilve, the site of Bletsoe's poem: "Hereof the country people of Somersetshire have good experience [with] the decoction of this Root. Others do take the infusion thereof in ale or such like, wherewith they purge themselves, and that unto very good purpose and effect" (Gerard 1597, 60). In his *Theatrum Botanicum* (or *Theatre of Plants*, published in 1640), the apothecarist-botanist John Parkinson noted the increasing ubiquity of the herb across England (Hatfield 2004, 89; Allen and Hatfield 2004, 332). However, with the advent of pharmaceutical alternatives and in the light of its toxic side effects—for instance, Grieve (1971, 434) reported gastro-enteritis, cardiac failure, blood vessel dilation, and pulmonary inflammation—stinking iris fell out of favor as a medicine.

Bioempathic emplacement makes possible an understanding of medicinal plants in terms of their complex relations. The principle, moreover, supplies a counterforce to the essentialization of herbal plants, such as stinking iris, into chemical isolates. As a second example from *Pharmacopœia*, let us briefly look at the final poem of the sequence, "Tormentil (*Potentilla erecta*) Dartmoor," which disperses syntactic elements more prominently across the page than "Stinking Iris" (Widger 2016, 378). "Tormentil" discloses the imbrications between the *mise-en-page* of a poem, the evocation of temporal movement, and the textures of the places about which the radical landscape/botanical poet writes (Tarlo 2011, 9; Widger 2016, 378). The compounding of words—consider the kenning "riverpebble" (Bletsoe 2010a, 111, l. 1)—is an *adéquation* of the flow of landscape and the activity of language:

>   riverpebble
>
> one side sharp
> enough to test the

reality of all this   & the body laid to sweat
                                  with Venice treacle

          astringent
      the savage crown of tors, sore
      lipped.
                                     (Bletsoe 2010a, 111, ll. 1–8)

Known as theriac, Venice (or Venetian) treacle was a fermented medicament consisting of more than 50 ingredients, depending on the recipe, but often including opium, cinnamon, fungi, gum arabic, viper flesh, and the roots of creeping cinquefoil (*Potentilla reptans*), a relative of tormentil (Griffin 2004). Needing to mature for 6 months to 1 year and regarded as a panacea if prepared correctly, theriac ranks as one of the most expensive concoctions in Western herbal history. In his *Complete Herbal*, first published in 1653, the physician Nicholas Culpeper advised using tormentil—also known as septfoil, thormantle, or Thor's mantle—in conjunction with theriac to balance the humors: "The juice of the herb and root, or the decoction thereof, taken with some Venice treacle, and the person laid to sweat, expels any venom or poison" (Culpeper 2006, 184). It is obvious that Bletsoe's phrase "the body laid to sweat" is meant to evoke Culpeper's description. The poem's concluding lines—"its vertue to part/all poison from the heart [no quotation marks in the original]" (Bletsoe 2010a, 111, ll. 16–17)—further accentuate the poetic quality of Culpeper's writing in *Complete Herbal*. Read in relation to the topographical specificity of the title, the final two lines of "Tormentil" express a prevailing sense of bioempathic emplacement. While acting therapeutically on the human body, tormentil, like so many other cosmopolitan medicinals, is able to propagate itself—with the aid of humans—ubiquitously across the British Isles.

Conclusion: Embracing Medicinal Futures

Narrativizing medicinal flora in relation to specific locales within the English countryside, *Pharmacopœia* stands out among contemporary British, American, and Australian examples of botanical poetry. The eclectic work uniquely traverses the heterogeneous exchanges that co-vitalize herbal and human natures. Bletsoe sees medicinal plants as relational agents whose historical voices reverberate in the present. While Tarlo theorizes radical landscape poetry as more focused on linguistic and structural experimentation than ecological politics and botanical activism, Bletsoe's poetry can be read otherwise. There is a dark pastoralism to her vegetal poetics that conveys a tacit sense of ecological degradation and calls attention to the disintegration of land-based knowledge and practices in Britain and elsewhere (Widger 2016, 380) (see Chapter 8 on John Kinsella's radical pastoralism). Poems such as "Stinking Iris," "Tormentil," and others intervene in the disruption of traditional botanical heritage and respond to the modern renunciation of cosmopolitan medicinals as unwanted and unloved plants-out-of-place. Radical vegetal poetry hence underscores the vital function of literary representation in attuning readers—and listeners—to botanical life and lives. In particular, *Pharmacopœia* facilitates perception, contemplation, and engagement with the vegetal world on its own terms and in its places of inhabitation, hence reversing the peripheralization of plants in literary discourse, everyday rhetoric, and popular consciousness (see Chapter 1 for background). Moving past the chemicalization of herbal nature, we might then begin to appreciate plants as active, responsive, embodied, and emplaced participants in the world alongside us (Widger 2016, 385). Bletsoe's radically empathic poetry nurtures this transformation of awareness by re-imagining commonplace healing species but without completely disavowing the language of plant science and technical herbalism, for instance, as denoted in the term *Venice treacle*. In this respect, Tarlo (2007) remarks that innovation and imagination—engendered in a radical landscape/botanical mode—"might be one of our ways out of ideological and ecological stalemates and stagnation" (para. 5).

I am inclined to agree with Tarlo that re-imagining plants is a crucial first step on the way toward devising means of empathically, reciprocally, and sustainably coinhabiting places with them. As I have thus far argued in *Plants in Contemporary Poetry*, however, an essential aspect of the human re-imagining of vegetal life—especially in our current epoch of exponentially accelerating botanical change and loss—is the obverse recognition that plants are already endowed with the intentionality, desires, affective states, future-directedness, and empathic resources required for them, in turn, to imagine a future with us and other non-vegetal beings. In deconstructing the cultural codes surrounding vegetality and human-plant relations—particularly with regard to healing flora—Bletsoe's botanical poetry marks a shift away from the reductive, utilitarian, and hierarchical approaches to plants that block the process of re-imagining from gaining momentum and critical mass in the first place. While this chapter theorized bioempathy as a generalized phenomenon of energetic exchange between beings in a place, it has not been my intention to do away with the significance of bioempathy as a value based in identification with other-than-human suffering. The future of many healing plants in Europe and across the world is uncertain. The authors of the *European Red List of Medicinal Plants* (Allen et al. 2014), for instance, assessed the extinction risk of 400 vascular plants native to the European region. Defining the term *medicinal plant* broadly to comprise those used in teas, spices, foods, nutritional supplements, and cosmetics, the report concludes that 31% of the plants assessed are declining while the status of 25% is unknown. Interestingly, whereas some plant populations are contracting, the collection and trade of medicinal species appear to be increasing on the whole (Allen et al.

2014, 32). In concluding this chapter on a global note, it is also important to acknowledge that in other parts of the world—such as Amazonia—botanical medicines harvested locally constitute the primary form of health care because pharmaceuticals are either not available or too expensive (Shanley and Luz 2003). Important to human wellbeing through history, herbal substances thus remain so for many cultures of the present. Bletsoe's *Pharmacopœia* reminds us of this global context and offers a poetic re-imagining of medicinal plant futures. In Chapter 5, Alice Oswald extends some of Bletsoe's themes through the practice of botanical humor.

Bibliography

Alexander, Neal, and David Cooper. 2013. "Introduction: Poetry and Geography." In *Poetry and Geography: Space and Place in Post-war Poetry*, edited by Neal Alexander and David Cooper, 1–18. Liverpool: Liverpool University Press.

Allen, David, Melanie Bilz, Danna J. Leaman, Rebecca M. Miller, Anastasiya Timoshyna, and Jemma Window. 2014. *European Red List of Medicinal Plants*. Luxembourg: Publications Office of the European Union.

Allen, David, and Gabrielle Hatfield. 2004. *Medicinal Plants in Folk Tradition: An Ethnobotany of Britain and Ireland*. Portland, OR: Timber Press.

Bennett, Bradley. 2007. "Doctrine of Signatures: An Explanation of Medicinal Plant Discovery or Dissemination of Knowledge." *Economic Botany* 61 (3): 246–55.

Berleant, Arnold. 1993. *Art and Engagement*. Philadelphia, PA: Temple University Press.

Bletsoe, Elisabeth. 1993. *The Regardians*. Nether Stowe, UK: Odyssey Poets Press.

———. 1994. *Portraits of the Artist's Sister*. Nether Stowe, UK: Odyssey Poets Press.

———. 2007. "Rainbarrows." *Poetry International*. Accessed 22 May 2017. www.poetryinternationalweb.net/pi/site/poem/item/9176

———. 2008. *Landscape from a Dream*. Exeter, UK: Shearsman Books.

———. 2010a. *Pharmacopoeia and Early Selected Works*. Exeter: Shearsman Books.

———. 2010b. "Votives to St. Witc." In *Towards Re-Enchantment: Place and Its Meanings*, edited by Gareth Evans and Di Robson. London: Artevents.

Bletsoe, Elisabeth, and Frances Hatch. 2013. *LPBmicros: Missal Birds*. Rhydyfelin, UK: The Literary Pocket Book.

Callicott, J. Baird. 1989. *In Defense of the Land Ethic: Essays in Environmental Philosophy*. Albany: State University of New York Press.

Culpeper, Nicholas. 2006. *Complete Herbal and English Physician*. Bedford, MA: Applewood Books.

Dale, Samuel. 1693. *Pharmacologia*. London: Sam Smith and Benjamin Walford.

Debes, Remy. 2015. "From *Einfühlung* to Empathy: Sympathy in Early Phenomenology and Psychology." In *Sympathy: A History*, edited by Eric Schliesser, 286–322. Oxford, UK: Oxford University Press.

Foucault, Michel. 2005. *The Order of Things: An Archaeology of the Human Sciences*. London: Taylor and Francis.

Gagliano, Monica. 2017. "Breaking the Silence: Green Mudras and the Faculty of Language in Plants." In *The Language of Plants: Science, Philosophy, Literature*, edited by Monica Gagliano, John Ryan and Patrícia Vieira, 84–100. Minneapolis: University of Minnesota Press.

Gerard, John. 1597. *Herball, or Generall Historie of Plantes*. London: John Norton.

Grieve, Margaret. 1971. *A Modern Herbal*. Vol. 1. Mineola, NY: Dover Publications.

Griffin, J.P. 2004. "Venetian Treacle and the Foundation of Medicines Regulation." *British Journal of Clinical Pharmacology* 58 (3): 317–25.

Grigson, Geoffrey. 1959. *A Herbal of All Sorts*. London: Phoenix House.

———. 2009. *The Shell Country Alphabet: The Classic Guide to the British Countryside*. London: Penguin.

Harborne, Jeffrey Barry, ed. 1984. *Phytochemical Methods: A Guide to Modern Techniques of Plant Analysis*. London: Chapman and Hall.

Harper, Douglas. 2017. "Flag." *Online Etymology Dictionary*. Accessed 22 May 2017. www.etymonline.com/index.php?term=flag

Hatfield, Gabrielle. 2004. *Encyclopedia of Folk Medicine: Old World and New World Traditions*. Santa Barbara, CA: ABC-CLIO.

Hechtman, Leah. 2012. *Clinical Naturopathic Medicine*. Sydney: Churchill Livingstone.

Heise, Ursula. 2008. *Sense of Place and Sense of Planet: The Environmental Imagination of the Global*. New York: Oxford University Press.

Hooker, Jeremy. 2011. "Spirit of the Place." *Resurgence* 267. Accessed 22 May 2017. www.resurgence.org/magazine/article3437-spirit-of-the-place.html

Jarvis, Charlie. 2007. *Order Out of Chaos: Linnaean Plant Names and Their Types*. London: Linnean Society.

Karban, Richard. 2015. *Plant Sensing and Communication*. Chicago: University of Chicago Press.

Kidambi, Sumanth, and Malek Massad. 2014. "On van Gogh and the Foxglove Plant." *Cardiology* 127 (3): 164–66.

Longfellow, Henry Wadsworth. 1867. *Flower-de-Luce*. Boston: Ticknor and Fields.

Lotze, Hermann. 1885. *Microcosmus: An Essay Concerning Man and His Relation to the World*. Translated by Elizabeth Hamilton and E.E. Constance Jones. Vol. 1. Edinburgh: T. and T. Clark.

Mabey, Richard. 2012. *Weeds: In Defense of Nature's Most Unloved Plants*. New York: Ecco.

Mahdi, Jassem. 2010. "Medicinal Potential of Willow: A Chemical Perspective of Aspirin Discovery." *Journal of Saudi Chemical Society* 14 (3): 317–22.

Marder, Michael. 2012. "The Life of Plants and the Limits of Empathy." *Dialogue* 51 (2): 259–73.

Marder, Michael, and Patrícia Vieira. 2013. "Writing Phytophilia: Philosophers and Poets as Lovers of Plants." *Frame* 26 (2): 37–53.

Martin, Mike. 2007. *Albert Schweitzer's Reverence for Life: Ethical Idealism and Self-Realization*. Aldershot, UK: Ashgate.

Miller, Joseph. 1722. *Botanicum Officinale*. London: E. Bell, J. Senex, W. Taylor, and J. Osborn.
Mortuza, Shamsad. 2013. *The Figure of the Shaman in Contemporary British Poetry*. Newcastle upon Tyne: Cambridge Scholars Publishing.
Nagel, Thomas. 1974. "What is it Like to be a Bat?" *The Philosophical Review* 83 (4): 435–50.
Noel-Tod, Jeremy. 2013. "Elisabeth Bletsoe." In *The Oxford Companion to Modern Poetry in English*, edited by Ian Hamilton and Jeremy Noel-Tod, 56. Oxford, UK: Oxford University Press.
Nowak, Magdalena. 2011. "The Complicated History of *Einfühlung*." *ARGUMENT: Biannual Philosophical Journal* 1 (2): 301–26.
Pardo-de-Santayana, Manuel, Andrea Pieroni, and Rajindra K. Puri, eds. 2010. *Ethnobotany in the New Europe: People, Health and Wild Plant Resources*. New York: Berghahn Books.
Pearce, J.M.S. 2008. "The Doctrine of Signatures." *European Neurology* 60 (1): 51–52.
Pendry, Barbara, ed. 2016. "Current Issue." *Journal of Herbal Medicine* 6 (4): 163–210.
Peverett, Michael. 2010. "Elisabeth Bletsoe, Landscape from a Dream." *Wintercapillary*. Accessed 22 May 2017. http://intercapillaryspace.blogspot.com/2010/08/elisabeth-bletsoe-landscape-from-dream.html
Pichersky, Eran, and David Gang. 2000. "Genetics and Biochemistry of Secondary Metabolites in Plants: An Evolutionary Perspective." *Trends in Plant Science* 5 (10): 439–45.
Pitman, Vicki. 2014. "Early Greek Medicine: Evidence of Models, Methods, and Materia Medica." In *Critical Approaches to the History of Western Herbal Medicine: From Classical Antiquity to the Early Modern Period*, edited by Susan Francia and Anne Stobart, 27–46. London: Bloomsbury.
Plants for a Future. 2012. "*Iris foetidissima*—L." Accessed 22 May 2017. www.pfaf.org/user/Plant.aspx?LatinName=Iris+foetidissima
Pulteney, Richard. 1790. *Historical and Biographical Sketches of the Progress of Botany in England, From its Origin to the Introduction of the Linnaean System*. Vol. 2. London: T. Cadell, In the Strand.
Randall, Rod. 2012. *A Global Compendium of Weeds*. 2nd ed. Perth: Department of Agriculture and Food of Western Australia.
Selles, Johanna. 2011. *Empathic Communities: Educating for Justice*. Eugene, OR: Wipf and Stock.
Shanley, Patricia, and Leda Luz. 2003. "The Impacts of Forest Degradation on Medicinal Plant Use and Implications for Health Care in Eastern Amazonia." *BioScience* 53 (6): 573–84. doi:10.1641/0006-3568(2003)053[0573:TIOFDO]2.0.CO;2
Spence, Steve. 2010. "Intoxication: *Pharmacopoeia and Early Selected Works*, Elizabeth Bletsoe (Shearsman)." *Stride*. Accessed 22 May 2017. www.stridemagazine.co.uk/Stride%20mag2010/march%202010/bletsoe.spence.htm
Stormonth, James. 1876. *Etymological and Pronouncing Dictionary of the English Language*. Edinburgh: William Blackwood and Sons.
Tarlo, Harriet. 1999. "Provisional Pleasures: The Challenge of Contemporary Experimental Women Poets." *Feminist Review* 62: 94–112.

———. 2000. "Radical Landscapes: Contemporary Poetry in the Bunting Tradition." In *The Star You Steer By: Basil Bunting and British Modernism*, edited by James McGonigal and Richard Price, 149–83. Amsterdam: Rodopi.

———. 2007. "Radical Landscapes: Experiment and Environment in Contemporary Poetry." *Jacket* 32. Accessed 22 May 2017. http://jacketmagazine.com/32/p-tarlo.shtml

———. 2011. "Introduction." In *The Ground Aslant: An Anthology of Radical Landscape Poetry*, edited by Harriet Tarlo, 7–18. Exeter, UK: Shearsman Books.

———. 2013. "Open Field: Reading Field as Place and Poetics." In *Placing Poetry*, edited by Ian Davidson and Zoë Skoulding, 113–48. Amsterdam: Rodopi.

Tobyn, Graeme. 2014. "An Anatomy of *The English Physitian*." In *Critical Approaches to the History of Western Herbal Medicine: From Classical Antiquity to the Early Modern Period*, edited by Susan Francia and Anne Stobart, 87–109. London: Bloomsbury.

Trewavas, Anthony. 2014. *Plant Behaviour and Intelligence*. Oxford: Oxford University Press.

———. 2016. "Intelligence, Cognition, and Language of Green Plants." *Frontiers in Psychology* 7: 1–9. doi:10.3389/fpsyg.2016.00588

Trewavas, Anthony, and František Baluška. 2011. "The Ubiquity of Consciousness." *EMBO Reports* 12 (12): 1221–25.

Vieira, Patrícia, Monica Gagliano, and John Ryan. 2016. "Introduction." In *The Green Thread: Dialogues with the Vegetal World*, edited by Patrícia Vieira, Monica Gagliano, and John Ryan, ix–xxvii. Lanham, MD: Lexington Books.

Vischer, Robert. 1994. "On the Optical Sense of Form: A Contribution to Aesthetics." In *Empathy, Form, and Space: Problems in German Aesthetics, 1873–1893*, edited and translated by Harry Francis Mallgrave and Eleftherios Ikonomou, 89–123. Santa Monica, CA: Getty Center for the History of Art and the Humanities.

Watkins, Frances, Barbara Pendry, Olivia Corcoran, and Alberto Sanchez-Medina. 2011. "Anglo-Saxon Pharmacopoeia Revisited: A Potential Treasure in Drug Discovery." *Drug Discovery Today* 16 (23–24): 1069–75.

Widger, Eleanore. 2016. "The 'Specific Evidentness' of Contemporary Radical Landscape Poetry: Innovative Form and Spatial Presence in *The Ground Aslant*." *English* 65 (251): 363–86.

Živković, Jelena, Dejan Stojković, Jovana Petrović, Gordana Zdunić, Jasna Glamočlija, and Marina Soković. 2015. "*Rosa canina* L.—New Possibilities for an Old Medicinal Herb." *Food Function* 6: 3687–92. doi:10.1039/C5FO00820D.

5 From Stinking Goose-foot to Bastard Toadflax

Botanical Humor in Alice Oswald's *Weeds and Wild Flowers*

> Finally she mentioned
> the name of her name
>
> which was something so pin-sharp,
> in such a last gasp of previously unknown language,
>
> it could only be spoken as a scent,
> it could only be heard as our amazement.
> —from "Violet" (Oswald 2009b, 17, ll. 14–19)

Molecular biologists tell us that the medical term *risus sardonicus*—also known as rictus grin or sinister smile—has an ominous botanical origin. According to ancient Latin and Greek accounts, the Nuragic civilization of pre-Roman Sardinia, between 1800 BCE and 800 BCE in particular, employed a toxic herb to inebriate elderly people no longer able to support themselves and criminals regarded as societal burdens. Resigned to their fate—or at least immobilized drunkenly before it—the condemned individuals, besotted by *herba sardonia*, were dropped from rock precipices or executed through other comparably violent means (Ribichini 2000). The pre- and post-mortality facial contortions produced by the mephitic plant hauntingly resembled a smile. As the English lexicographer William Smith wrote in the nineteenth century, the deadly species "was said to produce fatal convulsions in the person who ate it. These convulsions agitated and distorted the mouth so that the person appeared to laugh, though in excruciating pain" (1874, 367). With reference to this dreadful botanical history, the linguistic expression later entered mainstream medical rhetoric as a symptom of lockjaw, or *trismus*, the spasming of the masticatory muscles (Appendino et al. 2009). Through biochemical analysis, researchers have narrowed the identity of the infamous sardonic herb to hemlock water dropwort (*Oenanthe crocata*). Also known as water celery, the species is common to wetland habitats throughout Sardinia and resembles parsnips, carrots, and parsley. Denoting the paralytic state induced in human imbibers, *Oenanthe* literally means "wine flower." Hemlock water dropwort contains a central nervous system poison, oenanthotoxin, responsible for inhibiting physiological responses and triggering convulsions. Unlike most neurotoxic plants, however, *Oenanthe crocata* causes neither bitter nor burning sensations when ingested. Quite to the contrary, its highly poisonous roots are regarded as having an agreeable flavor and odor (Appendino et al. 2009, 963).

Writers of the Greco-Roman era frequently invoked the lore surrounding *herba sardonia* and the sinister smile it triggered. One of the earliest symbolic references to the stupefacient quality of water dropwort is found in the *Odyssey*, circa 800 BCE, during a tense exchange between Odysseus (or Ulysses) and the treacherous Ctesippus of Samos. In the epic's twentieth book, Ctesippus hurls an ox-hoof at the fabled king of Ithaca in disguise: "Ulysses gently bowed his head,/Shunning the blow, but gratified just/Resentment with a broad sardonic smile/Of dread significance" (Homer 1802, 216, ll. 356–59, translated by William Cowper). The nineteenth-century English poet-translator supplies some engrossing background detail in the footnotes to this incident from the *Odyssey*. Glossing the account of an unspecified scholiast or ancient commentator on classical literature, Cowper elaborated that, during a 3-day ceremony honoring Saturn, the early Sardinians "not only sacrificed the most beautiful of their captives, but also their elders whose age exceeded seventy years" (in Homer 1802, 216). If the victims accepted their circumstances and laughed, they were celebrated and cheered. As a consequence, "the laughter of a man in circumstances of misery came to be called sardonic laughter" (Cowper in Homer 1802, 216). As Cowper expounds further, the Greek geographer Pausanias from the second century CE derived the expression *risus sardonicus* "from a poisonous herb which, he says, grew in Sardis, of which whoever ate died laughing" (in Homer 1802, 216). To be certain, Pausanias in *Description of Greece* observed that Sardinia lacked noxious plants except for one that looked like parsley and caused "those who eat it to die laughing" (1824, 132). From this context, Homer formulated the idea of sardonic, or Sardonian, laughter as that "which conceals some noxious design" (Pausanias 1824, 132). The Greek physician and botanist Pedanius Dioscorides, who died 20 years before Pausanias was born, similarly observed that, when eaten, the herb "makes the victim lose his senses, and produces a certain spasm, so that it appears really as if they who eat are continually laughing" (qtd. in Emerson 1908, 466). The sixteenth-century herbalist John Gerard (1597) identified the deadly species as Illyrian crowfoot (*Ranunculus illyricus*) and noted that "it has seemed to some that the parties have died laughing, whereas in truth they have died in great torment" (953).

At this point in the introduction, I must concede that this is an unlikely and patently macabre way to open a chapter on botanical humor. Nevertheless, the brief overview of *herba sardonia* suggests the extent to which vegetal life is imbricated in comedy, laughter, levity, and—especially in relation to the scene from Homer—symbolically potent and historically resonant irony. In its tension between the false semblance of laughter and the actuality of death through brutal methods, the example of poisonous *Oenanthe crocata* also underscores the incongruity that is often essential to humor of different types (Apte 1985; Chandler 2014). As the misalignment between expectation and what really transpires or is represented, incongruity lies at the heart of diverse expressions of plant-related humor in Western literature. A prominent example is Erasmus Darwin's poetic narratives based on the sexualization of flowers central to mid-eighteenth-century Linnaean taxonomy. *The Loves of the Plants*, the second part of the long poem *The Botanic Garden* (Darwin 1798), animates the lascivious side of vegetal nature. The work dramatizes incongruous scenarios of plants falling desperately in love and jilting each another in their romantic matters. Canto I introduces the reader to the amusing possibility of amorous flowers, as perfected in images such as these: "With secret sighs the Virgin Lily droops,/And jealous Cowslips hang their tawny cups./How the young Rose, in beauty's damask pride,/Drinks the warm blushes of his bashful bride" (Darwin 1798, 11, ll. 15–18). In comparison, American transcendentalist Ralph Waldo Emerson's phrase "Earth laughs in flowers" (1880, 70, l. 13) is not exactly uproarious. While obviously less comical than Darwin's intercourse-obsessed lilies, roses, and cowslips, the flowers of Emerson's poem "Hamatreya" nevertheless elicit the provocative notion of blossoms expressing Gaian mirth. Rather than objects of humorous rhetoric, rendered amusing for narrative purposes, Emerson's flowers represent an innate capacity within vegetal nature for comedic or joyous states. Current developments in the field of plant behavior (Trewavas 2014) indeed make such a premise seem less preposterous. It is thus within the broad historical context of botanical humor and the comical plant—from *risus sardonicus* to Emerson's laughing flowers and additional examples presented later in this chapter—that I situate the work of contemporary British poet Alice Oswald.

Illustrated with etchings by Jessica Greenman, Oswald's collection *Weeds and Wild Flowers* (2009b) offers a focal point for theorizing botanical humor in the dialectic terms central to *Plants in Contemporary Poetry*. On the one hand, Oswald's collection positions plants as agents of humor that engender laughter in human subjects. Vegetal life accordingly provides a vehicle for comedy through caricature, parody, and other literary techniques leveraged to bring about humor through—or sometimes at the expense of—flora. On the other hand, Oswald's poetry figures plants as inherently funny personae who enact the forms of jocosity endemic to their being-in-the-world. The serious consideration of the comical plant hence underlies the dialectic of botanical humor developed in this chapter. Understanding the dialectic involves moving beyond the normative conceptual frame of botanical representation as the construction of plants in and through words. Such a move requires looking toward—and, indeed, embracing—the potentialities of vegetal being disclosed through language. We laugh at plants; do they laugh *at* or *with* us? If flora is funny, then what is funny *to* flora? These linguistic inversions are not merely flippant incitements intended to goad those of us indoctrinated in a mechanistic Cartesian or hierarchic Linnaean perspective of botanical life. These transposals are invitations to imagine—and re-imagine—the plants around, between, and within us. Vitalizing a cohort of ordinary weeds and everyday wildflowers—daisies, violets, roses—Oswald's verse offers her audience an uncommon glimpse into vegetal ontology. While enabling readers (and viewers) to gaze into the depths of botanical being, the humor of *Weeds and Wild Flowers* at the same time counterbalances the solemnity that is characteristic of weed discourse and invasive plant rhetoric. As a poet who has worked for stints as a professional horticulturalist and, in fact, is the daughter of a prominent garden designer, Oswald is intensely conscious of the cultural dichotomization of weeds (naturalized, exotic, invasive, out of place) and wildflowers (native, indigenous, balanced, place-adapted). I argue that Oswald's collection mediates the native-naturalized binary by disrupting rigid distinctions such as these. The poet-gardener's weeds and wildflowers form a pantheon of amusing plant-beings. Disclosing the abilities of plants and mediating indigenous-exotic oppositions, *Weeds and Wild Flowers* evokes the potential of poetry to act as a mechanism for coming to terms with the decline and disappearance of local flora. I conclude the chapter with the proposition that botanical humor supplies a means to respond to—and cope with—vegetal loss in an era of widespread ecological degradation.

On Becoming Bodily Implicated: Oswald as Gardener-Walker-Poet

From her debut collection, *The Thing in the Gap Stone Stile* (1996), to her most recent *Falling Awake* (2016), the poetry of Alice Oswald (b. 1966) is characterized by a profound interweaving of the poetic and the botanical. After reading classics at New College, Oxford (Porter 2014, para. 1), she studied at the Royal Horticultural Society at Wisley and has since worked periodically as a professional gardener. In 1994, Oswald received an Eric Gregory Award from the Society of Authors in recognition of her accomplishments as an emerging poet. *The Thing in the Gap Stone Stile* won the Forward Poetry Prize for Best First Collection and, in 1997, was short-listed for the coveted T.S. Eliot Prize. Her second book *Dart* (2002)—the result of 3 years of natural, cultural, and phenomenological research into the River Dart in Devon—garnered the T.S. Eliot Prize (Poetry Foundation 2017). As the poet explains in a side note that is quite relevant to a phytocritical reading of her work, the word *dart* is old Devonian for *oak* (Oswald 2002, 11). Subsequent collections, *Woods etc.* (2005b), *A Sleepwalk on the Severn* (2009a), and *Memorial* (2011), either won outright or were short-listed for a number of prestigious accolades, including the Forward Poetry Prize, the Warwick Prize, the Geoffrey Faber Memorial Prize, and the Ted Hughes Award. Oswald has been praised as England's "greatest living poet," one who "brings the characters and textures of antiquity to her work, embedded in the earth and water of the British countryside" (Runcie 2016, para. 3). She has been exalted as "an inheritor of some of Britain's greatest poetic voices, an heir to Ted Hughes, Seamus Heaney and Geoffrey Hill" (Campbell-Johnson 2002, 19). In-depth treatments of her work of the last 20 years, however, tend to emphasize either *Dart* or *Memorial*. Focusing primarily on these two collections, critics call attention to themes, for instance, of "echo-poetics," or the poetization of soundscapes (Pinard 2009, 18), ecology, time, and *enargeia* as "the capacity to make something vividly real" (Farrier 2014, 3), place, topography, and identity (Middleton 2015), polyvocality as the upshot of the intermingling of human and nonhuman worlds (Yeung 2015, 151–73), and *Dart* specifically as "a fluid model" of being and consciousness (Yeung 2015, 170). Oswald conceptualizes her own poems as "sound carvings" (qtd. in Armitstead 2016, para. 16).

Substantive treatments of her phytophilia (Marder and Vieira 2013) are peculiarly absent from the secondary literature. Mary Pinard's insightful and nuanced analysis of the influence of Oswald's horticultural interests on her poetic development does represent an exception to this overall trend. Pinard (2009) highlights the "blending of the ecological sensibilities learned through gardening with those of the poet" (18). However, in interviews (Armitstead 2016; Bunting 2012; Porter 2014; Runcie 2016) and in Oswald's prose itself—such as her introduction to *The Thunder Mutters* (2005a) and essay in *A Green Thought in a Green Shade* (2000)—we find that the discussion of plant life takes center stage. To be certain, Oswald is a botanophilist in lineage to American transcendentalist Henry David Thoreau, who invoked the term in an 1852 journal entry (1999, 35), and his contemporary, English poet John Clare, from whom she borrowed the phrase "the thunder mutters" for the title of her anthology of "poems for the planet" (2005a). In characterizing *Weeds and Wild Flowers* as a work of botanical humor in the tradition of Thoreau, Clare, Erasmus Darwin and other green-minded poets, it is important to consider the influence of observing and cultivating flora on Oswald's literary practice. Oswald is the third daughter of Mary Keen, a renowned garden designer who has been involved with several distinguished formal plantings including the walled garden at Eythrope, a country house owned by the Rothschild family since the 1870s (Dehn 2015). Her mother is also a prolific author of lavishly illustrated garden books including *Paradise and Plenty* (Keen and Hatton 2015). Mary Keen's steady recognition as a foremost garden designer resulted in an itinerant upbringing for young Alice, her two sisters, and brother as the family regularly relocated according to the demands of her mother's employment. With a sense of irony, Oswald remarks that "I felt I grew up in a series of gardens" (qtd. in Armitstead 2016, para. 12). After studying classics, she set her sights on becoming "a jobbing gardener in a park or something, to allow time for writing, but because my mother was quite a well-known gardener I kept being put into these high-powered jobs. I'm not as good a gardener as people think" (Armitstead 2016, para. 14).

Despite the understated self-characterization, Oswald has held positions at Chelsea Physic Garden at London and at Clovelly Court Gardens, Tapeley Park and Gardens, and Dartington Hall Estate, all at Devon in South West England (Pinard 2009, 18). Even with her reputation as one of the leading poets in the English language today, she regularly works at a local nursery near the River Dart in Devon where she lives with her husband and three children. Fostering immersive connection to plants, gardening has been indispensable to Oswald's trajectory as a poet. She explains that "when you're digging you become *bodily implicated* in the ground's world, thought and earth continually passing through each other. You smell it, you feel its strength under your boot, you move alongside it [emphasis added]" (qtd. in Pinard 2009, 21). In addition to gardening—yet closely related to it—walking is a technique of bodily implication and one which plays a formative role in Oswald's poetics. One of her preferred routes leads to where two tidal rivers, the Harbourne and the Dart, come together. An estuary path she perambulates at varying times each day according to tidal rhythms gives her "a very intimate idea of the lives of plants. I can watch every movement of the gesture of a leaf uncurling through a week. I'm addicted to this slow performance" (qtd. Porter 2014, para. 19). Accessing the lives of flora and striving to see the world from their stance are poetic techniques that interrupt the visual impulse to reduce the English countryside to beautiful, pretty, pleasing, or other aestheticized scenes. Rather than a romantic exercise in identifying with other-than-humans, though, adopting a plant's-eye perspective on things is not easy. It requires persuading "myself to look out from the flower's point of view at these great walloping humans coming down the path, and try, just try and feel it from their point of view because it's a different world to them" (qtd. in Bunting 2012, para. 4). In this context, her life-long preoccupation with Homer reached its apogee with *Memorial* (2011), an "excavation" of the *Iliad*. Oswald's rendering of the classic attempted to preserve the orality of the original and, thus, was written with performance in mind. She especially admires the Greek bard's penchant for animating plants in language and transmitting vegetal essence without a sense of mediation: "He describes a leaf and you don't just get a description of a leaf, you get a proper leaf.

That's always been my principle. You've got to make something living" (qtd. Porter 2014, para. 11).

For Oswald, the somatic modes of gardening and walking make possible the multisensorial implication with plants foundational to her botanical imagination. Pinard (2009) argues that her poetics "celebrates the primacy of physical work" as a mechanism "for bringing living things unmediated into the text" (26). The integration of seeing, sounding, and sensing constitutes a "participatory" approach to the natural environment in which "you look at it with your ear and with your body. You're walking through it and you're working in it" (Oswald 2013, para. 7). In exegetical snapshots such as this, Oswald's characterization of her poetics is redolent of Thoreau's principle of the "bodily eye" (1993, 26). Thoreau conceptualized the body as an instrument for unmediated corporeal perception and as an apparatus for acquiring knowledge via sensory participation in the world. Like Thoreau in the nineteenth century, Oswald values an approach to the natural environment "not restricted to one sense but fully engaged and physical [because] work, physical work, is a much more accurate form of perception" (2013, paras. 7 and 8). An openness and entrainment to the aural landscape renders the bodily eye a *bodily ear*—a corporeal medium for listening—particularly during the gardening act with its "free shocks of sound happening against the backsound of your heartbeat" (Oswald 2000, 35). Through carnal receptivity to the earth, gardening therein provides "a way of forcing a poem open to what lies bodily beyond it" (Oswald 2000, 37). Even so, Oswald abjures the tag *nature poet* and its association with landscape sentimentalization from a distanced standpoint. She instead embraces figures like John Clare whose poetry was shaped by direct visceral interaction with photosynthetic fellow-beings.

Despite a self-confessed reluctance to ally her writing to the Romantic literary tradition and its contemporary incarnations, Oswald nevertheless discloses a robust environmental outlook, notably in her prose and interviews. From the perspective of ethical time, David Farrier (2014) approaches Oswald's poetry as a lament for "the future passing of ecological diversity" and a "deeply-felt call not to turn away from the responsibility" (16) for the future. Delineated by the Devonshire region, her localized practice of gardening, walking, and writing internalizes the harrowing realization that humankind faces "the most extraordinary moment" of environmental crisis and subsequently "cannot afford to be complacent" (qtd. in Bunting 2012, para. 6). Acknowledging global concerns through bioregional rootedness, the poet aims to resist the complacency she calls out by reconfiguring the language that is used to construct and appropriate the nonhuman. To this end, polyvocality is consistently deployed throughout her work. This is true of *Dart*, "a sound-map of the river, a songline from the source to the sea [...] All voices should be read as the river's mutterings" (Oswald 2002, prefatory note). As a "poetic census" (Pinard 2009, 27) of the Dart River, the text is distinctive for its narration of diverse speakers' embodied interactions with the riverine landscape (Middleton 2015, 158). The river's story comprises the voices of the poet-narrator, rambler, swimmer, naturalist, fisherman, dairy laborer, oyster harvester, water nymph, and other characters. Rendered indistinguishable from one other, their heterogeneous enunciations meld to become the voice of the Dart. With "a gardener's sensibility and humility" (Pinard 2009, 31), Oswald unsettles the perceptual eye and reformulates the poetic "I" while the river supplies the narrative framework. Notwithstanding her overtures to the contrary, the poet refrains from didacticism, preferring in its place an approach to ecological politics based in the capacity of poetry "to change the aesthetic rather than to challenge the system" (Oswald qtd. Armitstead 2016, para. 18).

Oswald's debut publication, *The Thing in the Gap Stone Stile* (1996), was inspired not only by her gardening but also by sensory engagements with estuaries, rivers, the ocean, and local natural formations (Pinard 2009, 26). Poems like "The Glass House" and "The Gardeners in the Shed" present intimate portraits of plant cultivation while others, notably the "Sea Sonnet" cluster of three poems, disclose an affinity with the ocean and an intrigue for the nature of water (Oswald 2010, 5, 35, 18–20, respectively). Human and vegetal elocutions interleave, for example, in the poem generically titled "Poem" in which "I of the bluebells/laid on a succulent mattress, frown" (2010, 8, lines 3–4). The narrative "I" is rendered depersonalized, dehumanized, and distributed across beings and species. The interpenetration of voices in the first three couplets presages the corporeal transfiguration between the human and the plant in the lines "I run my fingers round my lip,/transmuted to a bluebell cup" (2010, 8, ll. 7–8). Movement toward a state of co-constitution between poet-speaker and bluebell reaches a crescendo as "my voice, a pollen dust, puffs out/the reason I remain" (2010, 8, ll. 17–18). From the same volume, "A Wood Coming into Leaf" narrates forest foliation as a symphonic movement of discrete arboreal articulations: "From the first to the second/Warily, from the tip to the palm/Third leaf (the blackthorn done)" (2010, 9, ll. 1–3). Vegetal temporality synchronizes with celestial phenomenality as "A greenwood through a blackwood/passes (like the moon's halves/meet and go behind themselves)" (2010, 9, ll. 12–14). The disquisition on plant ontology concludes by invoking floratemporaesthesia as a sense of time formulated through close attention to the physical registers of vegetal life in space. The forest coming into leaf signifies time's progression in intervals governed by the succession of species: "Birch, oak, rowan, ash/chinese-whispering the change" (2010, 9, ll. 16–17) (see Chapter 7 for a discussion of vegetal temporality in Judith Wright's poetry).

From her earliest to her latest collections, Oswald meditates on the temporality that is specific to plants and especially exalts their patient deportment. In the spirit of botanophilia, she concedes plainly that "I do love the company of plants. They are so expressive and patient" (qtd. in Porter 2014, para. 19). Her most recent volume, *Falling Awake*, enacts this declaration of affection in poems such as "Alongside Beans," which relates the experience of "Weeding alongside beans in the same rush as them/6 a.m. scrabbling at the earth" (Oswald 2016, ll. 1–2). As a participatory poetics, gardening harmonizes the poet-speaker with the botanical timescape. Although by a zoological standard vegetal movement appears drawn out, largely outside of the human perceptual frame, plants still pulsate according to the rhythms endemic to their modes of being, doing, and adapting:

> and after a while a flower
> turning its head to the side like a bored emperor
>
> and after a while a flower
>
> singing out a faint line of scent.
>
> (Oswald 2016, 27, ll. 20–23)

In addition to the dash of botanical humor in the aloof figure of "a bored emperor," Oswald's poem calls to mind Thoreau's attachment to his beanfield at Walden Pond: "I came to love my rows, my beans, though so many more than I wanted. They attached me to the earth, and so I got strength like Antæus" (Thoreau 1882, 241). Evocations of the time of plants similarly punctuate *Woods etc.* (Oswald 2005b). "Leaf" is a musing on the temporal dimensions of plant physiology. The poet-speaker apprehends:

> the slow through-flow that feeds
> a form curled under, hour by hour
> the thick reissuing starlike shapes
> of cells and pores and water-rods.
>
> (2005b, 8, ll. 4–7)

In the poignant and highly discerning representation of the plant as "a gradual fleshing out of a longing for light," the sonnet highlights the material inscription of time on the photosynthetic body (2005b, 8, l. 9). Attention to the forbearance of plants continues thematically in "A Winged Seed" as "I saw pollen pass through trees/in no rush/possessing nothing, not even weight" (2005b, 10, ll. 6–8) and again in "Sisyphus," comprising six sonnets, as the poet-narrator evokes the "smoky-headed grasses singing of patience" (2005b, 13, l. 68).

Laughing At and With Plants: Some History and Theory of Botanical Humor

Oswald's poetry reflects her horticultural inclinations and intrigue for vegetal ontology, exemplified by what she describes as the expressiveness and patience of plants. In *Weeds and Wild Flowers* (2009b), botanical humor and the comical plant find their completest expression within her oeuvre to date. Consider, as an example, the concluding poem in the collection, "Dense Silky Bent" (2009b, 60). The sonnet makes liberal use of imperfect rhyming to figure the plant incongruously as a cussing yogi "with long washed hair and a little beard cut square" who performs stretches at dawn but gets kicked from behind by passersby (2009b, 60, l. 2). While animating flora in a textual medium, humor in her poetry also helps to counterbalance the dreadfulness of the native-exotic rhetoric surrounding many species. To be sure, some amusing vegetal personae appearing in the illustrated collection—take, for instance, scarious chickweed and procumbent cinquefoil—could be classified as weeds, as out-of-place plants, especially when translocated beyond their native ranges. The following section historicizes the idea of botanical humor then reviews ecocritical perspectives on laughter in environmental writing before considering the typically humorless biosocial construct of *the weed*. Toward this end, the section presents examples from botanical verse (Darwin 1798; Nash 1985), environmental writing (Thoreau 1882, 1993, 2000), and contemporary fiction (Freeman 1954) in order to illustrate how plants become the subjects of—and substrates for—diverse comical forms. Through puns, quips, malapropism, irony, satire, and other techniques, writers make use of flora to produce amusing effects, sometimes with a view toward social, political, or environmental commentary. However, as argued through the case of Oswald's poetry, botanical humor can also be theorized in dialectic terms. A phytocritical approach to the humor of plants interrogates the extent to which a text brings to life—rather than merely constructs, depicts, or represents—the inherently comical qualities of vegetal being. A caveat is in order here. It is not my intention to anthropomorphize plants by claiming, in somewhat reckless terms, that they laugh and undergo states of jollity; and that humankind would understand their chuckles, chortles, gurgles, and snickers if only we shared a green sense of humor. In contrast, I do wish to emphasize that to proscribe plants from the affective realm—which includes laughter, joy, merriment, and levity—is to diminish vegetal being and to devitalize our potential to imagine plants outside of the reductionistic frameworks that condition human thinking about them.

In situating Oswald as an heir to the botanical humor tradition and underscoring the transformative potential of plant-based laughter in the Anthropocene, it is instructive to return, if only momentarily, to the verse of Erasmus Darwin, composed in the late eighteenth century. In the garden of Darwin's scientifically-informed and comically-inflected poetry, exotic species intermix with those considered originary to the English landscape (Browne 1989, 605). Darwin's levity thus serves as a medium for levelling the blunt distinction between native and naturalized flora. As the gardens and conservatories of his era received inflows of exotic flora from British colonies abroad, it follows that such ideological divisions would have assumed a prominent place in the botanical imagination of the populace. In this sense, Darwin's work intervened in the biopolitics of flora and reasserted the Linnaean prioritization of plant sexuality. Through the use of personification, the physician-turned-poet conferred to plants attributes of sensation, movement, psychological activity, and amusing behavior (Browne 1989, 603). Although some botanists of his time contested the idea of plant fertilization, Darwin considered the Linnaean scheme "an unexplored poetic ground" and "a happy subject for the muse" (qtd. in Browne 1989, 601). His preface to *The Loves of the Plants* (1798, first issued anonymously in 1789) begins with a synopsis of the "ingenious system" according to which Linnaeus "divided the vegetable world" (iii). Not merely a device to entertain his botanical readership, polyamory and hermaphroditism were encoded in the taxonomic hierarchy of natural orders devised by "the illustrious author of the sexual system of botany" (Darwin 1798, vii). As a "taxonomic poem," *The Loves of the Plants* stylized natural history and was designed to generate comedic effect while educating his audience in serious matters of Linnaean science (Browne 1989, 593). Darwin's extended narrativization of sexual behaviors shared by humans and plants involved depicting stamens and pistils as men and women in order "to introduce a real, physiological element into a highly abstract scheme" (Browne 1989, 602). Consequently readers of his verse discover reflective and affective flora embroiled in salacious affairs: "With vain desires the pensive Alcea burns,/And, like sad Eloisa, loves and mourns./The freckled Iris owns a fiercer flame,/And *three* unjealous husbands wed the dame [emphasis in original]" (Darwin 1798, 15, ll. 69–72).

Like Erasmus Darwin, though with far less voyeuristic focus on the sex lives of flowers, Henry David Thoreau in the nineteenth century understood plants as inherently amusing lifeforms and regarded human interactions with the vegetal world as occasions for levity. The American transcendentalist was also an adept botanical punster and frequently played on alternate connotations of specialized terms for plants. Through a mode of religious satire, Thoreau in the posthumous *Wild Fruits* (2000) posed amusingly barbed rhetorical questions intended to furnish readers an optic into the mysteries of vegetal life: "Who could believe in prophecies of Daniel or of Miller that the world would end this summer, while one milkweed with faith matured its seeds?" (198). The question generates pensive comical effect by juxtaposing stern end time prognostication incongruously to the seasonal dehiscence of a common—some would say weedy, gross, or profane—plant. What becomes apparent is that fully appreciating Thoreau's humor depends on comprehending his references: William Miller was an American Baptist preacher who predicted that the Second Coming of Christ would transpire in the 1840s while the Book of Daniel is the most apocalyptic of the Bible. While neither sidesplitting nor rib-tickling, his reflections on the beanfield portrayed in *Walden* are nonetheless amusing. Thoreau's witticisms exhibit self-awareness of his role in modifying the plantscape by expunging certain species to make way for others of a more desirable ilk. The labor of his summer was "to make this portion of the earth's surface, which had yielded only cinquefoil, blackberries, johnswort, and the like, before, sweet wild fruits and pleasant flowers, produce instead this *pulse* [emphasis added]" (1882, 129). While denoting a leguminous plant that produces edible seeds, a pulse, of course, also refers variously to a rhythmic contraction and expansion of an artery, a sharp change in voltage, and a vibration or throb. For the gardener-philosopher, cultivating beans was more than a physical transaction; the process fundamentally altered the pulse—the essential makeup or energetic character—of the earth that he tended. Suggesting a dialogical understanding of plants, he asks, "What shall I learn of beans or beans of me?" (1882, 129).

This mode of levity enabled Thoreau to bring attention to the role of the human hand in the botanical order, specifically in terms of the division between weeds and crops: "But what right had I to oust johnswort and the rest, and break up their ancient herb garden?" (1882, 129). Thoreau's "oblique wordplay" underscores "the inescapable ambiguity of language, its need for conscious interpretation" (West 2000, 184). The plant-based pun—a technique propagated by Thoreau in much of his writing—is invoked later by Richard Austin Freeman in the novel *The Penrose Mystery*, published originally in 1936. A letter signed by the missing antique collector Daniel Penrose is sent to a butler with the surname Kickweed. The writer oddly addressed the letter not to Kickweed but to Cerastium Vulgatum. As noted by John Thorndyke, the detective investigating the disappearance of Penrose, the peculiar Latinism used by the letter writer is the Linnaean name for the common chickweed and parodies the butler's real name. The botanical humor in this instance seems to call out the inadequacies of binomial nomenclature—a system of plant naming based on the pretense of universal applicability. Given the discomfiture of Kickweed and Thorndyke in response to the facetious wordplay, it becomes evident that "the botanical joke had produced a profoundly unfavourable impression" (Freeman 1954, 106). Earlier in the same chapter titled "Re-Enter Mr Kickweed," horticultural punning and the botanical riddle heighten the mystery of Penrose's disappearance, as Thorndyke asks, "'Are we not decipherers of cross-word puzzles and interpreters of dark sayings?'" (Freeman 1954, 101). One clue, written on a scrap of paper, contains the enigmatic inscription *hortus petasatus*, meaning "hatted garden." This proves to be a pun on Hatton Garden, a fictitious botanical garden in the novel but also a real-life street and area of Inner London. The narrator, however, disapproves of the plant-based wordplay that slows down the investigative efforts: "But what puerile balderdash it is. That man, Penrose, ought to be certified" (Freeman 1954, 102).

Other varieties of plant-based humor in poetic works during the twentieth century bring the natural and built environments into acute contrast. For instance, published in 1933, Ogden Nash's four-line "Song of the Open Road" amusingly disturbs the idealization of the environment by musing that "I think that I shall never see/A billboard lovely as a tree./ Indeed, unless the billboards fall/I'll never see a tree at all" (1985, 31). Nash's light-hearted yet iconoclastic short poem belies the reality of the industrialization of the American landscape during the 1930s as propelled by the advent of the motor vehicle industry and enshrinement of the United States System of Highways plan. It is not the lovely and innately funny trees themselves that provide comic relief; the effect is the upshot of the surprising collocation of tree and billboard as well as the unexpected inversion of the American pastoral idyll. To be certain, essential to the poem's effect is its satirization of the popular opening couplet of "Trees" by Joyce Kilmer: "I think that I shall never see/A poem lovely as a tree" (1914, 18). The environmental commentary latent in the poem by Nash points to the function of comedy in ecological writing and to studies of humor from ecocritical perspectives (Branch 2014; Chandler 2014; Meeker 1997; Peiffer 2000). As Michael Branch (2014) argues, environmental writing tends to foreground qualities of reverence, awe, piety, and numinous union with the natural world rather than the "creativity, spontaneity, flexibility, playfulness, and enjoyment that humor brings" (380). The precedent of Thoreau's comical sensibility—notable for its liveliness, historical depth, and critical force—prompts Branch (2014) to ask, "What new perspectives might humor provide, what new insights might it produce, what new pleasures might it enable?" (381). Correspondingly, in her reading of Barbara Kingsolver's *The Poisonwood Bible*, Katherine Chandler (2014) maintains that humor in the novel "supports environmentalist condemnations of American practices and policy" (331). Descriptions of abusive practices couched in frank and funny terms enable Kingsolver to position the figure of the capitalist as anathema to ecological wellbeing (Chandler 2014, 334).

Studies of humor since Aristotle identify incongruity as a key principle. Championed by Immanuel Kant, Arthur Schopenhauer, and others, incongruity is the dominant—though not sole—theory of humor in psychology and philosophy, and typically involves the violation of thought patterns and normal expectations (Morreall 2009, 10–11). Humor results from a psychological reaction to an unexpected, strange, or uncommon shift in a perceived regularity (Meyer 2015, 17).

Incongruity—recall Kickweed being addressed as Cerastium Vulgatum by a cheeky anonymous scrivener—emerges from the assemblage of ordinarily inappropriate or disparate elements (Chandler 2014, 330). Punning, nicknaming, mockery, mimicry, exaggeration, and reversal are consistent across cultures; they rely on incongruous images or language generated by techniques such as malaproprism (word misuse) and spoonerism (linguistic transposition) (Apte 1985, 178–79, 182). With regard to avant-garde and post-modernist poetry, Rosemary Huisman (1998, 221–22) maintains that individuals read humor into scenarios. Incongruity arises through the interaction of different verbal and nonverbal modalities. To this end, she cites the poem "Scared Cows"—a reversal of the term *sacred cows*—by Douglas Messerli, featuring an absurd image of "a kangaroo/pulling cigarettes/from pouch" (qtd. in Huisman 1998, 223). As an instance of behavioral incongruity—the kangaroo plucking cigarettes, rather than joeys, from her marsupium—the image signifies the prevalence of animals as comical subjects. (Counter to the zoocentrism of environmental humor in general, nevertheless, a cigarette-smoking cactus, cigar-puffing oak, or spliff-toking orchid would be equally amusing to this reader.) Although not specifically with incongruity theory in mind, other literary critics have investigated the function of comical effect in poetry. For instance, humor is a vital part of Horace's work (Connor 1987). What is more, all the major Romantic poets were concerned with the implications of humor as "one essential means of accommodating the self, especially the Romantic self, in poetry" (Storey 1979, x).

Notwithstanding the foregoing examples to the contrary, environmental humor on the whole has exhibited more zoological—and fewer botanical—proclivities over time. Consider, for instance, the archetypes of the laughing hyena (Enright 1953) and cackling kookaburra (Hooper and Hooper 1982, 44). We readily identify with such creatures' ability to evoke the sounds of human merriment; that is, to give the impression of laughing. Some historical commentators regarded humor as an attribute shared by humans and animals, as a trait revealing the commonalities—rather than affirming the distinctions—between species. In this vein, the American naturalist Samuel Lockwood (1876) remarked that "I think with animals, as with men, humor and gentleness go together" (259). Lockwood's (1876) zoological anecdotes—some of which abrade modern sensitivities, especially regarding animal welfare—nevertheless have the attributes of "incongruousness and surprise" (262) that are the pillars of comical narrative. The elision of the human and animal as discrete ontological categories is palpable in Bertrand Russell's oft-quoted sardonicism "it has been said that man is a rational animal. All my life I have been searching for evidence which could support this" (qtd. in Gordon 2014, 18). In *The Comedy of Survival* (1997, published originally in 1974), moreover, Joseph Meeker weighed aspects of animal behavior in support of the premise that comedy enhances survival and reduces alienation from other lifeforms. Furthermore, twentieth-century animal behaviorists identified in primates a "laugh like vocalization that accompanies a relaxed open-mouth play face, during tickling and rough-and-tumble play" (Morreall 2009, 41). As these instances reveal, the association of zoological life with humor—and the ascription of funny behavior to animals—have a range of precedents in history, philosophy, and science. In comparison, the recognition of botanical humor—as the humor produced by vegetal agents and the light-hearted affectivity possessed by plants on an intrinsic basis—is scarce. In the domain of popular culture and common parlance, the idea of botanical humor indeed appears shrouded in presuppositions about plants as unfeeling, unsensing, and uncommunicative automata.

In terms of botanical awareness and ecological conservation, there could be practical benefits associated with laughing *at, because of,* and *together with* plants. Humor is known to promote identification both with the rhetor and the subject matter of rhetoric (Meyer 2015, 34–36). Humor consequently can become a medium for appreciating plants, their worlds, and the variables impinging on both. As a response to an agreeable shift in mental outlook (Gordon 2014, 17), laughter can engender awareness of—and entrainment to—vegetal complexities. It can also provide an alternative to the well-trodden and sometimes soporific piousness of much environmental writing. While philosophers such as Schopenhauer and Nietzsche underscored the relevance of humor to societal thriving, there could also be value in it for human-plant relations too. As life on earth negotiates the grossly unamusing geological epoch of the Anthropocene, humor might become a more urgent resource for the future. Actualizing the ecological utility of humor necessitates going beyond the conception of botanical life as a comical pawn and embracing instead the radical possibility that plants undergo affective states, including something that could approximate joviality. Plant-based humor as such could moderate the buzzkilling—and plainly dreadful—rhetoric that frames the vegetal world in certain ways and promulgates techno-materialist conceptions of plants. In this sense, Oswald's *Weeds and Wild Flowers* intervenes in the vilification of select flora as exotics or weeds. Forwarding a playful view of botanical nature as a percipient force, the collection dispenses entirely with the binarism. This is not to suggest that Oswald is in denial of the scientific fact that invasive species trigger significant ecological upheavals and pose considerable risks to global biosecurity (Clout and Williams 2009). As a gardener and walker, she is intensely cognizant of the impacts precipitated by out of place species. Yet, to consign certain plants wholly to the weedy wastebin risks marginalizing their latent values, notably their artistic, cultural, and comical potential. It was Ralph Waldo Emerson who asked during a lecture, "And what is a weed?," and, receiving no satisfying reply from his listeners, answered himself: "A plant whose virtues have not yet been discovered, and every one of the two hundred thousand, probably yet to be of utility in the arts" (2001, 321). From Emerson's perspective, the weed is a construct of the human imagining of flora (or an indication of the human lack of imaginative ambit when it comes to plants) rather than an actual property of botanical being. Richard Mabey (2012) similarly comments that "plants become weeds when they obstruct our plans, or our tidy maps of the world" (1) and wonders "what positive features we might glimpse in their *florid energy* [emphasis added]" (3). Weeds, for Mabey (2012, 6), are more than plants in the wrong place; they are constructs of aesthetic nationalism.

It Could Only Be Spoken as a Scent: Oswald's Florid Energy

By bringing plants to life as personae, *Weeds and Wild Flowers* (2009) satirizes the exotic-native binary. With the aid of humor, the illustrated collection at the same time enables readers to acquire insight into vegetal being. Hence, the work intersects with companionable trajectories in neuro-botany (Baluška and Levin 2016; Gagliano et al. 2014; Gagliano et al. 2016; Trewavas 2014, 2016). The vegetal protagonists—24 in total, with the colloquial name of each plant furnishing the title of its respective poem (Oswald 2009b, 67)—are incongruent in their actions and habitually irreverent in their elocutions. Indeed, the diverse plant personae are "truculent, freakish, yearning, bored" (Brahic 2011, 423). Considering the traditional ascription of behavior to mobile organisms (humans, mammals, birds, insects), it rings as incongruent that the vegetal characters of Oswald's egalitarian coterie can behave in the first place, and with such self-determination and idiosyncrasy to boot. Not cast in opposition to one other, species intermingle equanimously as part of a heteroglossia of the florid world—as participants in a rowdy assemblage of expressive beings. Oswald's work epitomizes the etymological provenance of the term *anthology* as "a gathering of flowers." As with Erasmus Darwin's *The Loves of the Plants* written more than 200 years earlier, Oswald's flora unsettle orthodox ideas about plantness and disrupt the normative behavioral patterns to which we expect plants to adhere. Her text is both incongruous and confrontational: plants are not supposed to act *like that*. Provoked by the green personae of Oswald's universe, the reader begins to grasp the depth of vegetal ontology or, conversely, suffers the overturning of logocentrism, zoocentrism, and anthropocentrism. (Recalling *The Penrose Mystery* at this point, I expect that a few unsuspecting readers of her poetry will roar "that poet, Oswald, ought to be certified.") To heighten the incongruous effect of loquacious plant-speakers, instead of *wildflowers* (with no space between terms; flowering plants growing in uncultivated spaces), the protagonists are *wild flowers* (with a space between terms; flowering plants that are unruly and uninhibited in their mien, plants guided by terrene impulse rather than societal stricture). In her prefatory note to the collection, Oswald (2009b) remarks that "flowers are recognisably ourselves elsewhere."

Distinctly unlike the ominous mood of Louise Glück's *The Wild Iris* (1992) and the either despairing, melancholic, or argumentative voices of most of her garden speakers (see Chapter 6), *Weeds and Wild Flowers* has been characterized as a "comic Arcadia" (Brahic 2011, 422). Oswald's collection summons a multiplicity of techniques—assonance, alliteration, imperfect rhyming, parataxis, malapropism—and forms—light-hearted quatrains, free-verse stanzas, traditional sonnets—to generate comedic tenor. Floristic articulations oscillate between first-person intimacy and third-person distance, and between eccentricity and jolliness. In a manner evocative of Louise Glück's *The Wild Iris*, procumbent cinquefoil, for example, speaks directly to the reader in a serious tone of voice:

> I'll tell you how it looks
> without hope
> at the groundfloor level of a hedgerow
> lying staring at my handscape.
>
> (Oswald 2009b, 56, ll. 6–9)

Despite the nursery rhyme jingle of other poems, the collection on the whole departs stylistically from the plant-centered children's verse, for instance, of British illustrator Cicely Mary Barker whose work often depicts fairies and flowers (Moore 2009, para. 4). Like Oswald's volume, *A Flower Fairy Alphabet* (Barker 1934) adopts the common names of plants for the titles of poems, which also number 24. As a case in point, "Double Daisy" animates the flower—as many of Barker's poems do—but with a charming openness and innocence that is comparatively absent from Oswald's personifications: "In the smallest flower-bed/Double Daisy lifts his head,/With a smile to greet the sun,/You, and me, and everyone" (Barker 1934, 10, ll. 3–6). Whereas Barker's thrift (*Armeria maritima*) is a sprite relishing the freedom of living at the edge of the sea (1934, 42), Oswald's thrift is a lonely 40-year-old spinster who finds the sea boring and is hard of hearing (2009, 20–21). Oswald dramatizes the inner lives of vegetal protagonists as "ordinary folk, planted in some never-never land on the continuum between realism and allegory" (Brahic 2011, 425). In contrast to Brahic, I maintain that her plant personae are not merely allegorical; they signify the understanding of vegetal percipience she has acquired through gardening, walking, and musing. Oswald's "attention to the thing or person described never wavers" (Moore 2009, para. 8). Using "the names of flowers to summon up the flora of the psyche," the gardener-poet hopes that the experience of reading—and viewing—the work turns into "a slightly unsettling pleasure" (Oswald 2009b, prefatory note).

Notwithstanding her stylistic deviation from Barker, Oswald's verse has an instructive element heightened by comical nuances. Facilitating appreciation of plant behavior, humor in her writing—I argue—becomes a mode for transmitting botanical lives "unmediated into the text" (Pinard 2009, 26). In bringing ordinary weeds and wildflowers into clear focus, Oswald releases flora from the green perceptual field homogenized, in common speak, as landscape, countryside, environment, scene, or scenery. Rather than representing or constructing botanical identity and selfhood, poetry in this sense discloses the inborn capacities of flora—those qualities that already exist and which require no writerly embellishment or fabrication. More than narrative armature or humorous ploys, the 24 personae of *Weeds and Wild Flowers* mirror Oswald's embodied observations of plant behavior while engaged in horticultural, ambulatory, and other participatory activities on the land. What is more, the etchings of Jessica Greenman enliven the species poeticized by Oswald. Greenman remarks in a prefatory statement "the flowers themselves act on my mind in a way that reminds me of being similarly submerged [in acid]; they bite into me" (in Oswald 2009b). Calling for patience, the process of etching evokes the longue durée of plant temporality and parallels the slow tempo of vegetal inscription in space: "I can stare at a flower for weeks, and the ferric chloride takes many hours to work on the metal" (Greenman in Oswald 2009b). The variation of style, content, and perspective in the etchings harmonizes with Oswald's diverse poetic configurations. Twenty-five black and white images function as counterparts to the 24 poems. Greenman poses some flowers in vases or pots while others are positioned against empty backgrounds in a manner reminiscent of pressed herbarium specimens.

Greenman's images synergize with Oswald's poetry to produce light-hearted resonances. Excerpts from the works of canonical authors—William Shakespeare, William Blake, Andrew Lang, Beatrix Potter—occasionally included within the frame of the botanical etchings divulge the sources inspiring Oswald and Greenman's multimodal collaboration. As if the flowers are preparing to peruse the books, a pot of violets rests atop a stack of Potter's *The Tale of Samuel Whiskers* (1908, published originally as *The Roly-Poly Pudding*) and Lang's *The Green Fairy Book* (1906, originally 1892) (Greenman in Oswald 2009b, 16). Further along, the opening quatrain of Blake's "Auguries of Innocence" accompanies an image of a strawberry plant while lines from Shakespeare's *Hamlet* provide an epigraph to an etching of assorted flowers irrupting from a vase (Greenman in Oswald 2009b, 19, 62). Evoking the flower as a self-reflective entity able to recall the past, the sonnet

"Narcissus" begins with the line "once I was half flower, half self" (Oswald 2009b, 26, l. 1). Greenman's inscription of the whole poem on the facing page concretizes Oswald's assertion that "flowers are recognisably ourselves elsewhere" (2009b, prefatory note). In other words, poems and flowers partake in a florid energy; each diversifies rhizomatically while maintaining internal coherence and autopoietic self-determination. Writing a poem, producing an etching, and growing a plant are kindred material enactments of patience. "Snowdrop" underscores the forbearance of botanical life—a theme that, in interviews, Oswald admits to savoring (e.g. Porter 2014). Greenman mirrors the poet's interest in this dimension of plant behavior in an etching—the most intricate of the volume—that incorporates the poem's final two lines: "But what a beauty, what a mighty power/of patience kept intact is now in flower" (Oswald 2009b, 49, ll. 20–21). The snowdrop—perhaps *Galanthus nivalis*—is "a pale and pining girl, head bowed, heart gnawed,/whose figure nods and shivers in a shawl" (2009b, 49, ll. 1–2). As the tallest within an assemblage of different flowers posed on a table inside a house, the expressive snowdrop blossom nods in the viewer's direction while a pastoral landscape—with the appearance of a remnant orchard—appears through the window behind the flowers.

Through personification, Oswald humorizes—and as a result *de*humanizes—plants. Therein she enables the lived experiences of flora to be brought forth regardless of orthodox conceptions that would repudiate their aptitude for experience. Her poetry also enables us to think of personification not as the projection of human phantasies on the plant body but as the elicitation of vegetal being-in-the-world. What is more, the lyrical dramatization of the "wild-flower sense of wounded gentleness" (Oswald 2009b, 49, l. 14) brings to mind Louise Glück's snowdrop who "did not expect to survive,/earth suppressing me" (1992, 6, ll. 4–5). Correspondingly, Glück's Jacob's ladder (*Polemonium caeruleum*) who lives "in a lady's garden" (1992, 24, l. 4) communicates feelings of despair over being imprisoned by her domestic confines. While Oswald's snowdrop is patient and gracious, Glück's is impatient, agitated, and vocally disdainful of human sentiment. To be certain, the abovementioned instances are not, by any standard, uproarious but they do indicate the unwavering attention Oswald pays to her sprightly protagonists. The cantankerous hairy bittercress who "ought to drink less" because "she's so full of sadness" is more chuckle-worthy than other personae but just as dolorous as the snowdrop (Oswald 2009b, 36, ll. 2–3). The feminized bittercress mutters, curses, cogitates, weeps, and suffers loneliness. She is plagued by paroxysms of remorse and ghosts of memory:

> all round her house
> there's a fog and smell of old failure,

there's a dudness
fuzzing and shadowing round her.

'Blithering business!'

(Oswald 2009b, 36, ll. 15–19)

An amusing and eccentric character, hairy bittercress (*Cardamine hirsuta*) personifies plant intelligence. The species, however, is regarded as an extremely adaptable "weed of significance in many situations" across the globe (Vaughn, Bowling, and Ruel 2011, 1284). Counter to the perception of flora as passive, patient, and slow-as-molasses, bittercress deploys a ballistic seed dispersal mechanism. Even with a high-speed camera, it is difficult to capture the dispersion process, which launches the seed up to 5 m (or 16 feet) from the parent plant. The mechanism does not require a biotic or abiotic agent to be successful. Accordingly, Oswald's figuring of bittercress as a recluse could be said to have a scientific basis. The ballistic mechanism additionally enables the plant to impede aspiring predators. Research shows that bittercress can launch siliques, or seed capsules, at caterpillars several meters away (Vaughn, Bowling, and Ruel 2011, 1284). Regardless of whether the larvae shooting is intentional or not, it does appear that the orneriness of Oswald's bittercress is grounded, to some extent, in the actual lifeworld of the species. And as Erasmus Darwin showed us, humor inheres within plant science; the more we understand vegetal ontology and botanical conservation, the more we might laugh, or weep (as seen in Chapter 8 on the death of plants in John Kinsella's poetry).

Oswald figures other plants as dawdling old men with eccentric habits and bizarre mannerisms. In personifying plants, the humorous aspects of her poetry hinge on what John Morreall (2009, 46) posits as two fundamental techniques: the wild comparison and the wild exaggeration. Morreall underscores the essential role of language in potentiating these techniques and thus generating comical effect. In particular, *Weeds and Wild Flowers* develops a mode of corporeal humor focusing on comparisons between, and exaggerations of, vegetal bodies. For instance, red-veined dock or red sorrel (*Rumex sanguineus*) is sensorially present in the poem with his "soap-sweet hands," "bristly beard-shadow," "noisy nose-blow," and "grimly to-fro" (Oswald 2009b, 30–31, ll. 7, 29, 31, 32). Resembling spinach but with red-veined lanceolate leaves, red sorrel is a herbaceous perennial cultivated widely for ornamental purposes but also consumed in moderate amounts as an addition to sauces, soups, and salads. Unlike the domestic and weedy plants of Oswald's menagerie, such as red-veined dock and hairy bittercress respectively, interrupted brome (*Bromus interruptus*) is an annual grass endemic to southern and central England. The history of the species is fascinating. Last observed in the wild in 1972 and subsequently regarded for over 30 years as "Britain's best known extinct grass" (Lyte and Cope 2004, 296), it later became the first extinct plant in British conservation history to be reestablished in the wild (Randall 2005). Botanists accordingly regard brome as a symbol of "our own fragile British flora, and the responsibilities we have for its protection" (Lyte and Cope 2004, 298). While opinions differ as to whether the species is naturalized or endemic to the British Isles, conservationists agree that the continued restoration of wild populations of the grass is imperative.

From a humorous angle, Oswald reinterprets the narrative of the brome's disappearance from the wild between 1972 and 2005 as well as the taxonomic characterization of the species as *interrupted*, which specifically denotes the occurrence of seeds at intervals along the stem. The poems begins by recounting how the brome's lips turned blue while sweeping snow off his front door steps. He then transformed into an "ice-man [...] shock-still there" for years before thawing out and limping home (Oswald 2009b, 42, l. 15). The traumatic history of going extinct then coming back to life thus rendered his behaviors staccato and erratic: "Now every time he speaks he pauses./Halfway through a pause he freezes" (2009b, 43, ll. 23–24). Flashbacks cause the affected brome persona to cough and shed frozen tears that "last for several hours./Or is it years?" (2009b, 43, ll. 27–28). The reintroduction of interrupted brome of course happened only 1 year before the publication of *Weeds and Wild Flowers*. Through the use of humorous techniques, Oswald narrativizes the unusual yet momentous recent history of the plant. Another poem that plays on the amusing aspects of botanical monikers is "Scarious Chickweed." The vegetal protagonist is especially engrossed in peppermint candies. Scarious chickweed is an uncommon colloquial name for common chickweed (*Stellaria media*), an annual species originating in Europe but naturalized in parts of North America. The technical term *scarious* denotes the thin, dry, and membranous appearance of bracts, the specialized leaves that are usually smaller than the main foliage of the plant. In *All About Weeds* (1974, originally published in 1940), the biologist Edwin Rollin Spencer vilifies chickweed as "one of the meanest of the lawn weeds" despite its "heavenly" botanical name (126). Although not cruel, Oswald's chickweed is a "freakish," paranoid, and short-sighted man who "sucks his peppermints very hurriedly, very hurriedly,/one after another after another after another" (2009b, 53, ll. 9–10). The scarious bracts give the plant the appearance of donning a "full length coat buttoned up to the chin" and slumping "as if to hide his throat" (2009b, 53, ll. 5, 13). In all likelihood, the latter is a reference to lawn mowing, clipping, and other forms of expunging the weedy plants by decapitation. The final tercet heightens these insinuations with a postmortem image of chickweed: "Only his hands, poor wilted hands,/winding and strangling a sweetwrapper/while he tremblingly stands" (2009b, 53, ll. 17–19).

Conclusion: Botanical Humor as a Resource of Hope

This chapter approached botanical humor as a dialectic that encompasses, on the one hand, comical verse centered on plant subjects and, on the other, the innately amusing, playful, and plucky aspects of vegetal being. Of course, plants neither laugh nor vocalize as humans do, no matter how closely we listen and attune (that is, without psychotropic intervention). This does not mean, however, that flora should be debarred from the affective milieu to which laughter, mirth, and gaiety are essential. Nor should the human imagining of the botanical world hang suspended, waiting for experimental science to catch up with plant affectivities—emotions, moods, delights, joys, disappointments, aspirations—before such horizons can be explored and embraced. The reception of the kind of humor articulated in this chapter involves a sympathetic imagination that can engender feelings of kindredness with plants (Branch 2014, 389). In Oswald's poetry, humor is an important formation that serves as an outward sign of the liveliness—the *wild flowerness*—of flora, specifically their manifestations of intelligence, communication, and behavior. Introducing flora to the text as personae, *Weeds and Wild Flowers* at the same time tempers the dominant rhetoric that tends to split native (indigenous, endemic) species off from their naturalized (exotic, alien) counterparts. Whereas a localized plant like interrupted brome is exalted as a vulnerable icon of botanical conservation, others such as chickweed and bittercress become noxious invasives both within and outside their historical ranges. Oswald's collective, nonetheless, is an egalitarian one that acknowledges vegetal difference as a corporeal phenomenon rather than a biopolitical category. Underpinned by humor, *Weeds and Wild Flowers* renders accessible the dynamism of the botanical realm and the complexities of plant ontology. Humorous elements help to unshackle plants from their default place in the background of narrative history or as literary devices in service to human telos.

Although not as light-hearted as her other poems, "Tree Ghosts" from *Woods etc.* (Oswald 2005b) is "a ballad with footnotes (in which each letter commemorates a cut-down tree)" (42). The footnotes take the form of a tongue-in-cheek yet deadly serious nursery rhyme memorializing lost trees in alliterative lines such as "C is for both Copse and Corpse/as G is for both Grove and Grave" (Oswald 2005b, 44, ll. 5–6). Bearing in mind the poem as a quirky elegy, I suggest in closing that botanical humor can serve as an impetus for radical ecological change. Humor and its correlates present a means of responding to—and coping with—the loss of plants in the Anthropocene today. While accentuating vegetal capacities, humor engenders the resilience and fortitude that are vital to navigating the disconcerting epoch in which we all live. As biodiversity declines on a global scale—old forests evermore converted into plantations, botanical species evermore the specters banished to the margins of human imagining—cultivating the ability to laugh at, because of and together with flora could assuage the despair that plagues many of us. Oswald's poetry assists readers with the processes of grief and mourning. Indeed, the potency of the comical mode lies in its potential resistance to ecological exploitation and its capacity to reformulate the conceptual oppositions dividing beings, species, and communities (Branch 2014, 385). Laughter and its related emotions accordingly constitute a "resource of hope" for a future that morally considers people and plants (and animals, fungi, water, air, rocks, and so forth) (Williams 1989; and Chapter 9 of the present volume on hope in the poetry of Joy Harjo). As evident in *Weeds and Wild Flowers*, especially when read in relation to Oswald's interviews and prose, humor belies a "fierce moral seriousness" (Branch 2014, 386). Disclosing plant sensitivities and presenting a mechanism for coping with grief, humor also can encourage audiences to adopt ecological standpoints and move away from reckless utilitarianist conceptions of botanical nature (Chandler 2014, 343). In this regard, ecocritic Tim Morton (2017) speculates that "we simply cannot laugh at a fellow sufferer. Of course we might be able to laugh *with* one. Perhaps a whole new realm of humor could open up, akin to the humor of the survivor […] in which lettuces and humans bemoan their common lot [emphasis in original]" (174). Indeed, the opening up of such a realm foundationally depends on the recognition of plants as endowed with the capacity for both grief and humor. To this effect, Oswald's poetry leads the way forward toward a funnier and more satisfying future for plants and non-plants alike. On this note, Chapter 6 will look at another coterie of loquacious plants in Louise Glück's *The Wild Iris*.

Bibliography

Appendino, Giovanni, Federica Pollastro, Luisella Verotta, Mauro Ballero, Adriana Romano, Paulina Wyrembek, Katarzyna Szczuraszek, Jerzy Mozrzymas, and Orazio Taglialatela-Scafati. 2009. "Polyacetylenes from Sardinian *Oenanthe fistulosa*: A Molecular Clue to *Risus Sardonicus*." *Journal of Natural Products* 72 (5): 962–65.

Apte, Mahadev. 1985. *Humor and Laughter: An Anthropological Approach*. Ithaca, NY: Cornell University Press.

Armitstead, Claire. 2016. "Interview with Alice Oswald: 'I Like the Way That the Death of One Thing Is the Beginning of Something Else'." *The Guardian*. Accessed 21 May 2017. www.theguardian.com/books/2016/jul/22/alice-oswald-interview-falling-awake

Baluška, František, and Michael Levin. 2016. "On Having No Head: Cognition Throughout Biological Systems." *Frontiers in Psychology* 7: 1–19. doi:10.3389/fpsyg.2016.00902

Barker, Cicely Mary. 1934. *A Flower Fairy Alphabet: Poems and Pictures*. London: Blackie.
Brahic, Beverley Bie. 2011. "Review: Imaginary Gardens." *Poetry* 197 (5): 422–27.
Branch, Michael. 2014. "Are You Serious? A Modest Proposal for Environmental Humor." In *The Oxford Book of Ecocriticism*, edited by Greg Garrard, 377–90. Oxford: Oxford University Press.
Browne, Janet. 1989. "Botany for Gentlemen: Erasmus Darwin and 'The Loves of the Plants'." *Isis* 80 (4): 592–621.
Bunting, Madeleine. 2012. "Alice Oswald on the Devonshire Landscape: 'There's a Terror in Beauty'." *The Guardian*. Accessed 21 May 2017. www.theguardian.com/books/2012/jul/13/alice-oswald-devonshire-landscape
Campbell-Johnson, Rachel. 2002. "Rachel Campbell-Johnson Savours Seasonal Poetry." *The Times*, London, July 3., 19.
Chandler, Katherine. 2014. "Poisonwood Persuasion: Rhetorical Roles of Humor in Environmental Literature." *Interdisciplinary Literary Studies* 16 (2): 326–47.
Clout, Mick, and Peter Williams. 2009. "Introduction." In *Invasive Species Management: A Handbook of Principles and Techniques*, edited by Mick Clout and Peter Williams, v–x. Oxford: Oxford University Press.
Connor, Peter. 1987. *Horace's Lyric Poetry: The Force of Humour*. Berwick, Vic: Aureal Publications.
Darwin, Erasmus. 1798. *The Botanic Garden: A Poem, in Two Parts*. 5th ed. New York: T. & J. Swords.
Dehn, Georgia. 2015. "Mary Keen Interview: 'People Have Accused Me of Being Too Traditional'." *The Telegraph*. Accessed 21 May 2017. www.telegraph.co.uk/gardening/gardens-to-visit/the-world-of-mary-keen/
Emerson, Edward. 1908. *Beverages, Past and Present: An Historical Sketch of their Production, Together with a Study of the Customs Connected with Their Use*. Vol. 1. New York: Knickerbocker Press.
Emerson, Ralph Waldo. 1880. *Works of Ralph Waldo Emerson in Five Volumes*. Vol. 4. Boston, MA: Houghton, Osgood and Company; The Riverside Press.
Emerson, Ralph Waldo. 2001. *The Later Lectures of Ralph Waldo Emerson, 1843–1871*. Edited by Ronald Bosco and Joel Myerson. Vol. 2. Athens: University of Georgia Press.
Enright, D.J. 1953. *The Laughing Hyena and Other Poems*. London: Routledge and Kegan Paul.
Farrier, David. 2014. "'Like a Stone': Ecology, Enargeia, and Ethical Time in Alice Oswald's Memorial." *Environmental Humanities* 4 (1): 1–18.
Freeman, R. Austin. 1954. *The Penrose Mystery*. London: Pan Books.
Gagliano, Monica, Vladyslav Vyazovskiy, Alexander Borbély, Mavra Grimonprez, and Martial Depczynski. 2016. "Learning by Association in Plants." *Scientific Reports* 6 (38427): 1–9.
Gagliano, Monica, Michael Renton, Martial Depczynski, and Stefano Mancuso. 2014. "Experience Teaches Plants to Learn Faster and Forget Slower in Environments Where it Matters." *Oecologia* 175 (1): 63–72. doi:10.1007/s00442-013-2873-7
Gerard, John. 1597. *Herball, or Generall Historie of Plantes*. London: John Norton.

Glück, Louise. 1992. *The Wild Iris*. New York: HarperCollins Publishers.
Gordon, Mordechai. 2014. *Humor, Laughter and Human Flourishing: A Philosophical Exploration of the Laughing Animal*. Heidelberg: Springer.
Homer. 1802. *The Odyssey*. Translated by William Cowper. 2 ed. Vol. 2. London: J. Johnson.
Hooper, Toby, and Juliana Hooper. 1982. *The Laughing Australian: A Celebration of Australia's Best-Loved Symbol*. Melbourne: Nelson. Original edition, 1946.
Huisman, Rosemary. 1998. "Incongruous Means: Techniques of Humour in Avante-Garde and Post-Modernist Poetry." *Southern Review: Communication, Politics and Culture* 31 (2): 221–30.
Keen, Mary, and Tom Hatton. 2015. *Paradise and Plenty: A Rothschild Family Garden*. London: Pimpernel Press.
Kilmer, Joyce. 1914. *Trees and Other Poems*. New York: George H. Doran Company.
Lang, Andrew, ed. 1906. *The Green Fairy Book*. London: Longmans, Green, and Company.
Lockwood, Samuel. 1876. "Animal Humor." *American Naturalist* 10 (5): 257–70.
Lyte, Benedict, and Tom Cope. 2004. "Plants in Peril, 25. *Bromus interruptus*." *Curtis's Botanical Magazine* 16 (4): 296–300.
Mabey, Richard. 2012. *Weeds: In Defense of Nature's Most Unloved Plants*. New York: Ecco.
Marder, Michael, and Patrícia Vieira. 2013. "Writing Phytophilia: Philosophers and Poets as Lovers of Plants." *Frame* 26 (2): 37–53.
Meeker, Joseph. 1997. *The Comedy of Survival: Literary Ecology and a Play Ethic*. Tucson: University of Arizona Press. Original edition, 1974.
Meyer, John. 2015. *Understanding Humor through Communication: Why Be Funny, Anyway?* Lanham, MD: Lexington Books.
Middleton, Rowan. 2015. "Connection, Disconnection and the Self in Alice Oswald's *Dart*." *Green Letters* 19 (2): 157–69. doi:10.1080/14688417.2014.972427
Moore, Charles. 2009. "Alice Oswald Considers the Daisies and How They Grow." *The Telegraph*. Accessed 21 May 2017. www.telegraph.co.uk/comment/columnists/charlesmoore/5273262/Alice-Oswald-considers-the-daisies-and-how-they-grow.html
Morreall, John. 2009. *Comic Relief: A Comprehensive Philosophy of Humor*. Chichester: John Wiley and Sons.
Morton, Tim. 2017. "What Vegetables Are Saying about Themselves." In *The Language of Plants: Science, Philosophy, Literature*, edited by Monica Gagliano, John Ryan and Patrícia Vieira, 173–90. Minneapolis: University of Minnesota Press.
Nash, Ogden. 1985. *Candy is Dandy: The Best of Ogden Nash*. London: Methuen.
Oswald, Alice. 2000. "The Universe in time of rain makes the world alive with noise." In *A Green Thought in a Green Shade: Poetry in the Garden*, edited by Sarah Maguire, 35–48. London: The Poetry Society.
———. 2002. *Dart*. London: Faber and Faber.

———. 2005a. "Introduction: A Dew's Harp." In *The Thunder Mutters: 101 Poems for the Planet*, edited by Alice Oswald, ix–x. London: Faber.
———. 2005b. *Woods etc*. London: Faber and Faber.
———. 2009a. *A Sleepwalk on the Severn*. London: Faber and Faber.
———. 2009b. *Weeds and Wild Flowers: Poems by Alice Oswald, Etchings by Jessica Greenman*. London: Faber and Faber.
———. 2010. *The Thing in the Gap Stone Stile*. London: Faber and Faber. Original edition, 1996.
———. 2011. *Memorial: An Excavation of the Iliad*. London: Faber and Faber.
———. 2013. "Presiding Spirits." Accessed 21 May 2017. http://magmapoetry.com/archive/magma-26-questions-of-travel/articles/presiding-spirits/
———. 2016. *Falling Awake*. New York: W.W. Norton and Company.
Pausanias. 1824. *The Description of Greece*. Translated by Thomas Taylor. Vol. 3. London: Priestley and Weale, Library of Works on Art.
Peiffer, Katrina Schimmoeller. 2000. *Coyote at Large: Humor in American Nature Writing*. Salt Lake City: University of Utah Press.
Pinard, Mary. 2009. "Voice(s) of the Poet-Gardener: Alice Oswald and the Poetry of Acoustic Encounter." *Interdisciplinary Literary Studies* 10 (2): 17–32.
Poetry Foundation. 2017. "Alice Oswald." Accessed 21 May 2017. www.poetryfoundation.org/poems-and-poets/poets/detail/alice-oswald#poet
Porter, Max. 2014. "Interview with Alice Oswald." *The White Review* 11. Accessed 21 May 2017. www.thewhitereview.org/interviews/interview-with-alice-oswald/
Potter, Beatrix. 1908. *The Roly-Poly Pudding*. London: Frederick Warne and Company.
Randall, David. 2005. "Back From the Dead: Scientist Revives Lost Plant of Old England." *Independent*. Accessed 21 May 2017. www.independent.co.uk/environment/back-from-the-dead-scientist-revives-lost-plant-of-old-england-5346783.html
Ribichini, Sergio. 2000. *Il Riso Sardonico: Storia Di Un Proverbio Antico*. Sassari: Carlo Delfino.
Runcie, Charlotte. 2016. "Is Alice Oswald Our Greatest Living Poet?" *The Telegraph*. Accessed 21 May 2017. www.telegraph.co.uk/books/what-to-read/is-alice-oswald-our-greatest-living-poet/
Smith, William. 1874. *A Smaller Classical Dictionary of Biography, Mythology, and Geography*. 15th ed. London: John Murray.
Spencer, Edwin Rollin. 1974. *All About Weeds*. Newburyport: Dover Publications. Original edition, 1940.
Storey, Mark. 1979. *Poetry and Humour: From Cowper to Clough*. London: The Macmillan Press.
Thoreau, Henry David. 1882. *Walden*. Vol. 1. Boston, MA: Houghton, Mifflin and Company.
———. 1993. *Faith in a Seed: The Dispersion of Seeds and Other Late Natural History Writings*. Washington, DC: Island Press.
———. 1999. *Material Faith: Thoreau on Science*. Edited by Laura Dassow Walls. Boston, MA: Houghton Mifflin Company.
———. 2000. *Wild Fruits: Thoreau's Rediscovered Last Manuscript*. Edited by Bradley P. Dean. New York: W. W. Norton.

Trewavas, Anthony. 2014. *Plant Behaviour and Intelligence*. Oxford: Oxford University Press.
———. 2016. "Intelligence, Cognition, and Language of Green Plants." *Frontiers in Psychology* 7: 1–9. doi:10.3389/fpsyg.2016.00588
Vaughn, Kevin, Andrew Bowling, and Katia Ruel. 2011. "The Mechanism for Explosive Seed Dispersal in *Cardamine hirsuta* (Brassicaceae)." *American Journal of Botany* 98 (8): 1276–85.
West, Michael. 2000. *Transcendental Wordplay: America's Romantic Punsters and the Search for the Language of Nature*. Athens: Ohio University Press.
Williams, Raymond. 1989. *Resources of Hope: Culture, Democracy, Socialism*. New York: Verso.
Yeung, Heather. 2015. *Spatial Engagement with Poetry*. New York: Palgrave Macmillan.

6 Consciousness Buried in Earth

Vegetal Memory in Louise Glück's *The Wild Iris*

> Hush, beloved. It doesn't matter to me
> how many summers I live to return:
> this one summer we have entered eternity.
> I felt your two hands
> bury me to release its splendor.
> —from "The White Lilies," *The Wild Iris* (1992, 63, ll. 13–17)

The ability to recall past occurrences and anticipate future events has been valorized through the ages as belonging to the domain of organisms—from physiologically complex mammals to relatively simple invertebrates—possessing nervous systems and displaying outward signs of intelligent behavior. The seventeenth-century French philosopher René Descartes delineated memory unequivocally as a function of the brain and, in particular, emphasized the mneumonic centrality of the pineal gland: "The brain [is] the organ or the seat of the common sense, of the imagination, and of the memory" (qtd. in Clarke 2003, 79). In a letter to the theologian Marin Mersenne in late 1632, Descartes disclosed the anatomical basis of his theory of mind, mentation, and recollection: "I am dissecting the head of various animals at present to explain what the imagination, memory, etc. consist of" (qtd. in Clarke 2003, 78). More specifically, his notion of *plis de mémoire*—or "memory folds"—hypothesized that the immaterial contents of remembrance imprint physically on the brain "like creases left in a sheet of paper that has been folded" (qtd. in Bouton 1991, 52). Notwithstanding the unabashed zoocentrism of the neurosciences since Descartes, biologists in the late nineteenth and early twentieth centuries, including Charles and Francis Darwin and Jagadish Chandra Bose, respectively, have posited aneural—that is, non-neuron-based—models of memory that are independent of the exalted animal brain as the organ of information retrieval, processing, and integration.

Endlessly intrigued by vegetal memory, behavior, and learning, Charles Darwin examined the habituation of climbing plants to various stimuli (Trewavas 2014, 86). His disquisition *On the Movement and*

Habits of Climbing Plants (first published by the Linnean Society in 1865) provides a meticulous account of the twining habits of several tendril-bearing species, including three members of the Passifloraceae, or passion flower, family. Among them, crinkled passion flower (*Passiflora gracilis*) "exceeds all other climbing plants in the rapidity of its movements, and all tendril-bearers in the sensitiveness of its tendrils" (Darwin 1865, 89). Whereas stimuli such as thread, wire, and Darwin's own hand initiated curving, contact with tendrils of the same plant followed by gentle drops of water and a vigorously syringed water stream all failed to instigate tendril coiling. As a consequence, the English naturalist concluded that the "tendrils are habituated to the touch of other tendrils and to that of drops of rain" (Darwin 1865, 90). Minimizing the energy demands of repeated contraction during rain showers or blustery conditions when tendrils might cross, the passion flower observed by Darwin expressed tactile sensitivity and recollection involving the remembrance of touch, the ability to discriminate between stimuli, and the power of self-recognition. Although Darwin described this phenomenon in terms of habituation rather than memory, his experiments nevertheless point to the ability of vegetal life to recall previous light conditions and adjust behaviors in response. The insinuation that plants remember light—that memories of the sun are at work within their physiologies—decenters the predominance of phototropism. According to this principle, some growth in the botanical world is a reaction to light stimuli and is mediated by chemicals, namely auxin. A phototropic conception of movement constructs the plant as an assemblage of organs and compounds reacting mechanically to its environment rather than an agentic and embodied subject negotiating an ecological milieu. Implying the mediating role of memory in plant growth, Darwin also experimented with the cotyledons (embryonic leaves) of a cassia species. As expected, cotyledons placed in the darkest corner of a room remained closed while those fully exposed to sunlight expanded. When he placed both pots side-by-side in the middle of the room, however, cotyledons previously exposed to sunlight closed while the others unfurled. Despite exposure to equivalent solar intensity in the middle of the room, the young leaves moved in opposite directions and, hence, exhibited a memory of prior conditions as well as an awareness of relative states of darkness and light (Darwin and Darwin 2016, 414).

In the spirit of Darwin, contemporary plant scientists František Baluška and Michael Levin (2016) interpret memory—more inclusively in reference to the botanical kingdom—as a spatio-temporal feedback loop involving "experience-dependent modification of internal structure, in a stimulus-specific manner that alters the way the system will respond to stimuli in the future as a function of its past" (2). In contrast to the *plis de mémoire* of Descartes, an aneural model accommodates the behaviors of organisms—including plants—conventionally proscribed from the privileged sphere of recollection and, by association, the intelligent capacities of learning and consciousness. Indeed, current scientific thinking indicates that memory has increasingly become a prism through which botanists—especially those who, like Baluška and Michael, are located in the tendentious area of neuro-botany—rationalize their observations of vegetal life. It empirically has been demonstrated that plants monitor environmental changes, enacting the facility to both memorize and anticipate gradations in temperature, light, pressure, stress, and other ecological variables (Müller-Xing, Xing, and Goodrich 2014). Long- and short-term variations of vegetal memory support genetic selection by facilitating adaptation (Crisp et al. 2016, 5). For instance, young silver birches (*Betula pendula*) experimentally subjected to changes in intervals of solar exposure, which regulate the trees' maturation, modulate their growth by comparing the ratio of light to dark—as well as red to far-red light—in lab conditions similar to the ratios recalled from the sunrises and sunsets of previous days (Karban 2015, 33). As Michael Marder (2013) contends, "whereas humans remember whatever has phenomenally appeared in the light, plants keep the memory of light itself" (156).

The American poet Louise Glück (b. 1943) makes no explicit allusions to the science of plant consciousness, behavior, and learning. Her poetry, nonetheless, imaginatively mediates vegetal beings' memories of themselves, one another, and their ecological circumstances. In 1993, Glück received the Pulitzer Prize for Poetry for her heteroglossic collection *The Wild Iris* (1992)—the principal work from her oeuvre addressed in this chapter—and the Bollingen Prize in 2001 (Gosmann 2012, 18). From 2003 to 2004, she served as the U.S. Poet Laureat. Glück's botanical poetry engages a dialectic (as set out in Chapter 1 of *Plants in Contemporary Poetry*) of plants affecting both animate and inanimate things around them while, conversely, being impacted by their environments. More specifically, Glück's poetry moves contrapuntally between human remembrance (and memorialization) of the vegetal and the bold textualization of botanical memory and, with it, consciousness as intrinsic characteristics of vegetal subjects. A prominent narrative formation within *The Wild Iris* and other collections, botanical memory is nevertheless underemphasized or completely absent in critical discussions of Glück's work (for example, Diehl 2005; Gosmann 2012; Morris 2006). Yet, in her human speakers' recollections of flowers, Glück overcomes the reduction of the botanical (as an unfeeling and unspeaking aggregation of cellulose, hormones, organs, systems, and so on) by instead investing in the possibility that conscious plants with voices remember themselves, other beings, and their worlds. Accordingly, her work reflects—in lyrical form—the ontological claim that plants are temporally cognizant and "have a past, which they bear in their extended being and which they may access at any given moment" (Marder 2013,

155). This chapter moreover suggests that her poetic evocation of plant memory is inter-mnemonic, involving an exchange or "dialogue of memories" (Parks 1991, 57) between human, vegetal, and other speakers.

The Garden Admires: Inter-mnemonics and Glück as Cultivator

From her early collections *Firstborn* (1968) and *The House on Marshland* (1975) to her more recent *Averno* (2007) and *Faithful and Virtuous Night* (2014), Louise Glück's work consistently has been characterized as lean, unembellished, psychoanalytic, and, at times, strikingly stoic, reticent, and depersonalized. Unlike W.D. Snodgrass, Anne Sexton, Sylvia Plath, and other poetic predecessors in the contemporary confessional tradition, Glück's "postconfessional" lyricism constructs an authorial self that—while legibly intimate and porous—remains, at the same time, "muted by an amplified sense of the mythic" (Dodd 1992, 149). Although she began writing during the confessional upsurge of the 1950s and 1960s, Glück adopted a mode of "personal classicism" (Dodd 1992, 150–51) early in her career. As such, her poetry leverages a suite of techniques—mythologization, archetypes, polyvocality, linguistic economy, prominent blank space between lines and stanzas, as well as other literary and textual tools and motifs—to restrain the autobiographical immediacy and transparency typical of the confessional stance (Dodd 1992, 1–2). Considering the postconfessional orientation of her work, commentators tend to call attention to the "subtle, psychological moments captured by the austerity of her diction" (Diehl 2005, 1) and the elimination from her poetry of "any linguistic excess that blurs her sight" (Chiasson 2007, 139). Through its interweaving of mythic and personal voices, her poetry courageously thematizes harrowing memories; for instance, of "the tragedy of anorexia" during her adolescence (Glück 1994, 10) and the breakdown of an early marriage (as centralized in *The Wild Iris*, 1992). In *Proofs and Theories* (1994), Glück speaks frankly of her struggle with anorexia in the candid and, indeed, corporeal language one might expect of a confessional (or postconfessional) poet reflecting on her life experiences in prose: "I realized, logically, that to be 85, then 80, then 75 pounds was to be thin; I understood that at some point I was going to die [...] Even then, dying seemed a pathetic metaphor for establishing a separation between myself and my mother" (11). Notwithstanding the distinctly uninhibited self-analysis of this extract, Glück's intentional muting of personal memory through the amplification of myths and archetypes—including Persephone and her marriage to Hades in *Averno*—remains the foremost preoccupation of critical approaches to her work (Gosmann 2012, 18).

While the personal, psychoanalytic, and mythic dimensions of Glück's oeuvre have been well-articulated, analyses of the environmental facets of her poetry and, more specifically, her narration of the memory imbrications—or inter-mnemonics—between beings are less profuse. To be sure, ecocritical studies most commonly situate Glück within an ecofeminist framework (Azcuy 2008; Gordon 2002; Scigaj 1999, xiii). In *Sustainable Poetry* (1999, xiii, 7) Leonard Scigaj cites Glück alongside Joy Harjo, Mary Oliver, Adrienne Rich, Denise Levertov, and other female American poets whose writings investigate human affinities with the natural world assiduously while also exploring salient parallel questions posed by feminism or ecofeminism. Moreover, Maggie Gordon (2002, 222) observes that Glück's early career coincided with the emergence of American ecofeminism and that her poetry reflects a heterarchical—rather than hierarchical—understanding of the natural world as an interconnected web. Gorden sees Glück as aligning the female (personal) body with the earth (nonhuman) body through shared material being that reflects traditional ecofeminist concerns of corporeality, relationality, equipoise, and freedom from oppression. By narrating the voice of the persecuted plant—especially marked, for instance, in the poem "Witchgrass" from *The Wild Iris* in which a notoriously tenacious garden weed speaks directly of its oppression—Glück invokes the ecofeminist critique of the coterminous domination of women and nature (Gordon 2002, 225). In Gordon's analysis, Glück's principal focus ultimately remains "poetic rather than political. That is to say, her work is not driven *overtly* by themes of feminism and environmentalism [emphasis added]" (229). Similarly, Mary Kate Azcuy (2008) interprets the memory of an abortion, narrated in "The Egg" from *Firstborn*, as both a poetic indictment of the Western patriarchal legacy and a hopeful declaration for an "ecofeminist revisioning in nature" (63). Although without reference to ecocriticism or ecofeminism per se, Daniel Morris (2006, 178) regards *Ararat* as a work of nature poetry exhibiting Glück's indebtedness to the Romantic tradition for its unparalleled figurative—rather than literal—treatment of the environment. According to Morris, Glück's early writing positions the natural world as an adversarial counterforce to the full actualization of symbols in poetry. Subsequent collections such as *Ararat* and *The Wild Iris*, however, represent Glück's increasing openness to a material language of flowers that—despite sustained poetic attention—proves to be an imperfect vessel for grief, mourning, and traumatic memory (Morris 2006, 178).

One of the implications of the prevailing emphasis on the symbolic, postconfessional, and psychoanalytic elements of Glück's lyricism is the backgrounding of the materialities of the nonhuman agents in, and ecological contexts of, her poetry. For Serenella Iovino and Serpil Oppermann (2014), in contrast, material ecocriticism restores critical focus to such agents and contexts through the recognition that "the world's material phenomena are knots in a vast network of agencies, which can be 'read' and interpreted as forming narratives" (1). A critical perspective grounded in material ecocriticism shifts emphasis to the terrene genesis of poetic narratives by acknowledging that "human and nonhuman players are interlocked in networks that produce undeniable signifying forces" (Iovino and Oppermann 2014, 2). For the most part, though, the vegetal subjects and garden settings of Glück's work are regarded as symbolic structures or incidental signifying forces, even in the view of the poet herself who downplays the material foundations of the floristic poetics she enacts so grippingly. Published 2 years after *The Wild Iris*, Glück's exegetical *Proofs and Theories* (1994, 17) briefly alludes to her relocation from urban areas to rural Vermont where she wrote the Pulitzer-winning poems and commenced a fulfilling career as a university writing teacher. Yet, surprisingly, this volume of essays on poetry makes reference neither to the garden's significance as a locus for embodied participation and as a "vast network of agencies" (Iovino and Oppermann 2014, 1) nor to the attainment of horticultural knowledge through intensive observation, study, practice, and reflection. In copious detail, the opening chapter "Education of the Poet" (Glück 1994, 3–18) presents the poet's literary education but glosses over her apprenticeship to plant life. Considering the extensive botanical content of *The Wild Iris*—about half of the titles in the sequence bear the names of flowers—this represents a striking minimization of the vegetal foundations of Glück's poetry. Moreover, the de-prioritization that I call attention to seems out of step with critical reception of the volume underscoring the botanical tenor of the sequence. For instance, a review from *The New Republic* excerpted on the back cover of *The Wild Iris* characterizes the work as a *lieder* cycle "written in the language of flowers" that emphasizes the "vegetatively animate world" and even goes so far as to entreat the audience to "try to live like plants" (Vendler 1993, 36–38).

Insinuations of Glück's underlying interest in vegetal materialities and her acquisition of botanical knowledge tend to come, instead, in the form of brief reflections in interviews. As an example, in an interview in *Beltway Poetry Quarterly*, Glück quips that, after the publication of *The Wild Iris*, "I got a lot of horticultural inquiries, and I'm not a horticulturist" (Cavalieri and Glück 2006, n.p.). To the contrary, she acquired her considerable knowledge of plant ecology and behavior—as narrated in the *lieder* cycle—from the catalogues of White Flower Farm and "from growing flowers" (Cavalieri and Glück 2006, n.p.). In the 1930s, the amateur horticulturalists William Harris and Jane Grant founded White Flower Farm in Connecticut and, by the early 1950s, the company began mailing catalogues out countrywide "to expose their customers to the latest hybrids from Europe, Japan, and elsewhere" (White Flower Farm 2016, n.p.). Hence, Glück's botanical poetry enciphers her participation in the American folk tradition of growing ornamental flowers, marked by the circulation of practical knowledge through ephemeral publications, such as horticultural catalogues, and the first-hand experiences informally shared with fellow gardeners through observation, word of mouth, and other forms of convivial exchange. Moreover, I suggest that flower cultivation in the highly variable climate of Vermont engendered in Glück a consciousness of the seasonal cadences of plants, which in turn affected the structure of her writing. For instance, the placement of the poem "The Silver Lily" (Glück 1992, 59) toward the end of *The Wild Iris* reflects the flowering of the species at the close of summer and the beginning of autumn:

> If you are gardeners, you know that this [lily]—not the daylily, but the Asiatics and so on—[blooms] toward the end of summer, and in Vermont, where this garden was, at the very end of summer. And oftentimes they don't even get to bloom because the snow falls first.
> (Cavalieri and Glück 2006, n.p.)

Although "not a horticulturist"—a declaration that indeed underplays her practice of growing flowers during this period—in the interview excerpt Glück demonstrates an ability to distinguish between the daylily (*Hemerocallis* spp.) and Asiatic lily (*Lilium asiatica*).

Glück developed a passion for her backyard flower growing practice, which gradually began to intergrade with her poetic vision. Elsewhere, in another interview, she elaborates on the synergies between gardening, walking, music, reading, and writing that directed her development of *The Wild Iris* and the polyphonic mode of address, including the voices of plants, that typifies it. In the years preceding her writing of the sequence, during which she claims to have listened almost exclusively to Mozart and Da Ponte's opera *Don Giovanni*, Glück states that she limited her reading to flower catalogues in lieu of literary works:

> I was getting really passionate about the garden and I was writing nothing [...] I was walking in the garden and doing a little desultory reading, and I thought, 'Well, I'll try to write a poem spoken by a flower'. And immediately I thought—well, within two days, when I wrote another—I thought, 'This...I know what I'm doing'.
> (Glück 2013, n.p.)

She recalls the rapturous fusion of music, walking, growing, and reflecting into a synesthetic form lending shape and character to the poetic sequence. Rather than a tangential agent, the real garden Glück nurtured in Vermont came to offer a material locus of creativity and memory centered on human intimacy with cultivated flora. Unlike the sites of sublime encounter with the wild exalted by ecopoets in the tradition of Robinson Jeffers and Gary Snyder, Glück's garden helped to crystallize the domestic currents of *The Wild Iris* and, more specifically, the disintegrating relationship between a wife, husband, and son. Nevertheless, the integral narrative role of the garden and the practice of gardening is by no means specific to the Pulitzer-winning volume. Indeed, the garden as an agentic site of dialogue between percipient beings and elements is nascent in Glück's earlier works. For instance, the second part of the five-part poem "The Garden" from *Descending Figure* (Glück 1980, 5) invokes the conscious and self-directed nature of vegetal life:

> The garden admires you.
> For your sake it smears itself with green pigment,
> the ecstatic reds of the roses,
> so that you will come to it with your lovers.
>
> And the willows—
> see how it has shaped these green
> tents of silence [...]
>
> (pt. 2, ll. 1–7)

In these lines, the garden is more than an aesthetically pleasing backdrop that is acted upon by living things; instead, as a signifying force, it actively admires humans (experiences affective states), smears itself (exhibits self-awareness), and shapes the willows (modifies other species). In contrast to the poems of *The Wild Iris*, however, the percipient plants of *The House on Marshland*, *Descending Figure*, and other works do not address the reader directly.

The recognition of vegetal nature as animated—as infused with the divine and bearing the capacity of linguistic address—permeates *The Wild Iris*, published 12 years after *Descending Figure* and 17 years after *The House on Marshland*. Glück explains that the lieder cycle:

> takes its form from the arc of a summer in a garden. There are three types of speakers. The natural world speaks, and the poems spoken by the earth have the names of flowers: 'The Silver Lily', 'The Wild Iris', 'Field Flowers'. Then there are poems in which a human speaker addresses, occasionally the earth, I think, but mostly, whatever—I have no word to describe this divinity, or celestial presence—has animated [his or her] life.
>
> (Cavalieri and Glück 2006, n.p.)

Rather than following the relatively unified speaking position of her earlier works, the sequence exhibits a heterogeneity of voices in which the authorial-self negotiates "the border between the human and the not human, as under construction, and in a state of becoming" (Morris 2006, 200). During the course of *The Wild Iris*, the poet-gardener-supplicant, the earth, the wind, flowers, divine presence, and abstract ideas alternate speaking. Glück framed the text as a liturgical progression from

"Matins" (morning prayers, also used as poem titles) to "Vespers" (evening prayers) superimposed over the annual cycle of a Vermont garden. Fourteen flowering plant speakers—lamium, trillium, violets, witchgrass, red poppies, and others—address the poet-gardener-supplicant who, at times, implores an unnamed divinity. In turn, the supercilious god figure chastises the poet for her self-pity, solipsism, and anxious interrogation of nature, desire, values, and morality (Vendler 1993, 36). Critic Dan Chiasson's (2007) assertion that "Glück's poems often imitate forms of explicit address—prayer, hymn, confession" (144) provides an especially apt encapsulation of *The Wild Iris*. In a comparable manner, critics have distinguished the unusual lieder cycle succinctly as a "polyphonic theater," "heteroglossic text," "prayer sequence" (Morris 2006, 191), and "radically heteroglot volume" (Gordon 2002, 228).

Within *The Wild Iris,* and in the entirety of Glück's poetics, memory serves a vital narrative function. Such a textualization of memory, however, resists the sharply drawn subjectivity of the psychoanalytic optic through which her poetry—typecast as confessional or postconfessional—tends to be read. Constrained by an underlying psychoanalytic framing, Morris (2006, 160) emphasizes Glück's uncanny use of the present tense to confront, recover, and direct the content of recollection. In narrow terms, such a claim posits Glück's poetic memory as a mechanism for controlling the traumas of adolescence and early adulthood via the lyrical self. Uta Gosmann's comparative analysis of Glück, Sylvia Plath, Susan Howe, and Ellen Hinsey, (2012) forwards the concept "poetic memory" as the recognition that "the self is more than the compound of a person's remembered biography" (1). Whereas "historic memory" constitutes identity through the recollectable past, poetic memory positions the self as "dynamic, expansive, and full of potential" (Gosmann 2012, 1)—as more than an admixture of the previous sensations and experiences of the individual conjured in the poetic moment. In *The Wild Iris*, the expansive self—based on the principle that identity is more than an aggregation of one's memories—interbraids with the natural world and, more specifically, with botanical life. Yet, the volume goes beyond nostalgic recollection of plants, sentimental reflection on vegetal being, or the reduction of botanical life to malleable tropes in service to the psychological states of humans. As subjects with their own experiences, remembrances, and affective modes, plants speak in the first person. Gifted with the faculty of memory, the flower-beings of *The Wild Iris* collectively facilitate the transformation of Glück's poetic vision. No longer the privileged attribute of brained organisms, the power of recollection becomes a property of living and nonliving things, including plants and the environment construed broadly. The poet's immersion in the material realities of her Vermont garden, I argue, precipitates the movement within her poetry toward an understanding of memory as intrinsic to plants and indicative of their intelligence.

In contrast to this vision of plants as agentic, Glück's earlier volumes display the tendency to metaphorize and memorialize vegetal life. The "pared-down rhetoric" (Morris 2006, 179) of *Ararat* (1990) posits vegetal nature as a symbol for the emotional states and ideational deliberations of human subjects. The opening lines of "Yellow Dahlia," for instance, epitomize the distillation of botanical life into symbolic language in which a poem—despite its title—departs from the biological domain and bears almost no trace of real plants, their ecologies, and their companion species. No longer a vibrant presence, vegetality is appropriated as a metaphor to summon—in the textualization of memory—the speaker's strained relationship with a sibling while attempting to maintain, paradoxically, an aura of depersonalization in the narrative:

> My sister's like a sun, like a yellow dahlia.
> Daggers of gold hair around the face.
> Gray eyes, full of spirit.
>
> I made an enemy of a flower:
> now, I'm ashamed.
>
> (Glück 2012b, 228, ll. 1–5)

In likening her sister to a yellow dahlia, the speaker expresses ruefulness; how could she harbor a deep-seated aversion toward a lovely well-composed golden flower? Correspondingly, the poem "Birthday" employs roses to memorialize "the legend of [her] mother's beauty," especially in the eyes of a male admirer, while bringing the dispassion of her father into sharp relief:

> After ten years, the roses stopped.
> But all that time I thought
> the dead could minister to the living;
> I didn't realize
> this was the anomaly; that for the most part
> the dead were like my father.
>
> (Glück 2012b, 221, ll. 5, 11–16)

In a similar manner, the "The Shad-blow Tree" from an earlier collection, *The House on Marshland* (Glück 1975, 17), bears little resemblance in content or form to the titular shadblow serviceberry (*Amelanchier canadensis*), a common species to the wetland areas of the Atlantic coastal plain. In framing the tree as a medium for investigating the self through aspects of memory, time, seasonality, and the visual imagination, the poem re-inscribes the Romantic desire to cultivate nature for symbolic ends (Morris 2006, 160). "The Shad-blow Tree" comprises two parts: "The Tree" and "The Latent Image." On the threshold of the spring in the second part, the tree's mode of being is imbricated with the power of the human mind to form images and, in forging memories, to control nature:

> deep in the brain
> the shad-blow coins its leaf in this context,
> among monuments, continuous with such frozen forms,
> as have become the trained vine,
> root, rock, and all things perishing.
> (Glück 1975, 17, pt. 2, ll. 5–9)

The poet is noticeably restrained in her ascription of memory to the shadblow serviceberry. *The Wild Iris*, however, represents the evolution of Glück's approach to vegetal nature as a subject of poetry. The alternation between speaking positions accentuates the heterogeneous forms of memory enacted by nonhuman beings and natural elements. Whereas, in her earlier works, the poet remembers roses, dahlias, and shad-blow trees, imputing figurative resonances and symbolic meanings to them, in *The Wild Iris* the flowers defiantly reclaim both the faculty of memory and the power to direct the garden narrative. Indeed, of all her poetry, the Pulitzer-winning volume deviates from an anthropocentric psychoanalytic grounding and embraces a more ecocentric—or what I shall go on to characterize as inter-mnemonic—conception of memory as "the register of what a living being has undergone in its lifetime" (Marder 2013, 156).

Death-Spasm, Remembrance, and the Germ of Consciousness

As a locus of imaginative reflection and corporeal immersion, Glück's garden prompted a shift from the rhetorical depiction of vegetal life in *The House on Marshland* and in other collections to a vision of plants in *The Wild Iris* as endowed with memory, learning, behavior, emotions, and diverse sensitivities. I suggest that, through the practice of cultivating flowers over the course of the Vermont seasons, Glück began to internalize an understanding of the botanical kingdom as more percipient than conventional Western frameworks are capable of articulating. Especially since the experimentation of the physiologists Julius von Sachs and Jacques Loeb, a non-cognitive—or reactive—model has been the default standpoint for conceptualizing plants vis-à-vis their lifeworlds (Calvo 2016, 1323). The dominant theory propounds that vegetal life is mechanically "hardwired" for tropic (directional) and nastic (non-directional) responses to light, gravity, and other stimuli (Calvo 2016, 1323). Such a totalizing stance effectively rules out the prospect of intelligence, memory, and learning—characteristics regarded, instead, as the domain of motile beings. Accordingly, the Bengali biophysicist Jagadish Chandra Bose (1920) observed that "vegetable life has always appeared to us very remote, because that life is unvoiced. The plant, in its apparent immobility and placidity, stands in strong contrast to the energetic animal with its reflex movements and pulsating organs" (101). Notwithstanding the inherently "unvoiced" nature of plants posited by Bose, affective experiences and interspecies encounters in garden settings facilitate appreciation of the complex ecologies and behavioral modalities of the vegetal realm (Kiesling and Manning 2010; Nyberg and Sanders 2014). With gardens as sites of material engagement and gardening as an embodied practice, the peculiar registers and enunciations of plants can appear less "remote" to us over time.

Glück's work emphasizes that, not only are plants remembered, memorialized, and metaphorized by humans, they also actively integrate information, make decisions, and predict future circumstances by taking previous experiences into account. Michael Marder (2016) argues that to reject the possibility of vegetal memory is illogical because "without the recollection of past events, without forming patterns out of these, and without projecting them into the future via anticipation, survival is impossible" (para. 5). Energized by an exposure to plants in the continuously mutable New England garden setting, Glück's poetization of memory came to harmonize with a lineage of scientists, philosophers, writers, and polymaths across cultures who have acknowledged the percipient qualities of vegetal life. In particular, her work began to attend to the dialectic of botanical memory, to wit, the capacity of plant life to remember in converse relation to the vegetal as a focus—or object—of poetic memory. As an experimental biophysicist and poetic thinker, Bose (1858–1937) regarded plants in a similar manner as distinctly apperceptive organisms with memories, emotions, behaviors, and the ability to experience pain and pleasure. A close friend of the poet-artist Rabindranath Tagore, Bose developed an expansive and holistic conception of plants as able to negotiate their worlds, especially through sophisticated internal electrochemical signaling systems. The biophysicist devised a suite of apparatuses to disclose vegetal language, or what he characterized intriguingly as "plant-script" and "plant-autographs" (Bose 1914). His devices were designed to identify, through scientific means, the self-directed faculties making it possible for plants to participate in their environments, respond to stimuli, and interact with other beings. For instance, the crescograph measured variations in vegetal growth in accordance with temperature, pressure, chemicals, and other variables. The contemporaneous Scottish biologist Patrick Geddes (1920) extolled the "High Magnification Crescograph" assembled by Bose as "a veritable triumph in invention. The apparatus not only produces this enormous magnification, but also automatically records the rate of growth and its changes, in a period as short as a minute" (154). Advances in instrumentation allowed Bose to correlate fluctuations in the electric potential of a plant to patterns of growth, movement, and contractility.

Employing an integrative mode of scientific practice, Bose concluded that, while obviously devoid of the mammalian brain and the armature of zoological intelligence, plants have the equivalent of a nervous system as well as an electro-mechanical pulsation, or what he labeled affectionately the vegetal "heartbeat" (Shepherd 2009, 104). Concerned with demonstrating the responsiveness of botanical life in relation to the broader congruities between animal and plant physiologies, he moreover investigated the "death-point" as the correlate of bioelectric changes measured in the vegetal body (Bose 1906, 148–86). In experimentally scrutinizing plant death, Bose (1914) endeavored to bridge the gulf between kingdoms through the principle that the "simpler phenomena of irritability in the vegetal organisms" can illuminate the comparatively elaborate physiologies of animals (550). Although their deaths are characteristically less discernible to human subjects, plants nevertheless perish at an identifiable juncture that he termed the "death-spasm." In the essay "Plant Autographs and Their Revelations" (1914), Bose stated, "in man, at the critical moment, a spasm passes through the whole body, and similarly in the plant I find that a great contractile spasm takes place. This is accompanied by an electrical spasm also" (550). Elsewhere, in an address entitled "Death-Struggle and Memory Revival" (2007), Bose further elaborated that "the experiment consisted in finding whether the plant, near the point of death, *gave any signal* of the approaching crisis. I found that at this critical moment a sudden electrical spasm sweeps through every part of the organism [emphasis added]" (39). That the plant actively "gives" a signal implies some form of vegetal agency, intentionality, and communicativeness. Through indefatigable focus on the death-point and animal-plant correspondences throughout his career, Bose's conception of memory as an attribute of all things, including plants, increasingly crystallized.

In scientific works such as *Plant Response as a Means of Physiological Investigation* (1906), Bose infrequently summoned the term *memory*. Instead, he approached vegetal remembrance through the premise of habituation as the diminution or elimination of response following repeated exposure to a stimulus. As plants learn through trial and error—thus becoming more accustomed to, or remembering, a false stimulus conferring no discernible fitness advantages—habituation inherently engages features of learning, behavior, and recall. In rarer instances, Bose wrote more explicitly about nonhuman permutations of remembrance. During the death-spasm, he postulated, a flood of dormant memories besets the perishing plant, just as a concatenation of past experiences inundates a human being in the throes of death: "Such a strong and diffused stimulation—now involuntary—may be expected in a human subject to crowd into one brief flash a panoramic succession, of all the memory images latent in the organism" (Bose 2007, 39). In Bose's view, latent memory impressions can be restored or recalled not only by animals and plants but also by objects such as stones. As such, the biophysicist propounded a radically inclusive model of memory as inherent to animate and inanimate things—as part of the fabric of vibrant matter. As a consequence of this conception, the faculty of memory is not elevated as the rightful domain of humans, animals, and other creatures regarded as intelligent in their common mobility and analogous bodily structures (legs, arms, eyes, and brains). What is more, Bose's theory of memory upsets the prevailing model of time as a linear progression from event to event by enabling subjects—broadly conceived—to revitalize latent memories through the tracing of impressions from the present to the past:

> A question long perplexing physiologists and psychologists alike is that concerned with the great mystery that underlies memory. But now through certain experiments I have carried out, it is possible to trace 'memory impressions' backwards even in inorganic matter, such latent impressions being capable of subsequent revival.
> (Bose 1985, 25)

Bose's contemporary, Francis Darwin (1848–1925), postulated the existence of vegetal memory both before and after the publication of *The Power of Movement in Plants* (1880) with his father Charles. In his wide-ranging and nostalgic text *Rustic Sounds and Other Studies in Literature and Natural History* (1917), Francis reflected on the possibility of a "percipient region" at the tip of an embryonic grass responsible for coordinating the transmission of stimuli throughout the seedling (50). Echoing the late nineteenth century explorations of plant sensitivity conducted by the younger Darwin with his father, the section "The Movement of Plants" (36–54) characterizes vegetal mentation—including consciousness, memory, and desire—neither as a leap of human imagination nor a manifestation of rhetorical excess but, rather, as a salient question to be embraced by botanical scientists:

> We are, in fact, face to face with the question whether in plants there is anything in which we may recognise the faint beginnings of consciousness, whether plants have the rudiments of desire or of memory, or other qualities generally described as mental.
> (51)

Intimating what Marder terms "plant-thinking" (2013) as the interiority specific to vegetal life, Darwin warned that the "germ of consciousness" in the botanical kingdom should be approached "without assuming a psychological resemblance between plants and human beings, lest we go astray into anthropomorphism or sentimentality" (1917, 52). Suggestive of Bose's demonstration of vegetal memory through habituation, Darwin construed the faculty of remembrance in plants vis-à-vis habit, particularly following the idea of unconscious memory propounded by Victorian-era novelist Samuel Butler (1835–1902), physiologist Karl Ewald Konstantin Hering (1834–1918), and philosopher Karl Robert Eduard von Hartmann (1842–1906). In the lecture "The Analogies of Animal and Plant Life" delivered at the Royal Institution in 1878, Francis Darwin put forward a view of vegetal memory and mentation as a function of the enactment of habit: "[…] if it is allowed that the sensitive plant is subject to habit (and this cannot be denied), it must, in fact, possess the germ of what, as it occurs in man, forms the groundwork of all mental physiology" (qtd. in Cock and Forsdyke 2008, 544). In particular, Butler's *Life and Habit* (1878) and *Unconscious Memory* (1880)—the latter including a translation of the work of Hering and von Hartmann—propelled Francis Darwin toward a broad understanding of recollective agency as an attribute of all phenomena, including plants that "like all other living things, have a kind of memory" (1917, 51).

The foregoing overview of Francis Darwin and Jagadish Chandra Bose signifies—if only partially—the extent of historical interest in vegetal memory as well as the manner in which scientists approached the possibility of remembrance in the botanical world. From this overview, it is evident that the power of recollection is imbricated with learning (habit or habituation) and mentation (consciousness or mental physiology). Moreover, in the models of Bose and Francis Darwin, rather than confined to brained organisms, memory is a pulsation of all phenomenon—humans, animals, plants, and inanimate objects—as vibrant and agentic. Similarly, the plant physiologist Aldo Carl Leopold (2014) argued that "the existence of intelligent behavior may occur widely through biological systems, and is certainly not exclusively a feature of organisms that have defined brains" (4). This is not to claim that the impetus for Glück's loquacious flowers derived from the poet's "desultory reading" of Bose, Butler, Darwin, Leopold, or other forerunners of neuro-botany while cultivating a garden in Vermont and, as a consequence, becoming more attuned to the sensitivities of plants. On the contrary, the scientific context presented here aims to adumbrate the epistemological currents running parallel to and—at times—coalescing with contemporary botanical poetics. Indeed, recent investigations of plant cognition further substantiate, from various scientific perspectives, the practical intuitions of Glück and other poets, poet-horticulturalists, and poet-botanists. For instance, there is evidence of the transmission of memories—especially stressful or traumatic ones—between generations of plants. Thus, botanical progeny retain environmental memories from their predecessors. Research into the genes mediating the stress responses of mustard (*Brassica rapa*) identified the "multigenerational inheritance of stress memory" (Bilichak et al. 2015, 1). The study hypothesized that plants "maintain the memory of stress exposure throughout their ontogenesis [development] and faithfully propagate it into the next generation" (Bilichak et al. 2015, 1). Besides recollecting variable conditions and taxing events, plants exhibit a penchant for advantageous forms of forgetfulness. "Memory dissipation" involves the backgrounding or expunging of memory residues with potentially harmful effects for subsequent generations of the species (Crisp et al. 2016, 1). While plant researchers tend to conceptualize memory in positive terms as a vital adaptive mechanism, others assert that "forgetfulness and resetting may be the more successful evolutionary strategies under unpredictable environmental conditions" (Crisp et al. 2016, 10).

The view that the acquisition of information through learning depends on neuron-based processes inherently proscribes non-neural organisms, such as plants, from the province of behavior. In contrast to the neuronal model, vegetal learning and intelligence are defined by "a capability for beneficial adaptive behavior" (Leopold 2014, 4). Research into the garden pea (*Pisum sativum*) has shown that associative learning—the process by which an organism acquires knowledge of a connection between a behavior and a stimulus—is an integral dimension of both animal and vegetal behavior (Gagliano et al. 2016). Plants exploit environmental cues to identify and remember optimal food sources, developing associations that shape their foraging behavior. Notably in the study, "learned behavior prevailed over innate phototropism" (Gagliano et al. 2016, 1), hence weakening the emphasis on tropic responses pivotal to the reactive, non-cognitive model of plant physiology. In non-zoocentric terms, the authors concluded that "the ability to construct, remember and recall new relationships established via associative learning constitutes a universal adaptive mechanism shared by all organisms" (Gagliano et al. 2016, 5). Another study of vegetal behavior found that the sensitive plant (*Mimosa pudica*) adjusted the closure of its leaves over time in response to repeated dropping (Gagliano et al. 2014). Each potted plant was plunged a distance of about 6 inches 60 times successively at intervals of 5 seconds, causing the leaves to curl predictably into a defensive posture. Over the course of the experiment, some *Mimosa* no longer closed their leaves completely, thereby suggesting that the plants habituated to the cue by remembering the neutral consequences of dropping. Even when undisturbed—that is, not exposed to the dropping stimulus—for a month, the plants remembered their previously learned response. Recognizing that a stimulus has been encountered, *Mimosa* was shown to acquire a persistent memory of a past event. In the article "The Ubiquity of Consciousness" (2011), Anthony Trewavas and František Baluška point out a range of plant signals that induce memories lasting for hours, days, or years. Recollections of variable lengths ensure quicker, more efficient, and, in some instances, preemptive responses to subsequent stimuli.

Contemporary advances in plant signaling research return focus to the contention of anatomist Charles Sedgwick Minot (1902) that consciousness regulates "the actions of the organisms so as to accomplish purposes which on the whole are useful to the organisms" (11). In contrast to Trewavas, Baluška, Minot, and their intellectual forebears who conceptualized remembrance and consciousness as interbraided phenomena, Nietzsche (1999) considered memory "a primordial characteristic of things" but, ultimately, concluded that "the mimosa has memory, but no consciousness" (52). The philosopher regarded vegetal recollection as a characteristically non-imagistic and non-representational mode emerging independently of consciousness as "part of the essence of *sensation* [emphasis in original]" (52). Reflecting a Nietzschean frame, Michael Marder emphasizes the significance of embodied cognition and recollection for plant being. In his view, "memory need not be actualized in subjective consciousness or self-consciousness but can be inscribed in the bodies of organisms" (Marder 2014, 33). The bodies of plants archive past events including the trauma of injuries, acquisition of nutrients, and reception of light, hence retaining "a trace of light itself, rather than a representation of luminosity, in its cells" (Marder 2016, para. 4). Citing tree rings as representative of the corporeal inscription of memory in the plant realm, Marder (2016) avers that "vegetal memories *are* the plants themselves" and, similarly, that plants "*are* and *have* memories [emphasis in original]" (para. 4). In comparable terms but in literary form, Aldo Leopold elicited the somatic memory of trees in *A Sand County Almanac*, originally published in 1949. The ecologist envisioned the concentric rings of an oak as "the integrated transect of a century" that laid bare the chronology of the organism through the historical incidents—both natural and cultural—that impinged upon its body over time (Leopold 1989, 9).

Poeticizing the Rhizosphere: The Inter-Mnemonics of *The Wild Iris*

With its coterie of flower-speakers endowed with memory, Glück's *The Wild Iris* furthermore aligns with the tradition of sapient plants in English literature. A significant antecedent is the Anglo-Saxon poem, *The Dream of the Rood*, from the manuscript known as the Vercelli Book. Composed in the south-east of England in the tenth century yet associated with the northern Italian town of Vercelli where it was discovered in the eleventh, the devotional poem narrates the story of the crucifixion of Christ from the first-person perspective of the cross (Black et al. 2009, 31). The tree supplying the material for the cross appears to the narrator in a dream, recounting its experience of being felled and having to bear witness to the crucifixion: "It was so long ago—I remember it still—/that I was felled from the forest's edge,/ripped up from my roots.

Strong enemies seized me/there" (Black et al. 2009, 32, ll. 27–30). As the tree-cross-speaker comes to realize the significance of its appropriation for the crucifixion as a nonhuman observer of—and participant in—the divine death of Christ, it exhibits states of excitability and affect: "I trembled when he embraced me, but I dared not/bow to the ground,/or fall to the earth's corners—I had to stand fast" (ll. 42–44). Written in the early seventeenth century, John Donne's *Metempsychosis* (or *Infinitati Sacrum*, 1601) chronicles the soul's transmigrations through vegetal, animal, and human forms (Harvey 2007, 55). In the preamble to the long poem, Donne confers the faculties of remembrance and address to plants, despite the apparent immobility of vegetal life as a host for the comparatively motile soul: "And therefore though this soule could not move when it was a Melon, yet it may remember, and now tell mee, at what lascivious banquet it was serv'd" (Donne 2007, "Epistle").

Of note in nineteenth-century literature are the speaking tiger lily, rose, daisy, violet, and larkspur of "The Garden of Live Flowers," the second chapter of *Alice Through the Looking Glass* first published in 1871 (Carroll 2016, 15–21). Old Man Willow of *The Fellowship of the Ring* provides an illustration of a self-directed and percipient plant in twentieth-century literature. Although he sinisterly cackles but cannot speak in a human or humanoid tongue, the tree fiercely holds on to the memory of the desolation of the Old Forest of Eriador by the hobbits, and, as a consequence, tries to hypnotize and strangle Merry and Pippin as they enter the Withywindle Valley (Tolkien 1994, 108–17). In addition to the sapient flora of the English literary canon, a further context in which *The Wild Iris* can be situated encompasses the writings of poet-botanists (Mahood 2008) and poet-gardeners (Farr and Carter 2004; Martin 1984) as well as modernist verse taking gardens as subjects and settings, as, for example, in Amy Lowell's "In a Garden" (1913) and H.D.'s "The Garden" (1915). Notwithstanding her self-characterization as "not a horticulturist" (Cavalieri and Glück 2006, n.p.), I position Glück's work and, specifically, *The Wild Iris* within the poet-gardener and—to some extent, bearing in mind her limited technical knowledge of flora—the poet-botanist tradition. Paralleling this tradition is the science of vegetal memory pioneered by Charles and Francis Darwin, Jagadish Chandra Bose, and contemporary plant behaviorists, as elaborated in the previous section. Glück's poetic enactment of memory in the botanical kingdom engages the two-pronged notion that plants "*are and have* memories" (Marder 2016, para. 4)—that plants are remembered in literature, art, and culture but that they, at the same time, possess an ontological predisposition to recall past events. More precisely, the botanical memory of *The Wild Iris* is "inter-mnemonic" (Kirk 2015, 61; Parks 1991, 57) in that the recollections of the gardener-poet imbricate—in various ways, as will be explicated—with those of the flower-speakers. Glück's invocation of the past in the poetic sequence is a function of the phenomenological interpenetration of human and vegetal memories in the garden collective.

The poet-gardener's narration of botanical memory is central, in particular, to four poems—each titled "Vespers"—addressing a divine presence beyond the garden. Notably, the vegetal subjects of this grouping of poems do not speak for themselves but, instead, are construed as objects of human recollection. Named after the evening prayers of the Divine Office (or Liturgy of the Hours) of the Christian faith, the poems acts as a memory cluster positioned in the midsection of *The Wild Iris* and structurally approximating the episodic nature of memory in which a discrete recollection of the past instigates a chain of memory associations. In the first of the quartet, the speaker recalls—invoking the past tense, unlike much of the other poetry in the collection—her failed cultivation of a fig tree intended as a "test" of God's existence. Translocated to the garden—well outside of the hot Middle Eastern and Mediterranean climates ideal for growing the species—"if the tree lived,/it would mean you existed" (Glück 1992, 36, ll. 3–4). As an allegory for seeking the divine, the feckless planting of the tree "in Vermont, country/of no summer" overshadows the speaker's marginal attention to the climatic requirements of the species (ll. 2–3). In keeping with Glück's postconfessional bent, existential disenchantment accompanies the realization—mediated by the figure of the fig—that "by this logic, you do not exist" (l. 5). In this instance, the logic is hybridically human and vegetal. The failure to cultivate vegetal life and, by extrapolation, to apprehend numinous presence thematically continues in the second "Vespers," in reference to tomatoes:

> I planted the seeds, I watched the first shoots
> like wings tearing the soil, and it was my heart
> broken by the blight, the black spot so quickly
> multiplying in the rows. I doubt
> you have a heart, in our understanding of
> that term.
>
> (Glück 1992, 37, ll. 12–17)

The poet-gardener's botanical memory in the third "Vespers" intensifies her scornful address of God as a distant and absent father devoid of empathy for the human condition: "I climbed/the small hill above the wild blueberries, metaphysically/descending, as on all my walks" (Glück 1992, 43, ll. 9–11).

Detailing the estrangement of the poet-gardener from her brother during their childhood, the final "Vespers" of the cluster narrates memories of "embankments/netted with dark vinca" and "small things, flowers/growing under the hawthorn tree, bells/of the wild scilla" (Glück 1992, 44, ll. 5–6, 12–14). Yet, reading *The Wild Iris* as a whole, we are confronted with an inter-mnemonic "dialogue of memories" (Parks 1991, 57) between human, vegetal, and other subjects. Whereas the four "Vespers" metaphorize recollections of the vinca, hawthorn, fig, and tomato, the titular poem forcefully opens with the first-person address of the iris-speaker to the poet-gardener and reader. The flower possesses temporally deep memory—peculiar to the botanical life rendered in the sequence—transcending the narrow purview of human remembrance. Rather than one-dimensionally focusing on human recollections of plants, as in the "Vespers" quartet, "The Wild Iris" confers to the flower the sapient faculties of memory and consciousness. From her exertions in the garden and reading of horticultural catalogues, Glück would have become familiar with the particularities of species, such as the iris, that emerge from rhizomes or bulbs. In their perennial nature, irises archive the traces of each seasonal demise and resurrection, unlike human beings for whom the inadequate affordances of memory obfuscate the phenomenon of death. What is more, the iris exhibits sensory memory of its burial, as it awaits the return of the spring:

> Overhead, noises, branches of the pine shifting.
> Then nothing. The weak sun
> flickered over the dry surface.
>
> It is terrible to survive
> as consciousness
> buried in the dark earth.
>
> (Glück 1992, 1, ll. 5–10)

The stanzas are consistent with current understandings of the perception of visual, sonic, spatial, and proprioceptive stimuli by plants (Chamovitz 2012; Karban 2015). Counter to Nietzsche's contention that memory, but not consciousness, prevails in the vegetal kingdom, Glück figures the bulb in this opening poem of *The Wild Iris* as a nexus of reflective activity. Her poetization of vegetal intelligence also harmonizes with the Darwins' root-brain hypothesis in which the tip of the radicle "acts like the brain of one of the lower animals" and coordinates "impressions from the sense-organs" (Darwin and Darwin 2016, 419).

Invariably, however, the expansive quality of perennial consciousness brings into contrast the limited range of human recollection, bluntly underscored by the iris-speaker in its characterization of the poet-gardener as "you who do not remember/passage from the other world" (Glück 1992, 1, ll. 16–17). Such unembellished declarations from the flower personae of the sequence reflect the clear-cut syntax, austere diction, concision, and simplicity that typify Glück's style on the whole (Spiegelman 2005, 4). Indeed, the complex enactment of vegetal memory and consciousness in *The Wild Iris* has much to do with the voice of plants and, more precisely, the polyvocality of the work. The three principal personae of Glück as the poet-gardener, the flowers as vegetal-speakers, and God as divine presence converse with one another, and the reader listens in on them (Spiegelman 2005, 6). The flowers communicate directly about their inner lives—their emotions, memories, and states of consciousness—in poetic plant-script mediated by Glück. Just as Bose devised the crescograph as an apparatus for scientifically comprehending plant-autographs, so Glück deployed lyrical attention to garden plants as an instrument for intuiting aspects of vegetal intelligence and communication. In the opening lines of "Trillium," the ephemeral spring flower manifests consciousness as it awakes in a forest and perceives environmental cues: "The dark/seemed natural, the sky through the pine trees/ thick with many lights" (Glück 1992, 4, ll. 1–3). In depicting the return of the trillium from its unconsciousness, Glück joins a lineage of scientists and philosophers who recognized the occurrence of sleep in plants (Darwin and Darwin 2016; Hill 1762; Macnish 1838). For example, in *The Philosophy of Sleep*, the Scottish physician and philosopher Robert Macnish (1838) observed that "during night, plants seem to exist in a state analogous to sleep" (299), and even devoted a chapter to the subject in his book. Charles Darwin claimed that the leaves and cotyledons of some plants alternate between sleep states, but elsewhere in *The Power of Movement in Plants* the biologist questioned the appropriateness of the term as applied to vegetal life (Darwin and Darwin 2016, 232).

Glück reinvokes the depth and extent of plant memory in "Snowdrops" vis-à-vis one of the first bulbs to blossom in the American New England spring, in all probability the common snowdrop (*Galanthus nivalis*) or a relative within the same genus. To the "wonderfully petulant or hopeful or snide" (Chiasson 2007, 152) panoply of flower-speakers expressing their inner worlds freely throughout *The Wild Iris*, the poem adds a distinctive plant voice tinged with awe and verging on incredulity over the manifest potency of its own corporeal remembrance:

> I did not expect to survive,
> earth suppressing me. I didn't expect
> to waken again, to feel
> in damp earth my body
> able to respond again, remembering
> after so long how to open again
> in the cold light
> of earliest spring—
>
> (Glück 1992, 6, ll. 4–11)

The snowdrop's somatic recollection in wakening to the sensation of the earth with the stirring of spring aligns with the contention that memory "can be inscribed in the bodies of organisms" (Marder 2014, 33).

The intelligence and sensitivity of vegetal life even in light of its lack of neuronal infrastructure—to wit, what Trewavas (2002) terms "mindless mastery"—persists thematically through the middle and latter portions of the sequence. In "The Red Poppy," for instance, "the great thing" from the perspective of the plant "is not having/a mind" (Glück 1992, 29, ll. 1–3). Constituted instead by feeling, emotion, intuition, and corporeal sense, the ontology of the poppy represents plant-thinking as the "non-cognitive, non-ideational, and non-imagistic mode of thinking *proper* to plants [emphasis in original]" (Marder 2013, 10). This non-ideational proprioceptive awareness discloses the red poppy's memory as a function of seasonal cycles and bodily rhythms. Hence, in addition to the snowdrop's astonishment and the petulant, snide, and hopeful tenors of other flower-speakers, there is the empathic voice of the poppy. The flower nostalgizes a primordial epoch during which no classificatory demarcations—no subject-object binarisms—intervened between living things: "Oh my brothers and sisters,/were you like me once, long ago,/before you were human?" (Glück 1992, 29, ll. 12–14). Rooted in the far-reaching memory of vegetal being, empathic identification between the poppy and poet-gardener precipitates a sharing—a polyvocal melding—of voices by the poem's conclusion. What results is a lessening of the categorical distinction between human subjectivity and vegetal otherness, as heightened by a common inter-mnemonic language of affect: "I am speaking now/the way you do. I speak/because I am shattered" (29, ll. 18–20).

When approaching *The Wild Iris* as inter-mnemonic—characterized by a dialogue of memories—it is also vital to consider the ability of vegetal speakers to remember animals, insects, and other plants. To be sure, the flower-subjects of Glück's lieder cycle are not only aware of their corporeality, the garden milieu and its seasonal rhythms, and the presence of the gardener-poet. They also recognize and recall members of the same species (conspecifics) and those of different species (allospecifics). It was botanist David Rhoades (1983) who reported improved resistance in Sitka willows growing near herbivore-stricken conspecific plants and suggested that an airborne molecule transmitted between trees served as a warning signal. Before his research, in 1904, microbial ecologist Lorenz Hiltner coined the term "rhizosphere" to denote the thin zone of soil serving as the medium for the communicative secretions of plant roots (Gross 2016, R182) The "wooded web"—as the rhizosphere has been popularized in the twenty-first century—enables the exchange of information within populations of plants, and between plants and animals, insects, fungi, and humans (Gross 2016, R182). The phenomenon of allospecific recognition is poeticized in "The Silver Lily," located toward the autumnal end of the sequence (Glück 1992, 59). The lily's memories of snowdrop blossoms, maple seeds, birch trees, and daffodils correspond to scientific notions of rhizospheric and aerial signaling:

In spring, when the moon rose, it meant
time was endless. Snowdrops
opened and closed, the clustered
seeds of the maples fell in pale drifts.
White over white, the moon rose over the birch tree.
And in the crook, where the tree divides,
leaves of the first daffodils, in moonlight
soft greenish-silver.
(Glück 1992, 59, ll. 7–14)

The reflective voice of the silver lily is not solely a lyrical exploration of cross-species empathy and identification. Rather, the nostalgia of the flower-speaker has a scientific basis in plant communication where memory contributes to the fitness and survival of the plant. Hence, inter-mnemonic dialogue is both poetic and ecological in character.

Conclusion: Vegetal Memory, Ethics, and Justice

How might Glück's poetic enactment of vegetal memory overlap with issues of plant ethics, justice, and memorialization during a time of massive biodiversity loss on a global scale? An urgent context of phytocriticism—especially elucidated through the environmental humanities—is the ubiquitous decline of botanical populations in the Anthropocene, the present era characterized by pronounced anthropogenic disturbance of the climatic and biophysical features of the planet. Of the 500,000 terrestrial plant species estimated to exist around the globe—450,000 of which are angiosperms, or flowering plants—approximately one-third are at risk of extinction (Corlett 2016). The actual percentage, however, could be much greater if we consider the unknown or undescribed taxa excluded from estimates. Habitat fragmentation and loss, overexploitation, invasive plant and animal species, air pollution, nitrogen deposition, and climate change, including the perturbation of seasonal cycles, persist as major threats to floristic conservation (Corlett 2016, 12–13). Considering this dire outlook, we need, on the one hand, further theoretical and practical mechanisms for addressing issues of plant ethics and justice in order to conserve what is left (Hall 2009, 2014; Heyd 2012; Pouteau 2014; Swiss Confederation 2008) and, on the other, new ways to memorialize (Ginn 2014) and mourn (Ryan 2017) those plant specimens, species, communities, and landscapes that have been either severely altered or completely decimated. In this respect, I propose extending the concept of "memory-justice"—defined as resistance to the erasure of past events and individuals—to include the botanical realm (Booth 2006, 112–63).

As a voice countering the immoral effacement of remembrance, memory-justice in a phytocritical context would take into account the suffering and demise of plants. Vegetal memory-justice would signify the agentic position of botanical life in a myriad of historical or cultural formations, including poetry. Moreover, the concept would advocate the broader ethical regard for living plants as conscious, responsive, and memory-bearing entities. In this chapter, I have opted to read Glück's work, particularly her Pulitzer Prize-winning volume *The Wild Iris*, in terms of what I have described as the dialectic of vegetal memory, to wit, the self-aware capacity of the plant in relation to its objectification in human memory. Going beyond the monochrome rendering of plant life as a focus of human nostalgia, the poet endows flower-speakers with recollective agency and, in doing so, mediates their intelligence, sensitivity, and liveliness through the polyvocality of the writing. In my analysis, the work of Jagadish Chandra Bose, Charles and Francis Darwin, and contemporary plant behaviorists indirectly underlies Glück's mythologization of the flower-speakers and garden setting of *The Wild Iris*. The science-poetry crossover in relation to memory foregrounds the similarities between botanical science, philosophy, and poetry—fields traversing a shared terrain (that of the plant and its life-world) even though only remotely in open dialogue themselves. Indeed, reading the broader scientific and cultural currents that intersect with the lively rendering of vegetal life in contemporary poetry is essential to the practice of phytocriticism, as Chapter 7 demonstrates in relation to Australian poet Judith Wright and the temporality of plants.

Bibliography

Azcuy, Mary Kate. 2008. "Louise Glück, Feminism and Nature in *Firstborn*'s 'The Egg'." In *Women Writing Nature: A Feminist View*, edited by Barbara Cook, 57–66. Lanham, MD: Lexington Books.
Baluška, František, and Michael Levin. 2016. "On Having No Head: Cognition Throughout Biological Systems." *Frontiers in Psychology* 7: 1–19. doi:10.3389/fpsyg.2016.00902
Bilichak, Andriy, Yaroslav Ilnytskyy, Rafal Wóycicki, Nina Kepeshchuk, Dawson Fogen, and Igor Kovalchuk. 2015. "The Elucidation of Stress Memory Inheritance in *Brassica rapa* Plants." *Frontiers in Plant Science* 6: 1–17. doi:10.3389/fpls.2015.00005
Black, Joseph, Leonard Conolly, Kate Flint, Isobel Grundy, Don LePan, Roy Liuzza, Jerome McGann, Anne Prescott, Barry Qualls, and Claire Waters, eds. 2009. *The Broadview Anthology of British Literature: Volume 1: The Medieval Period*. 2nd ed. Peterborough, ON: Broadview Press.
Booth, William James. 2006. *Communities of Memory: On Witness, Identity, and Justice*. Ithaca, NY: Cornell University Press.
Bose, Jagadis Chandra. 1906. *Plant Response as a Means of Physiological Investigation*. London: Longmans, Green, and Co.
———. 1914. "Plant-Autographs and their Revelations." *Nature* 93 (2334): 546–50.

―――. 1920. "Plant and Animal Response." *Proceedings of the Royal Society of Medicine* 13: 101–28.
―――. 1985. *The Voice of Life*. Calcutta: P. Lal.
―――. 2007. "Sir Jagadis Chunder Bose: His Life and Speeches." *Project Gutenberg*. Accessed 22 May 2017. www.gutenberg.org/files/22085/22085-h/22085-h.htm#f34
Bouton, Charles. 1991. *Neurolinguistics: Historical and Theoretical Perspectives*. Translated by Terence MacNamee. New York: Plenum Press.
Butler, Samuel. 1878. *Life and Habit*. London: Trübner & Co.
―――. 1880. *Unconscious Memory*. London: David Bogue.
Calvo, Paco. 2016. "The Philosophy of Plant Neurobiology: A Manifesto." *Synthese* 193 (5): 1323–43. doi:10.1007/s11229-016-1040-1
Carroll, Lewis. 2016. *Alice Through the Looking Glass*. Online [Google Books]: Enhanced Media.
Cavalieri, Grace, and Louise Glück. 2006. "In the Magnificent Region of Courage: An Interview with Louise Glück." *Beltway Poetry Quarterly* 7 (4). Accessed 22 May 2017. http://washingtonart.com/beltway/gluckinterview.html
Chamovitz, Daniel. 2012. *What a Plant Knows: A Field Guide to the Senses*. Brunswick, VIC: Scribe Publications.
Chiasson, Dan. 2007. *One Kind of Everything: Poem and Person in Contemporary America*. Chicago: University of Chicago Press.
Clarke, Desmond. 2003. *Descartes's Theory of Mind*. Oxford: Oxford University Press.
Cock, Alan, and Donald Forsdyke. 2008. *Treasure Your Exceptions: The Science and Life of William Bateson*. New York: Springer.
Corlett, Richard. 2016. "Plant Diversity in a Changing World: Status, Trends, and Conservation Needs." *Plant Diversity* 38 (1): 10–16. doi:10.1016/j.pld.2016.01.001
Crisp, Peter, Diep Ganguly, Steven Eichten, Justin Borevitz, and Barry Pogson. 2016. "Reconsidering Plant Memory: Intersections Between Stress Recovery, RNA Turnover, and Epigenetics." *Science Advances* 2 (2): 1–14. doi:10.1126/sciadv.1501340
Darwin, Charles. 1865. *On the Movements and Habits of Climbing Plants*. London: The Linnean Society.
Darwin, Charles, and Francis Darwin. 2016. *The Works of Charles Darwin: The Power of Movement in Plants*. Edited by Paul Barrett and R.B. Freeman. London: Routledge.
Darwin, Francis. 1917. *Rustic Sounds and Other Studies in Literature and Natural History*. London: John Murray.
Diehl, Joanne Feit. 2005. "Introduction." In *On Louise Glück: Change What You See*, edited by Joanne Feit Diehl, 1–22. Ann Arbor: University of Michigan Press.
Dodd, Elizabeth. 1992. *The Veiled Mirror and the Woman Poet: H.D., Louise Bogan, Elizabeth Bishop, and Louise Glück*. Columbia: University of Missouri Press.
Donne, John. 2007. "Metempsychosis." *Luminarium Editions*. Accessed 22 May 2017. www.luminarium.org/editions/metempsycosis.htm
Farr, Judith, and Louise Carter. 2004. *The Gardens of Emily Dickinson*. Cambridge, MA: Harvard University Press.

Gagliano, Monica, Vladyslav Vyazovskiy, Alexander Borbély, Mavra Grimonprez, and Martial Depczynski. 2016. "Learning by Association in Plants." *Scientific Reports* 6 (38427): 1–9.

Gagliano, Monica, Michael Renton, Martial Depczynski, and Stefano Mancuso. 2014. "Experience Teaches Plants To Learn Faster and Forget Slower in Environments Where It Matters." *Oecologia* 175 (1): 63–72. doi:10.1007/s00442-013-2873-7

Geddes, Patrick. 1920. *The Life and Work of Sir Jagadis C. Bose: An Indian Pioneer of Science*. London: Longmans, Green, and Co.

Ginn, Franklin. 2014. "Death, Absence and Afterlife in the Garden." *Cultural Geographies* 21 (2): 229–45.

Glück, Louise. 1968. *Firstborn: Poems*. New York: New American Library.

———. 1975. *The House on Marshland*. New York: Ecco Press.

———. 1980. *Descending Figure*. New York: The Ecco Press.

———. 1990. *Ararat*. New York: The Ecco Press.

———. 1992. *The Wild Iris*. New York: HarperCollins Publishers.

———. 1994. *Proofs and Theories: Essays on Poetry*. Hopewell, NJ: The Ecco Press.

———. 2007. *Averno: Poems*. New York: Farrar, Straus and Giroux.

———. 2012. *Poems 1962–2012*. New York: Farrar, Straus and Giroux.

———. 2013. "Interview: Louise Glück, Former Poet Laureate of the United States." *Academy of Achievement*. Accessed 22 May 2017. http://prodloadbalancer-1055872027.us-east-1.elb.amazonaws.com/autodoc/page/glu0int-5

———. 2014. *Faithful and Virtuous Night: Poems*. New York City: Farrar, Straus and Giroux.

Gordon, Maggie. 2002. "A Woman Writing about Nature: Louise Glück and 'the Absence of Intention'." In *Ecopoetry: A Critical Introduction*, edited by J. Scott Bryson, 221–31. Salt Lake City: University of Utah Press.

Gosmann, Uta. 2012. *Poetic Memory: The Forgotten Self in Plath, Howe, Hinsey, and Glück*. Madison, NJ: Farleigh Dickinson University Press.

Gross, Michael. 2016. "Could Plants Have Cognitive Abilities?" *Current Biology* 26 (5): R181–R184.

H.D. (Hilda Doolittle). 1915. "The Garden." *Poetry: A Magazine of Verse* 5 (6): 267–68.

Hall, Matthew. 2009. "Plant Autonomy and Human-Plant Ethics." *Environmental Ethics* 31 (2): 169–81.

———. 2014. "Talk Among the Trees: Animist Plant Ontologies and Ethics." In *The Handbook of Contemporary Animism*, edited by Graham Harvey, 385–94. New York: Routledge.

Harvey, Elizabeth. 2007. "Donne's Metempsychosis and Early Modern Natural History." In *Environment and Embodiment in Early Modern England*, edited by Mary Floyd-Wilson and Garrett Sullivan, 55–70. Houndsmills: Palgrave Macmillan.

Heyd, Thomas. 2012. "Plant Ethics and Botanic Gardens." *PAN: Philosophy Activism Nature* 9: 37–47.

Hill, John. 1762. *The Sleep of Plants and Cause of Motion in the Sensitive Plant, Explained: In A Letter to Linnaeus*. 2 ed. London: R. Baldwin.

Iovino, Serenella, and Serpil Oppermann. 2014. "Introduction: Stories Come to Matter." In *Material Ecocriticism*, edited by Serenella Iovino and Serpil Oppermann, 1–17. Bloomington: Indiana University Press.

Karban, Richard. 2015. *Plant Sensing and Communication*. Chicago: University of Chicago Press.

Kiesling, Frances, and Christie Manning. 2010. "How Green is Your Thumb? Environmental Gardening Identity and Ecological Gardening Practices." *Journal of Environmental Psychology* 30 (3): 315–27. doi:10.1016/j.jenvp.2010.02.004

Kirk, Alan. 2015. "Memory Theory: Cultural and Cognitive Approaches to the Gospel Tradition." In *Understanding the Social World of the New Testament*, edited by Dietmar Neufeld and Richard DeMaris, 57–67. London: Routledge.

Leopold, A. Carl. 2014. "Smart Plants: Memory and Communication Without Brains." *Plant Signaling and Behavior* 9 (10): 1–5. doi:10.4161/15592316.2014.972268

Leopold, Aldo. 1989. *A Sand County Almanac, and Sketches Here and There*. Oxford: Oxford University Press.

Lowell, Amy. 1913. "In a Garden." *The New Freewoman: An Individualist Review* 1 (6): 114.

Macnish, Robert. 1838. *The Philosophy of Sleep*. Glasgow: W.R. McPhun Publisher.

Mahood, Molly. 2008. *The Poet as Botanist*. Cambridge, UK: Cambridge University Press.

Marder, Michael. 2013. *Plant-Thinking: A Philosophy of Vegetal Life*. New York: Columbia University Press.

———. 2014. *The Philosopher's Plant: An Intellectual Herbarium*. New York: Columbia University Press.

———. 2016. "Vegetal Memories." *The Philosopher's Plant: A Los Angeles Review of Books Channel*. Accessed 22 May 2017. http://philosoplant.lareviewofbooks.org/?p=172

Martin, Peter. 1984. *Pursuing Innocent Pleasures: The Gardening World of Alexander Pope*. Hamden, CT: Archon Books.

Minot, Charles Sedgwick. 1902. "The Problem of Consciousness in Its Biological Aspects." *Science* 16 (392): 1–12.

Morris, Daniel. 2006. *The Poetry of Louise Glück: A Thematic Introduction*. Columbia: University of Missouri Press.

Müller-Xing, Ralf, Qian Xing, and Justin Goodrich. 2014. "Footprints of the Sun: Memory of UV and Light Stress in Plants." *Frontiers in Plant Science* 5: 1–12. doi:10.3389/fpls.2014.00474

Nietzsche, Friedrich. 1999. *Unpublished Writings from the Period of Unfashionable Observations*. Translated by Richard Gray. Stanford, CA: Stanford University Press.

Nyberg, Eva, and Dawn Sanders. 2014. "Drawing Attention to the 'Green Side of Life'." *Journal of Biological Education* 48 (3): 142–53. doi:10.1080/00219266.2013.849282

Parks, Ward. 1991. "The Textualization of Orality in Literary Criticism." In *Vox Intexta: Orality and Textuality in the Middle Ages*, edited by A.N. Doane and Carol Braun Pasternack, 46–62. Madison: University of Wisconsin Press.

Pouteau, Sylvie. 2014. "Beyond 'Second Animals': Making Sense of Plant Ethics." *Journal of Agricultural and Environmental Ethics* 27 (1): 1–25.

Rhoades, David. 1983. "Responses of Alder and Willow to Attack by Tent Caterpillars and Webworms: Evidence for Pheromonal Sensitivity of Willows."

In *Plant Resistance to Insects*, edited by Paul Hedin, 55–68. Washington, DC: American Chemical Society.

Ryan, John Charles. 2017. "Where Have All the Boronia Gone? A Posthumanist Model of Environmental Mourning." In *Mourning Nature: Hope at the Heart of Ecological Loss and Grief*, edited by Ashlee Cunsolo and Karen Landman, 117–43. Montreal: McGill-Queen's University Press.

Scigaj, Leonard. 1999. *Sustainable Poetry: Four American Ecopoets*. Lexington: University Press of Kentucky.

Shepherd, Virginia. 2009. "Reflections on the Many-in-One: J.C. Bose and the Roots of Plant Neurobiology." In *Remembering Sir J.C. Bose*, edited by D.P. Sen Gupta, M.H. Engineer and Virginia Shepherd, 101–60. Singapore: World Scientific Publishing.

Spiegelman, Willard. 2005. "'Are You Talking to Me?': Speaker and Audience in Louise Glück's *The Wild Iris*." *Literature Compass* 2 (1): 1–6.

Swiss Confederation. 2008. *The Dignity of Living Beings with Regard to Plants: Moral Consideration of Plants for Their Own Sake*. Translated by Jackie Leach Scully. Bern: Federal Ethics on Non-Human Biotechnology ECNH.

Tolkien, J.R.R. 1994. *The Fellowship of the Ring: Being the First Part of The Lord of the Rings*. New York: Houghton Mifflin Harcourt Publishing.

Trewavas, Anthony. 2002. "Plant Intelligence: Mindless Mastery." *Nature* 415 (6874): 841. doi: 10.1038/415841a.

———. 2014. *Plant Behaviour and Intelligence*. Oxford: Oxford University Press.

Trewavas, Anthony, and František Baluška. 2011. "The Ubiquity of Consciousness." *EMBO Reports* 12 (12): 1221–25.

Vendler, Helen Hennessey. 1993. "The Wild Iris." *The New Republic* 208 (21): 35–8.

White Flower Farm. 2016. "About Us." Accessed 22 May 2017. www.whiteflowerfarm.com/about-us

7 That Seed Sets Time Ablaze
Judith Wright and the Temporality of Plants

> Among green shades and flowering ghosts, the
>   remembrances of love,
> inventions of the holy unwearying seed,
> bright falling fountains made of time, that bore
> through time the holy seed that knew no time–
> —from "The Two Fires" (Wright 1992, 20, ll. 1–5)

A vital aspect of the botanical imagination is plant time. Following Michael Marder (2013, 95), this chapter uses the term *plant time* to describe the temporalities that govern vegetal life and lives, and which differentiate plant being from its human and zoological counterparts. As Marder observes, "vegetal time passes in qualitatively distinct modes and rhythms" (2013, 107), resisting measurement in terms equivalent to our sense of time. In the light of the temporal otherness of vegetality, humans strive to imagine plants across vast biopaleontological scales (for instance, as living Gondwanan relics or fossils), through a myriad of events that corporeally trace the rhythms of our co-constituted lives (seeding, flowering, fruiting), and with the aid of technological interventions (consider, as a prime example, time-lapse photography) that supply lenses into their time topographies. The vegetal dialectics leveraged in *Plants in Contemporary Poetry* regarding the soul (Chapter 2), the body (Chapter 3), death (Chapter 8), hope (Chapter 9), and other themes also extends to the treatment of time, not as a monolithic singularity— sequentially proceeding from a distant past, to a perceptible present, and finally to an unknown future—but as an interwoven, multidimensional plexity (Wood 2003).

Vegetal being punctuates time's passage. In their bodily presence, plants instantiate temporality through material-semiotic processes of bringing forth and dying back. These processes produce signifiers of temporal movement. Yet, plants also have their own time. Increasingly, globalized society relies on adopting, scripting, appropriating, and engineering vegetal time in service to Enlightenment-fashioned ideals of progress. From greenhouse cultivation and quick-ripening hormones to genetically modified seeds and biotech crops, human technologies alter plant temporalities in a physical manner, reducing the place-specific complexity of vegetal time to a global homogeneity. In contrast, a more nuanced and dialogical approach to plant time—one which eschews impulses toward anthropocentrism and metaphorization—would seek the fruits of attending critically to "the time of the plants themselves" (Marder 2013, 94). In further distinguishing between the conscription of vegetal temporality for human ends and the empathic embracing of plant time as a multi-faceted plexity, Chapter 7 looks toward the botanical tendencies of Australian writer and activist Judith Wright (1915–2000).

Wright is arguably the most widely-read Australian poet of the twentieth century (Mead 2006). To be sure, critics have observed Wright's preoccupation with time (Griffiths 2006; Harrison 2000; McMahon 2007). Yet, notwithstanding her recognition as an ecological writer (Zeller 2000; Hutchings 2007; Brady 2007) and her pronounced influence on the history of Australian environmental activism (Mulligan and Hill 2001, 73), Wright's identification with plants and poetization of Queensland flora have received remarkably nominal attention. As a consequence, this discussion centers on the time of plants themselves in Wright's time-plexity (Siewers 2011, 109). The Australian poet envisages the Queensland environment through a framework steeped in the temporal nuances of plants. I will attempt to demonstrate that the time-space continuum of Wright's plexity encodes the particularities of the Australian landmass. On the whole, Wright's botanical poems evoke the primordial character of Australian species—some of the oldest on earth (Crisp and Cook 2013). As evident in her poetry, Wright's time-plexity takes shape and is poeticized in moments of encounter with Queensland flora, and in a manner distinct from human, animal, and geological timescales. For the poet, vegetal temporality is a stimulus for countering the marginalization of endemic forms of time—including Indigenous seasons—in the Australian biocultural landscape.

Vegetal Temporality: From Chronos to Kairos

In response to the "elusive time of plants" (Marder 2013, 98)—their propensity to defy ready alignment with human timescales—societies from diverse traditions around the world have endeavored to arrest or reformulate plant time (see, for example, Cumo 2016, 57–71). Through technological, chemical, horticultural, and other interventions, people manipulate the chthonic rhythms of vegetal nature, rendering plant time more decipherable and serviceable to human consciousness. An illustrative example is time-lapse photography, characteristically focusing on laboratory or greenhouse grown flowering plants since its inception in the late eighteenth and early twentieth centuries (Williamson 2015,

74–80). As plant physiologist Anthony Trewavas comments, "time-lapse photography has enabled the speeding up of plant movements, bringing them into a time frame familiar to us" (2014, 13). The nature documentaries *The Private Life of Plants* (BBC 1995), *Plants* (BBC 2009), and *Kingdom of Plants* (Williams 2012), narrated by David Attenborough, epitomize the contemporary use of three-dimensional time-lapse film techniques for transliterating plant temporality to the human lexicon. Condensing the stages of flowering into one seamless filmic sweep fosters a sense of enthrallment with widely distributed temporal incidents in the plant world, which would otherwise take days, months, or even years to fully unfold to perception. In the opening moments of *Plants*, for instance, Attenborough historicizes the botanical kingdom in dramatic terms, as possessing a "family tree stretching back nearly half a billion years" (BBC 2009). A high profile example, the famously long-lived bristlecone pine (*Pinus longaeva*) has endured "thousands of years to reach this size" and has witnessed "empires rise and fall—kings, queens, and presidents come and go" (BBC 2009).

The use of time-lapse in Attenborough's documentaries represents an evolution of the historical reformulation of plant time through imagistic technologies. In the mid- to late nineteenth century, Charles and Francis Darwin employed optical instruments to visualize the stages in the life of a plant (Williamson 2015, 78). In the 1890s, time-lapse studies of plant growth were carried out in Paris at the Marey Institute with a purpose-built camera designed by chronophotography innovator Lucien Bull (Williamson 2015, 77–78). Later, Percy Smith's eight-minute-long *The Birth of a Flower* (1910) became one of the earliest films to coalesce the opening of hyacinth, crocus, snowdrop, narcissi, anemone, and other commonplace blossoms into short time-lapsed cinematographic segments (Dixon 2011, 32–33). Visually poetic and accompanied by music, the footage incorporates minimalistic backgrounds to avoid distracting viewers from the operatic sequentiality of blooming, removed from its organic, ecological context. Yet, the reductionist emphasis on reproductive anatomies evident in *The Birth of a Flower* represents Londa Schiebinger's assertion that the "'scientization' of botany coincided with the ardent 'sexualization' of plants" enshrined in the Linnaean prioritization of stigmas, styles, ovaries, and other flowering parts (Schiebinger 2004, 12). What is more, the films of Smith and Attenborough replicate the *anth(r)o*-centric de-contextualization of the flower pictorialized on an empty background, which is also characteristic of historical forms of botanical art (Saunders 1995, 15). Hence, transposing plant time from a living biological milieu to a two- or three-dimensional representation has required the reconfiguration of vegetal embodiment in space and, in particular, the isolation of the flower from both its habitat and the wholeness of its own body (see also the discussion of the vegetal body in Mary Oliver's poetry in Chapter 3).

In impressing *chronos* upon vegetal rhythms, such visualizations appear to dismiss the potentialities of plant time and, instead, approach it as a technical problem to be overcome. However, to engage eco-poetically, phytocritically, and dialogically with plant-time, in a manner that resists the totalizing effects of human construction—as I will argue Judith Wright does in her poetry—is to interface with heterogeneous temporal modes. In Aristotelian thought, two terms discern between distinct yet imbricated facets of time: *chronos* and *kairos*. Chronos reflects a conception of time as a grid, as a measurable phenomenon with a quantifiable duration, rate, length, or age (Smith 1969, 1). Theorized as chronos, time encompasses and—even more—ordinally corresponds to the sequential procession of day to night, spring to winter, youth to old age, or flower to seed, making possible the logos of temporal designations such as *before* and *after*. In contrast, kairos foregrounds the qualitative, non-sequential character of time and the impregnation of events with meaning and *timeliness*. Kairos sensibility is latent in the expression *the right time*, the gerund *timing*, and the descriptors *too soon* and *too late*. Michael Northcott interprets kairos as special "moments in time which herald great or sudden change, or the need for change, in the flow of events and the passage of history" (2015, 107). As kairos, time signifies evental knots or constellations, the aptness of seasonal occurrences, or the rarity of opportunities that might not present again to our everyday perception (Smith 1969, 1). Nonetheless, despite their differing orientations, chronos and kairos are neither utterly distinct nor diametrically different. Just as quantitative time does not solely belong to the domain of the objective physical sciences, qualitative time is not exclusive to the subjective narratives of the humanities and creative arts. Instead, "kairos presupposes chronos" (Smith 1969, 2).

According to Smith's way of thinking, botanical events cannot be reduced to the terms of one mode of time or the other, but rather as the interpenetration of temporalities. By way of their evolutionary constitution, some plant species disrupt the chronos of annualism and biennialism for the kairos of unscripted perennialism at the distant margins of human awareness. An illustrative case in point is the endangered South American bromeliad, *Puya raimondii*, known as the Queen of the Andes, which typically blooms after an 80- to 100-year life cycle. The bromeliad yields a spectacular 12- to 18-foot spike composed of 15,000- to 20,000 flowers (Sgorbati et al. 2004, 222). In 1990, a puya on show at the University of California Botanical Garden astonished scientists and the public by blossoming a *mere* 24 years after being planted as a seed. The precocious puya became the first documented member of its species to flower in a cultivated setting outside of its high-elevation native habitat in Bolivia and Peru (Maclay 2014). The puya flowering instantiates vegetal kairos in both its biocultural rarity (as an event that might not be repeated in our lifetimes) and its constellatory alignment (as a *timely* convergence of temporally distributed factors, from pollination and freedom from predation to favorable climatic conditions and regular horticultural care). As a relatively unforeseen floristic happening, the puya bloom eschews characterization in terms of chronos ordinality. On the contrary, the puya embodies the condition of kairos inhering within chronos (and vice versa) in the interleaving of human and vegetal temporalities.

Aboriginal Dreamings: Plants, Time, Seasons, and Biocultural Rhythms

To appreciate the extent of Wright's engagement with plant time, it is essential to consider Australian influences—particularly Aboriginal time and endemic models of seasonality—on her poetry. Her rendering of plant time as a plexity—as a confluence of myriad, widely dispersed variables—points to Aboriginal time(s) as a foundation of her poetics. The following discussion, however, does not set out to align Aboriginal time neatly with plant time but rather to recognize the intricate overlays and intersections between the temporalities of plants and people in the Australian context. Bioregional configurations of seasons—the containers of time—have persisted for more than 50,000 years in parts of Oceania (Clarke 2009; Entwisle 2014; Prober, O'Connor, and Walsh 2011; Rolston 1905). At the moment of European settlement in 1788, an estimated 315,000 people from 250 nations occupied Australia (Entwisle 2014). Each group retained a distinct language as well as place-specific conceptions of time and the seasons. Wright would to some extent have been acquainted with Indigenous perspectives on time through her long-term friendship with poet-activist Oodgeroo Noonuccal, whose father Edward Ruska was of the Noonuccal group of the Quandamooka people of North Stradbroke Island, Queensland (Huggan and Tiffin 2010, 93–94). In traditional Aboriginal worldviews, vegetal lives can neither be separated from human lives and societies nor relegated exclusively to the domains of science (botany) or aesthetics (art). In fact, plants and people have nurtured one another synergetically over immense timescales through sustainable, land-based practices. For instance, fire-stick farming makes use of mosaic patterns of low-intensity burning to change the composition of the vegetation judiciously for the benefit of plants, animals, humans, and other beings (Hallam 1975; Wilman 2015). For this reason, Aboriginal time reflects the endemic rhythms of land not as a commodity but as *country*—a multidimensional signifier encompassing "people, animals, plants, Dreamings; underground, earth, soils, minerals and waters, surface water, and air," as well as sea, shoreline, and sky (Rose 1996, 8).

Mike Donaldson (1996) regards the temporal order of Aboriginal societies in general as premised upon an integrative conception of time spanning country, spirit, cosmic transactions, and supernatural beings. More specifically, his position counters the spurious assertion that Indigenous modes of time—enciphering the particularities of ecological regions, including plant rhythms—ceased with British colonization and the introduction of the mathematical, universalized schema of time dominating capitalist societies. Over the course of an astonishing 2,500 or more generations, the Dreamtime (or Dreaming) of Aboriginal culture has sustained relations between spiritual Ancestors—often in the form of animals, birds, reptiles, and plants—and living communities of people (Clarke 2009, 80). The Dreaming reflects a metaphysics of wholeness predicated upon the cadences of all that exists (relations and communities) and all that has existed (predecessors and ancestral beings). At the risk of generalization, given the diversity of cultural groups within Australia, Aboriginal consciousness can be said to formulate time in relation to seasonal cyclicality, human movements, and ancestral beings. By no measure eradicated from the Australian landmass, this primordial expression of time flourishes from region to region—from coast to coast—as a form of "counter-hegemonic" temporality (Donaldson 1996, 203). The counter-hegemonic facet of Aboriginal time, articulated by Donaldson, intersects with Michael Marder's characterization of vegetal time as a "locus of resistance" (2013, 103) and plant time itself as a plexity of elements distributed across cultures, worldviews, geographies, epochs, and species. Correspondingly, in his theorization of Aboriginal temporality, Warren TenHouten (2005, x) contends that the distinction between linear (chronos) and cyclical (kairos) time is instructive, to be sure, but there are subjective encounters with "primordial temporality" that resist both categories. In TenHouten's analysis, these non-categorical modes of time consciousness engage "episodic-futural" temporality propelled by what he calls the "knife-edged present" and the "immediate-participatory" dimension of experience (2005, x).

The prevailing Western perspective sees time as generally linear in character and calculable precisely as units of days, years, centuries, and millennia. In scientific thought, time commenced at the Big Bang—an estimated 14 billion years ago—and is expected to progress to a terminal point somewhere in the future. As a consequence, scientific discourse refers to climatic, geological, and evolutionary forms of time, depending on the scales and elements in question. In distinction to linear time, for the Nyoongar, the Aboriginal people of the south-west corner of Western Australia, "the past is always present" in that the spiritual reverberations of the past pervade all temporal possibilities (Robertson et al. 2016, 43). The anthropologist William Stanner (1979) used the intriguing neologism "everywhen" to denote the omnipresence of the past and inherence of the future within the Dreaming. Indeed, the past and future are neither distant concepts nor abstract denominations, but latent within the present, suggesting parallels between Aboriginal time and a kairos-based outlook. Moreover, in the Nyoongar language, there is no equivalent word for *time* that captures the abstract connotations of the English signifier (Robertson et al. 2016, 43). Additionally, Stanner (1979) described the perception of time among hunter-gatherer groups as cyclical and lacking abstraction. Instead, in traditional life, a sense of time arises in correspondence to the movements of the sun, moon, tides, animals, reptiles, insects, plants, humans, and the six (or more) seasons; or, in other words, via the "immediate-participatory" aspects of experience (TenHouten 2005, x).

Neither displaced nor erased by comparatively recent colonialist constructions of time, Aboriginal temporality marks an exceptional capacity to evolve as part of an Australian plexity amalgamating scientific precepts and traditional knowledge. For instance, the *Nyetting*—referring to "the cold, dark time" and "ancestral times" in Nyoongar—bears a likeness to the Ice Age of the early Permian geologic period of about 300-million-years ago (Robertson et al. 2016, 43). Arguably the oldest extant temporal sense of humankind, the time of Aboriginal people, exemplified in this instance by Nyoongar culture, is a time-plexity coalescing a broad range of elements—ecological, seasonal, cultural, ancestral, bodily—with the dominant paradigms of scientific thought and capitalist telos. Crucially for my focus on Wright's poetry, Nyoongar temporality—thriving in areas of country or *boodja* today—dialogically traces the time(s) of localised plants. Decisions, movements, ceremonies, festivals, gatherings, and the seasons themselves (as fluid demarcations of time) are determined in correspondence to, and in conversation with, the *timeliness*—the "knife-edged present" (TenHouten 2005, x)—of the flowering, fruiting, seeding, root-bearing, and other transactions of flora and botanical communities (Rusack et al. 2011). For the Quandamooka, the Aboriginal people of Minjerribah (North Stradbroke Island) where Wright collaborated in her later years with Oodgeroo Noonuccal on projects of environmental and social activism, time encompasses and integrates "knowledge of sky, land and waters, plants, animals and people, past and present. Shared memories construct *continuities between past, present, and future*, and between the specific and general [emphasis added]" (Harward-Nalder and Grenfell 2011, 496).

Seasonal calendars—otherwise known in the anthropological literature as Aboriginal, indigenous, bush, land-based, or endemic calendars—draw on environmental cues, rather than fixed numerical positions, to designate changes within and between seasons, and to encode the progression of time (Clarke 2009, 94). According to the Australian ethnobotanist Philip Clarke (2009, 95), in traditional Aboriginal societies, "different seasons are identified or signalled by distinct animal, vegetation, mythic and totemic associations, climatic events and patterns, and varied by intermittent landscape firings and floods." Across Australia, land-based seasons vary—according to cultural groups and natural environments—from two to seven per annual cycle. Most indigenous calendars have more than four divisions, but some have only two or three seasons, the timing and length of which fluctuate annually. For example, the Wik people of western Cape York Peninsula in northern Queensland divide the year into five seasons, each related to food procurement and each necessitating specific community responsibilities (Memmott 2007, 158). The Nyoongar of Western Australia recognize the six seasons of *birak, bunuru, djeran, makuru, djilba,* and *kambarang,* each designated by an ever-shifting mosaic of ecological and climatic factors. For example, the luminous golden blossom of the endemic West Australian Christmas Tree (*Nuytsia floribunda*) visually signals the beginning of the hot and dry first summer, or *birak* (Ryan 2015).

Furthermore, Clarke (2011, 55) notes the significance of "calendar trees" and "calendar plants"—species that herald the passage of time and the cyclical progression of the endemic seasons by virtue of their flowering, fruiting, and other ecological processes. The *timeliness* of the plants, accordingly, becomes *the right time* for community activities. Particular plants serve as bush calendars for monitoring seasonal progressions and for portending important cultural events. In the early 1900s, the Bigambul people of the Northern Tablelands and Border Rivers area, straddling the boundary between northern New South Wales and southern Queensland, were observed to reckon the seasons according to the flowering of trees; for instance, the Bigambul season *yerrabinda* is named after *yerra,* a tree species that blooms during September (Clarke 2009, 99). In the Brisbane area of southern Queensland, waterlily blossoms signify the optimum time for harvesting river mussels, while the ripening of wild passionfruit correlates to the highest amount of nourishing adipose in carpet snakes (Clarke 2011, 55). For the Lardil people of the Gulf of Carpentaria, between Queensland and the Northern Territory, the screw palm (*Pandanus spiralis*) is a calendar tree marking seasonal movements through its ripened red nuts, which coincide with the first influx of *dulnhu* fish (Clarke 2011, 55). Furthermore, among the Kuku Yalanji people of the rainforests of Far North Queensland, the ripening of black beans (*Castanospermum australe*) points to the appropriate time for catching wild fowl (Clarke 2011, 55). Aboriginal seasonalities concretize Marder's statement that "living at the rhythm of the seasons means respecting the time of plants and, along with them, successively opening oneself to various elements" (Irigaray and Marder 2016, 144).

Influenced by the endemic seasons—each appropriate to its respective cultural group and ecological region—botanist Tim Entwistle (2014) has proposed a decolonization of Australian time through a more botanically-nuanced, five-season model. The seasons of *sprinter, sprummer,* summer, autumn, and winter would replace the colonial four season paradigm and the codification of time it has put into effect since

British settlement. Rather than based upon fixed numerical reference points, Entwistle's schema takes into consideration the behaviors of local and introduced plants over the course of the year; in other words, the botanist seeks to reformulate seasonality—the container of time—in relation to the time(s) of flora. Spanning August and September, sprinter would coincide with the proliferation of flowers, especially those of wattles (*Acacia* spp.), throughout Australia. A short season, sprummer, would intervene between sprinter and summer, indicating weather variability and a second wave of blooms. Between December and March, Entwistle's summer would correspond to the emergence of hot weather plants. The cooling temperatures of autumn—approximately April to May—would involve a different set of taxa, including camellias and certain orchids, blossoming after the intensely hot and dry summer. Finally, a winter of 2 months would be marked by the physiological changes plants undergo during cold weather in preparation for sprinter and another annual cycle (Entwisle 2014, 43–46).

Across Timescales: Vegetal Temporality as a Plexity

In Western cultural traditions outside of the Australian context, there are diverse temporalities of relevance to the characterization of plant life and botanical communities as time-plex. Mara Miller refers to scientific, objective, subjective, and historical modes of time, especially applicable to cultivated garden landscapes (2010, 178). Codified by scientists and social institutions, scientific time, according to Miller, is largely objective, directional, and uniform (2010, 180). With its adherence to a chronos model, scientific time is essential to quantifying, for instance, the days until germination or the minimum number of sunlight hours necessary for fruiting. In a similar way, objective time is the shared experience of time within a family, community, or social group, structured by regularly occurring events, such as holidays or rituals. Objective time overlaps with historical time, or time as demarcated by historical occurrences. In contrast to these modes, subjective time refers to "time as it *feels* to us [italics in original]" and, unlike objective time, varies between individuals (Miller 2010, 182).

Significantly, these different temporal modes intersect with the time of vegetal nature in a garden setting through what Miller terms the "internal calendar" of plants (2010, 186). Alfred Siewers denotes the temporal intersection and knottiness evident in Miller's typology through the neologism *time-plexity*, denoting the entwining of chronos and kairos—of human and other-than-human modes of time. Time-plexity marks the co-passage of beings through instances of timing, timeliness, and timelessness, toward the experience of non-time (Siewers 2011, 109). In his analysis of non-Augustinian patristics (the study of the works of early Christian theologians), Siewers identifies the prevalence of at least four temporal modes articulated by early authors: human, non-human natural, created eternal (that of angels), and the non-time of uncreated natural divinities (Siewers 2011, 109). Building on philosopher Evan Thompson's research into neurophenomenology, Siewers goes on to suggest that ecopoetic narratives underscore time-plex human encounters with nature by upsetting reductionistic concepts of temporality and predeterminations of time's relationship to space.

In consonance with Smith's claim that "kairos presupposes chronos," Siewers asserts that the intellect's disposition toward ordering perception quantitatively is always counterbalanced by multidimensional entwinings of chronos logos and kairos indeterminacy (Siewers 2009, 53–54). Siewer's conceptualization of time also extends phenomenologist David Wood's elaboration of the plexity—or interwoven nature—of temporal scales that he suggests is foundational to human experience (2003, 213–17). A central feature of phenomenology, in dynamic interconnection to space, time makes possible the articulation of relationalities between beings and "a connectedness that transcends the moment" (Wood 2003, 213). To this end, Wood outlines four strands of an eco-phenomenology, also of relevance to Wright's poetization of the lives of plants: the invisibility of time; the celebration of finitude; the synchronization of rhythms; and the disruption and dissolution of temporal horizons (2003, 214). Wood begins by examining what he understands as the invisible features of time as a continuum. This first aspect of time-plexity involves engagement with time based on a recognition of "the true temporal extendedness of the object" and in which a "moment [of perception] would capture something importantly nonmomentary" (Wood 2003, 214). Presenting an arboreal example, Wood further elaborates that "[...] the life of the tree, the living tree, the tree of which we glimpse only a limb here, a trunk there, or views from various angles, this temporally extended persisting, growing tree, is *invisible* [emphasis added]" (2003, 214–15). Indeed, apprehending "the living tree" as a manifestation of the invisible within the visible necessitates "synthetic" attention that coalesces temporally distributed events within a perceptual instance, or whole (Wood 2003, 215). To appreciate time as a fountainhead of transformation is to orient consciousness to the potentialities inhering within the unseen: "There is an invisible in the heart of the visible to the extent that the essential temporal articulatedness of things is not itself obviously presented in their immediate temporary appearance" (Wood 2003, 215).

The second aspect of Wood's model of time-plexity, the celebration of finitude, involves the heightening of the infinite within the finite—a mode of time in which a "connectedness between individual events generates a kind of depth to every moment through which its very singularity is heightened" (Wood 2003, 216). The third aspect, the synchronization of rhythms, underscores the primacy of relational fields in which temporal pulses "interact, interpenetrate, interfere with one another, become locally coordinated and so on" (Wood 2003, 216). Here, the periodicity of time and harmonization of the rhythms of beings, organisms, elements, and things confer advantages to ecosystems and their human and more-than-human constituents. The coordination of temporal events has been an influential factor in the evolution of organisms through dynamic equilibrium, including states of mutualism and antagonism. As an example of rhythmic synchronization, the biotic interactions of the cycad are illustrative. Cycads are prominent vegetal subjects in Judith Wright's poetics of time, and among the oldest and most threatened plants on earth. Having existed for more than 280 million years—even before the emergence of dinosaurs—cycads attained their greatest diversity and extent during the Triassic and Jurassic periods. They are now regarded by naturalists and popular commentators as living, prehistoric fossils. Over vast scales of time, cycads and myriad insect species—especially microlepidoptera or micromoths—have developed elaborate pollination mutualisms moderated by the production of cycad sugars (Marler and Lindström 2015).

While ensuring the longevity of plant and insect species in coordinated states, the harmonization of rhythms between cycads and pollinators, conversely, amplifies the danger of coextinctions in the present Anthropocene scenario of intense biodiversity loss (Marler and Lindström 2015, 3). As a departure from this kind of synchronization, Wood's fourth aspect—the dissolution of temporal wholeness—points to discontinuities and upsurges in time, beyond the invisible within the visible or temporal alignments. As *physis* (the Greek term for nature, epitomized in the particular movements of vegetal life upward, downward, inward, outward), time is an irruptive phenomenon in which *any* conception of it eschews and confounds *any* conception that *can* be postulated (Wood 2003, 217). Although the time-plexities of natural phenomena—including plants—remain largely shielded from ordinary perception (*elusive*, in Marder's terms), eco-phenomenological attention can disclose the existence of heterogeneous temporalities, such as chronos, kairos, objective, subjective, scientific, historical, and vegetal modes of time.

For Marder, reformulating the Western metaphysical tradition with regard to vegetal life, botanical events mark the passage of time and the temporalization of human awareness through material-semiotic processes of "germination and growth, flourishing, dehiscence, blossoming, coming to fruition, and finally fermentation and decay" (Marder 2013, 94). However, a conception of time as announced by vegetal events—of plant being in service to human temporality—risks minimizing "the time of the plants themselves," defined as the endemic seasons, rhythms, pulsations, and scales of vegetal nature (Marder 2013, 94). In his analysis of the philosophies of Aristotle, Heidegger, and Hegel, Marder identifies three interpretations of plant time, which he calls "vegetal hetero-temporality" (95), the "'bad infinity' of growth" (107), and the "iterability of expression" (112). In particular, hetero-temporality aligns with Wood's eco-phenomenological tenet of the invisible within the visible. Widely disseminated loci of time(s) inhere within the present/presence of vegetal materiality: "[...] a mature plant, which has not yet developed by means of the qualitative articulations of growth, *is* the seed as its own not yet actualized potentiality [emphasis in original]" (Marder 2013, 97). In his discussion of the first interpretation, Marder echoes Wood's idea of invisibility and visibility but in parallel terms of potentiality and actualization, as to underscore the "futural modality of time (the not-yet) that resides in every present instant" (Marder 2013, 99). In contrast to rhythmic synchronization among beings, disjunctures and misalignments between the pulsations of plants and humans resonate with Wood's fourth principle of the dissolution of temporal wholeness. As stated by Marder, plant resonances are "often imperceptible to a conscious human observer" because divergent temporalities always govern different beings occupying one physical space (2013, 103).

As a consequence of the variations between the cadences of plants, animals, humans, and others, a temporal split—such as seeing a puya bromeliad again for the first time after a period spent away from the plant—perceptually accentuates the progression of time traced in the growth or decay of leaves, flowers, stems, trunks, roots, and so on. Accordingly, vegetal hetero-temporality centrally positions the plant corpus as "a loose alliance of multiple temporalities of growth" (Marder 2013, 104). Whereas a portion of a plant might flower and sprout toward greater self-actualization reflected in its spatial increase, another part might equally dehisce or rot, returning that segment of the plant body to an invisibility impregnated with re-emergent potential the following season or year. Although in consonance with the patterns and timings of certain genera, angiosperms will invariably flower, fruit, and seed; rather than a loss, the absence of a flower or other property entails a transfer of energy, resources, and movement from vital actualization to latent potentiality governed by seasonal return. Vegetal modularity—the distinct capacity of a plant to shed parts of its body without dying or diminishing in overall wellbeing (see Chapter 8 for further discussion)—reflects the interbraided modes of materialization and withdrawal that inhere within plant being-in-the world.

Marder's second facet of plant time—the "bad infinity" of growth—evokes the potentially limitless processions of spatial increase, efflorescence, seeding, and so on peculiar to vegetal life (2013, 107). In Marder's reading of Western metaphysics, plant fecundity has been conceptualized as monstrous, immoderate, indeterminate, and lacking both appropriate limits, as well as a precise beginning and end (2013, 107–11). The "reckless" limitlessness of growth expels the plant from temporal convention. As such, vegetal being is figured as wholly consumed with self-nourishment and unchecked proliferation. By implication, a monstrous plant lacks the nuanced mode of being required for intelligent discrimination. Marder asserts that this second dimension of plant time underlies, for instance, the treatment of plants as inexhaustible reserves. The third and final dimension—the iterability of expression—underscores how "the cyclical time of nature (the changing of the seasons, the alternation of day and night) intersects with the cycles of vegetal growth (the budding and shedding of foliage, the opening and closing of a flower)" (Marder 2013, 113). Plant temporality affirms cycles and repetition as the essential features of all pulsing life. In Marder's view, the leaf is "an ephemeral register for the inscription of vegetal time as the time of repetition" (2013, 114).

In conjunction with theorizations of chronos, kairos, and other temporal modes, the phyto-phenomenological frameworks of Marder, Wood, and Siewers underscore the plexity of the time of the plants themselves. A term leveraged from cognitive linguistics, *plexity* denotes a conceptual category based upon states of articulation between multiple elements (Evans and Green 2006, 519). Poeticizing the "elusive time of plants" (Marder 2013, 98)—as Wright does—requires lyrically orienting the writer across other-than-human timescales. One hence becomes enmeshed in the fabric of vegetal timescales and hetero-temporality. An expansion of imagination takes shape at the intersection of time elements. Glimpses arise of the shifting, poietic phenomena of vegetal presence—as the invisible imbricated within the visible, as actualization latent within potentiality, and of flower within seed. Wright's work troubles the reduction of plant time and resists the imposition of human timeframes on plants and other beings. Instead, she strives through her ecopoetic practice to responsively and dialogically attend to the time of plants—and particularly to render time in terms of her commitment to environmental consciousness, ethics, activism, and stewardship. For this reason, the relationship between time and plants in Wright's work illustrates Marder's notion of vegetal time as a "locus of resistance" (2013, 103) that troubles the capitalist paradigm and counters the conversion of plant difference into sameness.

Wright's Preoccupation with Time: Further Australian Contexts

Well before Entwistle's instigation of a new Australian seasonal regime based on flowering cycles, Wright had already provoked a parallel process of time decolonization in her poetry. By virtue of its lyrical engagement with time-plexity and vegetal hetero-temporality, Wright's work calls into question the mathematized, capitalistic temporality imposed on botanical nature. In its place, the poet embraces time as a plexity constituted—to a considerable extent—by the temporal modes of

Aboriginal traditions in conjunction with the time of Australian plants themselves. Poems, such as "The Cycads" (Wright 1963, 37), narrate the remarkable evolutionary longevity of Australian taxa, demanding of the writer a compositional purview that transcends the relatively contracted timescale according to which human consciousness normatively operates. Indeed, many early naturalists considered Australia "a habitat for living fossils," as a domain where species, which went extinct elsewhere in the world long ago, could survive because of the remoteness and harsh climate of the country (Stafford 1990, 81). Primordial vegetal life—notably the widespread Proteaceae (protea) family, including banksias, dryandras, hakeas, and grevilleas—figures appreciably into Wright's poetics of time.

To be sure, the venerability of Australian plants can be conceptualized in relation to both individuals and genera. For instance, Wollemi pine (*Wollemi nobilis*) specimens are known to have lifespans from 500 to 1000 years. The origin of the species itself is estimated to lie in the Late Cretaceous (Turonian) age, 89.8 to 93.9 million years ago (see, for example, Woodford 2012). In 1994, the highly-publicized discovery of the first Wollemi pine, merely 100 miles from Sydney, provided the third known, extant genus (in addition to *Araucaria* spp. and *Agathis* spp.) of the prehistoric Araucariaceae family of conifers (Macphailm and Carpenter 2014). Citing as illustrative the Araucariaceae (araucaria, from the Triassic period, 252 to 201 million years ago, or Ma) and Cycadaceae (cycads, from the Permian, 298 to 252 Ma) families, nineteenth-century British botanist Richard Owen argued that Australia reveals "a picture of an ancient condition of the earth's surface, which has been superseded in our hemisphere by other strata and a higher type of Mammalian organization" (Owen 1846, 69). The Gondwanan origin of many Australian species is the outcome of complex long-term interactions between climate, soils, symbionts, and the isolation of the landmass as a whole (Crisp and Cook 2013, 304).

Wright's time-plexity enfolds Aboriginal temporalities and the time of plants. The poet accentuates the primeval character and particular biotic rhythms of individuals and species according to the seasons. Critic Elizabeth McMahon (2007) intimates this lyrically-mediated enfolding of time in her analysis of "the temporality of composition" in Wright's work. For McMahon (2007, 15), time is a theme, preoccupation, and problematic with which Wright engages throughout her career. Her "temporal overlayering or patterning" intermeshes different modes of time, as outlined earlier in this chapter. Elements of historical time, the mythologized (chronos) time of nationhood, the non-linear (kairos) time of nature, and the experiential time of human individuals and generations, for instance, graft with the knife-edged immediacy of the time-conscious compositional present (2007, 16–17). McMahon's articulation of temporal plurality—of time as constituted by manifold cultural and environmental aspects—evokes the idea of time-plexity as the coalescing of broadly dispersed elements conventionally held as oppositional and irreconcilable. Invoking Julia Kristeva's (1986) three temporalities model of cyclical, monumental, and historical time, McMahon concludes that Wright's poetic corpus is "full of the present, full of the time of composition rather than [a sense of] realised completeness" (2007, 22). As a time-plexity—a splicing of human and other-than-human temporal dimensions—her writing enunciates "the complex relation of past and present to present and future readers" (McMahon 2007, 25). Moreover, the influence of Wright's understanding of Australian history—as the inherence of the past in present, of natural within cultural histories—in her dedication to environmental and social justice has been the focus of historians such as Tom Griffiths (2006). Despite their differing emphases, these observers of Wright's work concur that time consciousness is foundational to her politics and poetry.

Yet, unlike McMahon (2007) who suggests that Wright's preoccupation with temporal layering and patterning aligns her with the modernist poetics of figures such as T.S. Eliot, I contend that the poet's focus on the plexity of time corresponds to her affinities with Aboriginal worldviews, her interest in the rhythms of local plants, and her broader desire to disenchant the Anglocentric jingoism underlying Australia's deeply troubled colonial inheritance. Wright's article "The Battle of the Biosphere" (1969) coincided with the rise of the Australian green movement and lays out the ecological themes she explores later in her poetry. The essay "Learning to Look" from Wright's prose collection *Born of the Conquerors* (1991) supplies a pithy synopsis of the evolution of Australian flora since Gondwana, followed by an appeal for conservation based upon recognition of the inimitability of botanical species in the Antipodes. She appeals to the reader's senses: "Next time you see a moss or a lichened rock, try to stretch your mind around its past" (Wright 1991, 97). For Wright, the re-habituation of learning to see the land anew necessitates actively reorienting one's temporal disposition—"stretching your mind"—in order to apprehend plant time and the depth of evolutionary history. In this part of the world, commonplace encounters with flora render the enormous extent of plant time more immediate and accessible: "You can grow in your garden tree ferns whose ancestry lies in those times [the Ice Age of the Late Carboniferous period]" (Wright 1991, 97). Like Richard Owen in the nineteenth century and subsequent naturalists, the poet acknowledges the land's primordiality by figuring the vegetation as an extant relic—a living fossil—of a distant era: "The northern rainforests of Queensland today contain many living species of the earliest flowering plants" (1991, 97–98). However, Wright's appeal for sympathetic approaches to botanical conservation depicts Australian plants respectfully as primordial but not primitive and unaesthetic in the disparaging (or flabbergasted) sense found in some colonial-era writings (see, for example, the comments of botanist John Lindley in Ryan 2012, 87–109).

For the poet, the meta-narrative of Australian vegetation as ancient should be cause for more attuned consciousness as a means to counteract the injudiciousness of the past and progress anew toward an environmentally- and botanically-just future: "But now it is time to change. Walk into a forest of eucalypts and wattles (Australian plants both) and look again. Are these forests and plants and insects and birds and mammals yours to destroy?" (Wright 1991, 98). Notwithstanding the prominent vegetal themes of Wright's politics and writing—her "two fires," in critic Philip Mead's terms (2006) and her "double tree" in Zeller's (2000)—this kind of sustained engagement with the temporality of vegetal life has not been significantly foregrounded in studies of her bioregional poetics (Brady 2007; Harris 2009; Hutchings 2007; Zeller 2000), community environmental activism (Kinsella 2010, 160; Mulligan and Hill 2001, 73), and human rights advocacy (Brady 1998). Sue King-Smith does characterize one of the "spectres of the past" in Wright's work as the "indigenous landscape that existed prior to British occupation, with a substantial number of indigenous species of flora and fauna now extinct" (King-Smith 2007, 117–18). Katie Holmes (2005) has also written about the role of gardening in the poet's life and writing, commenting that "the cultivation of her peas and lettuce gave her as much joy as her bottlebrush, native jasmine, and mint bush" (1). Holmes reminds us that cultivated plants were as important to the phytophilic poet as the non-domesticated species existing before European colonization. Along with a love of the plants, animals, birds, waterways, and rock formations of *country*—in the Aboriginal sense of home rather than nation—gardening facilitated Wright's perceptive awareness of vegetal cadences (see also Chapters 4, 5, and 6 for further discussion of the importance of gardening to botanical poets).

Poetic Vegetal Temporality: Stretching One's Mind Around Time

Integral to Wright's poetization of vegetal temporality is a time-space continuum encompassing the northern New South Wales (Armidale area) and southern Queensland (Mount Tamborine) border region where she lived for periods during her life. Her first collection, *The Moving Image* (1946), heralds—in the titular poem—the preoccupation with time that characterizes her writing as a whole. In a tenor of direct appeal redolent of her essay "Learning to Look"—published 45 years later—Wright implores her audience to engage the plexity of time through embodied perception of place. As a many-sided phenomenon, time "speaks" through physical sensations and not solely in audible signatures. In linking temporality to breathing, the poet therein implies the vital, mediating presence of vegetal life in human relations to being and time:

> Listen then. Out of the mouth of time
> comes the inchoate sound, the inaudible sound
> only heard in the silence of our breathing
> when the heart stops and the listening nerve is tense.
> (Wright 1946, 4, pt 3, ll. 10–13)

In particular, Wright poeticizes Heidegger's idea of *call* as being-called by language, as waiting, attending, and reaching out to something through language (Hanly 2013, 248). In such terms, listening involves receptive and embodied presence in the world—presence animated by the autonomic act of respiring and its inextricable evolutionary relation to vegetal being. Although the botanical registers of *The Moving Image* are largely tangential to themes of colonial inheritance and Indigenous dispossession, the poem "The Hawthorn Hedge" alludes to a time-plexity weighted toward manicured, ornamental plant-scapes. Through its spatial accretion, the hawthorn temporalizes awareness but, at the same time, unsettles chronos as ordinal, quantifiable time: "How long ago she planted the hawthorn hedge—/she forgets how long ago" (Wright 1946, 22, ll. 1–2). Resonant in this context is Wood's (2003, 17) dissolution of time-wholeness and foregrounding of the importance of disjunctures and slippages within temporal consciousness. As Marder (2013, 103) also appositely claims, even when plants and people dwell in the same physical space, vegetal time can remain indiscernible and elusive; spatiotemporal breakages often allow us to see plants anew.

The entreaty to "stretch" one's consciousness around plant time is more palpable in "The Cycads," first featured in Wright's second collection *Woman to Man* (1949). The poem evokes the Carboniferous beginnings of cycads and the materialization of time-plexity in the bodily habitus of their seeds, roots, and foliage. The term *cycad* refers to a group of spermatophytes (seed plants) originating in the Carboniferous or early Permian periods—approximately 280 million years ago—and reaching their greatest profusion and diversity during the Mesozoic (Walters, Osborne, and Decker 2004, 3). In all likelihood, Wright is referring to *Macrozamia* (or zamia), a cycad genus comprising about 40 species of which 37 are endemic to Queensland (Forster 2004, 85). In *The Living Cycads* (1919), the first comprehensive account of the iconic plant group, the American botanist Charles Joseph Chamberlain characterized cycads as "the surviving remnants of a line reaching back through the Mesozoic into the Paleozoic" and also as fern-like or palm-like species of "great antiquity" (Chamberlain 1919, ix, 3). In his travels to Queensland, the botanist observed that, even after a prolonged drought of 8 months, cycads appeared "fresh and vigorous, with dark-green leaves and a wonderful display of cones" (Chamberlain 1919, 29). The large female cones of zamia species, such as *burrawang* (*M. communis*), noticeably turn bright red or yellow when ripe. Zamia nuts themselves bear divergent cultural histories; on the one hand, as a fatal or near-fatal toxin to early Australian settlers and livestock and, on the other, as a nutritious starch for Aboriginal people. Chamberlain (1919, 29) noted a paralytic affliction that pastoralists named "rickets." Cattle dragged their rear legs, displaying "a peculiar gait" and later starving to death. Numerous explorers—including Willem de Vlamingh in 1696, George Grey in 1839, and John McDouall Stuart in 1864—suffered from the ill consequences of ingesting unprocessed cycad nuts, a condition widely called *zamia staggers* for its pronounced neurotoxic effects (Carr and Carr 1981, 17). Despite the injurious properties, Aboriginal cultures throughout Australia developed efficient detoxifying processes—roasting, soaking, fermenting, or a combination of techniques—to transform the poisonous raw nut into a staple carbohydrate (Clarke 2011, 89–91).

In its lyricality, "The Cycads" coalesces these multifarious historical nodes of zamia in the first line, "Their smooth dark flames flicker at time's own root" (Wright 1963, 37, l. 1). The flickering flames—the stiff dark-green foliage rasping in the wind, the deep red nuts cast in stippled light, or the grafted quality of both anatomical effects—signify visually the depth of zamia ancestry, or what the poet calls the "strata of first birth" (1963, 37, l. 4). Wright paints an affective portrait of sullen "antique cycads [...] cursed by age" and isolated among "the complicated birds and flowers" of more recent evolutionary epochs (1963, 37, ll. 5, 7, 11). Unlike the impetuous avians that "cry in air one moment, and are gone," the zamia lean collectively—obdurate as monuments—toward the "countless suns" of time beyond the grasp of human temporal comprehension (1963, 37, ll. 15, 16). Prefiguring her much later injunction to "stretch your mind" across the temporal topographies of moss and lichen (Wright 1991, 97), the poet deploys an imperative verb connoting possession and encouraging readers to "take their [the cycads'] cold seed and set it in the mind" (1963, 37, l. 17). The allusion to "cold seed" marks a tacit invocation of the bifurcated pastoral history of zamia nuts as a declared poisonous species targeted for eradication throughout Queensland—an Australia-wide twentieth-century biopolitical campaign briefly cited by Chamberlain in his morphological assessment of "living" (as opposed to fossilized) Australian cycads (1919, 29). Contrastingly, the zamia seed Wright has in mind—and, indeed, advocates *being in mind*—is the nutritive blood-red-glistening nut consumed by Aboriginal Australian people for millennia. Thus, Wright's seed is a material-semiosis: an actual, presencing zamia organ not reducible to linguistic turns yet at the same time offering a poetic substance for detoxifying the dangerous residues of colonial inheritance. The attempt to expel zamia time from country overlapped with the broader historical campaign to supplant Aboriginal temporality with Anglo-European conventions (see, for example, Broome 2010, 57–80). Nonetheless, both forms survived respective genocidal campaigns and are thriving today. This disquisition on time concludes with the lengthening zamia roots penetrating the depth of plant temporality, coaxing one to "the unthinkable, unfathomed edge/beyond which man remembers only sleep" (Wright 1963, 37, ll. 20–21). As an evolutionary modality, plant time is not confined to the vegetal domain. Instead, it is latent within human consciousness and can be awakened through a process of imaginative, phenomenological stretching across the timescales of the primordial cycads.

The titular poem of the collection *The Two Fires* (1955) reinvokes the potent material-semiosis of the seed, presenting an extraordinary elemental meditation on plant time at the unfathomed edge of human awareness. Narrated as a creation story involving ghosts, death, love, rock, water, and, of course, fire, "The Two Fires" represents Wright's time-attentiveness as a preoccupation and problematic. The "inventions of the holy unwearying seed" are "bright falling fountains made of time, that bore/through time the holy seed that knew no time—" (Wright 1992, 20, ll. 3–5). Vegetal presence—signified by the burning blossoms of poiesis—of falling across, with, and into the plexity of time—pulsates in the dialogical relation between the seed and that which it yields. "For time has caught on fire, and you too burn:/leaf, stem, branch, calyx and the bright corolla/are now the insubstantial wavering fire/in which love dies" (Wright 1992, 20, ll. 8–11). In figuring the time of the plants themselves—of leaf and bright corolla—as fire, which generates the world but also consumes it, Wright summons the periodic burning practices of Aboriginal societies. At the same time, she elegizes the loss of the sacred interconnection between fire, time, seasonality, and flora since colonial occupation of Australia:

And walking here among the dying centuries—
the centuries of moss, of fern, of cycad,
of the towering tree—the centuries of the flower—
I pause where water falls from the face of the rock.
My father rock, do you forget the kingdom of the fire?
(Wright 1992, 20, ll. 30–34)

Time-plexity, for Wright, encompasses the temporalities of Aboriginal people, plants, geological elements, water, and the timeliness of seasons. Firing modified the landscape, encouraging desirable flora, such as edible yams (*Dioscorea* spp.), while suppressing the proliferation of undergrowth species that impeded bipedal movement (Gammage 2011;

Hallam 1975; Portenga et al. 2016; Wilman 2015). Lower-temperature, seasonally-responsive fires also diminished the potential for higher-intensity conflagrations. Indigenous people recognized *burn time* as an optimal juncture, during which firing would result in the most advantageous effects (Clarke 2011, 60–71). For them, as Bill Gammage observes in *The Biggest Estate on Earth* (2011, 164), "fire was a life study. Seasons vary, rain is erratic, plants have life cycles, fire has long and short term effects, people differ on what to favour." Yet, when the proper ecological circumstances occur—when the timing becomes *right*—the millennia-old cycle of fire resumes, re-enacting a landscape narrative of ancient provenance and affording a glimpse into the plants' timescape: "And now, set free by the climate of man's hate,/that seed sets time ablaze" (Wright 1992, 20, ll. 40–41).

As with "The Two Fires" and "The Cycads," Wright's poem "Phaius Orchid," first appearing in the collection *The Gateway* (1953), contemplates the extent of botanical temporality—in this instance, materialized by the ephemeral flower of the swamp orchid—within the primordial landscape. Also known as the swamp lily, lesser swamp orchid, and southern swamp orchid, the phaius orchid (*Phaius australis*) is one of three orchid species of this kind found in Australia. The genus nomination *phaius* derives from Greek term *phaios* for "dusky" or "swarthy," a reference to the dark brownish blossoms, the largest borne by any Australian orchid species (Clements 2013, 73). Inhabiting threatened coastal paperbark (*Melaleuca quinquenervia*) swamps, the phaius orchid is vital to the traditional botanical knowledge of the Aboriginal people of northern New South Wales and southern Queensland (McElroy 2011). Its wetland habitat is denoted early in the poem in the phrases "brackish sand" and "sand's poverty, water's sour" (Wright 1963, 71, ll. 1, 7). Unlike the cycad and other living relics of Carboniferous origin, however, the orchid is younger in its evolutionary constitution. In fact, the Orchidaceae family dates back to the Late Cretaceous, a (relatively) mere 100 million years ago. The temporal rhythms of the phaius, nevertheless, elude the poet—its multifaceted flower, rusting with time's entropic impulse, an "image I hold/and cannot understand" (1963, 71, ll. 9–10). Questions persist in the narrative. Is the telos of the intricate yet short-lived flower "to garland time—/eternity's cold tool/that severs with its blade/the gift as soon as made" (Wright 1963, 71, ll. 13–16)? Notwithstanding a tone of reserve throughout (unlike the more transcendental and uninhibited "The Two Fires"), Wright's discourse concludes with the surrendering of herself to time. She embraces—as an emergent quality of vegetal nature—time-plexity, which transgresses the chronos drive of settler consciousness: "Here like the plant I weave/your dying garlands, time" (1963, 71, ll. 19–20).

Instances from Wright's oeuvre reveal the enactment of time-plexity within the structure of her poems. The consideration of temporal poiesis takes the reader beyond the poet's representation of time to the articulation—and, indeed, bending—of time within her text. Rather than the forward march of chronos, the outcome is the weaving of temporality recursively onto itself. A classic illustration of the march of chronos is James Thomson's long four part poem *The Seasons* (1793), beginning with the spring, then moving sequentially through the summer and autumn, and concluding with the winter. Thomson's progressive arrangement of temporal consciousness parallels the idea of spring—especially in the northern hemisphere—as the season of birth and winter as the season of decline and death. Yet, in "The Cedars," Wright's concern with the possibility of "return"—of cyclical, kairos-infused time—is apparent at the structural level. Inverting the traditional order by beginning instead with winter (indeed, a period of intense growth and flowering for some Australian species), the poem's first stanza alludes to the robust constitution of plants during cold season desiccation and dormancy: "The dried body of winter is hard to kill [...] By the sunken pool/the sullen Sodom-apple grips his scarlet fruit" (Wright, 1963, 60, ll. 1, 5–6). In the second stanza, the narration proceeds to spring—the "returner, knocker at the iron gate" (l. 7)—but collapses the one-directional procession evident in Thomson's poem for a concept of time as a knot, as kairos inhering within chronos. "Locked in our mourning, in our sluggish age,/we stand and think of past springs, of deceits not yet forgotten" (ll. 9–10). The reflective "we" signifies cross-species collectivity: human and plant time are inextricably linked. "The Cedars" also constructs temporality as the state of being-called-by-time. Time's subjects, however, respond to the call differently in congruence with their bodies, in relation to their modes of percipience, and as a function of their broader environments: "Do not ask us to answer again as then we answered" (l. 13). In this example, Wright textualizes Wood's fourth ecophenomenological principle of the disruption and dissolution of temporal horizons.

Conclusion: Taking Your (Plant) Time

Michael Marder (2013) has argued that in their spatial articulations plants confer to human beings the temporalization of awareness. As this chapter has shown, flora is integral to the conception and perception of time. One of the ways in which humans become conscious of the progressions and dislocations of time is through the material-semiosis of plants: seeding, flowering, fruiting, rooting, proliferating, receding, coming into being, passing away, and flourishing within their dying. By multidimensionalizing temporality, an approach to plant time (as plexity) refuses the homogenization of vegetal difference. In the entwining of Western, Indigenous, and ecological modalities, the explosion of everlasting flowers in the Australian Outback, for instance, comes to signify not only the present immediacy of spring but also bygone seasons and those times (and episodes of timeliness) that lie ahead. The future inheres with the present—within the past. On the other side of the world, desiccated maple leaves drift to the ground in the American north-east, embodying the autumn while materializing time's inexorable movement, the inevitability of senescence, and the seasonal disclosure of arboreal being. Hence, to posit vegetal temporality in limiting terms, as merely an ordinal signifier of forward movement—of the passage of the days, months, years, seasons, and epochs that organize humanity's past, present, and future—is to risk expelling plant time to the periphery of consciousness and, therein, more broadly negating the potential of human-plant relations. As an alternative to appropriating vegetal rhythms or attempting to expunge botanical temporality altogether, there is a more dialogical mode of being, which Wright poetically intimates. This demands learning to exist relationally to the time of plants through the challenging—perhaps life-long—practice of stretching one's mind across their temporal terrains. Through a time-space continuum based in bioregions, the poet invites us to take our (plant) time.

The verse of Judith Wright offers a provocative stimulus—of ongoing contemporary relevance—for inspiring such an expansion, of attuning oneself to the timely pulsations of vegetal nature through spirited listening and looking. Wright's poetry lays bare the capacity of poetic language to mediate plant time and its myriad articulations with human temporalities. Yet, rather than "translating" vegetal temporality and hence chancing the appropriation of plant time, Wright instead attempts to patiently investigate, sensitively render, and lyrically enact the elusive time of the plants themselves. In her narrativization of the plexity of plant time, Wright facilitates her readers' consciousness of vegetal rhythms and brings the temporalities of the ancient Australian flora to the fore. Indeed, her enactment of plant time is linked to her sensory apprehension of vegetal life through the seasons. Thus, her poetry underscores the synergistic relation between mediation (reading about plants) and immediacy (experiencing the nonhuman world directly through the senses) in engendering awareness of botanical being. In contemplating, questioning, and surrendering to plant time, Wright also contributes to the decolonization of Australian temporality in a manner intersecting, for instance, with Tim Entwisle's call for a botanically-based, five season regime. Her lyricism provokes her readers' awareness of the formidable time topographies of ferns, cycads, orchids, and other Australian plant taxa. She reminds us that these species are the living, breathing portals to the outermost precipice of time as we know it, "beyond which man remembers only sleep" (Wright 1963, 37, ll. 20–21). While poeticizing evolutionary extent—for instance, the primordial nature of the cycads by virtue of their species' distant Carboniferous origin—Wright also examines the closer-at-hand temporal rhythms and dispositions of plants in the "knife-edged" depth of the compositional moment and the "immediate-participatory" (TenHouten 2005, x) aspects of her environmental consciousness, as presented in "Phaius Orchid" in particular. Wright's textualization of plant time invariably embodies a commitment to botanical ethics and locally-grounded activism on behalf of Aboriginal Australian people and the Queensland environment, which she indeed fervently pursued throughout her life. In the final analysis, her attention to plants can be understood as a locus of resistance to the appropriation of time and for its bold synchronization of the poet, the text, and the cadences of vegetal being and becoming, living and dying.

Bibliography

BBC. 1995. *The Private Life of Plants*. San Francisco: Kanopy Streaming. Film.
BBC. 2009. *Plants*. Accessed 23 May 2017. https://archive.org/details/LifeBBCDocumentry2009720pH264. Film
Brady, Veronica. 1998. *South of My Days: A Biograpy of Judith Wright*. Pymble, NSW: Angus and Robertson.
Brady, Veronica. 2007. "The Poetry of Judith Wright and Ways of Rejoicing in the World." In *The Littoral Zone: Australian Contexts and Their Writers*, edited by C.A. Cranston and Robert Zeller, 145–52. Amsterdam: Rodopi.
Broome, Richard. 2010. *Aboriginal Australians: A History Since 1788*. Crows Nest, NSW: Allen and Unwin.
Carr, Denis and Stella Carr. 1981. "The Botany of the First Australians." In *People and Plants in Australia*, edited by Denis Carr and Stella Carr, 3–44. Sydney: Academic Press.
Chamberlain, Charles Joseph. 1919. *The Living Cycads*. Chicago: University of Chicago Press.
Clarke, Philip. 2009. "Australian Aboriginal Ethnometeorology and Seasonal Calendars." *History and Anthropology* 20 (2): 79–106. doi:10.1080/02757200902867677
———. 2011. *Aboriginal People and Their Plants*. Dural Delivery Centre, NSW: Rosenberg.
Clements, Mark. 2013. *The Allure of Orchids*. Canberra: National Library of Australia.
Crisp, Michael, and Lyn Cook. 2013. "How Was the Australian Flora Assembled Over the Last 65 Million Years? A Molecular Phylogenetic Perspective." *Annual Review of Ecology, Evolution and Systematics* 44: 303–24. doi:10.1146/annurev-ecolsys-110512-135910
Cumo, Christopher. 2016. *Plants and People: Origin and Development of Human-Plant Science Relationships*. Boca Raton, FL: CRC Press.
Dixon, Bryony. 2011. *100 Silent Films: BFI Screen Guides*. Houndmills, UK: Palgrave Macmillan.
Donaldson, Mike. 1996. "The End of Time? Aboriginal Temporality and the British Invasion of Australia." *Time and Society* 5 (2): 187–207.

Entwisle, Timothy. 2014. *Sprinter and Sprummer: Australia's Changing Seasons*. Collingwood, VIC: CSIRO Publishing.

Evans, Vyvyan, and Melanie Green. 2006. *Cognitive Linguistics: An Introduction*. Edinburgh: Edinburgh University Press.

Forster, Paul. 2004. "Classification Concepts in Macrozamia (Zamiaceae) from Eastern Australia." In *Cycad Classification: Concepts and Recommendations*, edited by Terrence Walters and Roy Osborne, 85–94. Wallingford, UK: CABI Publishing.

Gammage, Bill. 2011. *The Biggest Estate on Earth: How Aborigines Made Australia*. Sydney: Allen and Unwin.

Griffiths, Tom. 2006. "Truth and Fiction: Judith Wright as Historian." *Australian Book Review* 283: 25–30.

Hallam, Sylvia. 1975. *Fire and Hearth: A Study of Aboriginal Usage and European Usurpation in South-western Australia*. Canberra: Australian Institute of Aboriginal Studies.

Hanly, Peter. 2013. "Dark Celebration: Heidegger's Silent Music." In *Heidegger and Language*, edited by Jeffrey Powell, 240–64. Bloomington: Indiana University Press.

Harris, Stephen. 2009. "'Narratives from Another Creek': Judith Wright and the Poetics of Water in Australia." *Journal of Ecocriticism* 1 (2): 11–20.

Harrison, Martin. 2000. "The Myth of Origins." *Southerly* 60 (2): 148–62.

Harward-Nalder, Glenda, and Margaret Grenfell. 2011. "Learning from the Quandamooka." *Proceedings of the Royal Society of Queensland* 117: 495–501.

Holmes, Katie. 2005. "Gardening at the 'Edge': Judith Wright's Desert Garden, Mongarlowe, New South Wales." *Australian Humanities Review* 36. Accessed 23 May 2017. www.australianhumanitiesreview.org/archive/Issue-July-2005/08Holmes.html

Huggan, Graham, and Helen Tiffin. 2010. *Postcolonial Ecocriticism: Literature, Animals, Environment*. New York: Routledge.

Hutchings, Ross. 2007. "Jung and the Wattle-Tree: Judith Wright and the Ecology of the Collective Unconscious." *AUMLA: Journal of the Australasian University of Modern Language Association* 107: 103–24.

Irigaray, Luce, and Michael Marder. 2016. *Through Vegetal Being: Two Philosophical Perspectives*. New York: Columbia University Press.

King-Smith, Sue. 2007. "Ancestral Echoes: Spectres of the Past in Judith Wright's Poetry." *Journal of the Association for the Study of Australian Literature*. Special Issue on Spectres, Screens, Shadows, Mirrors: 117–29.

Kinsella, John. 2010. *Activist Poetics: Anarchy in the Avon Valley*. Liverpool: Liverpool University Press.

Kristeva, Julia. 1986. "Women's Time." In *The Kristeva Reader*, edited by Toril Moi, 188–213. London: Basil Blackwell.

Maclay, Kathleen. 2014. "UC Botanical Garden Readies for Rare, Spectacular *Puya raimondii* Flowering." *Berkeley News*. Accessed 23 May 2017. http://news.berkeley.edu/2014/06/03/uc-botanical-garden-readies-for-rare-spectacular-puya-raimondii-flowering/

Macphailm, Mike, and Raymond Carpenter. 2014. "New Potential Nearest Living Relatives for Araucariaceae Producing Fossil Wollemi Pine-type Pollen

(*Dilwynites granulatus* W.K. Harris, 1965)." *Alcheringa: An Australasian Journal of Palaeontology* 38 (1): 135–39. doi:10.1080/03115518.2014.843145

Marder, Michael. 2013. *Plant-Thinking: A Philosophy of Vegetal Life.* New York: Columbia University Press.

Marler, Thomas, and Anders Lindström. 2015. "Article Addendum: Carbohydrates, Pollinators, and Cycads." *Communicative and Integrative Biology* 8 (2): 1–3. doi:10.1080/19420889.2015.1017162

McElroy, Amie. 2011. "Jidaanga Cultural Project, New South Wales: The Endangered Orchid 'Phaius Australis'." *Australasian Plant Conservation: Journal of the Australian Network for Plant Conservation* 19 (4): 19–21.

McMahon, Elizabeth. 2007. "Judith Wright and the Temporality of Composition." *Australian Literary Studies* 23 (2): 15–26.

Mead, Philip. 2006. "Two Fires: Poetry and Local Government." *Overland* 182: 30–35.

Memmott, Paul. 2007. *Gunyah, Goondie and Wurley: The Aboriginal Architecture of Australia.* St Lucia: University of Queensland Press.

Miller, Mara. 2010. "Time and Temporality in the Garden." In *Gardening— Philosophy for Everyone: Cultivating Wisdom*, edited by Dan O'Brien, 178–91. Chichester, UK: Wiley-Blackwell.

Mulligan, Martin, and Stuart Hill. 2001. *Ecological Pioneers: A Social History of Australian Ecological Thought and Action.* Cambridge, UK: Cambridge University Press.

Northcott, Michael. 2015. "Eschatology in the Anthropocene: From the Chronos of Deep Time to the Kairos of the Age of Humans." In *The Anthropocene and the Global Environmental Crisis: Rethinking Modernity in a New Epoch*, edited by Clive Hamilton, Christophe Bonneuil and François Gemanne, 100–111. New York: Routledge.

Owen, Richard. 1846. *A History of British Fossil Mammals, and Birds.* London: John Van Voorst, Paternoster Row.

Portenga, Eric, Dylan Rood, Paul Bishop, and Paul Bierman. 2016. "A Late Holocene Onset of Aboriginal Burning in Southeastern Australia." 44 (2): 131–34. doi:10.1130/G37257.1

Prober, Suzanne, Michael O'Connor, and Fiona Walsh. 2011. "Australian Aboriginal Peoples' Seasonal Knowledges: A Potential Basis for Shared Understanding in Environmental Management." *Ecology and Society* 16 (2): 1–16. Accessed 23 May 2017. www.ecologyandsociety.org/vol16/iss2/art12/

Robertson, Francesca, Glen Stasiuk, Noel Nannup, and Stephen Hopper. 2016. "*Ngalak Koora Koora Djinang* (Looking Back Together): A Nyoongar and Scientific Collaborative History of Ancient Nyoongar Boodja." *Australian Aboriginal Studies* 1: 40–54.

Rolston, William. 1905. "Aboriginal Methods of Determining the Seasons." *Nature* 72 (1860): 176.

Rose, Deborah Bird. 1996. *Nourishing Terrains: Australian Aboriginal Views of Landscape and Wilderness.* Canberra: Australian Heritage Commission.

Rusack, Eleanor May, Joe Dortch, Ken Hayward, Michael Renton, Mathias Boer, and Pauline Grierson. 2011. "The Role of Habitus in the Maintenance of Traditional Noongar Plant Knowledge in Southwest Western Australia." *Human Ecology* 39 (5): 673–82.

Ryan, John Charles. 2012. *Green Sense: The Aesthetics of Plants, Place and Language*. Oxford: TrueHeart Press.

———. 2015. "A Very Striking Parasite: Cultural History of the Christmas Tree." *Griffith Review* 47: 191–99.

Saunders, Gill. 1995. *Picturing Plants: An Analytical History of Botanical Illustration*. Berkeley: University of California Press.

Schiebinger, Londa. 2004. *Nature's Body: Gender in the Making of Modern Science*. New Brunswick, NJ: Rutgers University Press.

Sgorbati, S, M. Labra, G. Barcaccia, G. Galasso, U. Boni, M. Mucciarelli, S. Citterio, A. Benavides Iramategui, L. Gonzales, and S. Scannerini. 2004. "A Survey of Genetic Diversity and Reproductive Biology of *Puya raimondii* (Bromeliaceae), the Endangered Queen of the Andes." *Plant Biology* 6: 222–30. doi:10.1055/s-2004-817802

Siewers, Alfred. 2009. *Strange Beauty: Ecocritical Approaches to Early Medieval Landscape*. New York: Palgrave Macmillan.

Siewers, Alfred. 2011. "Ecopoetics and the Origins of English Literature." In *Environmental Criticism for the Twenty-First Century*, edited by Stephanie LeMenager, Teresa Shewry, and Ken Hiltner, 105–20. New York: Routledge.

Smith, John. 1969. "Time, Times, and the 'Right Time': 'Chronos' and 'Kairos'." *The Monist* 53 (1): 1–13.

Stafford, Robert. 1990. "Annexing the Landscapes of the Past: British Imperial Geology in the Nineteenth Century." In *Imperialism and the Natural World*, edited by John MacKenzie, 67–89. Manchester, UK: Manchester University Press.

Stanner, William. 1979. "The Dreaming." In *White Man Got No Dreaming: Essays, 1938–1973*, 23–40. Canberra: Australian National University Press.

TenHouten, Warren. 2005. *Time and Society*. Albany: State University of New York Press.

Thomson, James. 1793. *The Seasons*. London: A. Hamilton.

Trewavas, Anthony. 2014. *Plant Behaviour and Intelligence*. Oxford: Oxford University Press.

Walters, Terrence, Roy Osborne, and Don Decker. 2004. "'We Hold These Truths...'." In *Cycad Classification: Concepts and Recommendations*, edited by Terrence Walters and Roy Osborne, 1–11. Wallingford, UK: CABI Publishing.

Williams, Martin. 2012. *Kingdom of Plants 3D*. Kew, England. Film.

Williamson, Colin. 2015. *Hidden in Plain Sight: An Archaeology of Magic and the Cinema*. New Brunswick, NJ: Rutgers University Press.

Wilman, Elizabeth. 2015. "An Economic Model of Aboriginal Fire-Stick Farming." *Australian Journal of Agricultural and Resource Economics* 59 (1): 39–60.

Wood, David. 2003. "What is Eco-Phenomenology?" In *Eco-Phenomenology: Back to the Earth Itself*, edited by Charles Brown and Ted Toadvine, 211–33. Albany: State University of New York Press.

Woodford, James. 2012. *Wollemi Pine: The Incredible Discovery of a Living Fossil from the Age of the Dinosaurs*. Melbourne: Text Publishing Company.

Wright, Judith. 1946. *The Moving Image: Poems*. Melbourne: The Meanjin Press.

———. 1949. *Woman to Man*. Sydney: Angus and Robertson.

———. 1953. *The Gateway.* Sydney: Angus and Robertson.
———. 1955. *The Two Fires.* Sydney: Angus and Robertson.
———. 1963. *Five Senses: Selected Poems.* Sydney: Angus and Robertson.
———. 1969. "The Battle of the Biosphere." *Outlook* 13: 3–5.
———. 1991. *Born of the Conquerors: Selected Essays by Judith Wright.* Canberra: Aboriginal Studies Press.
———. 1992. "Poems: Judith Wright." *PN Review* 19 (1): 20–25.
Zeller, Robert. 2000. "The Double Tree: Judith Wright's Poetry and Environmental Activism." *Interdisciplinary Studies in Literature and Environment* 7 (2): 55–65.

8 On the Death of Plants
John Kinsella's Radical Pastoralism and the Weight of Botanical Melancholia

> Where the almond tree died, so died the wattle.
> That parabola can take no life for long. If borers
>   are below the surface,
> they will move on. They have killed the already dead.
> When the last leaves fell they flagged independence:
>   thin acacia leaf became the hearted leaf
> of the almond: it all added up in going.
>   —John Kinsella "Where the Almond Tree" from *Armour*
>   (2011a, 29, ll. 1–7)

Through the poetry of Australian writer and activist John Kinsella (b. 1963), this chapter emphasizes the actual, embodied—rather than metaphorical—dimensions of the death of plants vis-à-vis the pressing international context of accelerating botanical diversity loss (Hopper 2010) and the global anthropogenic disruption of plant communities (Pandolfi and Lovelock 2014). On many levels—scientific, ecological, social, and metaphysical—a fuller appreciation of plants necessitates an understanding of their decline, decay, and demise. Toward a more nuanced appreciation of vegetal lives, the discussion draws a distinction—but aims to avoid a binary—between *biogenic* and *anthropogenic* instances of plant death. Considering the correlation between vegetal existence, human wellbeing, and our co-constituted lives and deaths, I assert that a more encompassing and ecoculturally transformative outlook on plants—indeed, a principal aim of *Plants in Contemporary Poetry*—involves not only an acknowledgement of their qualities of percipient aliveness but also a recognition of their senescence and perishing.

Aristotle understood the vegetative soul in terms of growth and decay. As described in *De Anima*, plant ensoulment embodies the potential for movement in manifold orientations (see Chapter 2). Yet the materiality of plant death as an impactful and significant event emplaced in time has received limited attention in Western thinking. In the history of poetry, plant death predominantly has been constructed in metaphorical language as a trope for human mortality or the decline of social values, as examples presented in this chapter will demonstrate.

In contrast, the selection of John Kinsella's poetry examined here presents an exception. Kinsella attends to plant death as the negation of an interactively coproduced, regionally based, and multispecies life-world that closely engages vegetal being. His *botanical melancholia* derives from the gravely fragmented locus of his ecological consciousness: the ancient plantscape existing as small, disconnected remnants within the agro-pastoral Wheatbelt district of Western Australia. Consequently, rather than an incidental occurrence in his work, plant death is essential to Kinsella's enunciation of radical pastoralism. His poetry furnishes a counterweight to an idyllic textualization of botanical nature as existing in an unimpacted Arcadian state of happiness, harmony, balance, and equitable exchange with the built environment (Kinsella 2007, 1–46).

Shades of Plant Life and Death: Plurality, Resurrection, Neglect

Without a doubt, many of us as children or adults have formed potent bonds to the botanical world and have mourned the passing of cherished plants. (Visualize your favorite climbing tree, an ephemeral spring orchid, a luscious patch of rainforest moss, or other examples close to heart; now consider the destruction, defilement, and death of the plant or ecosystem.) Nonetheless, few of us—except for perspicacious botanical writers like Henry David Thoreau, Richard Mabey, and others—have substantively engaged with the intricacies of vegetal lives and deaths, apart from their emotional, decorative, scientific, or utilitarian importance. Why does a tree, shrub, or herbaceous plant die? And when should the death of a plant matter to us? These questions represent divergent—though not mutually exclusive—aspects of mortality in the vegetal kingdom. To begin with, it is necessary to disentangle the knottiness that is plant death, if only a little. Let me refer to one form as *biogenic* death. This entails the material decay and demise of plants: the withering of leaves, rotting of roots, shedding of bark, and falling of limbs as ecological occurrences central to the regeneration of biospheric systems and the proliferation of obligate species (Van der Valk 2009). The second form could be called *anthropogenic* death: the felling of trunks, poisoning of rhizomes, and destruction of botanical enclaves as acts of negligence, ignorance, or "ecocide," as promulgated by humans (White and Heckenberg 2014, 115). Whether anthropogenic or biogenic, plant death signifies the end of a single vegetal life, the demise of a vegetal collective, or the farther-reaching cessation of a species as the genetic matrix that underlies the (re)generation of plants. In the harrowing context of the Anthropocene (Steffen, Crutzen, and McNeill 2007), the Sixth Extinction (also known as the Holocene Extinction) (Kolbert 2014), and anthropogenic climate change (Parmesan and Hanley 2015) both forms of vegetal death take on an eerie significance.

According to *The State of the World's Plants Report*, one in five (or approximately 21% of), plant species on Earth is currently regarded by science as approaching extinction (Kew 2016, 3). Yet, only 5% of plants across the globe have been assessed for extinction criteria, potentially suggesting a much higher actual percentage of species facing total oblivion. The tragic irony is that, despite increasing threats to botanical taxa and communities the world over, researchers continue to identify previously unclassified plants on an annual basis. In 2015, there were 2034 new vascular plant species added to the International Plant Names Index (Kew 2016, 10), leaving us to speculate about the species already lost to the scientific record, as well as those that will be. Whether biogenic or anthropogenic, moreover, vegetal death can spur certain responses within human subjects in the wake of plants ceasing to live. Affective reactions of grief, mourning, and melancholia intermesh with symbolic modes of attachment to botanical nature. One permutation of the metaphorization of vegetal life is plant death standing in for something other than itself: the ultimate finitude of the human condition or the entropic decay of society, relations, love, knowledge, idealism, potentiality, or the future itself.

Regarding the poetic history of death in the plant kingdom, consider, for instance, the rhetorical timbres of Walt Whitman's meditation on death, "Scented Herbage of My Breast," a poem in which he addresses the rhizomatous sweet flag (*Acorus calamus*) as a plant persona:

> You are often more bitter than I can bear—you burn and sting me,
> Yet you are beautiful to me, you faint-tinged roots—you make me think of Death,/
> Death is beautiful from you—(what indeed is finally beautiful, except Death and Love?)
>
> (Whitman 1871, 122, ll. 10–12)

Notwithstanding gestures of empathic identification with the calamus, the poem obscures the real life and death of the plant through the rhetorical appropriation of its vegetality for the human subject's sentimental reflection. Also suggestive of the metaphorization of plant-death is American Romantic poet William Cullen Bryant's "The Death of the Flowers" (Bryant 1854, 101–2). The poem opens with, "The melancholy days are come, the saddest of the year" (Bryant 1854, 101, l. 1), enumerating in the third stanza the violets, roses, orchids, golden rods, asters, sunflowers, and other flowers that are "in their graves" during the saddest season (l. 14). In contrast to these historical instances and through the example of Kinsella's botanical imagination, I instead emphasize plant death absent of metaphoric totalization and in its manifold sensory and ecological impact—with only passing references to the dead plant body as an object of melancholic identification or as a rhetorical device deployed by poets, such as Whitman, through the ages.

To be sure, the questions of when and why a plant dies are rendered complex by the biological capacity of plants for adaptation through plurality—their innate predisposition toward "being singular plural" (Nancy 2000). A salient example is the colossal trembling aspen (*Populus tremuloides*) colony known as Pando—adopted from the Latin term for "I spread"—identified in 1968 by forest ecologist Burton Barnes and later characterized by geneticists as the world's largest organism (DeWoody et al. 2008; Rogers 2016). *P. tremuloides* is notable for reproducing vegetatively through root sprouting, or suckering, enabling the formation of genetically identical stems, known as ramets, thus constituting one ancient, sprawling, but living—not fossilized—plant body. The 47,000 stems of the Pando clonal colony weigh in at approximately 13-million pounds. What is more, the organism encompasses one hundred acres in the western U.S. state of Utah; and scientific estimates of its age range wildly from 80,000 to 1 million years old. In this instantiation of vegetal longevity and resilience, the death of a single aspen tree—as we recognize it visually—need not signify the demise of the entire clonal system. As a result of its persistence for millennia by virtue of a tenacious root system, Pando seems at once inconceivable, limitless, and immortal from a narrow human temporal perspective (see Chapter 7 on vegetal temporality). Nonetheless, empirical studies indicate that the intensive grazing of domestic and wild herbivores, in conjunction with prolonged drought conditions, have led to a pronounced absence of young ramets and the overall senescence of the Pando colony (Rogers 2016).

The clonal propagation of *P. tremuloides* ensures that the loss of an individual aspen's life is unlikely to precipitate the demise of the colony. Whereas the Pando epitomizes a coordinated systemic capacity to endure, in other instances plants display the uncanny aptitude to return from the brink of ordinarily death-dealing conditions, specifically drought and dehydration. This is acutely so for resurrection plants—a small grouping of species that occur globally and can survive complete desiccation, resuming normal physiological function when rehydrated. Although the exact mechanism of reverting metabolic arrest has not been fully identified, a subset of resurrection plants, characterized as poikilochlorophyllous, make use of protein-mediated biochemical pathways to disassemble their chloroplasts and degrade their chlorophyll, which are then resynthesized during rewetting (Challabathula, Puthur, and Bartels 2016). A well-known example, the rose of Jericho (*Selaginella lepidophylla*), a species native to the Chihuahua Desert of the United States and Mexico, returns to green approximately 24 hours after rehydration as photosynthesis and respiration recommence normal levels (Lambers, Chapin, and Pons 2008, 213). In biodiverse Western Australia, the pincushion lily (*Borya nitida*)—the subject of Kinsella's poem "Resurrection Plants at Nookaminnie Rock" (2011a, 53), later discussed—withstands dehydration to below 5% of its typical leaf moisture content, as signaled by the orange color of the leaves that revert to green within a day of receiving rain (Hopper, Brown, and Marchant 1997). Resurrection plants exemplify the courting of death by paring back—then resuscitating— physiological processes in correspondence to fluctuating ecological circumstances.

In contradistinction to these plants and the Pando, other expressions of plant mortality entail the cessation of vegetal lives deprived of their intrinsic right to exist and flourish independently of human will. Anthropogenic in origin, such deaths derive less from environmental circumstances and more from human disregard, the absence of an ethics of care, distorted modernist visions of progress, myopic anti-environmentalist attitudes, and pervasive misconceptions about the ways flora adapt to stress over time. A story from a Perth, Australia, newspaper captures the harsh finality of careless human instigated plant death as well as the response of outrage that tends to ensue once botanophilic members of the community become aware of local plant-related injustices. The government agency, Main Roads Western Australia, which manages the implementation of policies on road access in the state, chainsawed a healthy jarrah tree (*Eucalyptus marginata*) showing faint indications of decay. Estimated at between 500 and 1000 years in age, the specimen's final transgression was its harboring of a supposedly dangerous beehive. As a result, Main Roads deemed the jarrah a public hazard and furtively targeted the tree for removal. A prominent botanist, Hans Lambers, interviewed about the travesty likened the felling of the jarrah to "ecological vandalism" and "burning the Mona Lisa" (qtd. in Young 2016).

Indeed, the massive eucalypt was one of only 13 remaining in the Swan Coastal Plain of Perth—an area noted for plant diversity but which has lost approximately 70% of its species since European colonization in the early nineteenth century (Seddon 2004). This is the broader biogeographical and biopolitical context in which Kinsella's radical pastoralism is situated and provoked. The impetus of the agency could have been to incite—through the indiscreetly public and brashly cruel gesture of the tree's felling—the removal of native vegetation to open the way for the controversial Roe 8 highway development project (Rethink the Link 2016). In this instance, the death of the jarrah mattered, on the one hand, to a government bureaucracy because the colossal specimen posed a physical and symbolic impediment to the capitalistic drive and, on the other hand, to local conservationists who recognized the age, size, stature, rarity, endemism, and ecological role of the tree. For the latter group, the decaying appearance of the jarrah signified its potential to nourish the wellbeing of other species, as Lambers relates, but within the abruptness of its death echoes the glaring absence of an irreplaceable ecological presence: "half-dead trees and trees with dead branches with hollows provide important nesting space for our parrots and cockatoos" (qtd. in Young 2016). In addition to provoking ethical deliberation on plant death, the story of the jarrah underscores the question of temporality: given the particular ontological modes of the vegetal—its uncanny capacity to integrate death into being—when does life in the botanical kingdom actually cease? For Michael Marder, the consideration of plant death reflects the "decentralized and nonorganismic" nature of vegetal existence. The event of death does not consolidate the decentralized plant subject into a perceptibly dying organism—like an animal in the throes of death, eyes rolling back and breath sputtering—nor does death bring about the end of life for plants with the relatively clear-cut finality we observe when animals die (Marder 2014, 187).

> [...] Diggings
> around termite scaffolding at the foot
> of died-and-reborn York gums. Roots.
>
> The dead have been gathering.
> And, to be frank, accruing.
> They are phenomenally heavy,
> like self-doubt or self-belief.
> —from "Harsh Hakea (or Elements of the Subject's Will)"
> (Kinsella 2011b, 132, ll. 9–15)

Toward a Philosophy of Plant Death: Modularity, Desire, and Dignity

Whereas the death of animals has been hotly debated in the field of critical animal studies (Taylor and Twine 2014), the death of plants has been treated as tangential or metaphorical in posthumanist and ecocritical studies. After all, if a plant is construed as lacking sentience—and is, thus, inferior to animals and humans in the great chain of being—then its death should matter to us neither personally, socially, nor intellectually. On a practical level, plants are the nuisances we eradicate (weeds) or the nutriment we consume (fruits, vegetables, herbs) on a regular basis: their deaths make life (and the pleasure of living) possible. In contrast to a utilitarian perspective, my intention in this chapter is to consider these nuances through the poetry of John Kinsella; and to position poetry as a vital medium for enunciating the lives of silent, so-called sessile nonhumans beyond the use-value of their deaths. Not merely a symbol of human mortality or social decline, plant death is the immanent, embodied expression of vegetative ensoulment (see Chapter 2). To understand plant death is to acknowledge its intricate ecological manifestations. Although from widely ranging corners of the globe, the Pando colony, resurrection plant, and jarrah eucalypt emblematize three permutations of plant death essential to locating Kinsella's radical pastoralism vis-à-vis Western Australian flora.

The example of Pando conveys the inherent capacity—or *dunamis*, to adopt a term from Aristotle (Marder 2013b, 36)—of plants for decay, as the poietic correlate of growth, but also the ways in which vegetal being uniquely conscripts death and its mechanisms of senescence and decay for survival. The *dunamis* of Pando for vegetative multiplicity and anatomical repetition perpetuates the arboreal collective regardless of the death of an individual plant or loss of a body part (leaf, stem, root, and flower). One of the defining features of vegetal life of particular interest to thinkers historically has been its pronounced modularity: the recurrence within the corpus of a plant of basic units—or functionally analogous structures—of growth (Trewavas 2014, 50). In relation to a plant's "body plan" (Baluška et al. 2006), the principle of modularity describes the repetition of growth units. In fact, modularity is the basis for why plants can survive intensive grazing by herbivores by sacrificing parts—leaves, flowers, stems—without perishing. In contrast, the loss of an anatomical segment for most animals is typically catastrophic because their (our) bodies are not agreeable to being nibbled. For seed-producing flowering plants, known as angiosperms, repeated patterns of leaves, branches, nodes, buds, flowers, fruits, and root meristems constitute their modularity. The metamer—the structural subunit replicated over the lifetime of a plant—comprises an internode and a node with associated leaves and meristems as the foundation for larger modules, including branches and stems (Herrera 2009, 2). Considering this unique evolutionary mechanism, physiologist Anthony Trewavas (2014) maintains that plants are "intensely modular" (42). In classical antiquity, Aristotle's pupil, Theophrastus (circa 371–287 BCE), noted plant modularity in his treatise *De Causis Plantarum* (*On the Causes of Plants*)—one of the most important early botanical texts in Western philosophy. He commented that "every tree has many starting-points for sprouting and fruiting. This [...] is of the essence of a plant, that it also lives from a multitude of parts, which is why it can also sprout from them" (Theophrastus 1976, 85). Much later reflecting Theophrastus' observations, the polymath and early plant morphologist, Johann Wolfgang von Goethe (1749–1832), in his long poem *The Metamorphosis of Plants* (1790), conceptualized plant foliage as the homologous basis— the repeated structural unit—of flowers and fruits: "Like unto each the form, yet non alike;/And so the choir hints a secret law,/A sacred mystery" (Goethe 2009, 1, ll. 5–7).

Unlike the clonal reproduction of the long-lived aspen, the resurrection plant returns from a provisional state of metabolic arrest that would spell the end for less hardy plant species. This unusual example lays bare the particular vegetal dynamic of life (and living) within their deaths (and dying) as integrated ecological processes involving minimal human intervention. In Aristotelian entelechy, the vegetative soul is characterized by the dual movement of the plant toward liveliness, nourishment, and growth—and toward decline, decay, and death. The latent potential for aliveness inheres within the potential for death, and the reverse remains true. In Aristotle's triadic hierarchy, plant ensoulment constituted "an originative power through which they increase or decrease in all spatial directions" and live out their lives through the continuous absorption of nutriment (Aristotle 2011, 700). Moreover, the nutritive soul of the plant—"possessed by everything that is alive" (Aristotle 2011, 732)—conferred the basis for the birth, existence, and death of the higher-order lives of the sensitive and intellective souls. Without the somatic surrendering of the plant to other organisms (being grazed, harvested, pruned), life on earth as we know it could not exist. According to Aristotle, like animals and human beings, plants grow, mature, and decay in relation to sustenance received from the environment, including photosynthetically from the sun. In his treatise "On Youth, Old Age, Life and Death, and Respiration," the philosopher recognizes that plants vegetatively circumvent the finality of death and, in doing so, ingeniously proliferate through their own process of dismemberment: "[...] plants when cut into sections continue to live, and a number of trees can be derived from one single source" (Aristotle 2011, 791). The ability of some plants to propagate profusely through vegetative division signified, for Aristotle, the corresponding entelechy of the vegetative soul in its multiplicity: "It is true that the nutritive soul, in beings possessing it, while actually single must be potentially plural" (Aristotle 2011, 791).

However, as Chapter 2 discussed, the Aristotelian theory of ensoulment privileges the sensitive (animal) and intellective (human) over the nutritive (plant). In a similar vein, contemporary philosophies of death reinscribe the pernicious presumption that plants bear neither mental life nor sentience worth considering and that, hence, their ceasing to live should matter less than animal and human deaths. Reflecting the conceptual conventions and terminologies of Western philosophy of death, Christopher Belshaw (2013) invokes the Aristotelian order in discerning between a desire view (as true) and a life view (as false) approaches to ascertaining whether death is a "good" or "bad" outcome for a living thing. For Belshaw, the desire view reflects categorical desires—those unconditional desires that arise independently of our living long enough to see them eventuate or materialize. A desire view depends on a being's capacity to desire: life is something a subject wants to live. In contrast, a life view suggests that death can be bad even when such desires are absent or (in the case of plants) cannot readily be identified—but when life, health, and pleasurable experience are present—because death prevents more life regardless of the desires a being has. Belshaw concludes that having "future-directed categorical desires is a necessary condition of my death's being bad for me [or, I add, for other beings]" (2013, 278).

A glaring presupposition within the desire view is that plants lack mentation, sentience, and categorical desires: a plant desiring sunlight, nutrition, water, comfort, or proliferation is superficial metaphor from this bleak perspective of life. An activity, such as felling an ancient jarrah with bravado, understood as compromising vegetal wellbeing, for Belshaw, reflects a life view of plant death, which is false. Even if one were to adopt a life view, "from conceding that death is bad for the plant it doesn't at all follow that we should be exercised about plant death, regret its occurrence, or make any sacrifices to prevent it" (Belshaw 2013, 290). Yet, as the field of plant signaling and behavior indicates through quantitative evidence (for example, Trewavas 2014), plants have a kind of inner life—the exact nature of which we are not yet completely sure—affirmed by their ability to learn and remember. In light of this burgeoning science and hastened by the exponential loss of plant species across the globe, a more nuanced consideration of plant death and, more generally, human-plant relations has been forwarded by environmental ethicists (Hall 2009; Heyd 2012; Marder 2013a; Pouteau 2014; Koechlin 2009). If plants have a mental life and can experience pain—which we cannot and should not rule out—then death is bad for them, as it is for us; and while we must nonetheless eat, drink, and otherwise use plants for our benefit, their deaths can matter to them and us, and their living and dying can have dignity. As a contentious example of plant ethics in the public domain, the Swiss government's Federal Ethics Committee on Non-Human Biotechnology report *The Dignity of Living Beings with Regard to Plants* (Swiss Confederation 2008) was inspired by emerging scientific studies of plant sensitivities. For the authors of the report, codified in the Swiss constitution, that plants distinguish between self and non-self implies their subjectivity and cognition, notwithstanding the general socio-political "refusal to understand plants as something other than living automatons" (Koechlin 2009, 79).

Kinsella's Radical (Vegetal) Pastoralism: Melancholia and Plant Mortality

Having considered the manifestations of death in the plant kingdom—biogenic, anthropogenic, and the interplay of both—as well as the dignity of plants, it is an appropriate point to ask: How have plant death and its ethical consideration impacted the landscape poetry of Western Australian writer John Kinsella and his practice of radical pastoralism? The possibility of plant ethics brings us closer to the consideration of our lives and deaths, including the embodied, emotional, and spiritual effects on humans as plants cease to exist. Regardless of the myriad forms human responses take (desperation, withdrawal, indifference, anger, impoverishment, malaise, disease), there remains at the center of plant death the demise of an actual nonhuman entity—the termination of a vegetal life, the cessation of the possibility for further life and experience—as definitive and final as the toppling of the 500 year old jarrah. Let us remain a while longer with the idea of our own deaths inhering within vegetal otherness. In comparison to the Pando and resurrection plant (which I conceptualized—albeit crudely—as exemplifying biogenic modalities of death and life-within-death), the jarrah instantiates the direct, injurious interference with plant being that, at once, reduces the capacity of companion species—including ourselves and our kith and kin—to actualize our full potential of ecological interrelatedness. More simply put, as plants die, so do we, though our deaths might not necessarily be physical and can, instead, manifest as an obdurate sense of loss and malaise. As the comments of Lambers suggest, the anthropogenic death of plants can often lack ethical grounding (Young 2016). This kind of wanton plant death can incite outrage over the despoliation of vegetal nature, followed by the weight of botanical melancholia including lingering feelings of personal helplessness and community fragmentation.

An ethics of botanical life conspicuously figures into Kinsella's ecopoetic corpus—which combines acute sensory awareness of habitats and meticulous ecological knowledge of loca flora (Ryan 2012, 254–56). Although figured in terms of the beautiful and sublime, Kinsella's Wheatbelt plantscape reflects intense rupture and stark polarization between human and other-than-human actants in the Western Australian context. Kinsella's sense of ecological ethics involves a poetics of fragments in which his rupturing of the whole (of the poem, of the landscape representation) calls the writerly self into question. From Kinsella's perspective, "language contains all possible meanings in the fragment as much as entirely" (2007, 237). Hence, his radical pastoralism—pivoting, to a significant extent, on the poetization of plant death—often makes use of fragmentary sequences that upend narrative lyricism while maintaining a sense of movement within the text (2007, 133). Notwithstanding the tenor of ecological despondency echoed in his fragments, Kinsella also introspectively revels, at times, in the complexities of vegetal living and dying, revealing a multifaceted view of plant death and dying as a source of hope for positive change. An illustrative case is *Jam Tree Gully* (2012b), titled after the raspberry jam tree, *Acacia acuminata*, for the fragrant odor of the cut timber. Jam Tree Gully is also the name of Kinsella's residence near the Avon Valley of Western Australia in "York gum and jam tree country" (Kinsella 2013, 66). The collection expresses an acute attachment to place and an ethics grounded in kinship and empathy with local vegetation. Through epigraphs and other allusions, the poetry also strikes a temporally distributed intertextual dialogue with the nineteenth-century American botanophile, Henry David Thoreau, whose intellectual-experiential investigations of plant life feature in his posthumous *Faith in a Seed* (1993) and *Wild Fruits* (2000) (see also Chapter 5). In the poem "First Lines Typed at Jam Tree Gully," Kinsella notes with haptic resonances the "rampage/of dead and living trees,/entire collapsed structures,/signs of fire as jam-tree bark/blackened crumbles with touch" (Kinsella 2012a, 79, ll. 15–19), but the reader is left to contemplate the probable causes of the burning.

I situate Kinsella's botanical poetics within the context of a radical pastoralism that recognizes the demise of the vegetal as a source of botanical melancholia: the poet's intersubjective response to plant death not as an externalized phenomenon but as one with tangible repercussions for his or her personal welfare. Rather than a trivial consideration or insignificant event, plant death—as expressed in Kinsella's oeuvre—is implicated in the fragmentation and degradation of the once remarkably plant diverse and sustainably managed 140,000 km^2 (8700-mile) Wheatbelt region (for historical background, see Beresford et al. 2001). In the beginning years of European colonization, the Wheatbelt principally consisted of an intricate mosaic of salmon gum (*E. salmonophloia*), York gum (*E. loxophleba*), and wandoo (*E. wandoo*) woodlands. Since the mid-1800s, the ecological devastation of the Wheatbelt and surrounding areas has been precipitated by the removal of native woodland vegetation for the production of wheat, barley, canola, and sheep. As poignantly portrayed in the documentary *A Million Acres a Year* (2002), by 1968, over 130,000 km had been cleared through a relentless campaign that continued into the late 1980s (Rijavec, Harrison, and Bradby 2002). In the central part, known as the Avon Botanical District, more than 93% of the native flora has been removed, and up to 97% of the eucalpypt woodlands erased (Bradshaw 2012, 112–13). Apparent in the preternatural glow of salt ponds, the eradication of well-adapted floristic communities—particularly endemic gums that held salt levels in check underground—triggered the salinization of the topsoil, or what analysts call "the salinity crisis" (Beresford 2001). Other factors impinging on the remaining vegetation include industrial mining activities (Latimer 2012), diseases such as the root-rot fungus *Phytophthora cinnamomi* (Environment Australia 2001), and introduced plant species that swiftly displace local counterparts (Prober and Smith 2009).

Regarding Kinsella's ecopoetics of plants, the distinction I have posited between biogenic and anthropogenic death collapses through the interpenetration of human and vegetal living and dying. For Kinsella, the plant mirrors back to us the exigencies of our demise, mourning, and melancholia. Yet the physicality of its death remains. As the regional context of Kinsella's poetics, the Wheatbelt poignantly underscores the historical and contemporary shortening of the potentialities of local plants—their deaths rendered *in toto* (as the 95% rate of clearance grimly attests), largely without ethical deliberation or expressions of care; and their lives socially constructed as impediments to modernist techno-industrial progress. Within this bleak ecological—and, arguably, anti-ecological—milieu, Kinsella characterizes his ecopoetic practice as "radical pastoralism" (a term synonymous with "poison pastoralism" and a variant of "anti-pastoralism"). To be sure, Kinsella's radical pastoral is one in a long line of different conceptualizations of the pastoral by theorists. In *The Machine in the Garden* (1964) and, later, in the essay "Does Pastoralism Have a Future?" (1992), the critic Leo Marx identified a peculiarly American version—the so-called complex pastoral—in which the pastoral idyll of the landscape intersects with ecological counterforces that destabilize the idyll. Ecocritic Greg Garrard (1996) later proposed the term *radical pastoral* as a poetics of resisting the marginalization of nature and engendering "a genuine counter-hegemonic ideology" (464). Garrard built upon critic Terry Gifford's (1995) contemporaneous identification of the anti-pastoral as a counter-tradition embodying the principal tension of "how to find a voice that does not lose sight of authentic connectedness with nature, in the process of exposing the language of the idyll" (55). More recently, Gifford (2014) has underscored the proliferation of versions of the pastoral—including the anti-pastoral, postmodern pastoral, post-pastoral, and others—highlighting the incidence of historical shifts in meaning. Whereas the term *pastoral* came to denote, in the history of English literature, any work describing the countryside in distinction to the city or court, the post-pastoral attempts to reach beyond the original restraints of the pastoral (Gifford 2014, 19, 26). In particular, post-pastoral works depict a collapse of the human/nature divide alongside an awareness of the problems triggered by such a collapse (Gifford 2014, 26).

As representative of the pastoral, consider the idyllic depiction of botanical harmony in the image of Wordsworth's "[...] host of dancing Daffodils;/Along the Lake, beneath the trees,/Ten thousand dancing in the breeze" (qtd. in Robinson 2010, 38). In sharp relief, Kinsella's radical pastoralism plants fuses lyrical responses to the Wheatbelt environment and a naturalist's firsthand observations of flora with a prevailing sense of the disruption of the vegetal idyll through "linguistic disobedience," often enacted through the insertion of poetic fragments into the text (Kinsella 2007, 127). Kinsella's botanical imagination is equally rooted in the regional (Phillips and Kinsella 2001) and global (Gander and Kinsella 2012) ecological crises. Deeply personal and observationally rigorous, his botanical poetics is not delimited by speculative, objective distance but, instead, involves corporeal connectivity to native plantscapes and histories of place (Kinsella 2007, 223). The long-term biopolitical campaign to eradicate local flora is but an extension of the region's troubled colonial past. Despite being an ecocidal locus for plants, the Wheatbelt, and Southwestern Australia more generally, retain vestiges of floristic diversity as islands within the pastoral, enabling

Kinsella to maintain "authentic connectedness with nature," in Gifford's original terms, while subverting the literary tradition of botanical idyllicism and problematizing the regional Anglo-Australian histories of habitat destruction.

Indeed, Kinsella re-interprets the radical pastoral for an Australian context. In *Disclosed Poetics* (2007) and elsewhere, he sharply differentiates between the anti-pastoral and radical pastoral. For Kinsella, the Australian anti-pastoral characterizes poets located in (or writing about) rural spaces who challenge the bucolic myths promulgated by colonial culture and literary heritage (Kinsella 2007, 9). Although in Kinsella's analysis few pastoral Australian poets can be described as radical, most poets exhibit acute awareness of the history and limitations of the genre as "an idyllicised representation of the rural world, most often for the allegorical delectation of urban or town audiences" (Kinsella 2007, 11). Critic Dennis Haskell characterizes the anti-pastoral aesthetics of Kinsella's *The Silo: A Pastoral Symphony* (1995) as "an exorcism" (Haskell 2000, 94) of the colonialist history of land appropriation and the poet's personal remorse in partaking in the devastation during his youth. As Kinsella comments on his awareness, "Death was a fantasy/made real/in the bush enclaves" (qtd. in Haskell 2000, 94). In contrast to the anti-pastoral, the radical pastoral upends "the norms of pastoral telling, of pastoral singing, and pastoral convention" and expresses a desire for "radical change" (Kinsella 2007, 10). In the former, "the clearing of native vegetation [and] the poisoning of land, water, and air" are textualized in their full extent and affect—rather than codified through linguistic sleights of hand—as "an active undoing of the [pastoral] tradition" (Kinsella 2007, 10–11). Additionally, for Kinsella, the Australian pastoral tradition is "a vehicle of nationalist yearning" and "the ultimate tool of nationalistic sentiment" (Kinsella 2013, 191)— and, for that reason, a subject of poetic subversion at least partially enacted through engagement with the deaths of plants. His practice of radical ecopoetics forms a piercing critique of the pastoral as a tradition underlying the ecological devastation of the Wheatbelt and the related displacement of Aboriginal cultures throughout Australia (Reed 2010).

Kinsella's poetic engagement with vegetal death reflects, on the one hand, the ruination of the Wheatbelt ecosystem, while on the other, the positive and negative environmental memories from his predominantly rural upbringing. Although Kinsella mostly grew up in the suburbs of Perth, his family regularly retreated to a farm outside York, Western Australia, where he nurtured a naturalist's ability to observe the flora, fauna, and fungi of his immediate environs (Hughes-d'Aeth 2012, 20) but also committed acts of ecological transgression, including the wanton shooting of birds (Kinsella 2007, 39). A mechanic and farm manager, his father worked in the open country where industrial-scale broadacre farming eventually supplanted the unique sandplain vegetation known as kwongan (Lambers 2014). An early immersion in rural places and the engendering of environmental awareness based on the interplay between life and death—"I wandered the bush as a child quoting Keats" (Kinsella 2007, 223)—certainly appears to have counterweighed any inclination toward plant blindness during his upbringing. Formulated by environmental educators, this term denotes the prevalent inability to notice the flora of one's surroundings or the ingrained understanding of vegetal life as the stationary backdrop to animal and human activities (Wandersee and Schussler 1999). To the contrary, Kinsella's ecopoetics exhibits pronounced botanical attunement, but within the delimitations of the Wheatbelt and as a function of a radical pastoral ethics, in the manner he has conceptualized it. Instances from his non-fiction writings point to an abiding consciousness of flora, particularly the Wheatbelt eucalypts that sustain ecological relationships in a state of death-within-life. He comments on "the straggling York gums with their mud-encrusted termite colonies wrapping around their trunks, winding up through *the dead wood the living wood embraces* [emphasis added]" (Kinsella 2013, 106). Here, we are reminded of the vegetal capacity—particularly manifested by the gum trees of Southwestern Australia—to exist in a condition of death-within-life that is internally supportive (of its living wood) while also externally imbricated (with termite colonies). Indeed, as Aristotle noted, plants "increase or decrease in all spatial directions"—a mode of being facilitated by their vegetative entelechy (2011, 700).

If the dead wood of the York gum is emblematic of biogenic death—the decline, decay, and demise of plants as adaptive, ecological beings—then the slaying of the Swan River jarrah is representative of anthropogenic death. Kinsella's ecopoetics of plants intersects with both forms of death in the Wheatbelt. Yet, to understand the poet's textualization of human impacts on vegetal life further, it is crucial to consider botanical melancholia as a plant-inflected expression of environmental melancholia (Lertzman 2015) and solastalgia (Albrecht 2010, 2005). Renee Lertzman defines environmental melancholia as "a condition in which even those who care deeply about the wellbeing of ecosystems and future generations are paralyzed to translate such concern into action" (2015, 4). For Lertzman, following Freud's well-known analysis of unresolved mourning, environmental melancholia can involve anxiety, ambivalence, sadness, loss, and despair, as well as an anticipatory sense of mourning the ecological losses to come (2015, 6). Moreover, one can be locked in a state of inactivity and isolation as a result of the general social lack of recognition of such losses. Although ecological threats have the potential to shatter traditional certainties (such as air, water, seasons, and the existence of flora), Lertzman argues that, in due course, environmental melancholia can become a source of active engagement in the protection of human and nonhuman wellbeing. Correspondingly, solastalgia recognizes "the pain or sickness caused by the loss or lack of solace and the sense of isolation connected to the present state of one's home and territory" (Albrecht 2005, 48). Defined as the "homesickness one gets when one is still at 'home'" (Albrecht 2005, 48), solastalgia entails emotional distress that is intensified through the first-hand experience of one's home-place (for Kinsella, the Wheatbelt) deteriorating in the past, present, and future.

Following Lertzman and Albrecht, botanical melancholia can be defined as a solastalgiac condition in which people who intimately identify with plants are either paralyzed or called to action by the anxiety, despair, and grief of witnessing the loss of individual specimens (the jarrah) or whole botanical communities (the Wheatbelt). The model I put forward aims to offset an object-cathexis paradigm of environmental mourning, which risks relegating plant-death to a signifier of human mortality, of societal decline, or of "hyperobjects" (Morton 2013), particularly climate change and species extinction. Shunning a human-centered paradigm of ecological grief, botanical melancholia recognizes the imbrications between biogenic and anthropogenic processes of plant death. In certain instances, the manner in which a plant dies might not entirely concern a human mourner: the life of a plant disappears undetected. What is more certain is that the widespread annihilation of plant individuals and assemblages for long-standing, botanically-minded occupants of a place, such as Kinsella's Wheatbelt, can be an ongoing and seemingly inexhaustible source of despair. In acknowledging plants as percipient subjects, the model of melancholia I present conceptualizes their deaths as events that terminate the potential for more of their lives to be led with dignity. This entails the distinction between "plant life" (biology, species, abstraction, generalization—the social construction of the vegetal) and "the lives of plants" (ontology, experience, materiality, sensoriality—their lives to live independently of human desires and interventions). As the following section elaborates, botanical melancholia is pivotal to appreciating Kinsella's radical pastoralism as a wellspring of indignation, activism, reflection, and, at times, wonderment in relation to the demise of plants.

Poeticizing Plant Death: Gums, Almonds, Wattles

I have suggested that plant death is an imprecise designation and have, therefore, attempted in this chapter to discern between contrasting nuances of death in the vegetal world by applying the biogenic-anthropogenic typology. Whereas biogenic death involves the demise of plants as an ecological event, anthropogenic death signifies human extermination of the entelechy of vegetal ensoulment (remember the jarrah), as well as the burden of botanical melancholia. Anthropogenic death can mirror back to us—as the perpetrators or witnesses—our complete reliance on the vegetal foundations of human existence. The perilous neglect and senseless maltreatment of botanical life can precipitate the physical, social, and spiritual decline of human beings. Of course, the biogenic deaths of plants can also prompt mourning and melancholia, but, I assert, to a lesser degree than anthropogenic (or anthropogenically-exacerbated biogenic) forms. Kinsella's poetry textualizes plant death and the unforeseen transactions between both sides of the typology. The four-part "Idyllatry" (Kinsella 2011a, 34–43), from the collection *Armour*, is representative. The poem's title amalgamates the words *idyll* and *idolatry*, signaling Kinsella's critique of the fetishization of techno-industrial agriculture in contradistinction to the traditional Indigenous ecological knowledge and practices of the Wheatbelt.

The opening of "Idyllatry," a 14-line sonnet variant titled "*Laetiporus portentosus*," centralizes the presence of the white punk bracket, a species of polypore fungus traditionally used by Aboriginal Australians as tinder and to transport fire between camps (Clarke 2011, 64). A saprotroph that consumes the dead heartwood of living trees (Fagg 2013), the fungus has "injected rot into the heart/of the eucalypt" (Kinsella 2011a, 34, ll. 2–3). Conversely, the surface of the fungus "is breached by numerous/invertebrates, larvae that will interphase/with our sense of space, the air/we breathe" (Kinsella 2011a, 34, ll. 5–8). The opening sonnet of "Idyllatry" reminds us that the omnipresence of death in nature is the upshot of ongoing evolutionarily-grounded exchanges between organisms. Ecology as a function of lives-within-deaths and deaths-within-lives means that all things—animal, vegetal, fungal—are in dynamic relation and equipoise. Rather than the neocolonialist images of pastoral idolatry of the poem's successive three parts, the sonnet in its last six lines culminates with the fungus as an object of environmental veneration—a "halo we might walk beneath" (Kinsella 2011a, 34, l. 12)—with parallels to Les Murray's poetic ecology of the sacred in Chapter 2. End rhymes punctuate the final sestet: "distract from grief" (l. 11) and "walk beneath" (l. 12), then a decisive imperfect end rhyme with "carried fire" (l. 13) and "smouldering tinder" (l. 14). Kinsella emphasizes that, for Indigenous cultures across Australia, the fungus was—and, in places, still is—a "companion species" (Haraway 2008) that, like many plants and animals, furnishes precious means of sustenance while reinforcing cultural identity and heritage. And, so, the final two lines—"the first people here carried fire/in its smouldering tinder" (Kinsella 2011a, 34, ll. 13–14)—plainly but potently invoke the 50,000-or-more-year history of Nyoongar people's sustainable inhabitation of the Wheatbelt. For Kinsella, the region's pastoral idyll collapses under the weight of a traumatic history of interlinked ecological devastation and cultural genocide. While prefigured in the sonnet, these postcolonial dimensions are more fully drawn out in contemporary terms, as we later learn of the Western Australian government's convenient forgetting of Kinsella's proposal for a "'wheatbelt forum'/where indigenous communities/could discuss their issues with white/farming communities" (2011a, 39, ll. 15–18). The poet's desire for reconciliation stands in startling alignment with his young son's innocent yearning to shed his Anglo-Australian identity and become Nyoongar after some exposure to the indigenous language in school (2001, 40, ll. 4–9).

With the Aboriginal underpinnings of Kinsella's radical pastoralism rendered ostensible, the poem's second part, "The View from Here and Now," consists of seven quatrains and intensifies the consideration of belonging and nativeness in the Wheatbelt plantscape. The poet relates his gazing over the Avon River from a touristic viewing platform assembled from "treated-pine" (Kinsella 2011a, 43, l. 2)—a plantation species that, in its presence as a material in the built landscape, poignantly emblematizes the near total eradication of native eucalypts. The seventh quatrain laments the plant blindness (Wandersee and Schussler 1999) of the non-Indigenous, settler culture in the concluding lines, "And what breaks/the bursts of wattlebloom, takes/paperbarks for granted, insert/of amenities, these local assets" (Kinsella 2011a, 36, ll. 25–28). Allusions to the wattle (*Acacia* spp.) flowers and paperbarks (*Melaleuca* spp.)—two plant icons ubiquitous throughout Southwestern Australia—embody the fragmentation of the native plantscape as a consequence of an entrenched privileging of a narrow Anglo-Australian perspective on botanical (dis)order. Indeed, denigrative attitudes toward the flora of the Australian landmass—as strange, straggly, scrubby, prickly, ugly, worthless—reinscribe historical biases based in European landscape aesthetics (Ryan 2012, 88–109). However, Kinsella affirms that the "amenities" and "assets" are the phenomenally well-adapted and primordial plants themselves, not the puerile by comparison colonialist infrastructures and mechanisms. The critique of pastoralist consciousness and convention accelerates in the third part, "An Idea of Disorder," comprising 23 quintets exposing the gruesome face of everyday country life, especially appalling for a self-confessed "vegan anarchist" (Kinsella and Lucy 2010, 11). For instance, at the edge of a woodland reserve, the carcasses of sheep have been unceremoniously dumped, "[...] Flesh and clumps of wool/detached from the frame" (Kinsella 2011a, 37, ll. 18–19).

A prevailing tone of disillusionment closely connected to the effects of botanical melancholia is evident in the mid-section of "Idyllatry" as Kinsella scrutinizes the normalization of perverse anti-ecological (and, specifically, anti-botanical) values. What emerges is a radical pastoral manifesto and poetic act of catharsis that troubles the ingrained logic of agricultural production:

>[...] Anyway, it's all lies.
>I've spent half my life living

in the middle of this and don't believe
any of it. I don't believe in growth,
and I don't believe anyone's being fed.
(Kinsella 2011a, 38, ll. 39–43)

The scene surrounding the ever-more brackish, poisoned, and desiccated river approaches botanical apocalypse, with:

> [...] stands of York gum
> with track-marks set by termites, jam tree
> weighed down by mistletoe, a black-
> shouldered kite circling above the dead
>
> York gum, just skin and bones [...]
> (Kinsella 2011a, 40–41, ll. 92–96)

Kinsella insinuates that the anti-pastoral prospect of devastation is not biogenic but anthropogenic. The unspoken agreements between trees, termites, and parasites that upheld dynamic balance over vast expanses of time have been disrupted by the same colonialist forces that have rendered the river more saline and sent its guardian spirit, the Wagyl, into retreat. As the York gum "loses bones/proportional to the blast" of storms (41, ll. 97–98), Kinsella's evocations reflect Renee Lertzman's analysis of environmental melancholia as one being "paralyzed to translate such concern into action" (2015, 4). The poet's self-conscious dread of inaction and anxiety over ineptitude to galvanize radical change immediately follow the succession of bleak plant death images. In a last melancholic concession, he states, "I feel no guilt not being out there, helping./I cherish the action of the flora and fauna,/but have nothing to observe that might/traumatise those around me into/preserving the habitat" (Kinsella 2011a, 41, ll. 102–106).

Yet, when all else fails, it is poetry that serves as the activist's medium, as Kinsella paradoxically observes himself claiming to observe nothing, as an expression of his feeling ineffectual when confronted with regional botanical ecocide. Before the fourth and final part, "Idyllatry" (titled after the poem itself), the third part, "An Idea of Disorder," concludes with a prodding allusion to a navigation marker on a hill where a rare orchid species grows—an image so resonant that the botanically melancholic poet "can't bear to look/back at it" (41, ll. 110–11). Affective identification with native and naturalized flora is similarly palpable in the poem "Where the Almond Tree" (Kinsella 2011a, 29) in which the poet grieves the interrelated deaths of an almond tree and a wattle as a corollary of prolonged drought in the Wheatbelt. "Where the Almond Tree" evokes plant death as a relational phenomenon contingent on the activities of other organisms (i.e., insect larvae and parrots). In its very exclusion of the word "died," the title reveals emotional reluctance to acknowledge the death of cherished flora as well as a pronounced absence of existential resolution—a negation of the possibility that humans can eventually come to terms with plant death particularly when it is precipitated on a widespread basis by ecological calamity. In the poem, plant death is an intimate event analogous to the sudden sickness and decline of a family member at home. Moreover, the almond tree and wattle are deprived of dignity because of the intensity and totality of their deaths. The elegiac meditation opens with:

> Where the almond tree died, so died the wattle.
> That parabola can take no life for long. If borers
>   are below the surface,
> they will move on. They have killed the already dead.
>   (Kinsella 2011a, 29, ll. 1–4)

Although exhibiting an affinity in his writings for the native flora of the Wheatbelt, Kinsella here spurns botanical nativism as an ideology strictly opposing invasive, exotic, or non-indigenous plants (Coates 2007, 76). Instead, in their lives and deaths, the almond and the wattle created an equilibrium, which was then fragmented by the pastoral juggernaut and cut short by the effects of climate disturbance. Kinsella continues, "[...] *It bothers me*/the almond tree died so intensely/it lost all moisture. And the wattle/died just as entirely [emphasis added]" (Kinsella 2011a, 29, ll. 20–23). By the final lines, the paralysis of melancholia is not overcome by the textualized progression of grieving but by the feathers of parrots flying "at half-mast" (29, l. 27), implying an expansive, cross-species concept of mourning in which the poet is not alone in his being troubled by vegetal death.

> because death is the most alive district
> to inhabit. We could say so much more
>   if only we had the time.
>   "Resurrection Plants at Nookaminnie Rock"
>   (Kinsella 2011a, 53, ll. 20–22)

Conclusion: On Vegetal Living and Dying

In closing this chapter's assaying of the significance of vegetal decay and demise in Kinsella's radical pastoralism, I want to underscore that not all evocations of plant death in his ouevre are weighed down by feelings of botanical melancholia. For instance, "Resurrection Plants at Nookaminnie Rock" (Kinsella 2011a, 53) presents a different version of vegetal death and the potential for new life through the narrativization of the resilient mechanisms of the pincushion lily (*Borya* spp.), known for its ability to endure episodes of dehydration through metabolic arrest

(Nikulinsky and Hopper 2008, 24). Sequestered at Nookaminnie, a boulder enclave near Quairading in the Wheatbelt, the *Borya* defy, through their physiological adaptations, the "belief that the dead will stay dead/and there will be no lift, no rebirth" (Kinsella 2011a, 53, ll. 11–12). What emerges in the midst of the poet's biogeographically articulated contemplation of life, senescence, birth, and regeneration in the natural world is a plant ethics centering on intimate ecological knowledge, profound regard for endemic flora, and a recognition of the limits of proximate human-plant encounters. One must always tread conscientiously in fragile rock outcrop environments, stepping "carefully around these/wreaths hooked into granite sheen, holdalls/for a soil-less ecology" (Kinsella 2011a, 53, ll. 14–16). The pincushion speaks to the poet—and speaks of the courting of death and the return from its brink—through a haptic, material presence, at once soft and bristly. Nevertheless, the plant "would say so much more if your boots/were off" (Kinsella 2011a, 53, ll. 17–18)—that is, if physical exchange could be consummated. Undergirded by sensitivity toward the granite outcrop habitats, the poet's ethics of stewardship come to restrain his impulse to sink more deeply into the inevitable mystery of co-constituted human-plant deaths. In its defiant brinkmanship, the resurrection plant exemplifies the contention that the event of death does not necessarily spell out the end of a plant's existence (Marder 2014, 187).

More subtle in its radical pastoral subtext than "Idyllatry," "Resurrection Plants" textualizes vegetal death and near-death, principally, as a process of embodied, ecological wonderment and, secondly, as suggestive of the possibility of ecosystemic renewal and social hope through respectful and reciprocal engagements with the plant inhabitants of one's place. Despite admissions of melancholic paralysis elsewhere in his oeuvre, further examples from Kinsella's botanical poetry resound with the call to rejuvenate the ill-treated Wheatbelt through attentive interaction with local plants. An activist poetics resounds in the long poem, "Harsh Hakea (or Elements of the Subject's Will)," which is interspersed with fragments of an account of planting the shrub *Hakea prostrata*, native to Southwestern Australia. "I will check the Harsh Hakea/planted hopefully restoratively/on the steep incline of Bird Gully" (Kinsella 2011b, 151, pt. 15, ll. 6–8). Foregrounding the percipience of the hakea as a subject with its own will in the poem's title, Kinsella enunciates an ideal of radical pastoralism that spurns cynicism, inaction, and melancholy in favor of collaboratively working with the inherent intelligence of the vegetal world. After all, those plant taxa that have endured the harsh, arid, and nutrient-deficient Western Australian landscape must have stories to tell, lessons to impart, and actions to inspire, if only the human masses could learn to listen. As such, we find in the radical pastoral poetry of John Kinsella an empathic attentiveness to plant life and plant lives that does not recoil from their deaths and dying—biogenic (e.g., "Resurrection Plants" and "Harsh Hakea"), anthropogenic ("Idyllatry" and, to a lesser extent, "Where the Almond Tree"), and the expressions of life and death along the spectrum between both. Circumscribed in part by the botanical denizens of the Wheatbelt, Kinsella's pastoral vision recognizes the region's traumatic legacy of the abuse and eradication of other-than-humans—a history in which he himself once participated—while conveying, with clarion hope, the potential for more sustainable and ethically-grounded relations to the Wheatbelt biota for the benefit of all inhabitants. The next and final chapter will pursue the idea of vegetal hope in Joy Harjo's poetry.

Bibliography

Albrecht, Glenn. 2005. "'Solastalgia': A New Concept in Health and Identity." *PAN: Philosophy Activism Nature* 3: 44–59.

———. 2010. "Solastalgia and the Creation of New Ways of Living." In *Nature and Culture: Rebuilding Lost Connections*, edited by Sarah Pilgrim and Jules Pretty, 217–34. Hoboken: Taylor and Francis.

Aristotle. 2011. *The Complete Works of Aristotle*. Hastings: Delphi Publishing.

Baluška, František, Dieter Volkmann, Andrej Hlavacka, Stefano Mancuso, and Peter Barlow. 2006. "Neurobiological View of Plants and Their Body Plan." In *Communication in Plants: Neuronal Aspects of Plant Life*, edited by František Baluška, Stefano Mancuso, and Dieter Volkmann, 19–35. Berlin: Springer-Verlag.

Belshaw, Christopher. 2013. "Death, Value, and Desire." In *The Oxford Handbook of Philosophy of Death*, edited by Ben Bradley, Fred Feldman, and Jens Johansson, 274–96. Oxford: Oxford University Press.

Beresford, Quentin. 2001. "Developmentalism and its Environmental Legacy: The Western Australia Wheatbelt, 1900–1990s." *Australian Journal of Politics and History* 47 (3): 403–15.

Beresford, Quentin, Hugo Bekle, Harry Phillips, and Jane Mulcock. 2001. *The Salinity Crisis: Landscape, Communities and Politics*. Crawley: University of Western Australia Press.

Bradshaw, Corey. 2012. "Little Left to Lose: Deforestation and Forest Degradation in Australia Since European Colonization." *Journal of Plant Ecology* 5 (1): 109–20. doi:10.1093/jpe/rtr038

Bryant, William Cullen. 1854. *The Complete Poetical Works of William Cullen Bryant*. London: Knight and Son, Clerkenwell Close.

Challabathula, Dinakar, Jos Puthur, and Dorothea Bartels. 2016. "Surviving Metabolic Arrest: Photosynthesis During Desiccation and Rehydration in Resurrection Plants." *Annals of the New York Academy of Sciences* 13651 (1): 89–99. doi:10.1111/nyas.12884

Clarke, Philip. 2011. *Aboriginal People and Their Plants*. Dural Delivery Centre, NSW: Rosenberg.

Coates, Peter. 2007. *American Perceptions of Immigrant and Invasive Species: Strangers on the Land.* Berkley: University of California Press.

DeWoody, Jennifer, Carol Rowe, Valerie Hipkins, and Karen Mock. 2008. "'Pando' Lives: Molecular Genetic Evident of a Giant Aspen Clone in Central Utah." *Western North American Naturalist* 68 (4): 493–97.

Environment Australia. 2001. *Threat Abatement Plan: For Dieback Caused by the Root-Rot Fungus* Phytophthora cinnamomi. Canberra: Environment Australia and Natural Heritage Trust.

Fagg, Murray. 2013. "Fungal Ecology: Wood Rotting Fungi." *Australian National Herbarium.* Accessed 21 May 2017. www.anbg.gov.au/fungi/ecology-woodrot.html

Gander, Forrest, and John Kinsella. 2012. *Redstart: An Ecological Poetics.* Iowa City: University of Iowa Press.

Garrard, Greg. 1996. "Radical Pastoral?" *Studies in Romanticism* 35 (3): 449–64.

Gifford, Terry. 2014. "Pastoral, Anti-Pastoral, and Post-Pastoral." In *The Cambridge Companion to Literature and the Environment*, edited by Louise Westling, 17–30. Cambridge: Cambridge University Press.

———. 1995. *Green Voices: Understanding Contemporary Nature Poetry.* Manchester: Manchester University Press.

Goethe, Johann Wolfgang von. 2009. *The Metamorphosis of Plants.* Cambridge, MA: MIT Press.

Hall, Matthew. 2009. "Plant Autonomy and Human-Plant Ethics." *Environmental Ethics* 31 (2): 169–81.

Haraway, Donna. 2008. *When Species Meet.* Minneapolis: University of Minnesota Press.

Haskell, Dennis. 2000. "Tradition and Questioning: The Silo as Pastoral Symphony." In *Fairly Obsessive*, edited by Rod Mengham and Glen Phillips, 89–102. Fremantle, WA: Fremantle Arts Centre Press.

Herrera, Carlos. 2009. *Multiplicity in Unity: Plant Subindividual Variation and Interactions with Plants.* Chicago: University of Chicago Press.

Heyd, Thomas. 2012. "Plant Ethics and Botanic Gardens." *PAN: Philosophy Activism Nature* 9: 37–47.

Hopper, Stephen. 2010. *Sir John Crawford Memorial Address: Plant Diversity at the Turning Point.* Saint Louis: Federal Reserve Bank. Accessed 21 May 2017. www.crawfordfund.org/wp-content/uploads/2014/01/2010-SJCM-Hopper.pdf

Hopper, Stephen, Andrew Brown, and Neville Marchant. 1997. "Plants of Western Australian Granite Outcrops." *Journal of the Royal Society of Western Australia* 80 (3): 141–58.

Hughes-d'Aeth, Tony. 2012. "Salt Scars: John Kinsella's Wheatbelt." *Australian Literary Studies* 27 (2): 18–31.

Kinsella, John. 1995. *The Silo: A Pastoral Symphony.* Fremantle, WA: Fremantle Arts Centre Press.

———. 2007. *Disclosed Poetics: Beyond Landscape and Lyricism.* Manchester: Manchester University Press.

———. 2011a. *Armour.* London: Picador.

———. 2011b. "Harsh Hakea (or Elements of the Subject's Will)." *Literary Review* 54 (3): 132–55.

———. 2012a. "First Lines Typed at Jam Tree Gully." *Iowa Review* 41 (3): 79–81, 189.
———. 2012b. *Jam Tree Gully: Poems*. New York: W.W. Norton.
———. 2013. *Spatial Relations, Volume Two: Essays, Reviews, Commentaries, and Chorography*. Amsterdam: Rodopi.
Kinsella, John, and Niall Lucy. 2010. *Activist Poetics: Anarchy in the Avon Valley*. Liverpool: Liverpool University Press.
Koechlin, Florianne. 2009. "The Dignity of Plants." *Plant Signaling and Behavior* 4 (1): 78–79. doi:10.4161/psb.4.1.7315
Kolbert, Elizabeth. 2014. *The Sixth Extinction: An Unnatural History*. London: Bloomsbury.
Lambers, Hans, ed. 2014. *Plant Life on the Sandplains in Southwest Australia: A Global Biodiversity Hotspot, Kwongan Matters*. Crawley: University of Western Australia Publishing.
Lambers, Hans, F. Stuart Chapin, and Thijs Pons. 2008. *Plant Physiological Ecology*. 2nd ed. New York: Springer.
Latimer, Cole. 2012. "Western Australia's First Uranium Mine Approved." *Australian Mining*. Accessed 21 May 2017. www.australianmining.com.au/news/western-australias-first-uranium-mine-approved/
Lertzman, Renee. 2015. *Environmental Melancholia: Psychoanalytic Dimensions of Engagement*. London: Routledge.
Marder, Michael. 2013a. "Is It Ethical to Eat Plants?" *Parallax* 19 (1): 29–37.
———. 2013b. *Plant-Thinking: A Philosophy of Vegetal Life*. New York: Columbia University Press.
———. 2014. *The Philosopher's Plant: An Intellectual Herbarium*. New York: Columbia University Press.
Marx, Leo. 1992. "Does Pastoralism Have a Future?" In *The Pastoral Landscape*, edited by John Dixon Hunt, 209–23. Washington, DC: National Gallery of Art.
———. 1964. *The Machine in the Garden: Technology and the Pastoral Ideal in America*. Oxford: Oxford University Press.
Morton, Tim. 2013. *Hyperobjects: Philosophy and Ecology after the End of the World*. Minneapolis: University of Minnesota Press.
Nancy, Jean-Luc. 2000. *Being Singular Plural*. Stanford, CA: Stanford University Press.
Nikulinsky, Philippa, and Stephen Hopper. 2008. *Life on the Rocks: The Art of Survival*. Fremantle, WA: Fremantle Press.
Pandolfi, John, and Catherine Lovelock. 2014. "Novelty Trumps Loss in Global Biodiversity." *Science* 344 (6181): 266–67. doi:10.1126/science.1252963
Parmesan, Camille, and Mick Hanley. 2015. "Plants and Climate Change: Complexities and Surprises." *Annals of Botany* 116 (6): 849–64.
Phillips, Glen, and John Kinsella. 2001. "An Extract from Watershed: A Discussion about the Avon River Catchment Region of the Western Australian Wheatbelt from York to Lake Grace." *Literary Review* 45 (1): 11–16.
Pouteau, Sylvie. 2014. "Beyond 'Second Animals': Making Sense of Plant Ethics." *Journal of Agricultural and Environmental Ethics* 27 (1): 1–25.
Prober, Suzanne, and F. Patrick Smith. 2009. "Enhancing Biodiversity Persistence in Intensively Used Agricultural Landscapes: A Synthesis of 30 Years

of Research in the Western Australian Wheatbelt." *Agriculture, Ecosystems and Environment* 132 (3-4): 173-91.

Reed, Marthe. 2010. "John Kinsella's Anti-Pastoral: A Western Australian Poetics of Place." *Antipodes* 24 (1): 91-96.

Rethink the Link. 2016. "About Us." Accessed 21 May 2017. www.rethinkthelink.com.au

Rijavec, Frank, Noelene Harrison, and Keith Bradby. 2002. *A Million Acres a Year*. Sydney: Snakewood Films and SBS. DVD.

Robinson, Daniel. 2010. *William Wordsworth's Poetry: A Reader's Guide*. London: Continuum.

Rogers, Paul. 2016. "Saving Pando: Humans Are Taking Measured Steps To Rejuvenate an Ailing Giant." *Natural History* 124 (2): 32-37.

Royal Botanic Gardens, Kew. 2016. *The State of the World's Plants Report*. Kew: Royal Botanic Gardens.

Ryan, John Charles. 2012. *Green Sense: The Aesthetics of Plants, Place and Language*. Oxford: TrueHeart Press.

Seddon, George. 2004. *Sense of Place: A Response to an Environment, the Swan Coastal Plain, Western Australia*. Melbourne: Blooming Books. Original edition, 1972.

Steffen, Will, Paul Crutzen, and John McNeill. 2007. "The Anthropocene: Are Humans Now Overwhelming the Great Forces of Nature?" *Ambio* 36 (8): 614-21.

Swiss Confederation. 2008. *The Dignity of Living Beings with Regard to Plants: Moral Consideration of Plants for Their Own Sake*. Translated by Jackie Leach Scully. Bern: Federal Ethics on Non-Human Biotechnology ECNH.

Taylor, Nik, and Richard Twine. 2014. "Introduction: Locating the 'Critical' in Critical Animal Studies." In *The Rise of Critical Animal Studies: From the Margins to the Centre*, edited by Nik Taylor and Richard Twine, 1-15. New York: Routledge.

Theophrastus. 1976. *De Causis Plantarum: In Three Volumes*. Translated by Benedict Einarson and George K. K. Link. London: Heinemann.

Thoreau, Henry David. 1993. *Faith in a Seed: The Dispersion of Seeds and Other Late Natural History Writings*. Washington, DC: Island Press.

Thoreau, Henry David. 2000. *Wild Fruits: Thoreau's Rediscovered Last Manuscript*. Edited by Bradley P. Dean. New York: W.W. Norton.

Trewavas, Anthony. 2014. *Plant Behaviour and Intelligence*. Oxford: Oxford University Press.

Van der Valk, Arnold, ed. 2009. *Forest Ecology*. Dordrecht: Springer.

Wandersee, James, and Elisabeth Schussler. 1999. "Preventing Plant Blindness." *The American Biology Teacher* 61 (2): 82-86.

White, Rob, and Diane Heckenberg. 2014. *Green Criminology: An Introduction to the Study of Environmental Harm*. New York: Routledge.

Whitman, Walt. 1871. *Leaves of Grass*. New York: J.S. Redfield.

Young, Emma. 2016. "Outrage After Centuries-Old Jarrah Tree Cut Down in Coolbellup." *WA Today*. Accessed 21 May 2017. www.watoday.com.au/wa-news/outrage-after-centuriesold-jarrah-tree-cut-down-in-coolbellup-20160114-gm5run.html

9 Every Leaf Imagined With Us

Vegetal Hope and the Love of Flora in Joy Harjo's Poetry

> Everything was as we imagined it. The earth and stars, every creature and leaf imagined with us.
>
> * * *
>
> The imagining needs praise as does any living thing. Stories and songs are evidence of this praise.
>
> * * *
>
> The imagination conversely illumines us, speaks with us, sings with us.
> —from "A Postcolonial Tale" (Harjo 1994, 20, sects. 6–8)

In an epoch of pronounced biodiversity loss and psychoterratic disturbance (Mcmanus, Albrecht, and Graham 2014), vegetal life can arouse a vital sense of hope in individuals, communities, and societies. Plants can become, as Raymond Williams (1989) put it, "resources of hope" for a more ecocentric—or, at least, less anthropocentric—future that figures nonhuman lives equitably into its calculus. Such a bold claim for a vegetally-inflected form of ecological hope is tacit in stories of plant resilience, recovery, and renewal that continue to surface in the public domain despite a prevailing mood of dread and helplessness over the state of the planet. For instance, ponder the rediscovery of plant species once regarded as either globally extinct or eliminated from particular locales or regions. In 2015, botanists confirmed the presence of the critically endangered grass, *Dichanthelium hirstii*—previously limited to two small populations in the eastern United States—in Georgia after a 67 year hiatus in the state (McAvoy, Patrick, and Kruse 2015). In another intriguing case of vegetal revival, scientists identified a new species of extinct plant from fossilized flowers captured in amber chunks between 15- and 45-million years ago (BBC Science and Environment 2016; Poinar and Struwe 2016). The neotropical flower, *Strychnos electri*, belongs to an extant genus whose living members are infamous for producing the alkaloid strychnine. The fossil species, moreover, is a representative of the asterids—a massive lineage comprising in excess of 80,000 (or nearly 20% of all known) flowering plants, including potatoes, sunflowers, mint, and coffee.

Stories of rare grass populations countering the scientific consensus and primordial flowers unsettling the fixed logos of human temporality signify the importance of hope as a galvanizing resource for sustainability, plant justice, and other ecological ideals. In addition to the return of wild species from the brink of extinction, community gardens present a compelling example of vegetables, fruits, and herbs mediating the development of social capital and inspiring hope, especially for marginalized or disadvantaged individuals. Indeed, studies underscore the health benefits of community gardening, specifically in maintaining lower body mass indexes for male and female gardeners in comparison to non-gardeners in their neighborhoods (Zick et al. 2013). Also of note are the distinct biopsychosocial benefits: more robust social solidarity, increased community participation and interaction, and a clarified sense of personal purpose and direction (George 2013). While enhancing the physical and mental health of participants, community gardens also contribute to the empowerment of women and the leveling of gender disparities, as strongly evident in the case of Abalimi Bezekhaya, or Planters of the Home, an urban agriculture initiative located in Cape Town, South Africa (Small 2007). It has been shown that inner city greening through community garden programs reinforces civic engagement and fosters neighborhood stability while countering trends toward youth violence and crime (McCabe 2014). Plants in conjunction with soil, microorganisms, insects, birds, and other companion species transform the disused lots of urban communities into flourishing multispecies loci that help to counter the entrenched linkage between violence and prolonged exposure to environmental health hazards (McCabe 2014). Through sensory immersion and corporeal participation—seeing, touching, smelling, tasting, hearing, and learning to cultivate plants—community gardens inscribe the hope that botanical life confers to humanity regardless of the trying social, political, and environmental circumstances in which we and our fellow photosynthetic beings find ourselves.

More than inspiring hope by overcoming the odds of extinction and facilitating hope in community garden settings, botanical life is linked to a vast symbology in the Anglophone poetry tradition that figures seeds, flowers, roots, and trees as signifiers of renewal (Knewitz 2015, Mahood 2008). As a consequence, the vegetal becomes a trope for hope—an intimation of transcendent release from the vicissitudes of everyday consciousness and the immediacies of the earthbound present. When the speaker in Wordsworth's famous poem beholds "[...] a crowd,/A host of golden Daffodils;/Beside the Lake, beneath the trees,/Fluttering and dancing in the breeze" (1815, 328, ll. 3–6), an instance of euphoric reverie, catalyzed by a glimpse of the animated flowers, banishes the sense of melancholic isolation and detachment from the world declaimed in the opening two lines. In analogous terms, though in less adorned language, the nineteenth-century American poet Lucy Larcom construed the tree as a portico to the sublime when she wrote, "He who plants a tree,/ Plants a hope./Rootlets up through fibers blindly grope;/Leaves unfold into horizons free" (2014, 35, ll. 1–4). Uncannily mirroring Larcom's sentiment, moreover, the speaker in Robert Frost's "Birches," from 1916, imagines the act of climbing the black branches of birch tree heavenward up its white trunk as an antidote to world-weary moments when "[...] life is too much like a pathless wood" and, more frankly, when "I'd like to get away from earth awhile" (2006, 224, ll. 44, 48). In his seventies, Williams Carlos Williams wrote the four part pastoral poem "Asphodel, That Greeny Flower"—named after the perennial plant *Asphodelus*—as an affirmation of regeneration and renewal. The beginning of the third book of the long poem foregrounds the perennial resolve of the flower emerging in spring as indicative of love's persistence: "I have invoked the flower/in that/frail as it is/after winter's harshness/it comes again" (William Carlos Williams 1955, 371, ll. 8–12).

Of note among contemporary poets who look toward hope through the optic of the vegetal world is Joy Harjo, a Native American writer, musician, and screenwriter of Muscogee Creek heritage. Harjo's work over 40 years has perceptively attended to the plants, mammals, birds, reptiles, waterways, geological features, and ecological issues of the American Southwest (Bryson 2002; Jossa 2007; Lang 1993). Distinguished for its "highly political" orientation (Hussain 2000), Harjo's lyricism pivots to nature, dreams, the imagination, and the mythic as counter-forces to the pervasive techno-industrialization of contemporary American society (Dowdy 2007, 89). Her poetic critique of neo-imperialism's devastating impacts on Native American cultures consistently returns to the importance of prayerfulness in sustaining hope for a culturally and environmentally equitable future. What is more, her verse tends toward prayer-like structures and content (Bryson 2002; Gibson 2002), as especially evident in her early poem "Remember" (Harjo 1983, 40). Although largely overlooked by critics of her work, vegetal nature is essential to Harjo's ecological poetics and vision of social renewal. Before turning to the plant-inflected prayerfulness of her poetry, I begin this final chapter of *Plants in Contemporary Poetry* by characterizing Harjo as a botanical poet who resists what she calls the "dehumanization" of plants. She engages vegetal life not as aesthetic background or cultural commodity, but as a vibrant agent in the process of writing, composing, and valuing language. Her empathic outlook on the vegetal kingdom—grounded in ideas of kinship with and respect for the other-than-human—reflects Native American cosmographies as well as firsthand sensory experiences:

> I remember Oklahoma springs in childhood. I felt like a small plant and knew myself as part of the earth. I'd get up before anyone else. I liked the smell of the medicine of plants [...] The front [yard] was

carpeted in clover patches and dandelions. I knew these plants intimately and practically lived in them in the spring and summer.
(Harjo and Winder 2011, 110)

Rather than a symbolic structure or lyrical object emptied of material-semiosis, plants are poeticized by Harjo as living manifestations and pulsating embodiments of hope. Acknowledging the immanence of plants in everyday life, her writing centralizes an Indigenous ontology of interrelation between things, ideas, and potentialities. In particular, the emergence of botanical hope takes shape through Harjo's triangulation of poetry as prayer as plant. In the poem "The Book of Myths," for instance, Harjo declares that "every day is a common/miracle of salt roses, of fire in the prophecy wind" (2008, 1892, ll. 18–19). Her poetics ultimately reminds us that the vegetal is more than a symbol or incarnation of human aspiration. In addition to representing and embodying hope, plants can be understood to *have* hope—a claim I will expound in relation to scientific evidence of emotion, affect, and desire in the botanical world. I argue that the intelligent propensity of plant life for greater self-actualization manifests the existence of hope as both inherent to vegetality and indispensable to the resilience of ecological communities over time.

Harjo's Vegetal Poetics: Against the Dehumanization of Plants

Born in Tulsa, Oklahoma, in 1951 and raised in New Mexico, Joy Harjo (née Joy Foster) adopted the last name of her grandmother, painter Naomi Harjo, in 1970 as an affirmation of her paternal Native American ancestry (Van Dyke 2005, 96). Harjo's father Allen Foster was of the *katcv*, or tiger clan, of the Muscogee Creek while her mother Wynema Baker Foster had Cherokee, French, and Irish heritage. Harjo's paternal forebears include the distinguished tribal leader Chief Menawa (born Hothlepoya) who propelled the anti-assimilationist "Red Sticks" against General Andrew Jackson at the Battle of Horseshoe Bend during the Creek War of 1813–1814 (Coltelli 2005, 283). Inspired by the artistic practices of her grandmother, Naomi, and her great aunt, Lois Harjo, as well as her mother Wynema's singing, she studied dance, art, and painting at the Institute of American Indian Arts before pursuing creative writing at the University of New Mexico (Giacoppe 2002, 168). As a young writer, Harjo was mentored by the Laguna Pueblo novelist Leslie Marmon Silko whom she once visited "outside her Tucson home while [Silko] tenderly watered a garden she had fortressed against predators" (Harjo and Winder 2011, 98). Following the publication of her first chapbook, *The Last Song* (1975), while still an undergraduate, Harjo went on to complete an MFA degree at the University of Iowa's Writers'

Workshop. Since the 1970s, she has published more than 12 poetry collections including *She Had Some Horses* (1983), *In Mad Love and War* (1990) and, most recently, *Conflict Resolution for Holy Beings* (2015). Her prose poetry book, *Secrets from the Center of the World* (1989), is a collaboration with the astronomer and photographer Stephen Strom on the landscapes of the American Southwest. The collaborative work alludes to vegetal life, for instance, in a tree's bearing witness to a meteorite impact: "That cedar tree marks the event and the land remembers the flash of its death flight" (Harjo and Strom 1989, 24). She has also written a memoir, *Crazy Brave* (2012), and co-edited an anthology of contemporary Native American women's writings, *Reinventing the Enemy's Language* (1997).

Harjo embraces Native American imagery, motifs, forms, politics, and spiritualities, particularly of the Creek, Cherokee, Navajo, and Pueblo cultures. As Craig Womack (1999, 224) suggests, although Harjo's focus is "pan-tribal," her immersion in Muscogee Creek tribal heritage invigorates her craft of writing. Concerning the literary effects of Indigenous identity, she observes that Creek heritage "provides the underlying psychic structure, within which is a wealth of memory. I was not brought up traditionally Creek, was raised in the north side of Tulsa [but] I know when I write there is an old Creek within me that often participates" (Harjo and Coltelli 1990, 57). Her poems tend to integrate the oral cadences, breaks, and other elements of traditional Native American storytelling (Adamson 2001, Lang 1993, 41). Intimately linked to her politics, Harjo's creative work as a poet, artist, musician, screenwriter, and filmmaker articulates the concerns of Indigenous people, women, minorities, and other groups historically excluded from the masculinist Anglo-American literary mainstream (Goodman 1994). She proclaims the importance not only of pan-tribalism on her poetics but of African-American and Chicano literature and music. Her writing thematizes the painful legacies of cultural isolation, identity loss, community and family disintegration, alcoholism, drug addiction, and domestic violence (Coltelli 2005, 284–85). Also expressed in her poetry are collective memories of genocidal policies. These include the forced relocation of Indigenous people from their traditional homelands (culminating, but not ending, in the Trail of Tears of the Southeastern United States), the imposition of Eurocentric educational standards, and the institutionalization of discriminatory practices geared toward assimilation (Lang 1993, 42). In communicating the unique experiences of Native American women, the beautiful young alter ego Noni Daylight of Harjo's early collections *What Moon Drove Me to This?* (1979) and *She Had Some Horses* (1983) represents a feminist reconfiguration of the typically male figure of the trickster (Holmes 1995). The peripatetic Noni Daylight, perpetually moving from place to place in the southern United States, parallels the government removal of the poet's Creek and

Cherokee ancestors from their tribal homelands to Indian Territory in Oklahoma during the 1830s.

Harjo's poetry draws—directly and indirectly—from a lineage of Muscogee Creek and other Native American poets for whom plants provided vital subject matter for poetic reflection. Most notably, she is a descendent of the Creek poet, journalist, and politician Alexander Posey (or Chinnubbie Harjo, 1873–1908), who founded in 1901 the first Native American newspaper, *Eufaula Indian Journal*, and continues to be recognized today by the Indigenous people of the American Southeast and Southwest as "the poet laureate of Indian Territory" (Peyer 2007, 181). The regional emphasis, cultural allusions, and political voice of Posey—whose mother was a member of the extensive Harjo family—has markedly influenced succeeding generations of Creek poets. The collection, *Song of the Oktahutche* (Posey 2008), exhibits a range of Romantic, botanically-inflected poems narrating human-plant intimacies. Expressing empathic sentiment for the kindred vegetal life of indoor environments, "Death of a Window Plant" laments the demise of a common houseplant: "My window-friend,/I'll dig thy grave,/Inter thee grandly" (Posey 2008, 18, ll. 37–39). Likewise, in the elegy "Daisy," the speaker respectfully addresses the deceased flower in humanized terms as "[…] a friend, and true;/A closer brother, too,/Than some who've shook my hand" (2008, 43, ll. 21–23). The theme of befriended plants resurfaces in "To a Daffodil" in which a dead flower is mourned. The speaker addresses the vegetal persona as a fellow percipient being, intimating that flowers and humans are held to a common fate: "A true friend still,/Although I'll never know thee till the Judgment Day" (2008, 174, ll. 5–6). And in the eclogue "The Flower of Tulledega," a rare plant vocalizes its preference for its native habitat through dialogue with thrushes and the Oktahutchee—or North Canadian—River (2008, 218–19).

Among Harjo's other culturally and personally proximate literary influences are the Muscogee Creek poet Louis Oliver (Littlecoon or Wotkoce Okisce, 1904–1991) and the Acoma Pueblo writer Simon Ortiz (b. 1941). Louis Oliver was born in Indian Territory 3 years before Oklahoma became a state. Harjo acknowledges his poetization of Creek folklore and furtherance of Native American intellectualism as leaving lasting imprints on her own work (Harjo and Coltelli 1996, 107). The principal foci of Oliver's writing—specifically the search for an integration of moral, spiritual, intellectual, and geographical concerns (Womack 1999, 187)—are comparably palpable in Harjo's verse throughout her career. For instance, "In Honor of Ya'ha" from *Chasers of the Sun* (1990, 83) typifies Oliver's attention to the effects of the Creek environment on his writerly activities and philosophical deliberations. The search for literary knowledge—and, more broadly, for Creek cultural identity—is likened to wildcrafting the grapes, persimmons, and other (actual and metaphorical) fruits specific to one's locale. Also featured in Alexander Posey's work, the Oktahutchee River lyricized by Oliver is central to the traditional activities of Muscogee Creek people. As an example, "Deep Fork" from *Caught in a Willow Net* (Oliver 1983, 14) emphasizes the river's other-than-human life and ecological workings. It was the poetry of Simon Ortiz, however, that guided Harjo most profoundly and directly when, early in her artistic development, she focused more on the visual and performing arts (Harjo 2004b, 48). Ortiz enabled the young poet to conceptualize the possibility of identifying as a Native American writer at a time when this kind of self-characterization was unusual and, in fact, radical: "As I watched Simon work I had to admit that I was amazed at the creation of a poem, how a kernal of meaning and sound condensed to one page could stagger the world with meaning" (Harjo 2004b, 48). The Pueblo poet assisted Harjo in coming to see poetry as a mechanism for advancing social justice for Indigenous and other marginalized groups. Like Oliver and Posey before him, Ortiz elucidates the intimate, ancestral relations between Native American people and flora. Notwithstanding the juggernauts of oil drilling and uranium mining depicted in the opening lines of "Returning It Back, You Will Go On," vegetal life and the process of cultivation embody the poet's vision of hope, renewal, and regeneration for the future: "When you plant something,/watch it grow, nourish it,/so carefully, so gently, sing, talk" (Ortiz 1992, 331, ll. 29–31).

In addition to the ecological poetics of Ortiz, Oliver, Posey, and others, music has facilitated Harjo's creative work and, specifically, her enchantment with the aurality of language. In this regard, she cites Patsy Cline, Nat King Cole, John Coltrane, Miles Davis, Bob Dylan, Billie Holiday, and the Kaw-Muscogee jazz saxophonist and composer Jim Pepper as formative influences (Harjo and Winder 2011, 41). Harjo's poetry is distinctive both for its musicality and its regular allusions to songs, music, and musicians. Yet, she also sets her spoken poetry to a fusion of jazz, blues, and traditional rhythms with her band Joy Harjo and Poetic Justice. Their album, *Letter from the End of the Twentieth Century* (2003), contains melodic interpretations of "She Had Some Horses," "A Postcolonial Tale," and eight other poems recited by Harjo as lyrics. The synthesis of written language and musical performance infuses her literary work with the traditional oral dimensions of Native American cultures (Coltelli 2005, 291). Harjo's preoccupation with music and sound begins to become most apparent in the collection *In Mad Love and War* (1990) in poems such as "Rainy Night" (40) dedicated to Billie Holiday and "We Encounter Nat King Cole as We Invent the Future" (51) (see also, Bryson 2002, 187). The predominance of prose poems in the same volume enables her to approximate the narrative directness of storytelling without completely jettisoning poetic convention (Coltelli 2005, 291). Hence, Harjo's invocation of the prose poem form mediates Native American orality and Anglo-American textuality.

"Javelina" (Harjo 1990, 31) makes use of the first person prose observational style of nature writing but with characteristically poetic interpolations. The botanical imagination of the poem takes shape through the synaesthesiac effects of listening to sensation—the speaker *hearing* the coolness and spininess of plants vicariously—vis-à-vis the acknowledgement of nonhuman (porcine) vocalization: "A renegade turtle hides beneath damp runners of a plant with red berries; tastes rain. I imagine the talk of pigs and hear them speak the coolest promise of spiny leaves" (para. 3).

As an ecological poet, Harjo positions the other-than-human—including the plant—as a counterforce to the alienation, placelessness, despondency, and resentment of life in contemporary technocratic society, especially for Native American people (Bryson 2002, 170). Notwithstanding the deconstruction of technological fundamentalism apparent throughout her verse, vegetal nature for Harjo is reverberant with hope. The plant is a source of optimism for the future. Embracing a non-dualistic purview—in which all life is seen as interdependent—she foregrounds her pan-tribal cultural identity without romanticizing, idealizing, or nostalgizing Indigenous interactions with a supposedly prelapsarian botanical environment. Her poetry hence recognizes that the poet's "true self exists in a bio-social relationship with the natural world" (Bryson 2002, 176) and enacts—in lyrical form—an "ontology of connectivity" (Rose and Robin 2004, para. 3) drawn predominantly from Creek, Cherokee, and Pueblo cosmographies. Harjo's ecopoetics centralizes "radical intersubjectivity" between humans and others (Bryson 2002, 186). In contrast to Murray, Oliver, Bletsoe, Oswald, Glück, Wright, Kinsella, and other contemporary botanical poets, however, the preponderance of her poems eschews a focus on a single species and, instead, aims to disclose the reciprocal interrelations between humans, plants, animals, birds, insects, cities, and the cosmos from an Indigenous perspective. Harjo nonetheless remains exceedingly conscious of vegetal life as essential to Native American cultures. It is noteworthy, then, considering the foundational role of plants in her poetics and politics, that studies of Harjo emphasize, for instance, the mythic zoological protagonists of her work (deer, horse, crow, rabbit) (Bryson 2002; Holmes 1995) and her poetic pursuit of a hybridic land-based alternative to standard American English (Adamson 2001, 116–27). Even though Joni Adamson equates Harjo's attention to linguistic self-determination to "a gardener engaged in the act of cultivating her garden" (126), the vegetality of her poetry remains a noticeable oversight in many ecocritical commentaries.

For Harjo and other Muscogee Creek poets and artists, corn especially embodies hope; but not in the mode of Romantic self-actualization according to which a plant is converted into a symbol of human longing—a process, I argue, that strips vegetal life of its agential presence and signifying power. The material-semiosis of corn evident in Harjo's poetics derives from the biocultural heritage of the species and—specifically for Creek and other Native American people of the Southeastern United States—the annual *boskita* (or *busk*), known as the Green Corn Ceremony. Performed on behalf of entire communities, the ceremony celebrates the ripening of a new crop of maize, or green corn, marking the beginning of a new year (Hudson 1984, 19–21; Wright 1986, 22). For the Muscogee Creek people, maize retains "both its real and symbolic significance" (Wright 1986, 22). Occurring sometime between June and early September, the ceremony serves as the means for Native American societies of the region to purify themselves. A bitter emetic made of button snakeroot (*Eryngium cuneifolium*) and a black decoction of the parched leaves of yaupon holly (*Ilex vomitoria*) were historically consumed (Hudson 1984, 21, 35). The festivities concluded with feasting, dancing, games, and mock fighting between warriors. Indeed, Alexander Posey's poem "Fus Harjo and Old Billy Hell" (2008, 191–97) alludes to the location of ceremonial stomp dances occurring during the boskita and incorporates references to the foods *apusky* and blue dumplings, both made from corn meal. This familial sacredness of corn for Creeks recurs frequently in Harjo's writing. The essay "Family Album" (1992) details her trip to the Tallahassee dance ground in north-eastern Oklahoma for the Green Corn Ceremony. A family history rather than an ethnographic account, the essay characterizes boskita as "a rite of resonant renewal, of forgiveness" (Harjo 1992, para. 1). Recalling the journey to the sacred ground, Harjo (1992) notes that "the trees and tall reedlike grasses resounded with singing" (para. 2). The insects' singing moreover "helps the growing corn remember the climb to the sun" (Harjo 1992, para. 3).

The harmonization of plants, insects, earth, sound, and memory in Harjo's account has an ancestral basis. Some traditional Creek stories involve humans talking and chanting to plant beings who, in turn, express themselves aurally through songs, rhythms, and forms of direct utterance (Chaudhuri and Chaudhuri 2001, 33). In contrast, Harjo cautions against the interlinked "dehumanization" of people and plants as a technocratic juggernaut that "flatlines us to think and be in one dimension, or one mind" and which simultaneously reduces the vegetal to a voiceless and institutionalized artifact (Harjo and Winder 2011, 103). In an interview from 2009 with Anishinabe scholar Loriene Roy, Harjo poignantly explains the implications of dehumanizing plants by denying them song and disregarding their innate powers:

> There are over five hundred indigenous nations and cultures [in the United States], each with helpers. There are established relationships. Plants are beings and require respect and singing if they are to be helpful. We all owe our lives to the helpfulness and sacrifice

of plants. Corn is very powerful. Corn has managed to be included as an ingredient in almost every manufactured 'food' item in this country. The impetus of corn therefore is very powerful. If we enslave plants, disrespect them, abuse them, we get the same in return. (Harjo and Winder 2011, 64–65)

The dehumanization of corn takes place in the manufacturing of corn syrup and other derivatives. No longer a nutritious staple or community centerpiece, the industrially-processed sweetener becomes a principal factor in the diabetes epidemic. For Harjo, the widespread addiction to denatured corn-based sweetener is evidence that "the essence and the meaning of corn and our relationship to it gets lost and perverted in the process" (Harjo and Winder 2011, 102). Tobacco is another case of the modern dehumanization of a spiritually potent plant. Many Native American people revere tobacco as a sacred and life-affirming persona that mediates between the human and supernatural worlds (Winter 2000, 3). In an article "Dehumanization Flatlines," first published in the *Muscogee Nation News* in 2007, Harjo problematizes the modern maltreatment of tobacco and its transmutation into an addictive commodity: "Consider tobacco and how it has served us traditionally. It too has been dehumanized by process, by lack of respect in its use" (Harjo and Winder 2011, 102). In the same interview with Loriene Roy, she characterizes tobacco as an entity necessitating loving, respectful, and judicious use: "It is a beloved plant for my people, and is actually a different plant than used in the manufacture of tobacco products. We used to use it sparingly. It's a powerful plant. The power gets angry when misused" (Harjo and Winder 2011, 65). Harjo's botanical poetry thus can be understood as a lyrical means to restore respectful relations with vegetal nature through song and prayer.

Tendrils of Poetry Coiling into the Future: On Botanical Hope

This chapter approaches Joy Harjo's poetry through the prism of botanical hope. This non-oppositional dialectic comprises, on the one hand, the formulation of vegetal life as an object, abstraction, or material expression of human hope and, on the other, the principle that plants themselves possess desire, aspiration, or states of hopefulness innately as part of intelligent awareness of self and world. Parallelling Michael Marder's explication of vegetal memory as three-pronged—"memories are not only *like* plants, and vice versa, but plants also *are* and *have* memories [emphasis in original]" (2016, para. 4)—I put forward the premise that hope is not only *like* a plant, and vice versa, but plants also *are* and *have* hope. In other words, while *standing in* for hope in the Wordsworthian sense alluded to earlier and *embodying* hope as percipient beings dynamically emplaced in relation to other living things, plants also *have* hope for advantageous future outcomes that ensure both their individual fitness and the wellbeing of their biosocial communities. Harjo's poetry most explicitly inflects the former two dimensions (of plants representing and materializing hope) but the latter dimension (of plants having a capacity for hopefulness independent of their construction as symbols or embodiments of human desire) is implied in her poetics and philosophy. Rather than inscribing a staunchly utilitarian discourse on the vegetal—as one-dimensionally exploited, for better or worse, by animals and other motile creatures for food, medicine, fiber, and adornment—Harjo heartens readers to consider the capability of the botanical domain to influence our bodies, minds, and spirits beneficently and indeed dialogically. More than mere resources, plants are helpers. The selfless assistance perpetually granted by the botanical world to other beings expresses a yearning for familial exchange and a hope for kinship with the non-plant. In an interview "Becoming the Thing Itself," Harjo recognizes the vegetal desire for relation by articulating the understanding that:

> the trees *want* to share as do the plants. And when we share with anyone, whether they are plant, animal, mineral, we make a familial relationship, or maybe the word is we acknowledge it, because it's innately there.
> (Harjo and Winder 2011, 24 [emphasis added])

The dehumanization of vegetal life at the fore of Harjo's appraisal of the industrial rendering of corn, tobacco, and other spiritually- and culturally-potent species internalizes the values of empathic identification with nonhumans (bioempathy) (for example, see "In Defense of the Land Ethic" in Callicott 1989) and love for plants (phytophilia) (Marder and Vieira 2013). Notwithstanding its grounding in an animist ontology of kinship between beings, the idea of dehumanization does not need to involve the acknowledgement of plants as persons. Put differently, the process of humanization (and dehumanization) invoked by Harjo does not need to be contingent on the concept of personhood (and its converse), especially as applied in Anglo-European theoretical contexts. My claim is at odds with the extension of personhood to vegetal nature as "a crucial, all pervading concept—for as persons, plants are recognized as volitional, intelligent, relational, perceptive, and communicative beings" (Hall 2011, 100). The linkage propounded by Hall attempts to level the ingrained inequities between plants and other beings through the specious application of personhood, therein risking the marginalization of vegetal alterity and diminishing the vital need for humans to engage creatively—and lovingly—with the intelligent otherness of plants. In contrast to the perils of personhood, bioempathy and phytophilia offer viable anchor points for conceptualizing the pernicious dehumanization alluded to by Harjo. The corporeal basis of bioempathy elucidates the shared worlds of human and plant beings according to which the denaturing of one (the processing of maize into an addictive sweetener) reciprocally impacts on the bodily wellbeing of the other (the epidemic of diabetes) (Chapter 4 pursues the enactment of bioempathy in the medicinal plant poetics of Elisabeth Bletsoe). The pairing of these principles discloses that the forces dehumanizing people—techno-industrialization, globalization, postcolonialism, neocolonization—simultaneously underlie the widespread societal disregard and exploitation of plants lamented by Harjo. Without pivoting to personhood, Harjo's writing reminds us that intrinsically-relational entities have biosocial environments, kinship networks, and corporeal impulses in common.

Attentive to the emergent being-in-the-world of vegetal life, Harjo's praxis as a phytophile poet is shaped and deeply inspired by a love of plants (Marder and Vieira 2013) but is equally appalled by their maltreatment and imprudent use. Not constructing *plants as persons*, however, Harjo's poetic intervention in the pervasive dehumanizing of the botanical world—particularly via empathy and philia—gathers impetus through the configuration of *plants as poetry*. As a perennial issue in ecocriticism and environmental writing (for example, Buell 1995, 83–88; Oppermann 2014), the question of language's capacity to represent or express the factical world is usually addressed critically by elevating the function of narrative and author in approximating—to varying degrees of effectiveness—the being-in-the-world of nonhumans, including flora. The contention that plants *are* poems disrupts the status of the text as a privileged artifact mediating the perceptible domain of vegetal nature and the inward-looking processes of human ideation. Yet, despite its apparently radical re-imagining of language, the formulation of plants as poetry has precedents within the Anglophone poetry tradition. For instance, the English poet Ebenezer Elliott (1781–1849) asserted that "poetry, like truth, is a common flower. God has sown it over the earth, like daisies, sprinkled with tears or glowing in the sun" (qtd in Adams 1844, 139). From Elliott's standpoint, poetry is not *like* a flower but *is* a flower disseminated by a divine creator. The alignment of poetry and flower is not merely a switch from simile to metaphor. Rather than a linguistic code to be deciphered or symbolic structure to be unraveled, the textuality of vegetal life is immanent and self-disclosing. Vis-à-vis contemporary poetry, we only need to return to the third book of "Asphodel, That Greeny Flower." The concluding stanzas of the poem ask, "Are facts not flowers/and flowers facts//or poems flowers/or all works of the imagination,/interchangeable?" (William Carlos Williams 1955, 382). Through the aggregation of imagination, facticity, and vegetality, the speaker implores his forgiving wife to accept his flower—his poem—of regret not as a figurative gesture but as a material-semiosis propelling forward the revitalization of their once-fraught interpersonal relationship.

Above and beyond their profoundly deep symbolic dimensions, plants are always already a vibrant, affective, resonant presence in the world—and so too are poetry and the imagination. Like poems, vegetal beings speak palpably by inscribing meaning through the lyrical articulations of their bodies in space and time. While provoking our imagination—for instance, of a more sustainable green future that fully embraces renewable energy forms—plants, moreover, as cognitive entities, imagine future possibilities for themselves, fellow creatures, and their ecological milieu. In "I Used to Think a Poem Could Become a Flower," her introduction to an issue of the literary magazine *Ploughshares* from 2004, Harjo reflects on the congruities between poetry and plants that—as a young, idealistic writer—molded her appreciation of literature's potential to engender and convey hope. She recalls discovering poetry through song "under the huge elm sheltering my childhood house [...] I used to think that the elm, too, was poetry, as it expressed the seasonal shifts and rooted us" (Harjo and Winder 2011, 133). For Harjo, the "tendrils of songs [and, hence, of poems] coil into the future" (2011, 133). Despite the harrowing history of interlinked environmental devastation and cultural usurpation in the United States, compounded by the seemingly endless global military campaigns of the post-9/11 era, for the Muscogee Creek poet "the elm is still growing there in that yard" (2011, 133). Harjo looks toward the poetic imagination and the sheltering world of plants as gifts of hope, "for inspiration, for sustenance" (2011, 133). Plants as poetry, and vice versa, nevertheless, is one component of the triad—poetry as prayer as plant—that I suggest is integral to Harjo's poetics of botanical hope. The correspondence between poetry and prayer, and vice versa, reflects her emphasis on song in the context of Indigenous practices of orality and conceptions of the sacred. In diverse Native American cultures, a firm demarcation between poetry, prayer, and song is not strictly observed (Parker 2003, 178; Swann 1996). As an example, "Eagle Poem" adopts the form of a prayer and, through its chant-like cadence and use of parallelism, communicates a prevailing sense of optimism. The poem opens with, "To pray you open your whole self/To sky, to earth, to sun, to moon/To one whole voice that is you" and concludes with, "We pray that it will be done/In beauty/In beauty" (Harjo 1990, 65, ll. 1–3, 24–26).

The conjunction of poetry, prayer, and plant in Harjo's thought enables readers to appreciate language less as a representational medium and more as a performative impetus inspiring the vegetal domain and its relations. For Muscogee Creek and other Native American people and their botanical kin—as articulated by Harjo—poetry and its correlates of song and prayer constitute a medium of hope. Entrusting in the prospect of societal renewal through flora and other nonhuman entities, she intimates that hope is a potentiality common to sentient beings. Through poetic intervention, Harjo refuses the dehumanization of plants as well as the anthropocentric focus of most theorization in which—excluded a priori from consciousness, desire, and a futural disposition—the vegetal is thus debarred from the privileged sphere of hope. To be sure, the preponderance of conceptualizations of hope disregards the possibility that other-than-human beings could possess innate forms of desire for favorable outcomes for themselves, their communities and, more abstractly, for the future. Marxist philosopher Ernst Bloch's seminal three volume work, *The Principle of Hope*, originally published in 1959, articulates an excessively humanist vision of hope based on an ontology of not-yet-being. Indeterminate and open-ended, the world in Bloch's conception is not yet finished—for humanity but not necessarily for plants—because it continually encloses objective possibilities for the future. In the introduction to the first volume of his *magnum opus*, Bloch exalts the value of unbounded imagination, "so that the wheat which is trying to ripen can be encouraged to grow and be harvested" (Bloch 1986, 4). Notwithstanding the alluring hint of an ecology of hope based on cross-species relation—in which the imaginative drive facilitates the actualization of vegetal life, to flower, to grow, to ripen, to be harvested, to emerge *poietically* through seasonal shifts—the not-yet-being central to Bloch's ontology appears to proscribe the other-than-human from a future-oriented consciousness. The presumption that hope is the rarified province of human experience continues in more recent work on the philosophy, sociology, and economics of hope, namely the edited volumes *The Resilience of Hope* (McDonald and Stephenson 2010) and *The Economy of Hope* (Miyazaki and Swedberg 2017).

A predominantly anthropocentric focus underlying the absence of the nonhuman is moreover evident in *Hope*, a volume of interviews by Mary Zournazi with leading contemporary theorists, notably Julia Kristeva, Brian Massumi, Michel Serres, Gayatri Spivak, and Isabelle Stengers. The deep-rooted supposition of the collection is that hope is a temporal projection carried out by the human imaginer in the incandescent moment. For anthropologist Michael Taussig, hope is "a type of sense or something like a sense. A sense which we [humans] are not very conscious of—unlike seeing or smelling or hearing, where there are anatomical sense organs and receptors" (Taussig and Zournazi 2002, 43). Imbricated with healing, grace, miracles, and metamorphosis, hope entails the potential to transform a negative situation into something good (Taussig and Zournazi 2002, 55). The third section of the book, entitled "Revolutionary Hope," omits the possibility of vegetal desire despite the most radical form of hope issuing from the selfless recognition that it is not only the cognitive human subject who can invest in hope. That animals, plants, insects, mushrooms, and other lifeforms could express an abstract ideal—regarded as one of the hallmarks of consciousness—is beyond the purview of the contributors. A humanistic interpretation of hope is unmistakable in an interview with Michel Serres, author of *The Natural Contract* (1995), who avers that the duty of philosophy should be to inculcate optimism in the public domain. As a pathway for doing so and in place of an ontology of the state of things, Serres proposes a desmology—from the Greek term *desmos* meaning "connection" or "link"—alert to the relations, the interstices, between things (Serres and Zournazi 2002, 204). Although, from the largely sanguine outlook of Serres, "relations come before being" (Serres and Zournazi 2002, 204), nothing is mentioned of the nonhuman agents connected to and, indeed, enacting hope for the benefit of themselves, others, and their environments. What is more, vegetal life is granted no explicit place in Stengers's paired concepts of "cosmo-politics" and "ecology of practices," the latter concerned with the overlays between different forms of knowledge (Stengers and Zournazi 2002, 262). It seems that, in devising the language to enunciate hopelessness, mourning, and grief while envisioning hope and grace in relation to the profound environmental loss of the Anthropocene, theorists including contributors to the volume *Mourning Nature* (Cunsolo and Landman 2017) have neglected to recognize the prospect of nonhumans experiencing comparable affective states (despair, mourning, hope) (see also Chapter 5 on humor as plant affect in Alice Oswald's poetry).

Therein lies the expansiveness of Harjo's vegetal poetics. Inviting contemplation of the obverse of the botanical hope dialectic, Harjo enables her readers—and listeners—to imagine plants as bearers of the forward-leaning consciousness necessary for hope. If the hope of the other-than-human has been overlooked in philosophical discourse and unsurprisingly transfigured into a symbol in Anglophone verse, Harjo's lyricism restores hope as a latent property of all life—as something that cannot be ruled out or presumed not to exist, as something that is essential to envisioning a more equitable future on the planet. "The earth and stars, every creature and leaf imagined with us" (Harjo 1994, 20, sect. 6). Rather than a fanciful leap forward, however, Harjo's decentering of humanistic hope has intriguing parallels with neuro-botany. Vegetal being has been shown to have a temporal sense—of integrating memories of previous events and outcomes in order to make sensible choices about the future (Bilichak et al. 2015; Crisp et al. 2016; Karban 2015; Leopold 2014; Müller-Xing, Xing, and Goodrich 2014). Intelligent behavior in plants is characterized by the selection of the most beneficial choice among various options. Involving environmental awareness, spontaneity, counting, and error correction, the process of decision-making signifies the likelihood of consciousness in plants (Trewavas 2016). Vegetal behaviors driven by awareness reflect the perception of dangers and opportunities as well as the desire for a full life. While it is ever more possible to demonstrate the choices, perceptions, and decisions of plants through empirical methods, the question of vegetal emotion, desire, fear, and hope remains open-ended but should not be dismissed as implausible (Trewavas 2014, 259). After all, if plants are cognitive beings, then by all accounts they should have feelings and emotions—inspirations and aspirations—that influence the decisions they make in seeking optimal circumstances for themselves and others. Not reducible to an isolated biological mechanism aimed at enhancing the "fitness" of the organism, hope encompasses the totality of being—from intellection and sensation to pleasure and desire. Indeed, Jagadis chandra Bose (1906, 1914) understood the electrical impulses registered by the crescograph as indications of the emotional states of plants. Almost 100 years later, the forester Peter Wohlleben (2016), in speaking of the associations between trees and fungi, observes that:

> a tree must be very open—literally—because the fungal threads grow into its soft root hairs. There's no research into whether this is painful or not, but as it is something the tree wants, I imagine it gives rise to positive feelings.
> (39–40)

How We Become Plants: Seeds of Renewal

As critics have claimed, in spite of a withering stance toward the technocratic and anti-environmentalist Anglo-American status quo, Harjo's poetry remains inherently hopeful (Adamson 2001; Jossa 2007; Womack 1999). Steadfastly optimistic, her writing not only critiques, through a form of lyrical intercession, the oppressive discourses privileging technocratic progress "but she is able to imagine their absence" (Womack 1999, 230). Decolonizing one's thinking, engendering ecological consciousness, and participating in activist initiatives all commence with the will to imagine alternatives to the historical objectification of women, Indigenous people, ostracized social groups, nonhuman life, and the environment (Womack 1999, 230). For Harjo, vegetal nature is foundational to the political impulse of her poetry—not peripherally as a narrative backdrop or aesthetic object, but agentically as "an interlocutor, a witness, and a source of consolation" (Jossa 2007, 587). Emphasizing the desmologies between human, animal, vegetal, telluric, and cosmological domains, she attempts to generate "a new harmony capable of restoring the universe denied to the Creek woman" and other peripheralized people (Jossa 2007, 589). The botanical imagination thus integral to Harjo's hope-filled poetics is not the end result of wistful longing or starry-eyed idealism regarding flowers, but is instead part and parcel of the enduring practice of renewal rooted in pan-tribal oralities, cosmogenies, and ethnobotanical knowledge (Womack 1999, 235). The countering of biocultural oppression through song, prayer, poetry, and plant is the overarching telos of Harjo's ouevre (Womack 1999, 246). Healing emerges where imagination transforms language—conceived broadly as textual, sonic, corporeal, animate, and animating (Adamson 2001, 122).

This penultimate section further examines the confluence of plant, prayer, and poetry in relation to Harjo's poetization of botanical hope as a multidimensional phenomenon. While symbolizing, inspiring, and materializing hope as percipient interlocutors, at the same time plants resist totalization through their intrinsic desires for nutriment, growth, wellbeing, and reciprocal exchange with the non-plant. In other words, vegetal desires exist independently of the conceptualization of flowers, roots, leaves, herbs, orchids, and trees as symbols of hope in service to human longing. As previously ventured in this chapter, I propound that hope is not only *like* a plant, and vice versa, but that plants also *are* and *have* hope. Some of these themes coalesce in one of Harjo's best-known poems, "Remember," first published in *She Had Some Horses* (1983). The deployment of repetition and parallelism—propelled by the commanding refrain "remember"—transfigures the poem into a prayer or chant: "Remember the plants, trees, animal life who all have their/ tribes, their families, their histories, too. Talk to them,/listen to them. They are alive poems" (Harjo 1995, 307, ll. 15–17). The poet humanizes the vegetal not through the mode of affective fallacy but by recognizing plants as relational beings with their own tribes, families, and histories. As a result, vegetality becomes more than a well-trodden trope of hope. Harjo entreats her readers and listeners to embrace dialogue with the botanical world by speaking with and listening to plants—by attending sensitively to their specific desmological modes. There is also an implication in the poem of vegetal desire for connection with the non-plant. This potentiality is latent within the plant's anticipation of exchange with the human. Harjo posits the practice of remembering as a powerful mechanism for reinvigorating ancestral traditions hinging on close engagement with plants—traditions that existed prior to the intrusion of capitalist Anglo-settler culture and the ensuing conversion of plants into voiceless commodities. In an even more expansive alignment, for Harjo, vegetal life *is* a living poem signifying meaning through its sensuous being-in-the-world. She radically departs from the expropriation of vegetality for lyrical artifice; the reading of the poem *is* the direct apprehension of the plant, tree, or animal by the audience.

A spirit of hopefulness via remembering thus emerges through the union of plant, prayer, and poetry in Harjo's verse. Though poeticized as catalysts of hope, transformation, and renewal, plants nonetheless remain vulnerable to the same exploitative capital-driven forces that can devalue human lives. Principles of bioempathy and phytophilia converge in her vegetal poetics to expose plants as the victims of rampant technocratic dehumanization, particularly within the broader context of nuclear testing in the arid reaches of the American Southwest (Kuletz 2016). The poem "Are You Still There?," originally published in *What Moon Drove Me To This?* (1979), opens with an allusion to the miles and miles of telephone cables materializing—through rectilinear inscriptions on the desert landscape—the discourse of capitalist progress. The modernist communication infrastructure, nevertheless, is incorporated into the exchanges between Native American people as an expression of pan-tribal adaptation and resilience. Harjo juxtaposes wires, phones, bridges, and highway exits to wind, cliffs, sandstone, and flowers in order to call attention to the invariable hybridities between human and nonhuman beings—between animate and inanimate things—in the American neocolonial context:

> hello
> is a gentle motion of a western wind
> cradling tiny purple flowers
> that grow near the road
> towards laguna
> i smell them
> as i near the rio puerco bridge
> my voice stumbles
> returning over sandstone
>
> (Harjo 2004b, 49, ll. 9–17)

The redolent purple flowers impart sensory orientation to the otherwise miasmic scene of highways and bridges representing hypermodernization. What is more, the nameless blossoms are an expressive presence enabling both the poem and its speaker to become cognizant of the human-plant relationships that have sustained the deserts of New Mexico for millennia. Comparably, Harjo's more recent poem "Insomnia and the Seven Steps to Grace" (2014) refers to plants as percipient agents in the world and witnesses to societal transactions. Vegetal life is negatively affected by the machinations also complicit in the denigration of women ("a young mother who is looking for a job," l. 11), Indigenous people, and other socially excluded groups. "The stars take notice, as do the half-asleep flowers, prickly pear and/chinaberry tree who drink exhaust into their roots, into the earth" (Harjo 2014, 34, ll. 26–27). Like the stars, the cactus, tree, and drowsy flowers that take notice are situated within a cosmogeny recognizing nonhuman beings and elements as conscious participants in the world. Whereas some people are trapped by addiction, enslaved by poverty, and denied a future, others resolve to "eat cornmeal cooked with berries/that stain their lips with purple while the tree of life flickers in the sun" (Harjo 2014, 34, ll. 16–17). Notwithstanding the severity of themes confronted boldly in the poem, the overriding note is of hope.

Life sustaining sensory exchanges with plants—eating and tasting cornmeal, feeling the sensation of berry stains on lips, apprehending the flickering tree of life—thus have the potential to heal those (including the plants) who have been dehumanized by the neocolonial apparatus. Composed 1 month after the 9/11 attacks, the dystopian "When the World as We Knew It Ended," initially published in *How We Became Human* (Harjo 2004a), employs chant-like refrain and parallelism, in a manner similar to her early poem "Remember," to signify unwavering commitment to the value of botanical hope irrespective of prevailing sociopolitical circumstances (terrorism, religious ideologies, racial conflicts, war, and war-like posturing). In a somewhat hyperbolic tenor heralding planetary apocalypse, the poet implicates those who scheme:

> to be king or emperor, to own the trees, stones and everything
> else that moved about the earth, inside the earth
> and above it.
>
> We knew it was coming, tasted the winds who gathered intelligence
> from each leaf and flower, from every mountain, sea
> and desert, from every prayer and song all over this tiny universe
> floating in the skies of infinite
> being.
>
> (Harjo 2007, 34, ll. 25–32)

The collective percipience of leaf, flower, mountain, and sea exceeds the limited reach of human knowledge. In particular, the enumeration of nouns in lines 29 and 30 elides the conceptual demarcation between biological entities, geological elements, and sacred utterances (prayers and songs)—all of which in the poem are active contributors to the innate intelligence of the world. From Harjo's perspective—one of course reflecting a Muscogee Creek belief system—intelligence is not the exclusive province of beings endowed with brains but instead is woven into all that exists. Narrative tension—mounting incrementally through phrasal repetition and the first-person plural "we"—reaches a denouement in the collective lament over the dehumanization of vegetal nature and the environment (as ecology, home, or *oikos* rather than an appropriable substance or resource). The diminishment of prayer and song in the rally to war is implicated in the degradation of the natural world, which "we had grown to love/for its sweet grasses [...] for the shimmering possibilities/while dreaming" (Harjo 2007, 35, ll. 33–36). By all accounts, the affective milieu bemoaned in Harjo's botanical imagination had been permeated with phytophiliac interconnection (people loving plants, and vice versa)—the loss of which underlies interminable mourning that is not confined to human emotion. Plants also desire connection and grieve its absence. The contrapuntal movement in "When the World as We Knew It Ended"—from the specifics of leaves, flowers, grasses, and seeds to the possibilities of being, dreaming, infinity, and imagination—is characteristic of Harjo's vegetal poetics and in particular her configuration of plant as prayer as poetry. Following the anticipation of apocalypse in miasmic images early in the poem, the more tranquil concluding stanzas embed hope within the possibility of sensuous return to the earth: "But then there were the seeds to plant" (Harjo 2007, 35, l. 34). Hence, as a revitalizing potentiality, the plant and its seed constitute a "locus of resistance" (Marder 2013, 103) that provokes hope in bleak times.

This chapter has argued that the vegetal poetics of Joy Harjo engages the dialectic of plants both giving and possessing hope. Botanical hope is moreover a desmology between plants, animals, humans, natural elements, the cosmos, mythic beings, prayers, songs, desire, abstractions, and ideals. Hence, in distinction to the vegetal verse of Kinsella, Wright, Glück, Oliver, and others, Harjo's lyricism attends to the energetic transactions between things. This is not to claim that other poetries lack a relational conception of plants but rather that Harjo enacts such a view more faithfully and compellingly in her work. In lieu of a focus on single specimens or floristic species extracted from their biocultural exchanges—an approach that I suggest reflects, to some extent, the effects of a poet's awareness of natural science on his or her praxis—Harjo's vegetal poetics foregrounds the plant's being-in-the-world in the broadest possible ambit of the term. As a consequence, poems such as "It's Raining in Honolulu"—ostensibly about rain—also have much to say about the percipience of vegetal life. As the mist comes:

> Each leaf of flower, of taro, tree and bush shivers with ecstasy.
> And the rain songs of all the flowering ones who have called for the rain
> Can be found there, flourishing beneath the currents of singing.
> Rain opens us, like flowers, or earth that has been thirsty for more than a season.
> (Harjo 2007, 35, ll. 1–4)

In this extract, Harjo frames the taro, tree, and bush as entities capable of joy and pleasure in response to the arrival of rain. The plants are not presented as the silent constituents of the poetic narrative but are affected participants who join the speaker in cathartic renewal. Spiritual purification takes shape through the symphonization of rain, plant, and song. In the final line, the hope for regeneration, flourishing, *and* resistance through the will to plant seeds bears implications for Indigenous people in neocolonial societies: "We will plant songs where there were curses" (Harjo 2007, 35, l. 11). As Michael Marder claims in the essay "Resist Like a Plant!" (2012), vegetal being holds promise as a model for political engagement. In its capacity to wither and flourish—die and live—at the same time, unlike the animal, the plant resists binary logic and destabilizes the principle of non-contradiction (Marder 2012, 30). For Harjo, the hope of plants resides in their countering—through their very being—the dehumanizing forces that, for instance, tend to render the complex world of sensation one-dimensional and homogenous.

Vegetal nature defies metaphorization by enacting hope in space and time. Harjo textualizes this assertion in other poems through the interrelated ideas of kinship, consanguinity, and bioempathy. Beginning in dread but ending in hope, "Equinox" parallels the progression of "When the World as We Knew It Ended." The former poem, also published in *How We Became Human* (2004), forcefully opens with references to the grief, war, and death emanating from an oppressive past and pervading the present. Seeking personal and societal renewal, as many of Harjo's poems do, the speaker finds in the natural world—of mountains, birds, and plants—a fountainhead of hope transforming the oppressive legacy of colonialism and its techno-utopianist residues:

> I keep walking away though it has been an eternity
> And from each drop of blood
> Springs up sons and daughters, trees
> A mountain of sorrows, of songs.
>
> I tell you this from the dusk of a small city in the north
> Not far from the birthplace of cars and industry.
> Geese are returning to mate and crocuses have
> Broken through the frozen earth.
>
> (Harjo 2007, 36, ll. 5–12)

Trees are kin who alchemize the haunting tyrannies of the past into an emergent sense of relationality. The seasonal bringing forth of the crocuses through the snow is the co-resurrection of plant and human, nature and culture, song and prayer. Therein, Harjo's vegetal poetics shows us that the hope inhering poietically in the vegetal world entails the rejuvenation of the primordial, life-sustaining nodes between plants and non-plants. Harjo's bioempathic orientation to the botanical world and its relations consequently reveals the multidimensionality of hope as an affective state of humans, plants, and the complex lines of connection between both. In a comparable way, the prose poem "Grace" from *In Mad Love and War* invokes the spring as the time during which botanical hope materializes in the body of the corn: "We once again understood the talk of animals, and spring was lean and hungry with the hope of children and corn" (Harjo 1989, 380, sect. 3). In traditional Muscogee Creek thought, the inborn hopefulness of the vegetal manifests in the agency of potent plants like corn in alleviating disease and fostering community cohesion by appealing to the bodies, minds, spirits, and relations of people (Hudson 1976, 156–57). Botanical hope thus inheres in the nexus of plants, prayer, and language, which are indissoluble in Harjo's poetics and fundamental to her vision of societal revitalization.

Conclusion: Imagining Hope Through and With Plants

Michael Marder frames plant-thinking as an instance when human thinking, "altered by its encounter with the vegetal world" (10), is made plantlike. This chapter has asserted that the transformative encounter with the botanical kingdom in Joy Harjo's poetry centers on the ability of plant life to represent (through symbols), materialize (through its corporeality), and enact (through its percipience and futural sense) the resource of hope. The flowering of plants in particular has been appropriated frequently by poets of the past and present in order to symbolize fecundity, beauty, and the renewal that is brought forth following the barrenness of winter. From the vantage point of human anticipation and expectation, plants usher in hope through their promise of food, medicine, healing, ornamentation, enjoyment, and the other yieldings of their bodies. Harjo, however, affirms that, alongside the poetic narrativization of botanical hope, there is the intrinsic hopefulness of the vegetal anticipating seasonal changes, awaiting release from the stasis of metabolic arrest, seeking exchange with the non-plant, and making decisions informed by memories of prior experiences that go on to affect the integrity of the ecological community of which it is part. While selflessly supplying hope to humans and other-than-humans, the plant also has needs, wants, intentions, and desires—intimated by the science of neuro-botany—that are not contingent on the poet's figuring of hope in their image. The dialectic of vegetal hope is thus essential to understanding Harjo's botanical imagination and, more specifically, her integration of pan-tribal cosmogenies as it relates to flora. Her poetics enables readers to resist a one-dimensional appreciation of plants as aesthetic objects or pleasant accoutrements to the human dramas rendered in lyrical narratives.

Countering an anthropocentric conception of vegetality and infusing the botanical world with agency, Harjo confers hope to plants, elevating them as sensitive beings connected intimately to the lives of Indigenous people and integral to the future of social and ecological justice. As we imagine plants, so they at the same time imagine us.

The poet conceives of hope *through* and *with* plants, and in conjunction with other beings: "The earth and stars, every creature and leaf imagined with us" (Harjo 1994, 20, sect. 6). While recent work in the environmental humanities has highlighted "the importance of grounding hopes in communities of actual living animals, plants, and microbes" (Kirksey 2014, 296), hope nonetheless remains tethered—in the preponderance of discussions of the concept—to the ideation of the human. Another recent example, primatologist Jane Goodall's popular book *Seeds of Hope* (2014), examines hope in terms of sustainable food production, organic gardening, medicinal plants, seed banks, botanical conservation, and genetically modified organisms. In Goodall's approach, botanical hope connotes the mode of human hope inspired by plants. While such an orientation is valid and important, a radical conception and praxis of hope—for a commensurately radical transformation of human consciousness in the Anthropocene era of unbridled botanical loss—would take into account the possibility that desire is not the sole province of human or animal telos. As a resource for the Anthropocene, botanical hope embraces the idea of the plant as a bearer of hope for a more equitable future on earth for itself and us.

Bibliography

Adams, Henry Gardiner. 1844. *Flowers; Their Moral, Language, and Poetry*. London: H.G. Clarke and Co.

Adamson, Joni. 2001. *American Indian Literature, Environmental Justice, and Ecocriticism: The Middle Place*. Tucson: University of Arizona Press.

BBC Science and Environment. 2016. "Extinct Plant Species Discovered in Amber." *BBC News*. Accessed 22 May 2017. www.bbc.com/news/science-environment-35582991

Bilichak, Andriy, Yaroslav Ilnytskyy, Rafal Wóycicki, Nina Kepeshchuk, Dawson Fogen, and Igor Kovalchuk. 2015. "The Elucidation of Stress Memory Inheritance in *Brassica rapa* Plants." *Frontiers in Plant Science* 6 (5): 1–17. doi:10.3389/fpls.2015.00005

Bloch, Ernst. 1986. *The Principle of Hope*. Vol. 1. Oxford. B. Blackwell.

Bose, Jagadis Chandra. 1906. *Plant Response as a Means of Physiological Investigation*. London: Longmans, Green, and Co.

———. 1914. "Plant-Autographs and their Revelations." *Nature* 93 (2334): 546–50.

Bryson, J. Scott. 2002. "Finding the Way Back: Place and Space in the Ecological Poetry of Joy Harjo." *MELUS* 27 (3): 169–96.

Buell, Lawrence. 1995. *The Environmental Imagination: Thoreau, Nature Writing, and the Formation of American Culture*. Cambridge, MA: Belknap Press of Harvard University Press.

Callicott, J. Baird. 1989. *In Defense of the Land Ethic: Essays in Environmental Philosophy*. Albany: State University of New York Press.

Chaudhuri, Jean, and Joyotpaul Chaudhuri. 2001. *A Sacred Path: The Way of the Muscogee Creeks*. Los Angeles: UCLA American Indian Studies Center.

Coltelli, Laura. 2005. "Joy Harjo's Poetry." In *The Cambridge Companion to Native American Literature*, edited by Joy Porter and Kenneth Roemer, 283–95. Cambridge, UK: Cambridge University Press.
Crisp, Peter, Diep Ganguly, Steven Eichten, Justin Borevitz, and Barry Pogson. 2016. "Reconsidering Plant Memory: Intersections Between Stress Recovery, RNA Turnover, and Epigenetics." *Science Advances* 2 (2): 1–14. doi:10.1126/sciadv.1501340
Cunsolo, Ashlee, and Karen Landman, eds. 2017. *Mourning Nature: Hope at the Heart of Ecological Loss and Grief*. Montreal: McGill-Queen's University Press.
Dowdy, Michael. 2007. *American Political Poetry in the 21st Century*. New York: Palgrave Macmillan.
Frost, Robert. 2006. "Birches." In *The Oxford Book of American Poetry*, edited by David Lehman, 223–24. Oxford: Oxford University Press.
George, Daniel. 2013. "Harvesting the Biopsychosocial Benefits of Community Gardens." *American Journal of Public Health* 103 (8): e6.
Giacoppe, Monika. 2002. "Joy Harjo (1951–)." In *Contemporary American Women Poets: An A-to-Z Guide*, edited by Catherine Cucinella, 168–72. Westport, CT: Greenwood Press.
Gibson, Eliza Rodriguez. 2002. "Love, Hunger, and Grace: Loss and Belonging in the Poetry of Lorna Dee Cervantes and Joy Harjo." *Legacy* 19 (1): 106.
Goodall, Jane. 2014. *Seeds of Hope: Wisdom and Wonder from the World of Plants*. New York: Grand Central Publishing.
Goodman, Jenny. 1994. "Politics and the Personal Lyric in the Poetry of Joy Harjo and C.D. Wright." *MELUS* 19 (2): 35–56.
Hall, Matthew. 2011. *Plants as Persons: A Philosophical Botany*. Albany: State University of New York Press.
Harjo, Joy. 1975. *The Last Song*. Las Cruces, NM: Puerto Del Sol.
———. 1979. *What Moon Drove Me to This?* New York: Reed, Cannon & Johnson Co.
———. 1983. *She Had Some Horses*. New York: Thunder's Mouth Press.
———. 1989. "Grace." *Rhetoric Review* 7 (2): 380.
———. 1990. *In Mad Love and War*. Middletown, CT: Wesleyan University Press.
———. 1992. "Family Album." *The Progressive* 56 (3): 22–24.
———. 1994. "A Postcolonial Tale." *The American Poetry Review* 23 (6): 20.
———. 1995. "Remember." In *The Oxford Book of Women's Writing in the United States*, edited by Linda Wagner-Martin and Cathy Davidson, 307–8. Oxford: Oxford University Press.
———. 2004a. *How We Became Human: New and Selected Poems, 1975–2002*. New York: W.W. Norton.
———. 2004b. "Poetry Can Be All This: All of You, All of Me, All of Us." *Studies in American Indian Literatures* 16 (4): 47–50.
———. 2007. "Four Poems." *World Literature Today* 81 (6): 34–36.
———. 2008. "Joy Harjo, 1951–." In *Women's Worlds: The McGraw-Hill Anthology of Women's Writing*, edited by Robyn Warhol-Down, Diane Price Herndl, Mary Lou Kete, Lisa Schnell, Rashmi Varma and Beth Kowaleski Wallace, 1887–92. New York: McGraw-Hill Higher Education.
———. 2012. *Crazy Brave: A Memoir*. New York: W.W. Norton.
———. 2014. "Insomnia and the Seven Steps to Grace." *America* 210 (11): 34.

———. 2015. *Conflict Resolution for Holy Beings: Poems*. New York: W. W. Norton.

Harjo, Joy, and Gloria Bird, eds. 1997. *Reinventing the Enemy's Language: Contemporary Native Women's Writing of North America*. New York: W.W. Norton.

Harjo, Joy, and Laura Coltelli. 1990. "Joy Harjo." In *Winged Words: American Indian Writers Speak*, edited by Laura Coltelli, 55–70. Lincoln: University of Nebraska Press.

Harjo, Joy, and Laura Coltelli. 1996. *The Spiral of Memory: Interviews*. Ann Arbor: University of Michigan Press.

Harjo, Joy, and Stephen Strom. 1989. *Secrets from the Center of the World*. Tucson: Sun Tracks and The University of Arizona Press.

Harjo, Joy, and Tanaya Winder. 2011. *Soul Talk, Soul Language: Conversations with Joy Harjo*. Middletown, CT: Wesleyan University Press.

Holmes, Kristine. 1995. "'This Woman Can Cross Any Line': Feminist Tricksters in the Works of Nora Naranjo-Morse and Joy Harjo." *Studies in American Indian Literatures* 7 (1): 45–63.

Hudson, Charles. 1976. *The Southeastern Indians*. Knoxville: University of Tennessee Press.

Hudson, Charles. 1984. *Elements of Southeastern Indian Religion*. Leiden: Brill.

Hussain, Azfar. 2000. "Joy Harjo and Her Poetics as Praxis: A 'Postcolonial' Political Economy of the Body, Land, Labor, and Language." *Wicazo Sa Review* 15 (2): 27–61.

Jossa, Emanuela. 2007. "The Colors of the Earth: Nature and Landscape in the Poetry of Joy Harjo and Humberto Ak' Abal." *Journal of the Southwest* 49 (4): 585–601.

Joy Harjo and Poetic Justice. 2003. *Letter from the End of the Twentieth Century*. Glenpool, OK: Mekko Productions.

Karban, Richard. 2015. *Plant Sensing and Communication*. Chicago: University of Chicago Press.

Kirksey, Eben. 2014. "Hope: Living Lexicon for the Environmental Humanities." *Environmental Humanities* 5: 295–300.

Knewitz, Simone. 2015. "'The Fading Memory of Those Flowers': Poetic Selves and Metaphorical Lineages in William Carlos Willams's Later Poetry." In *Recovery and Transgression: Memory in American Poetry*, edited by Kornelia Freitag, 55–70. Newcastle upon Tyne, UK: Cambridge Scholars Publishing.

Kuletz, Valerie. 2016. *The Tainted Desert: Environmental and Social Ruin in the American West*. New York: Routledge.

Lang, Nancy. 1993. "'Twin Gods Bending Over': Joy Harjo and Poetic Memory." *MELUS* 18 (3): 41–49.

Larcom, Lucy. 2014. "Plant a Tree." In *Over the River and Through the Wood: An Anthology of Nineteenth-Century American Children's Poetry*, edited by Karen Kilcup and Angela Sorby, 35. Baltimore, MD: Johns Hopkins University Press.

Leopold, A. Carl. 2014. "Smart Plants: Memory and Communication Without Brains." *Plant Signaling and Behavior* 9 (10): 1–5. doi:10.4161/15592316.2014.972268

Mahood, Molly. 2008. *The Poet as Botanist*. Cambridge, UK: Cambridge University Press.

Marder, Michael. 2012. "Resist Like a Plant! On the Vegetal Life of Political Movements." *Peace Studies Journal* 5 (1): 24–32.
———. 2013. *Plant-Thinking: A Philosophy of Vegetal Life*. New York: Columbia University Press.
———. 2016. "Vegetal Memories." *The Philosopher's Plant: A Los Angeles Review of Books Channel*. Accessed 22 May 2017. http://philosoplant.lareviewofbooks.org/?p=172
Marder, Michael, and Patricia Vieira. 2013. "Writing Phytophilia: Philosophers and Poets as Lovers of Plants." *Frame* 26 (2): 37–53.
McAvoy, William, Thomas Patrick, and Lisa Kruse. 2015. "Rediscovery of *Dichanthelium hirstii* (Poaceae) in Georgia." *Phytoneuron* 7: 1–8.
McCabe, Art. 2014. "Community Gardens to Fight Urban Youth Crime and Stabilize Neighborhoods." *International Journal of Child Health and Human Development* 7 (3): 223–36.
McDonald, Janette, and Andrea Stephenson, eds. 2010. *The Resilience of Hope*. Amsterdam: Rodopi.
Mcmanus, Phil, Glenn Albrecht, and Raewyn Graham. 2014. "Psychoterratic Geographies of the Upper Hunter Region, Australia." *Geoforum* 51: 58–65.
Miyazaki, Hirokazu, and Richard Swedberg. 2017. *The Economy of Hope*. Philadelphia: University of Pennsylvania Press.
Müller-Xing, Ralf, Qian Xing, and Justin Goodrich. 2014. "Footprints of the Sun: Memory of UV and Light Stress in Plants." *Frontiers in Plant Science* 5: 1–12. doi:10.3389/fpls.2014.00474
Oliver, Louis. 1983. *Caught in a Willow Net: Poems and Stories*. Greenfield Center, NY: Greenfield Review Literary Center.
Oliver, Louis. 1990. *Chasers of the Sun: Creek Indian Thoughts*. Greenfield Center, NY: Greenfield Review Press.
Oppermann, Serpil. 2014. "From Ecological Postmodernism to Material Ecocriticism: Creative Materiality and Narrative Agency." In *Material Ecocriticism*, edited by Serenella Iovino and Serpil Oppermann, 21–36. Bloomington: Indiana University Press.
Ortiz, Simon. 1992. *Woven Stone*. Tucson: University of Arizona Press.
Parker, Robert Dale. 2003. *The Invention of Native American Literature*. Ithaca, NY: Cornell University Press.
Peyer, Bernd. 2007. *American Indian Nonfiction: An Anthology of Writings, 1760s–1930s*. Norman: University of Oklahoma Press.
Poinar, George, and Lena Struwe. 2016. "An Asterid Flower from Neotropical Mid-Tertiary Amber." *Nature, Plants* 2. doi:10.1038/nplants.2016.5
Posey, Alexander. 2008. *Song of the Oktahutche: Collected Poems*. Lincoln: University of Nebraska Press.
Rose, Deborah Bird, and Libby Robin. 2004. "The Ecological Humanities in Action: An Invitation." *Australian Humanities Review* 31–32. Accessed 22 May 2017. www.australianhumanitiesreview.org/archive/Issue-April-2004/rose.html
Serres, Michel. 1995. *The Natural Contract*. Translated by Elizabeth MacArthur and William Paulson. Ann Arbor: University of Michigan Press.
Serres, Michel, and Mary Zournazi. 2002. "The Art of Living: A Conversation with Michel Serres." In *Hope: New Philosophies for Change*, edited by Mary Zournazi, 192–208. Pluto Press: Annandale, NSW.

Small, Rob. 2007. "Organic Gardens Bring Hope to Poor Urban Communities." *Appropriate Technology* 34 (1): 18–24.

Stengers, Isabelle, and Mary Zournazi. 2002. "A 'Cosmo-Politics'—Risk, Hope, Change: A Conversation with Isabelle Stengers." In *Hope: New Philosophes for Change*, edited by Mary Zournazi, 244–72. Annandale, NSW: Pluto Press.

Swann, Brian, ed. 1996. *Native American Songs and Poems: An Anthology*. Mineola, NY: Dover Publications.

Taussig, Michael, and Mary Zournazi. 2002. "Carnival of the Senses: A Conversation with Michael Taussig." In *Hope: New Philosophies for Change*, edited by Mary Zournazi, 42–63. Annandale, NSW: Pluto Press.

Trewavas, Anthony. 2014. *Plant Behaviour and Intelligence*. Oxford: Oxford University Press.

Trewavas, Anthony. 2016. "Intelligence, Cognition, and Language of Green Plants." *Frontiers in Psychology* 7: 1–9. doi:10.3389/fpsyg.2016.00588

Van Dyke, Annette. 2005. "Women Writers and Gender Issues." In *The Cambridge Companion to Native American Literature*, edited by Joy Porter and Kenneth Roemer, 85–102. Cambridge, UK: Cambridge University Press.

William Carlos Williams. 1955. "Of Asphodel." *The Kenyon Review* 17 (3): 371–82.

Williams, Raymond. 1989. *Resources of Hope: Culture, Democracy, Socialism*. New York: Verso.

Winter, Joseph. 2000. "Introduction to the North American Tobacco Species." In *Tobacco Use by Native North Americans: Sacred Smoke and Silent Killer*, edited by Joseph Winter, 3–8. Norman: University of Oklahoma Press.

Wohlleben, Peter. 2016. *The Hidden Life of Trees: What They Feel, How They Communicate—Discoveries from a Secret World*. Carlton, VIC: Black Inc.

Womack, Craig. 1999. *Red on Red: Native American Literary Separatism*. Minneapolis: University of Minnesota Press.

Wordsworth, William. 1815. *Poems by William Wordsworth: Including* Lyrical Ballads, *and the Miscellaneous Pieces of the Author*. Vol. 1. London: Longman, Hurst, Rees, Orme, and Brown.

Wright, J. Leitch. 1986. *Creeks and Seminoles: The Destruction and Regeneration of the Muscogulge People*. Lincoln: University of Nebraska Press.

Zick, Cathleen, Ken Smith, Lori Kowaleski-Jones, Claire Uno, and Brittany Merrill. 2013. "Harvesting More than Vegetables: The Potential Weight Control Benefits of Community Gardening." *The American Journal of Public Health* 103 (6): 1110–15.

Index

Abalimi Bezekhaya 215
Abrams, M. H. 36
adéquation 62, 74, 100
Adorno, Theodor 15
Alice Through the Looking Glass (Carroll) 152
alterity: and poetry 12
anima nutritiva 4
anima sensitiva 4
animal studies 14, 195
animality 1, 36
Anthropocene 29, 116, 121, 128, 157, 173, 191, 228, 236
Aquinas, Saint Thomas 28, 34–6, 41, 43, 45, 46
Aristotle 4, 37, 43, 45, 49, 68, 72, 196, 197, 203; *De Anima (On the Soul)* 34–6, 190; *scientia de anima* 34; and time 166
Attenborough, David 165
Australian flora 29–30, 164, 176–8, 182–4, 191, 193–4, 206–9; loss of 48–9, 194, 199, 200–3

Bachelard, Gaston 1, 9, 21; material imagination 9
banksia 44, 176
barberry (*Berberis communis*) 3
Barker, Cicely Mary 123
Bauplan (body plan) 62, 66–9, 70, 196
Bergson, Henri: *Creative Evolution* 1–2
Bhaskar, Roy 15
binomial totalization 99
bioempathic emplacement 75, 81, 90–7, 100, 101; definition of 93; *see also* empathy
biomechanics 1
biopolitics 117, 128, 180, 194, 201

Blackstone, Bernard 12–3
Bletsoe, Elisabeth 6, 75, 83–90, 94–103; as herborizer 20
Böhme, Jakob 64
Bose, Jagadis Chandra 4, 146–8; and memory impressions 148; and plant-script 146–7
botanical criticism 9–10, 12; *see also* phytocriticism
botanical hope 217, 223–33; *see also* hope
botanical humor 107–9; definition of 121; as a dialectic 109–10, 116; and environmental loss 110, 128–9; and plant names 118; as a resource of hope 128
botanical imagination 1, 7–8, 21, 48, 55, 62, 67, 117, 128, 163, 192, 201, 229, 233, 235
botanical life: in comparison to botanical lives 16, 102, 204
botanical melancholia 190–1, 199–200, 203–4, 206, 208; definition of 200, 204
botanical nativism 19, 30, 208
bristlecone pine (*Pinus longaeva*) 165
Bryant, William Cullen 192
Buell, Lawrence: *The Environmental Imagination* 7, 11

calendar trees 170
Canadian goldenrod (*Solidago canadensis*) 72
Cartesian rationalism 29
cerebrocentrism 2, 5
Chamberlain, Charles Joseph 179–80
chickweed (*Stellaria media*) 127
chronos 166, 168, 171, 176, 182–83; *see also kairos*
circumnutation 3

Clare, John 111, 113
Clarke, Philip 40
climate change 5, 96, 157, 191, 204
Coles, William 64
Comedy of Survival, The (Meeker) 120–1
Commentary on De Anima (Aquinas) 35
community gardening 215
companion species 59, 144, 199, 205, 215
confessionalism 57, 138; and postconfessionalism 138, 153
Consecrated Urn, The (Blackstone) 10
corn 221–3, 235
corporeal semiosis 16
critical plant studies 5–6
Culpeper, Nicholas 64, 65, 101
cycads 173, 176, 179–81

Darwin, Charles 135–36, 165; *The Power of Movement in Plants* 3, 53–4, 148, 155
Darwin, Erasmus 13, 70, 109, 116–7, 122
Darwin, Francis 148–9, 165
De Causis Plantarum (Theophrastus) 196
death of plants 147; anthropogenic 190, 191–2, 194, 198–9, 200, 203–5, 207; biogenic 190, 191–2, 198, 200, 203–5, 207; philosophies of 197–8
Descartes, René 135–6
dialectics 15; and alterity 16; *see also* vegetal dialectics
digitalin 82–3
Dioscorides 63–4, 108
doctrine of signatures 62–5, 67, 83
dog-rose (*Rosa canina*) 82
Douglas fir (*Pseudotsuga menziesii*) 27
Dream of the Rood, The 151–2

Eclogues (Virgil) 30, 33
eco-cosmopolitanism 87, 96
ecocide 191, 207
ecocriticism 11; and anthropocentrism 7; of forests 10; of plants 17
Eliade, Mircea 33, 38–9
Ellacombe, Henry 9
Elliott, Ebenezer 225
Eggleston, Edward 65
embodied cognition 58, 75

Emerson, Ralph Waldo 109
empathy 71, 75, 84, 90–6, 102, 156, 163, 199, 224–5, 230, 234; and environmental ethics 92
endocannabinoids 53
Entwistle, Tim 170–1
environmental humanities 14, 157, 236
essentialization 100
eucalypts 41–4
extinction 29, 102, 157, 173, 191, 192, 204, 215

Fellowship of the Ring, The (Tolkien) 152
Fichte, Johann Gottlieb 38
flower-de-luce 97
Freeman, Richard Austin 118
Frost, Robert 216

geocriticism 14
Gerard, John 60, 94, 100, 108
Glück, Louise 125, 137–45; ecofeminism 139; gardening 19, 140–2, 143; memory 143–5; Romanticism 139, 144–5; the use of myths 138
Goethe, Johann Wolfgang von 60, 62, 63, 66–8, 196
Gondwana 30, 163, 176–7
Goody, Jack 39
Graham, Mary 40
Greenman, Jessica 124–5
Grigson, Geoffrey 94
Grindon, Leopold Hartley 9

Haraway, Donna 16
Harjo, Joy 6, 18, 19, 216–36; Green Corn Ceremony 19–20, 221–2; musical influences 220; pantribalism 218, 221, 231, 235; upbringing 217–8
healing 20, 44, 63, 64, 81, 84, 89, 102, 227, 230, 232, 235
Hegel, Georg Wilhelm Friedrich 15–6, 37–8, 173
Heidegger, Martin 173, 179
hemlock water dropwort (*Oenanthe crocata*) 107–8
herba sardonia 107–9
herbalism 63, 81, 83–4, 102
hierophany 33, 38–9
Holocene Extinction 191
Homer 108–9, 112

hope 214–36; philosophies of 227–8; of plants 217, 228; in poetry 215
humor 109–110; benefits of 121; ecocriticism 119; incongruity 109, 119–20, 123; Romanticism 120; *see also* botanical humor

Indigenous people: Australian Aboriginal cultures 32, 37, 38, 39–40, 42, 180–1, 202, 205; Dreaming 168; fire 181–2; lightning 44–5; temporality and seasons 167–70; North American cultures 216–34; *see also* Muscogee Creek, Nyoongar, Worimi
Indigenous studies 14
inter-mnemonics 138, 139, 145, 152–3, 154–7
intercorporeality 55, 57, 61, 71–5
International Plant Names Index 192
interrupted brome (*Bromus interruptus*) 126–7

jarrah (*Eucalyptus marginata*) 194–6, 198–9, 203, 204

kairos 164, 166, 168–69, 176, 183
Keats, John 10, 13; *see also The Consecrated Urn*
kinaesthesia 92
Kinsella, John 190–2, 194–6, 198–210: activism 207; botanical nativism 19, 208; *see also* radical pastoralism
kinship: with plants 20, 199, 216, 224, 225, 234
Koller, Dov 4

land-based calendars 169–70
Larcom, Lucy 215–6
leaves-dropping 70
Leopold, Aldo Carl 149–50
Life Movements in Plants (Bose) 4
Linnaeus 67, 165; and binomialism 18, 60, 99, 117
Lipps, Theodor 91–2
Lockwood, Samuel 120
Longfellow, Henry Wadsworth 97
Lotze, Hermann 91
love of flora 18, 178, 216, 223, 224, 225

Mabey, Richard 191
Macnish, Robert 155

Marder, Michael 12, 16, 146, 151, 163, 168, 173–5, 183, 223, 234, 235
material ecocriticism 13, 139–40; *see also* ecocriticism
material-semiosis 32, 59, 163, 173, 180, 181, 183–4, 217, 222; *see also* corporeal semiosis
Memorial (Oswald) 112
memory-justice 157–8
metamer 196
Metamorphosis of Plants, The (Goethe) 66, 196
Metempsychosis (Donne) 152
Miller, Joseph 98
mimosa 4, 150–1
Morton, Timothy 15–6
moss 58–9
Murray, Les 18–9, 28, 34–49; Christian faith 45–6; embodiment and sensoriality 39; *The Ilex Tree* 30; *The Paperbark Tree* 31; theory of cultural convergence 29, 30, 32–3, 37, 44, 48; *Translations from the Natural World* 32, 39; upbringing 31
Muscogee Creek 216–22, 226, 232, 235
mycorrhiza: networks 27

Nash, Ogden 119
nastic movement 2–3, 4, 145
Naturalis Historia (Pliny) 63
Negative Dialectics (Adorno) 15
neuro-botany 5, 7, 11, 122, 137, 149, 198, 228–9; *see also* plant neurobiology
neurocentrism 2
Nietzsche 121, 151, 154
nomenclature 18, 46, 55, 60–1, 67, 94, 99, 118
Noonuccal, Oodgeroo 167, 169
Nyoongar 168–9, 170, 205–6; *see also* Indigenous people

olfaction 39, 55, 63, 69–71, 99
Oliver, Louis 219
Oliver, Mary 54, 68–75; embodiment 54, 55, 57, 58, 62, 69, 71, 72, 74, 75; transcendence 54, 56, 57, 60, 62; Romanticism 60, 62; upbringing 56–7
Ortiz, Simon 220

244 Index

Oswald, Alice 6, 109–16, 122–8; gardening 19, 110, 111–5; as nature poet 113; Romanticism 60, 113; Thoreau 60–1

Pando (*Populus tremuloides*) 193, 195–6
Paracelsus 64, 94
passion flower 136
Pausanias 108
Penrose Mystery, The (Freeman) 118
personification 18, 32, 117, 123, 125
Pharmacopœia (Bletsoe) 83–4, 90–103; plant naming in 18, 87, 98–9
phototropism 136, 150
phytochemical reductionism 84, 96
phytocriticism 11–5, 157–8, 166
phytophenomenology 12
phytophilia 90, 111, 115, 224–5, 230, 233
phytosemiotics 11
pilpil (*Boquila trifoliolata*) 27
pincushion lily (*Borya nitida*) 193–4, 208
plant: affectivity 121, 128; agency 75; ballistics 2, 126; behavior 109, 124, 127, 136–7, 150; blindness 5, 6, 206; body 54, 62–7, 71, 74, 165; consciousness 150, 154–5, 228; dehumanization 216, 222–3, 224, 227, 232; desire 229, 230, 233, 235; dignity 208; ensoulment 27–31, 34–6, 37–9, 42–9, 197; ethics 13, 15, 56, 157, 185, 198–9, 209; forgetfulness 150; habituation 147, 149; heartbeat 147; intelligence 5, 28, 126, 156; loss 190, 192; love 90, 224; materiality 9, 35, 174; medicine 81–4, 94–103; memory 135–58; metamorphosis 36; modularity 174, 196; morphology 66; movement 3–4; neglect 5–6, 75, 202–3, 225; neurobiology 2, 4–5, 11, 13, 21, 27, 37, 53–4, 55; otherness 8; patience 6, 58–9, 115–6, 124–5; persona 109, 116, 122, 123, 128, 143, 154, 192, 219, 223; personhood 8, 224–5; physiology 53, 65–7, 115, 149–50; place 86; as poetry 225–6, 230; puns 118–9; seasons 167–71; sessility 35; sexualization 109, 165; sleep 155; temporality 114–5, 124, 163–71, 195

plant-thinking 12, 94, 148, 156, 235
Pliny the Elder 63, 65, 94
Poetics of Reverie, The (Bachelard) 1, 21
poetisphere 20–1
poetry: botanical 13, 15, 16, 29, 55, 61, 83, 89, 90, 97, 98, 101, 102, 137, 140 209, 223; Christianity 33; as an ecosystem 16–7; embodiment 55, 58, 75; empathy 96; ensoulment 32; gardening 19, 152; humor in 120; modernism 85–6; open-form 89; pastoral tradition 30, 88, 101, 201; place 86–7; radical landscape mode 85, 88, 99, 102; sacred 33–4; shamanism 85–6; temporality 86
polyvocality: in Murray's work 32; in Oswald's work 111, 113; in Glück's work 141–3, 155–6
Posey, Alexander 219–20
post-pastoralism 201; *see also* radical pastoralism
Priestley, Joseph 18
prose poetry 220–1

Quandamooka 169; *see also* Indigenous people
Queen of the Andes (*Puya raimondii*) 166–7, 174

radical pastoralism 17, 19, 101, 191, 194, 196, 198–9, 200–2, 204, 206, 208–9
resurrection plants 193, 196–7
rhizosphere 156
risus sardonicus 107–8
Robbins, William 5
Romanticism 36, 60, 62, 74, 84, 85, 89, 113, 120, 139, 144, 192, 219, 221
root-brain hypothesis 3, 53–4, 55, 65–6, 154
Rose, Deborah Bird 40
rose of Jericho (*Selaginella lepidophylla*) 193
Rustic Sounds and Other Studies in Literature and Natural History (Francis Darwin) 148

sacred ecology of plants 28–32, 36–41, 43, 47, 49; definition of 29
Sand County Almanac, A (Aldo Leopold) 151
Schweitzer, Albert 92–3
Seasons, The (Thomson) 183

secondary metabolites 53, 83, 95
Shakespeare 124; and flora 9–10
Silko, Leslie Marmon 217
skunk cabbage (*Symplocarpus foetidus*) 69–70
Smith, James Edward 3
solastalgia 203–4
soul: of plants 28, 29, 34–8, 40, 43, 46–8; intrinsic and extrinsic 29, 41
subjectivity 36, 46, 54–5, 57, 61, 143, 156; alternative modes 32; distributed 41; and embodiment 57; of plants 40, 44, 59, 156, 195, 198

Tarlo, Harriet 87–8, 97, 101
temporality 86, 114–5, 124, 158, 163–4, 215; objective 171; scientific 171; subjective 171; *see also* time-plexity, plant temporality
Theophrastus 35, 196
Thoreau, Henry David 60, 62, 74, 111, 113, 115, 117, 191, 199–200
time-lapse photography 164–5
time-plexity 163, 167, 169, 171–3, 175–7, 178–9, 181–4
tobacco 223
totalizing vitalism 93
touch-me-not (*Mimosa pudica*) 4
translation 33
Translations from the Natural World (Murray) 32, 45–8

Umwelt (life-world) 4, 11, 16, 17, 19, 21, 158, 191; *see also* phytosemiotics

vegetal dialectics 14–6, 37, 55, 137, 146, 158, 163, 223, 228, 233, 235
Venice treacle 101–2
Venus flytrap (*Dionaea muscipula*) 27
Virgil: *Eclogues* 30, 33; *Georgics* 31
Vischer, Robert 91
von Sachs, Julius 4, 65, 145

walking 19–20; and Bletsoe 20; and Glück 141; and Oliver 20, 57, 59; and Oswald 112–3, 123; and Wright 181
Walser, Robert 20
weeds 84, 95–6, 97, 110, 115–6, 118, 121–2, 126, 195
Weeds and Wild Flowers (Oswald) 109–10, 111, 122–8
Wheatbelt (Western Australia) 200–10; *see also* Australian flora
white mulberry (*Morus alba*) 2
Whitman, Walt 192
Wild Iris, The (Glück) 19, 123, 129, 137–8, 140–5, 151–8
Williams, Raymond 214
Williams, William Carlos 216, 225–6
willow 81, 83, 142, 152, 156
Wollemi pine (*Wollemi nobilis*) 176
Wordsworth, William 10, 19, 60, 201, 215, 223
Worimi 28–9, 32, 37, 38, 46
Wright, Judith 164, 175–85; environmentalism 177, 185; gardening 178; modernism 177; temporality 164, 175–76; *see also* plant temporality

zoocriticism 14, 68, 120, 135